JIM
MORRISON

LIFE, DEATH, LEGEND

JIM MORRISON

LIFE, DEATH, LEGEND

STEPHEN DAVIS

GOTHAM BOOKS

GOTHAM BOOKS

Published by Penguin Group (USA) Inc.
375 Hudson Street, New York, New York 10014, U.S.A.
Penguin Books Ltd, Registered Offices: 80 Strand, London WC2R 0RL, England
Penguin Books Australia Ltd, 250 Camberwell Road, Camberwell, Victoria 3124, Australia
Penguin Books Canada Ltd, 10 Alcorn Avenue, Toronto, Ontario, Canada M4V 3B2
Penguin Books (N.Z.) Ltd, Cnr Rosedale and Airborne Roads, Albany, Auckland 1310, New Zealand

Published by Gotham Books, a division of Penguin Group (USA) Inc.

First printing, July 2004
10   9   8   7   6   5   4   3   2   1

Gotham Books and the skyscraper logo are trademarks of Penguin Group (USA) Inc.

LIBRARY OF CONGRESS CATALOGING-IN-PUBLICATION DATA
Davis, Stephen, 1947–
    Jim Morrison : life, death, legend / by Stephen Davis.
        p.   cm.
    ISBN 1-592-40064-7 (hardcover : alk. paper)
    1. Morrison, Jim, 1943–1971.   2. Rock musicians—United States—Biography.   I. Title.
ML420.M62D38   2004
782.42166'092—dc22

                                                                        2004003139

Printed in the United States of America
Set in Cremona Regular with Trajan and Abbess
Designed by Sabrina Bowers

This book is printed on acid-free paper. ♾

For
JIM MORRISON
1943–1971

ΚΑΤΑ ΤΟΝ ΔΑΙΜΟΝΑ ΕΑΥΤΟΥ

Ex-fan des sixties
Ou sont tes années folles?
Que sont devenues toutes tes idoles?

—Jane Birkin

CONTENTS

INTRODUCTION

H E'S BEEN DEAD FOR DECADES, but he's still causing trouble.
Jim Morrison was a mesmeric figure in the American sixties, a
rebel poet and godhead in snakeskin and leather. He lived fast, died
young, and left a less-than-exquisite corpse in Paris while hiding out from
the law. In his prime the writers and critics went nuts trying to do his
weird mojo some measure of justice. (One called him "an angel in grace
and a dog in heat.") Jim was the greatest American rock star of his era,
and one of its most publicized celebrities, but—more than three decades
later—his life and works have yet to yield all their secrets and enigmas.

Jim Morrison tried to set the night on fire. As lead singer of the
Doors, he was an acid evangelist on a suicide mission to deprogram his
generation from what he saw as a prisonlike conformity to social and sexual norms. He was a seer, an adept, a bard, a drunk, a bisexual omnivore.
Jim styled his band "erotic politicians," and relentlessly urged his huge
audience—at the height of the dangerous sixties—to break on through
the doors of perception, to free themselves from robotic familial condi-
tioning, to seek a higher, more aware consciousness. Doors concerts—
throbbing with war-dance rhythms and superheated intimacy—were as
close to the experience of shamanic ritual as the rock audience ever got.
The Doors captured the unrest and the menace that hung in the air of
the late sixties like tear gas, and they did it with hypnotic cool.

Between 1965 and 1971 Jim Morrison wrote a hundred songs, recorded seven platinum albums, wrote and published four editions of poems, made three films, recorded his poetry, wrote screenplays, and filled dozens of notebooks with verse and notations. He played more than two hundred concerts with the Doors. He established himself as a sex icon and the major American rock star of the sixties. He violated all of puritan America's sexual taboos and—in a frenetic burst of political energy—even threatened the vindictive Nixon administration with his blatant invitations to protest and revolt.

Jim Morrison, as it turns out, was much more important than anyone realized at the time. Critically dismissed as a has-been Bozo/Dionysius before his death, Morrison's poetic visions have stayed on the radio for more than thirty years, and on into the new century. They have become the classic texts of classic rock, reaching out to generations beyond the one that first understood the deepest meanings, the organic unity, and the transcendent qualities of his greatest work.

Jim Morrison was the last incarnation of that quintessential late-romantic figure, the demonically aroused poet shaking with rage at his world and his contemporaries; a prophet with terrible eyes and rigid features, clad in black leather. He was arguably *the* major poet to emerge from the turmoil of the legendary American sixties. Decades later, Jim Morrison has materialized as the true avatar of his age. His words are burned into the brains of three American generations—the emergency telegram of "Break On Through," the visionary cadences of "L.A. Woman," and the mysterious whispered verses of "Riders on the Storm." His voice echoes on classic-rock stations from coast to coast. His image haunts dorm walls everywhere, emblazoned: JIM MORRISON / AMERICAN POET / 1943–1971. The Doors' album sales, as of this writing, are over fifty million units, and climbing.

Today, more than thirty years after Jim Morrison died, important new revelations are emerging concerning his tumultuous life, his tragic death, and his enduring legend. And the questions about him still linger. Who was he really? Why did he destroy himself? Why was he failed by everyone who knew him?

* * *

I T WASN'T ALL GREAT, being a rock god in the sixties. The tours were primitive and disorganized. The groupies were pretty, but they gave you herpes and the clap. The drugs and alcohol turned you into an imbecile. Your old lady slept around while you were on tour. The critics hated you when you got huge, and suddenly the press that had built you up into a deity began to tear you down. The Doors at their best were about as good as rock music ever got. At their worst, they were one of the most pretentious bands on the planet. But no one had a clearer grasp of the complexities and ironies of the age than Jim Morrison.

Living the times as he did, in full senses-deregulated consciousness, Jim understood the American sixties for what they were: an era of new religious visions, spiritual crisis, political unrest, race riots, assassinations—as well as a rare opportunity for change and reform. The decade's promises were never fulfilled, but some of its goals—such as integration, civil rights, the "global village," and the bringing of East and West into closer harmony—are clearly still in process. Jim Morrison hitchhiked along this psychic landscape like a killer on the road, and the Doors' music still has the uncanny power to poison every new class of ninth graders with its dark messages and raw power. What thirteen-year-old today can play "People Are Strange" and not hear it as a postcard of comfort from beyond the grave? How many dead rock stars have an annual riot at their tomb?

I N ONE OF HIS UNPUBLISHED SPIRAL NOTEBOOKS, sometime in 1968, Jim penned his credo in blue ink: "I contend an abiding sense of irony over all I do."

Jim Morrison's famous "Lizard King" persona was a joke, but it was a serious joke, a cosmic put-on. Jim's serial evocation of the American desert and its reptilian underworld was part of his existential drive to include in the experience of life the omnipresence of impending death. In another notebook entry he wrote: "Thinking of death as the climactic point of one's life."

John Densmore, the Doors' drummer, who was often frightened and bewildered by Jim Morrison's behavior, later observed that all the other California bands of the sixties preached the raising of consciousness toward a state of enlightenment. But the Doors' message, he wrote, had been all about "endarkenment."

No rock singer ever sounded more like he meant it than Jim Morrison. No one else could have released a subversive, antimilitarist song like "The Unknown Soldier," with its hellacious screams of violence and despair, amid the brutality of the Vietnam War. Alone of his generation, Jim's power depended not just on the surge of his poetry with the blinding charisma of his amplified performances, but also on the sheer, cussed rebel energy it took to stand up to society and challenge its hypocritical, constipated moral values in a time of dangerous upheaval.

Alone of the sixties rock stars, Jim Morrison didn't see his mission as a show. "For me, it was never an act, those so-called performances," he said. "It was a life-and-death thing—an attempt to communicate, to involve many people at once in a private world of thought."

Jim Morrison took the inherent dread of the American sixties and made it even crazier, more desperate. Then he made it into a joke, and Jim's volatile essence was a rocket destined to burn out. Drugs would destroy the bravest and craziest of the rock stars. "Revelation would turn into delusion." When his spiritual drive was exhausted, sapped by addiction, dementia, and legal battles, Jim's body followed soon after. Jim Morrison's tragic death at twenty-seven in 1971 was the last in the sequence of rock extinctions that began with Jim's hero Brian Jones (at twenty-seven) in 1969, and continued with Janis Joplin and Jimi Hendrix (both also at twenty-seven) in 1970. The rock movement never recovered. The surviving heroes would carry on, new ones were born (and also would die), but the midnight hour had passed when Jim Morrison flamed out. Those whom the gods love die young.

THE THEATER IS DARK AND SMOKY. Outside, police sirens scream as the cops teargas the kids who can't get in. Suddenly a white-hot light pierces the gloom and a jellied scream rips open an abyss of despair and fury. The Doors are in town tonight, and Jim Morrison is acting out his epic pathos, the lead singer as an illuminating angel from hell.

Looking beyond the lip of the stage, he sees a dark jumble of chaos and disorder as the convulsive young mob of teenagers pulses violently before him. The energy the band is putting out may be awesome, but it is nothing in comparison to what is happening down in the audience, where the chaos is not an act, and often gets much crazier than it does onstage. Jim Morrison's experience of the concert was the inverse of the audience's, as he witnessed nightly scenes of mass rapture, anxiety, lust, fear, and joy. Jim learned early on that the real energy in the room belongs to the audience. It's this knowledge that compelled him to document these Bosch-like fantasias for posterity in his film, *Feast of Friends.*

THERE IS SOMETHING AWFUL, deeply moving, and terribly human in the tragical history of Jim Morrison. On the surface, it's a story of how the excess of fame and unlimited freedom ruined a young American poet. Looking closer, it becomes clear that Jim Morrison's early fury and mania gradually evolved into a kind of artistic maturity, one that was more keenly experienced and aggressively lovely—and prophetically fatal. This book seeks to replace the myths and the lies that have overwhelmed the legend of Jim Morrison with new reporting and a reconsideration of both the known facts and the wild, unsubstantiated rumors. The portrait that emerges in the end reveals a damaged, fiercely loving, compassionate man who overcame his self-destruction through a body of darkly beautiful work that echoes down to us today, with its romantic glamour and spiritual power intact. Mr. Mojo—still rising.

Is everybody in?

The ceremony is about to begin.

BOOK ONE

JIMMY

CHAPTER ONE

THE
LIZARD KING'S
SCHOOL DAYS

*The devotion of the greatest is to encounter risk and
danger, and play dice with death.*

—NIETZSCHE

INDIANS SCATTERED

NYONE INQUIRING MORE THAN SUPERFICIALLY into Jim Morrison's life immediately realizes that the story of his childhood is crucial to understanding what happened to him later. First, he remained very childish his entire life. (Of course, for the rock stars who came to fame and fortune very young, what else was there for them to do?) Second, when Jim joined the Doors and began performing in public, he abruptly severed all contact with his family and never saw his parents again. Third, his early act was a graphic, pull-no-punches rewrite of the ancient Oedipus legend, in which he sang of killing his father and fucking his mother in front of tens of thousands of his fans.

Why did Jim Morrison hate his parents so much? Why did he hate himself? How was he able to create such pure American music out of his own anguish? Why did he end up with a crazy girlfriend who was an even heavier character than himself; who tried in vain to control him; who may have killed him in the end? How could it have happened that this cool, talented guy—one of the great artists of his generation—morphed into a monster, and then immolated himself?

The problem with answering these questions is that Jim Morrison's troubled and problematic post–World War II childhood within the sheltered, close-knit world of military families has been one of his story's most closely guarded mysteries. His parents, Admiral George S. Morrison and Clara Clarke Morrison, have never commented publicly on their notorious firstborn son. Jim's brother and sister have been equally reluctant to speak of their brother. Whether fear of scrutiny or a desire for privacy drives this steely reticence, any inquiries to the Morrison family concerning the late rock star and poet Jim Morrison are parried by California attorneys claiming to represent his estate. The Morrison family's wall of silence has immured Jim's childhood, especially his tense and unhappy adolescence, since the day he died.

This shouldn't be surprising, since Jim Morrison tried to convince the media that his parents were dead, and that his siblings never existed. He probably thought he was doing them a favor.

Here's what is known about Jim's first twenty years.

His father, George Stephen Morrison, known as Steve, was born in Georgia in 1920 and raised in Leesburg, Florida. The Morrison family was descended from Scottish settlers who arrived in America in the late eighteenth century. The name Morrison is thought by some scholars to derive from the Latin root of *Moorish*. In Roman times soldiers from far-flung provinces were moved around to guard different parts of the empire. Thus Celtic troops from Britain would be sent to guard Morocco, while Moors from North Africa maintained order in Britain. Folklorists say, for example, that the quaint English custom of the Morris dance can been traced to a Moorish antecedent. In this context, Morrison could mean "Moor's son." Late in his life, Jim would visit Morocco at least twice, searching for something he was unable to describe to his traveling companions.

Steve Morrison's parents were hardworking, God-fearing, nondrinking southern Presbyterians, and Steve followed the family's tradition of military service and entered the U.S. Naval Academy in the late 1930s. He was a trim young man, short of stature and serious, with an air of quiet authority. With World War II about to begin, his class was hustled through an early graduation in 1941, and Steve Morrison was posted to Hawaii for flight training. Later that year, just before the Japanese attack on Pearl Harbor, he met Clara Clarke at a military dance. Blond, bubbly, very pretty and slightly heavy, she was the daughter of a Wisconsin lawyer and political maverick who defended union activists and had run for political office as a socialist candidate. It is interesting that Jim Morrison's maternal grandfather came from the great populist/progressive/socialist strain of American radicalism, a powerful sector of dissent and anger that challenged the two-party establishment from a strong political base in the upper Midwest and produced national leaders like Robert La Follette.

After a brief and war-torn courtship typical of thousands of young couples in that dangerous time, Steve Morrison and Clara Clarke were married in April 1942. They moved to Pensacola, Florida, where Steve continued flight training before shipping out on a vessel laying mines in the waters around Alaska. Their first child, named James Douglas Morrison, was born in Melbourne, on Florida's Atlantic coast near Cape Canaveral, on December 8, 1943, amid the greatest burst of military energy his country ever experienced. He was called Jimmy by his family, and answered to that name all his life, at least to those who knew him intimately.

His father was soon flying Hellcat fighters in the South Pacific, and spent the next eighteen months on duty. While her husband was overseas, Clara lived with her husband's parents, Paul and Caroline Morrison, who operated a laundry in Clearwater, on the Gulf of Mexico. Jimmy lived in his grandparents' house until he was three, and Clearwater remained the family's hometown of record during Jimmy's childhood.

Steve Morrison emerged from the war a decorated Navy pilot and an ambitious officer devoted to his career. His first postwar assignment was in Washington, but, determined to rise in the naval hierarchy, he moved his young family around with very little notice as he earned promotions and his assignments changed. Correctly guessing in 1947 that quick advancement lay in the new technologies that were reshaping the world, Steve Morrison transferred into nuclear weapons systems in the period when the hydrogen bomb was being developed at Los Alamos and tested at the White Sands proving grounds in the deserts of New Mexico. His new duties required a high-level security clearance that specified that his work was never discussed at home. Obscured by official secrecy (references to Lieutenant Morrison's duties during this period are still heavily censored in copies of his naval records made available to the public), all that is known about this era is that the Morrison family lived in naval housing in the vicinity of Albuquerque. Jim's sister, Anne, was born there when he was three years old.

If his sister's arrival was traumatic for the quiet only child, something else happened in New Mexico that left a profoundly vivid impression on

Jimmy. Early one morning the family was driving in the desert some-where between Albuquerque and Santa Fe. According to Jim, his mother and father were in the car, along with his grandparents. At one point his father pulled off to the side of the two-lane road, and he and Jimmy's grandfather got out of the car. Jimmy looked up and saw the grisly re-mains of a very recent head-on collision between another car and a truck carrying some Pueblo or Hopi Indians, "scattered on dawn's high-way bleeding," as he later famously remembered. Dead and injured peo-ple were lying in the road, and from somewhere rose the anguished voice of a woman wailing in pain and hysteria.

Fascinated by the bloody spectacle, Jimmy tried to get out of the car to follow his father, but his mother held him back. So Jimmy pressed his face to the window, taking in the gory aftermath of the fatal traffic acci-dent. His grandmother blurted that she'd always heard that Indians didn't cry, but these people were wailing in anguish. Jimmy shuddered and strained to get a last look at the carnage as his father climbed back in the car and pulled onto the road again. A few miles farther, they stopped at a filling station and called the highway patrol and an ambu-lance. Jimmy was visibly disturbed and kept asking questions. He got so upset that his father finally said, "Jimmy, it didn't really happen. It was just a bad dream."

But he never forgot the dying Indians. "It was the first time I discov-ered death," he recounted many years later, as tape rolled in a darkened West Hollywood recording studio. "I'm just this little ... like a child is a flower, man, whose head is just floating in the breeze. But the reaction I get now, thinking back, looking back, is that, possibly, the soul of one of those Indians, maybe several of them, just ran over and jumped into my brain. . . . It's not a ghost story, man. It's something that really means something to me."

After this encounter on a desert highway, Jimmy began to wet his bed at night. It drove his mother crazy. As an adult he remembered go-ing to his mother's bed when it happened, and being forced to go back to his room and sleep in his wet sheets. *Shame city.* He tried to hide it when it happened, but she always found out. Then he started to be afraid to sleep in his own bed at all. Some nights he fell asleep curled in a ball on the floor. (The bedwetting may also have been connected to a childhood bout with rheumatic fever, which Jim told his doctor about in 1970. This illness might have, additionally, weakened Jimmy's heart.)

IF JIM MORRISON'S TRUSTED LAWYER is to be believed, Jimmy was introduced early to sexuality. In 1969, while preparing for the obscenity and lewd conduct trial that could have resulted in a prison term for his client, Beverly Hills attorney Max Fink debriefed Jim Morrison on his sexual history. According to a transcript of a taped interview later conducted by Fink's wife, Margaret, the lawyer said that he asked Jim why he had chosen to expose himself onstage in his home state of Florida. "I thought it was a good way to pay homage to my parents," Jim replied.

Taken aback, and mindful of the abyss that seemed to separate Jim Morrison from his family, Fink then asked what his parents had done to him. Jim reportedly mentioned the bed-wetting trauma, then let slip that he'd been molested by a man when he was a boy. Jim refused to tell Max Fink who had molested him, except to say it was someone close to the family. When Jimmy tried to tell his mother, Fink claimed, she had gotten angry, called him a liar, and insisted such a thing never could have happened. Fink said that Jim began to cry as he told him the story, and claimed Jim had said that he could never forgive his mother for this. (For the record, the Morrison family's attorneys categorically denied that any of these incidents or "this alleged behavior" ever occurred.)

IN 1948 THE FAMILY MOVED AGAIN, to Los Altos in northern California. Here Jimmy Morrison started public school as a shy and chubby boy who hated getting on the bus in the morning. Cold War paranoia was in the air amid fear of nuclear attack by the Soviet Union. Schoolchildren of Jimmy's generation were indoctrinated about the omnipresent threat of thermonuclear annihilation and required to practice duck-and-cover routines during monthly air raid drills, sometimes squatting under their desks, sometimes lining the darkened halls of their school buildings to be beyond the range of shattering glass as phantom A-bombs pulverized their world. Television—viewed on tiny, seven-inch black-and-white screens—made a deep impression on Jimmy. In second grade, Jimmy and his buddy Jeff Morehouse—another son of a navy family whose wanderings roughly kept pace with the Morrisons—were avid viewers of Dumont's *Captain Video* and paid-up members of his fan club, the Video Rangers.

Jimmy's younger brother, Andrew, was born in Los Altos the following year, 1949. Then this fairly typical navy family's transient wanderings began in earnest. They went back to Washington, D.C., for a year before moving to Claremont, California, where they lived while Steve Morrison was serving in Korea. Jim attended Longfellow Elementary School. In sixth grade he was a slightly chubby, asthmatic natural leader, the best kickballer in the school, and president of the student council, which required him to open morning assemblies by reciting the pledge of allegiance. But then Jimmy got in trouble. He was asked to leave his Cub Scout pack after he refused to follow directions and was unruly with the den mother.

In 1955, the Morrisons returned to Albuquerque, New Mexico, where, family members recall, they noticed a change in Jimmy. He gave up his piano lessons and refused to spend time with the family. Living on the edge of the desert, Jimmy became fascinated with the mysterious, prehistoric-looking desert reptiles—lizards, snakes, armadillos—that scurried around the hot, dry landscape. The horned toads fascinated him, little scaly dragons with flicking tongues and nightmare eyes. He hunted them down, seeking their lairs, reading books about them. Desert reptiles became Jim's personal totem, making dozens of appearances in his notebooks on their way to what became a national fetishization at the behest of the future Lizard King.

In 1955 Commander Steve Morrison was assigned to the aircraft carrier USS *Midway*, and the family relocated again, this time to San Francisco. They moved into a big shingled house in suburban Alameda, where Jimmy began the eighth grade amid the convulsive birth of rock and roll and the epic milestones of juvenile delinquency—Elvis censored on *Ed Sullivan*, Bill Haley's irresistible "Rock Around the Clock," Little Richard's savage jungle rhythms, Fats Domino's gutbucket New Orleans R & B, Chuck Berry's clever three-minute high school anthems, black leather motorcycle jackets, switchblade knives—a James Dean maelstrom of 1950s rebellion amid Eisenhower-era conformity, repressed sexuality, and the political stresses and apocalyptic threats of the Cold War.

POSTER CHILD

EXPERTS HAVE LONG OBSERVED that some children of military families may be at risk for various social problems and psychological disorders. Military families are called upon to move often and on short notice. There isn't much time to cultivate friendships before the family moves on to the next post or assignment. In the navy, with the ambitious, on-the-move father often away at sea, the mothers did the bulk of the child raising, and often had to cope with rootlessness, emotional disorders, and alcoholism. Jimmy's family moved four times before he was four years old, and this lack of stability may have engendered a physical restlessness and a sense of profound alienation that stayed with Jim Morrison for the rest of his life. The adult Jim Morrison often didn't know where he would sleep each night, and he preferred it that way. Even after the royalty checks for "Light My Fire" started in 1967, Jim never owned a house or rented an apartment, preferring instead to live with girlfriends, crash in motels, or just pass out on the beat-up sofa at the Doors' office.

Discipline was a problem for Jimmy, and the despair of his mother. Resentment, on the boy's part, was built into the situation. An ambitious officer had to put the navy ahead of his family. It was the way things were in the services, and the families had to accept it. With his father mostly absent, his mother was the authority figure in the family constellation. She was all he had to rebel against. When his father came home from sea duty, Jimmy would overhear his mother complaining bitterly to his father about him, enumerating all his mistakes, malicious pranks, and fuckups.

Years later, Jimmy's friends wondered why he liked to throw darts at naked *Playboy* pinups (taped upside down) on his bedroom walls.

When his father was home, the atmosphere was often tense. Steve Morrison was known in the navy as charming, soft-spoken, forceful, and extremely intelligent. At home this battle-tested sea officer tended to bark orders at his children. Is it any wonder that ten years later his son created the Vietnam era's greatest antiwar song, "The Unknown Soldier"? Jim's younger brother told interviewer Jerry Hopkins that Clara bossed Steve around at home, and was clearly the dominant personality in the family. Early on the couple had decided not to hit their children, so punishment was dished out verbally, with—in Jimmy's case at least—lashes of guilt and shame added to the standard military dressing down. Andy Morrison said that while this would make him cry, Jimmy took this verbal punishment with dry eyes.

Jimmy's behavior was a family flashpoint, with his mother as the lightning rod and designated scapegoat. In 1969, at a chaotic Doors concert in Seattle, a drunk and upset Jim Morrison waved the band to a ragged halt, stopped the show, and told the audience: "I've been reading about the problems kids have with their parents. Yeah. That's right. And I'm here to tell you—*I didn't get enough love as a kid!*"

Intelligent and articulate, Jimmy also had a dirty mind and a vivid imagination, and he'd often blurt out things in school that got him in trouble. An early pastime was cutting up comic books to rearrange Donald Duck and Daisy in sexual positions with new dialogue. When *Mad* magazine began publishing its surreal parodies and sick humor in 1956, Jimmy was an early subscriber. He read his issues of *Mad* till the pages wore out, and tried to duplicate the harsh comic screams and outbursts that peppered the texts, driving everyone around him crazy. Jimmy's slouched deportment, extreme lack of eye contact, and sarcastic and insolent attitude drove his parents to distraction. His sniggering and public antics (nose-picking, spitballs, snide remarks) embarrassed the family at navy functions, and they soon learned to leave him home when they could.

Andy Morrison indicated that Jim began to bully his siblings when he was about thirteen. His brother suffered the most. Andy would be watching TV and Jimmy would lumber in, get him in a headlock, turn him over, sit on his head, and fart in his face. Or pin him down and let a gob of spit hang over his face. Outdoors Jimmy would pick up a rock and tell his brother, "I'll give you ten," which meant Andy should start running. The little boy learned quickly that Jimmy wasn't kidding. He would throw the rock. In 1955 the Morrisons were on a ski holiday when Jimmy put his brother and sister on a toboggan and pushed off downhill, aiming for the side of a barn. The sled picked up speed but Jimmy didn't brake. Faster, *faster*. His sister started crying. His mother was shouting. A horrified Steve Morrison had to sprint to save his children from injury. Jimmy told his furious, disbelieving father that he'd only been kidding around.

Conventional wisdom might nominate Jim Morrison as a poster child for the instability of military families. The lack of roots, the father's continual absence, the mother's uneven discipline, the difficulties that a bright but socially isolated child encountered in receiving approval from friends, teachers, and parents, all can be used to explain Jim's urges to rebel in order to get the attention he needed. Yet some observers counter that these peripatetic military families form a larger, extended family that often provides a secure enclave for its own and produces flexible, well-adjusted children. Military families often moved together, and the women who kept their families going amid such dislocation often forged bonds that survived for years and even for generations.

Jimmy Morrison was obviously exceptional, a piece of work, a pistol. No one could really control him. He was a kid with a rocket in his pocket. Early on, Jimmy learned how to push people's buttons to get the recognition he craved. Later on, as his father rose in the ranks and was able to spend more time at home, he reasserted his role in the family with a program of strict rules and discipline, which was deeply resented by both Andy and Jimmy.

S EVERAL IDEAS TAKEN FROM THE FIELDS of psychology and child development might help to illuminate Jim Morrison's behavior later in life. "Attachment Theory," for instance, suggests that children who receive insensitive, neglectful, or inconsistent care can develop difficulties with controlling their emotions, and often turn to drugs and alcohol to soothe themselves. Such children often have trouble with trusting other people and maintaining consistent relationships, and may also become impossible to control. They often exaggerate their behavior to get the attention they crave, with negative attention being better than none.

Insensitive or neglectful care can also result in young children relying upon fantasies of grandiosity to protect against anxiety. Some display a tendency to break away from their families prematurely. This independence can make them feel powerful and untouchable, as if nothing will hurt them. As they grow, unprotected, they become self-destructive, accident-prone, and are often the victims of their own poor judgment.

While no one can say for certain that Jim Morrison fit into all of these criteria, they way he conducted himself later on makes anyone interested in him wonder what lay beneath his permanent state of rebellion.

IN 1955 JIMMY WENT to see James Dean in the movie *Rebel Without a Cause. Rebel,* directed by Nicholas Ray, was the archetypal juvenile-delinquency film, pitching its restless hero Jim (called "Jimbo" by his alcoholic father) into an affluent California high school milieu of anxiety, conflict, and despair. Dean's riveting performance as the rebel Jim was set against visually exotic Los Angeles locations like the observatory in Griffith Park, and Sal Mineo's tragic sacrificial death at the film's end made a deep impression on Jimmy.

Rebel Without a Cause also began Jim Morrison's deep and obsessive love of movies, and his often-stated desire to learn how to make them. *Rebel* is the first film mentioned in Jim's surviving notebooks. He also mentions *Giant,* James Dean's next film, released the following year after Dean's death in a car crash. It's also possible that the movies, especially the westerns that flooded American theaters in the 1950s, played a crucial role in moving Jim to write. His first poem, "Pony Express," now lost, was probably based on a Hollywood western that he caught at a Saturday-afternoon matinee while living in Alameda. It was definitely in Alameda that Jimmy Morrison first caught the beatnik poetry virus, which infected him for the rest of his life.

THE BEAT POETS

FROM 1956 TO 1958 the Morrisons lived in a big shingled house with an Edwardian turret at 1717 Alameda Avenue in the leafy island suburb of Alameda, the site of the navy's biggest air station. It was a relatively quiet time in Jim's life—his mother was very content there and was fondly remembered by neighbors—and would subsequently prove to be highly influential in terms of Jim Morrison's artistic aspirations.

Jim lived by himself in an attic room at the top of the old house, listening to Elvis and Ricky Nelson, while downstairs his mother played her own music—Harry Belafonte, Frank Sinatra, and the original cast albums from *South Pacific* and *My Fair Lady.* Jim was popular in school, darkly handsome and no longer chubby, friendly and very funny, able to banter with teachers who were impressed with a reading level and intelligence rarely encountered in young teenagers. At thirteen Jim's favorite writer was Norman Mailer, and he could roll out entire *Mad* magazine parodies from memory. Yet his school records indicate his teachers' frustrations at Jim's hyperactivity, and in some classes he was forced to sit alone so he wouldn't bother the other students or disrupt the class with his loud interjections and joke accents.

Inspired by *Mad* and the other satiric magazines of the new "sick humor" genre (*Cracked, Sick, Trump,* etc.) Jim's notebook sketches became wilder and more deeply cynical. He specialized in obscene drawings of people with surreally exaggerated sexual organs and enormous assholes, obsessively inking in bodily fluids, especially excrement, menstrual blood, mucus, and sperm. With his father's big reel-to-reel tape recorder Jimmy made fake radio commercials promoting masturbation. (One reel of these survives and is of almost professional quality, complete with sound effects.) He liked to answer the family's phone with broad Negro dialect copied from the *Amos 'n' Andy* show or cheesy Oriental accents. Jimmy spent hours in his quiet attic room cutting and pasting comics into ever-more-complex lewd collages, relettering the texts, going the sick humor mags one step further:

LUCY: "I'll give you fifty cents if you'll fuck me, Charlie Brown!"
CHARLIE BROWN: "Throw in your trycicle [sic] and it's a deal, Baby."

His best friend in Alameda was a street-smart neighbor his age, Fud Ford, who was as reckless and fun loving as Jimmy was. Jim had access to the navy's gyms, pools, and athletic facilities, and the boys would get into trouble on the diving board at the officers' club swimming pool and embarrass the family. (Ford said that Jimmy's father beat him with his belt for one of these incidents when some officers' wives felt they'd been insulted.) All the streets in Alameda led down to the beach, so in the warm months there was a lot of swimming and clowning around. There was a pretty girl they used to go swimming with. Jimmy discovered a way to sneak into her family's boathouse so they could watch her change into her swimsuit.

In September 1957 Jimmy started the ninth grade at Alameda High. He made the swim team, specializing in the butterfly stroke. He was good in class, and always had the answers even though he'd never deign to put his hand in the air. He was a charismatic clown, a troublemaker, very funny and loud, a clever mimic and practical joker whose grating, outrageous pranks caused "Morrison stories" to float around the school ten years before they surfaced in the media.

One of his favorite stunts was to pretend to collapse on the staircase at school and lie there, unconscious, while the others had to step around him. He did this a lot at Alameda, and apparently kept it up at his next school since it was a major attention-getter. It was like Jimmy's big joke. Classmates recalled that Jimmy would actually lie there a long time (according to Fud Ford, "pretending he was dead"), seemingly oblivious to attempts to rouse him. When he was satisfied that the game was played out, he'd pick himself and his books up off the floor, accept the inevitable detention ticket from the hall monitors, and carry on with his usual smirk and swagger.

But was this really a joke? Or was this Jimmy's method of faking his way through a mortifying disorder that left him prostrate on the floor, with embarrassing minutes lost from his life? Or was it what the ancients called "the falling sickness," the malady of kings and prophets? Anyone familiar with Jim Morrison's later life and career knows that losing consciousness and passing out was a regular occurrence for him. He fainted or fell down during rehearsals, recording sessions, photo shoots. He collapsed during concerts, poetry readings, bar crawls. He passed out on car rides, in airports, and during plane trips. Shattering theatrical collapses were incorporated into the Doors' stage act, a drama Jim Morrison later refined into the apex of rock theater.

Was it all really an act? Put together, the anecdotal and visual evidence could suggest that Jim Morrison suffered an undiagnosed case of petit mal epilepsy that may have begun at the age of fourteen, if not earlier. In high school, it cost him a lot of time in the principal's office. And everyone talked about Jimmy Morrison and all the funny, outrageous shit he liked to pull.

Jim started tenth grade in the fall of 1958, but he preferred to cut school and visit beatnik hangouts in San Francisco. The year earlier, two significant events had shaken America. First the Soviet Union launched Sputnik, the first satellite to orbit the earth. This sensational event provoked spasms of American self-doubt and recriminations about being beaten into space by the Russians. It began the so-called missile gap debate that later helped put John Kennedy in the White House. The second event was the publication of Jack Kerouac's second novel, *On the Road,* the stream-of-consciousness saga of existentially aware youth, adrift on the vast highways and midnight streets of American cities, that turned an entire generation on to the Beat subculture. The book became a best-seller and media icon, and cracked the corporate, conformist façade of the 1950s wide open. On America's two coasts, Sputnik anxiety was allayed by beatnik cool, offering an alternate way of righteous existence in the late fifties.

The Beats traced their style to French symbolist poets, existentialist philosophers, and Zen masters. Jazz, drugs, nonconformity and Buddhism were cool. Gray flannel suits were uncool. Beat writers like Kerouac on the West Coast, William Burroughs in Paris, and Allen Ginsberg in New York became overnight culture stars.

The Beat poets were the legatees of Dylan Thomas, the brilliant Welsh poet whose magical Celtic cadences and lush imagery had spread via the new technology of long-playing phonograph records as much as through printed books, before he drank himself to death in Greenwich Village in 1953. They were also in the tradition of radical American writers like Walt Whitman and Mark Twain, and modernist poets like William Carlos Williams, with whom Ginsberg particularly identified.

In the Beat universe, Paris was philosophy, New York was jazz, and San Francisco was poetry. Ginsberg called this flowering "the San Francisco Renaissance." Often accompanied by bongo drummers, star beatniks could be heard declaiming in the jazz clubs seven nights a week. Allen Ginsberg premiered his Beat epic *Howl* in San Francisco in 1955, and the other Beats, many of them identifiable characters in *On the Road*—Robert Duncan, Robert Creeley, Tom Parkinson, Lawrence Ferlinghetti, Gary Snyder, Kenneth Patchen, Philip Whalen, Kenneth Rexroth, Michael McClure—often gave public readings of new work in the coffeehouses, art galleries, and bookstores. San Francisco was the third corner of the Beat international, a city where poets, not athletes, were local heroes. In San Francisco and neighboring Sausalito and North Beach, poetry ruled.

When Jimmy and Fud skipped school and headed into the city, their first stop was usually Ferlinghetti's City Lights Books at 261 Columbus Avenue. A sign in the window boasted "Banned Books." Jimmy liked to hang out there in his beatnik uniform of sweatshirt, sandals, and jeans, hoping to meet any of the poets who might show up. Once Jimmy said hello to Ferlinghetti, and when the poet and author of *A Coney Island of the Mind* returned his greeting, Jimmy turned red with pleasure. He and Fud would go to Stairway Records in Oakland to buy Dylan Thomas LPs on Caedmon, or comedy albums by Tom Lehrer or Lenny Bruce. Fud took Jimmy to Duo Records, an R & B record store in Oakland, where Jimmy first heard Chicago blues stars Muddy Waters and Howlin' Wolf, and New Orleans legends like Professor Longhair. Jimmy and Fud read *On the Road* and plugged into its Beat Generation dreams, talking endlessly about the unimaginable joys of hitchhiking, inexpensive Mexican whores, and the endless highways of America illuminated by Zen flares of enlightenment.

Jimmy fell in love with Dean Moriarty's ferocious American energy, and Kerouac's concept of Dean as one of "the mad ones, the ones who are mad to live, mad to talk, mad to be saved, desirous of everything at the same time, the ones who never yawn or say a commonplace thing, but burn, burn, burn like fabulous roman candles exploding like spiders across the stars." He practiced Dean's speed-addled laugh—"heeeee-heeeee-heeee"—until it made his mother nuts. Jimmy's facial hair began to grow, and he tried to develop a proper beatnik goatee until his mother ordered him to shave it off and get a haircut too. She would shout at Jim and he'd just laugh at her. Once she went to grab him and he put her into a headlock and, still laughing, grabbed a pen and scribbled on her arm. Even Clara had to laugh at this. "You don't fight fair!" she yelled at her son.

A S THE SCHOOL YEAR PROGRESSED Jimmy kept up his serial provocations. Because he was so funny and had this weird presence, he was the kind of kid who could get away with being a jerk and no one would call him on it. But he also had an unexpected compassionate side. He had a classmate, Richard Slaymaker, who was seriously ill with leukemia. Jimmy liked to visit him after school, bringing him comics and comedy records to keep his spirits up. He'd take Richard for walks in his wheelchair and do wheelies with him. It seemed to Fud that

Jimmy, who was fascinated with death, was almost studying Richard as the disease progressed and his skin turned different colors. When he died after six months of almost daily visits, Jimmy Morrison cried.

Late in 1958, halfway through the school year, Steve Morrison was promoted to captain and reassigned. His parents told Jimmy that the family was moving to Alexandria, Virginia, right after Christmas. According to Fud Ford, Jimmy was crushed and didn't want to go. On the last day of classes, Ford said, Jimmy walked up to the homeroom teacher's desk and announced that his family was moving away, and that he wanted to leave with a bang. Then he lit a cherry bomb, and sauntered out of the room before it exploded.

Jimmy came over to Fud's house to say good-bye on the day the Morrisons left Alameda. Then Jimmy got in the captain's ugly green Packard and didn't look back as his father pulled away. Fud Ford would later recall: "Jimmy felt bad, because he didn't want to go to Virginia. It was one of the few times in my childhood that I cried. They were taking my best friend away."

Jimmy was sent to Virginia, ahead of the rest of the family, so he could resume high school there in January 1959. For a few weeks he stayed with the Morehouse family, who had a son, Jeff, his own age. It would be five years before Jimmy was able to return to his beloved California for good.

NIETZSCHE AND BO DIDDLEY

IN 1959 ALEXANDRIA, VIRGINIA, was a sleepy suburb of Washington, D.C. Populated mostly by the families of government employees and ranking military personnel, it was less affluent than neighboring Arlington, but was still respectable enough. In January the Morrisons moved into a comfortable house at 310 Woodlawn Avenue in the upscale Braddock Heights neighborhood, an address that Jimmy was able to call home for an unprecedented two and a half years. That month, Jimmy enrolled in George Washington High School to finish the tenth grade. Rather than charm (or alarm) his schoolmates like he'd done at

Alameda, he tried to blend in quietly. He refused to try out for the swim team. He told some kids who tried to talk to him that he was an orphan who'd been carried off by Gypsies. He seemed nervous, ill at ease, and anxious, and when he wasn't roaming the back streets and old wharves of Alexandria, or shoplifting comics and candy on Main Street, he preferred to read or sketch in his notebooks alone in his basement bedroom, which had its own separate entrance so he could come and go at will. He told one of his new friends that he sometimes could go for weeks without contact with his family.

Ten years later, trying to describe his high school experience in Virginia to an interviewer, Jim recalled his feelings of foreboding. "I just had this . . . underlying sense that something was not quite right. I felt blinders being put on me as I grew older. I and all my friends were being channeled down a long, narrowing tunnel. When you're in school, you're taking a risk. You can get a lot out of it, but you can get a lot of harm too."

Alameda High had been relaxed and easy compared to racially segregated, uptight, status-conscious George Washington High. Classmates vividly recall that, early on, Jimmy stunned some of his teachers with his wide reading and erudition. After the first marking period he made the honor roll. Then a teacher saw Jimmy reading black writer James Baldwin's controversial novel *Giovanni's Room* in the lunchroom and told him to get that "nigger trash" off the school grounds. That was probably when Jimmy lost interest in school.

Lonely, depressed, isolated from his family, Jimmy liked to stay up late listening to Bible radio, mesmerized by the southern evangelist hellfire preachers and the riffing deejays of zillion-watt AM rock and roll stations broadcasting to all of North America from just south of the Mexican border. One night Jimmy thought about killing himself, but then Bo Diddley came on the radio, singing "Crackin' Up," a jokey song about being nuts. Jimmy had to laugh, and that made him feel better, made him feel that life could be worth living. Bo Diddley, protean and streetwise inventor of black rock and roll, had saved Jimmy's life that night.

"FRIEDRICH NIETZSCHE KILLED JIM Morrison," said Doors cofounder Ray Manzarek, who claimed to have watched it happen. It was from the writings and legendary career of the mad German philosopher that Jimmy got the idea that anything that doesn't kill you just makes you stronger.

In the first paragraph of *On the Road,* Jack Kerouac cites Friedrich Nietzsche as the guiding spirit of his book. In the summer between his sophomore and junior years, Jimmy delved into Nietzsche's astonishing work and tragic life, and what he read changed him in profound, even perhaps fatal, ways. If Nietzsche didn't exactly kill Jim Morrison, his radical thoughts set Jim on a course that provided its own tragic momentum.

Nietzsche was the first modern writer to break away from two thousand years of inherited moral and metaphysical beliefs. As an alternative to the Christian precepts he found contemptible, Nietzsche invented an absurd and disturbed mythology of his own. In his superheated writing style, and with the unshakable fervor of a visionary comfortable with his own often contradictory views, Nietzsche tried to break through conventional rationality and proclaim a new way of thinking. For Nietzsche, mankind and the totality of his history were only justified by the birth of genius, and his highest goal was the flourishing of culture. His adventurism and rhetorical cadences were so monumentally influential that they inspired an even darker strain of Germanic mysticism fifty years later, when Adolf Hitler began his rise to power.

But just as Nietzsche was beginning to enjoy the first real recognition of his brilliance, he suffered a nervous and physical collapse in the Italian city of Turin. In January 1889, watching in horror as a hansom cabdriver flogged his lame horse in the street, Nietzsche collapsed in a paroxysm of mental anguish. He never recovered from the trauma, spending the next eleven years as a mental invalid until he died in 1900. One of the great mysteries of the philosophical world is why he fell so quickly from the heights of creativity into a state of abject mental helplessness. His modern biographers claim he was syphilitic, a closeted homosexual, and suffered from manic-depressive psychosis that gave way to chronic madness.

According to one notebook, Jimmy read *The Birth of Tragedy* twice that summer, and then kept reading: Nietzsche's *Beyond Good and Evil.* William S. Burroughs's *Naked Lunch,* which he got from an odd little bookstore in Georgetown. Norman Mailer's *The Deer Park.* The Marquis de Sade's writings, newly published by Grove Press. John O'Hara's *Butterfield 8.* But nothing he read left a more lasting impression on Jimmy Morrison than his encounter with Friedrich Nietzsche. Just as Nietzsche had opened the door of modern consciousness, he also opened a portal in the consciousness of a young writer in the Virginia suburbs in 1959.

THE LIZARD KING'S SCHOOL DAYS

JIMMY SEEMED TO PERK UP in the eleventh grade. Once he felt more familiar in school he started falling down again, playing jokes, talking in class, passing out in the halls, balancing precariously on high ledges. Dean Moriarty's hyena laugh echoed down the halls of George Washington High, channeled through Jimmy's powerful lungs. He talked too much in class, bothered other kids. "They made me sit at a special table by myself," he told an interviewer. He dominated discussion in the classes he liked—history and English—and debated with the teachers, did the minimum required work, and had a B+ average. (School records indicated that his IQ was 149. His college board scores were 630 verbal, 528 in math.) Despite his oddball inclinations, his natural charisma and pithy catchphrases drew others to him, and in school he moved with the elite group of brains, athletes, and predebs. But Jimmy steadfastly refused to take part in sports or school activities, or join any clubs. He was recruited by the elite student fraternity, but told the BMOCs that he wasn't interested. He showed some of his poetry (including probably the earliest version of "Horse Latitudes," which dates from this period) to the editor of the literary magazine, who refused to let him publish it. He mocked and mimicked his teachers, and cheated openly in math and science classes. During a chemistry exam, he suddenly jumped on a lab table, wildly swinging his arms. "Sorry ma'am," he drawled to the startled teacher. "Ah's jes' chasin' a bee!" He got out of a detention one day by telling the teacher he was being operated on for a brain tumor. His mother had to field a call from the concerned principal the following morning. The kids who didn't like him dismissed him as someone who was always playing a role.

After school he went home and read with the radio on. Elvis sang "It's Now or Never." Frankie Avalon. Percy Faith. The Kingston Trio. He heard the ethereal voice of nineteen-year-old Boston folksinger Joan

Baez on the radio, and couldn't get enough of her. He also took up painting after stealing a set of brushes and paints from an art supply store, executing several primitive self-portraits in which his face is a contorted rictus of demented mirth, and he's wearing a crown. He worked at this obsessively for a while, and his brother asked him why. "You can't read all the time," Jimmy replied. "Your eyes get tired." Most weekdays at five-thirty, he watched *American Bandstand,* the teen dance program broadcast live from Philadelphia that featured pop stars lip-synching to their hits. *Bandstand* got even more interesting in 1960, when Chubby Checker's hit record "The Twist" spawned increasingly sexual dance crazes (the Hully Gully, Watusi, Monkey, etc.) that sparked a national debate in the early sixties about whether African mating customs should be performed by white kids in the suburbs.

Jim also got a girlfriend. She was a year younger than Jimmy, and was introduced to him by Jeff Morehouse. Tandy Martin lived in the neighborhood and was pretty and petite, with curly brown hair, and for a while they were inseparable. He told her he wanted to be a writer, and loaned her some of his notebooks with the sketches and poems that he worked on. They'd walk to school together. Jimmy told her constantly that he wanted to kiss her toes. At night he appeared under her bedroom window, tossing coins at the glass to try to wake her up. When she came downstairs, he'd be gone. The next morning he would deny he'd been there. A lot of his show-off public antics—declaiming poetry, balancing on things, wading in fountains—embarrassed her. He affected a mock-Virginian drawl. "Tandeh, Ah thank Ah'm a-gonna go ovuh and pee-yuss on that there fahr hydrant," he'd say, as he started to unzip his chinos. Mortified, she would scream at him until he laughed at her. She asked him why he played games with her all the time. He told her, "Nobody would stay interested in me if I was normal."

Soon he was bullying Tandy the way he bullied his younger brother. Jim and Tandy would take the bus into Washington together, and he would suddenly ditch her and disappear, leaving her crying and confused until he showed up again, seemingly out of nowhere. He swore in front of her mother. When Jimmy was in one of his black moods, he made those around him suffer, and years later everyone remembered that it was Tandy Martin who bore the brunt of Jimmy Morrison's pain. Once he told her he had a problem, one that he couldn't talk to his parents about, and she got him to see the youth counselor at Westminster Presbyterian Church. But Jim never told her what they talked about.

I N 1997, a California woman named Linda Ashcroft published an account of her relationship with Jim Morrison, one that she claimed lasted from 1967 to 1970. Among the confidences she claims Jim shared with her was Jimmy's story of being raped by his father during a disciplinary beating while he was in high school, presumably in Alexandria. Jim, she claimed, told her that he missed dinner one night and that his father took him upstairs for a man-to-man talk that ended in a depraved sexual assault. Ashcroft's book, *Wild Child: Life with Jim Morrison,* was published first in London with this allegation, but when the book was published in America in 1998, the allegation was deleted from the text, presumably for legal reasons.

CANCEL MY SUBSCRIPTION

I N THE SUMMER OF 1960, something in Jimmy Morrison changed. Classmates remembered he seemed to undergo a change of personality. He appeared depressed and angry, and neglected his studies. His teachers noted his "irrational tendencies" and "impulsive behavior." He took no interest in the November presidential election—hotly debated in his politically conservative school—in which John Kennedy beat Richard Nixon and injected a new vigor into American political life. Jimmy later wrote in a notebook that he was both a fool and the smartest kid in class. As the identified beatnik of George Washington High, Jimmy tramped around in an old pair of worn desert boots, wrinkled khakis, and striped shirts so threadbare that one of his teachers asked him if the family was on welfare. If his mother gave him money to buy a new shirt, Jimmy would get a thrift shop shirt for a quarter and spend the rest on books. His collection of paperbacks—the only possessions he cared about— covered the walls of his room on shelves he had built himself out of boards and cinder blocks.

He continued to torture his brother and his girlfriend. (He'd recently taped up Andy's mouth while he was sleeping because Jimmy said Andy's breathing was bothering him.) He became even more of a loner, haunting Alexandria's used bookshops and decaying waterfront, where he hung out with old black men who fished from the rotting piers. Some people later claimed that Jimmy Morrison was seen in the rough soldier bars along Route 1, near Fort Belvoir, that featured black R & B bands, but this appears to be more legend than established fact. If Jimmy was trying to write poetry, on the evidence of "Horse Latitudes" they involved nautical imagery, inhuman cruelty, and a deep fear of drowning. Given a camera for his seventeenth birthday on December 8, 1960, Jimmy began photographing the most grim and depressing things he encountered in his solitary meanderings. None of these photographs are known to survive.

Jimmy's relationship with Tandy began to deteriorate under the cloud of his restless spirit and petty cruelties. He was alternately courtly and abrasive toward the thoroughly confused girl, and her concerned mother eventually asked Tandy to stop seeing him. Sometimes she thought he was just using her. Once he and Tandy were at his house when they heard his parents' car pull up. Jim dragged her up the stairs to his parents' bedroom, where he mussed up the sheets. Tandy got up and ran out, her own clothes in disarray, and Jim had a satisfied look on his face as he greeted his startled parents as though they had interrupted them making love. It's possible that Clara had voiced concerns about Jim's sexuality and that Jimmy wanted to dispel any doubts his parents had.

No one knew what was behind Jimmy's obvious downward spiral. As he became more sullen and defiant, his parents' attempts at discipline increased. His mother nagged him. He told friends (and an interviewer in 1970) that his father once chased him around the kitchen with a baseball bat. With Captain Morrison living at home for the first extended period in Jim's adolescence, the tension in the household between the brusque, somewhat preoccupied officer and the renegade teenaged beatnik may have been unbearable. Even the father's attempts to interest his son in his career by taking him aboard his ships were disastrous, as Jimmy found the unquestioned authority accorded his father distasteful.

Years later, Jim described his teenaged self as "an open sore." He described with weary resignation his impulses to screw up any situation in which he found himself. Jim Morrison recognized the impulses within himself with a poet's exactitude, knew exactly what he was doing, understood with wonderment and not a little sadness that he utterly lacked the Apollonian interior-control mechanisms that could make him stop behaving like a crazed Dionysius with a chip on his shoulder.

THINGS GOT EVEN WORSE as Jimmy was about to graduate from high school in the spring of 1961. Steve Morrison's early wish that his son follow him to the Naval Academy was plainly absurd in light of reality. It's possible that a clinically depressed Jimmy Morrison didn't bother to apply to any colleges or universities, but this level of neglect seems unlikely. There are no extant school records indicating that he did apply anywhere, however, and if he did he either wasn't accepted or didn't respond in time.

In the months when his classmates were excitedly preparing to take the next step in their lives, Jimmy Morrison didn't seem to have any specific plans. He had to be forced by his parents to put on a coat and tie and have his yearbook picture taken. (James Douglas Morrison's yearbook entry lists a solitary accomplishment: "Honor Roll 2.") In May, when the seniors had their prom, Jimmy refused to go. Jeff Morehouse took Tandy Martin to the prom instead. He failed to show up at his class's graduation ceremonies, infuriating his father, so the school mailed the troubled loner his diploma, and forgot about him until his first biographer came to George Washington High looking for his ghost twenty years later.

That summer Steve Morrison was reassigned to the aircraft carrier USS *Bonhomme Richard,* based in California. For whatever reasons, Steve and Clara Morrison decided that Jimmy would not go with them to the family's next home in Coronado, near San Diego. Arrangements were made instead for Jimmy to live with his grandparents back in Clearwater, and attend St. Petersburg Junior College, about ten miles away, beginning in September 1961. So, not yet eighteen, Jimmy Morrison— walking impulse disorder, shoplifting sociopath, public nuisance, human fly, family outcast, voracious reader—was exiled to rural Florida where, hopefully, he couldn't cause any more trouble.

It didn't end well with Tandy either. On what was, unbeknownst to her, their last Friday night date, Jimmy got drunk, and then started to cry when she called him on his behavior. Sobbing in her lap, he told her that he loved her.

"*Sure* you do," she said with sarcasm.

Suddenly he grabbed her arm and twisted it behind her back.

"You're so *smug,*" Jimmy hissed, and threatened to cut her face so no one else would look at her—probably something he'd seen in an old noir movie.

The next afternoon, Saturday, he called again to apologize and ask if he could see her. She told Jimmy that she had a long-standing date for a formal dance with someone else. There was a long silence. "But . . . I'm moving to Florida tomorrow," he blurted. "Tomorrow I'm gonna be gone—*for good.*" Tandy was stunned. It was the first she'd heard of this.

Jimmy arrived at her house a few minutes later, in a rage. She later told journalist Jerry Hopkins that Jimmy stood outside under a tree, and bawled, "At least I'll be *free* of you. . . . I'm leaving, and I'll *never* write you. . . . I won't even *think* of you!"

She tried to calm him down, but he was insistent and frantic to get back the notebooks he'd given her to read. Late Sunday night, she woke up and thought Jimmy was standing under her window. When she went downstairs and opened the back door, she saw a familiar figure walk quickly away, get into a car that looked like the Morrisons', and drive off into the night.

CHAPTER 2

CANCEL MY SUBSCRIPTION

Behind the laughing mask is a crying mask
Behind the mask of drunkenness is the mask of wisdom
Behind the mask of a criminal is the mask of a sojourner
Behind the mask of a revolutionary is the mask of a
movie director

—TERAYAMA SHUJI

SHOW YOUR MEAT

COASTAL FLORIDA BACK IN THE EARLY SIXTIES was still quiet, charming, and uncrowded. It was a subtropical realm of crystal springs, tannin-black rivers, and white houses with red-tiled roofs peeking above the royal palms and mangrove that opened onto white sand beaches. Jimmy loved the Gulf Coast landscape, which he later described as "a strange, exotic, exciting place." Returning to the first home he'd ever known, Jimmy Morrison moved in with his grandparents, Paul and Caroline Morrison. In September 1961 he began classes at St. Petersburg Junior College, a conservative institution that required Jimmy to wear a blazer and the striped school tie to class every day.

He hated it. He was bored out of his mind. A notebook records him alleviating the tedium of the bus rides between St. Pete and Clearwater by rubbing his book bag in his lap until he got hard.

The Morrisons lived in a small house near the town's library. Jimmy and several cartons of his books occupied the lone guest room. Jimmy loved his grandparents and generally treated them with southern deference and respect. No, he informed them, he wouldn't be joining them at church. In the year he lived with them, he spent as little time at their house as he could, and conducted himself with enough discretion that his drunken antics didn't touch their lives. When his grandma asked him about the empty beer and wine bottles she found in his wastebasket, he just laughed at her. He kept teasing them that he was going to bring a "nigger girl" home to meet them.

"We just didn't understand him, any of us," Caroline Morrison later said, meaning the extended Morrison clan. "There were so many sides to Jimmy.... You never knew what he was thinking."

His marks at school were only satisfactory. His A in English came on the strength of an essay on Albert Camus's 1942 existentialist novel, *The Stranger,* in which a faceless man in Algiers commits a senseless murder while in the helpless grip of life's absurdities. School records indicate he was thought of as impulsive, inconsistent, somewhat shy, and hypercritical of social institutions—like the school itself.

St. Petersburg had an arts community that flourished with the coming of the winter season, and as the autumn wore on Jimmy soon found out about the Contemporary, the area's beatnik coffeehouse, located in Pinellas Park just south of Clearwater. The Contemporary Arts Coffeehouse and Gallery was a hangout for local artists and bohemians. The owner, Tom Reese, was openly homosexual and reveled in his camp personality, so for the younger clients there was an element of risk and danger in just being seen there. (The Contemporary was officially off-limits for junior-college dorm residents.) Jimmy loved the place. Given a broad interpretation, his performing career could be said to have begun at the ramshackle clapboard house shaded by overgrown palmetto trees on the edge of a bayou.

He began going to the Contemporary on weekends with a boy who lived in his neighborhood, and then began going alone. Reese picked up on him immediately and tried to get him to pose nude for the life-study drawing classes held in the gallery. "[Jimmy] was very aware that he was attractive," Reese later recalled. "He just had that sexy feeling about him—very raw. Everybody wanted to go to bed with him.... Whether it was the boys or the girls, they were all attracted to him."

Jimmy would just shake his head and decline the modeling proposal. He was more interested in the Contemporary's film program that screened foreign movies ordered from Janus Films in New York. Reese showed Swedish art films like *Wild Strawberries,* French films with a little nudity like Roger Vadim's *And God Created Woman,* and early underground films such as Robert Frank's *Pull My Daisy,* a pantheon of Beat poets narrated by Jack Kerouac. This is probably where Jim got his first serious taste of non-Hollywood movies. An undated notebook entry thought to be from this era mentions Jean-Luc Godard's 1961 *Une Femme est une Femme.*

More important, the Contemporary held an open-microphone night on Sunday evenings, when anyone could get on the little stage and do their thing. Mostly folksingers signed up, but there were also some Beat poet/bongo combos, and Jimmy Morrison, this weirdo kid from the junior college who showed up with a ukulele and just let it rip with freeform poetics that seemed to spontaneously erupt from his mind and that no one really got. This was Jimmy's first experience performing for a live audience. "He would strum somewhat like [Allen] Ginsberg did," Reese remembered. "He'd sign up in advance, but I always felt he just made it up as he went along, based on whatever philosophy he was reading, because he read that stuff all the time."

After a few months of doing this, Jimmy even began to attract a tiny following at the Contemporary. Tom Reese became a sort of mentor and was probably the first person with any artistic credibility to convince Jimmy that he had real talent. "You're rather musical when you do your lines," he told Jimmy. "They may not rhyme, but they're very poetic." Reese and others convinced Jimmy to apply to Florida State University in Tallahassee, two hundred miles to the north, where his creative instincts could be brought along in a more progressive atmosphere. Reese also said he offered Jimmy some timeless showbiz advice: "Show Your Meat."

In the late spring of 1962, something happened that caused Jimmy to stop hanging out at the Contemporary. Whatever it was remains a mystery tinged with scandal. One of Steve Morrison's brothers was called in to extract Jimmy from some kind of trouble he'd gotten into, something that the Morrisons found shameful enough to refuse to discuss with anyone outside the family. Years later, during the 1969 obscenity trial preliminaries, while insisting he wasn't a homosexual, Jim told his lawyer Max Fink that he had been intimately involved with a man during his junior college days. He described this man as an older friend, the owner of a nightclub who had encouraged him and acted as a mentor.

Contacted about this thirty-five years after these events occurred, Tom Reese said, "Well . . . it certainly *sounds* like me." Asked if he had intimate relations with Jimmy Morrison, he paused before replying, "Well, let's put it this way. Everyone *wanted* to."

* * *

S PRING 1962. Jimmy was on his way to a party with some friends in Clearwater and they stopped at the Kallivokas brothers' house to pick up some beer. The youngest brother, Chris, couldn't come to the party because he had to finish a term paper on Elizabethan history, specifically Lord Essex's rebellion in 1601, so he could graduate from high school. "The earl of Essex?" Jimmy mused. "Yeah, I know all about him." Forgetting about the party, Jimmy spent the evening writing Chris's term paper, typing a clean eight-page draft, even creating a bibliography from memory. The paper earned an A from a teacher who had earned a master's degree in Elizabethan studies.

This paid off for Jimmy too. Chris was joining his older brother at FSU in August, and there was a spare room in the off-campus house they rented. Jimmy Morrison could live with them if he wanted. And there was another bonus. During the summer of 1962 Jimmy was introduced to a friend of Chris's girlfriend, a sixteen-year-old Clearwater high school student named Mary Werbelow. Mary was slight with long, auburn-colored red hair, a luminous smile, and a dancer's figure blessed with full breasts. She was from a good Catholic family, and, best for Jimmy, she was intelligent and inquisitive. He introduced her to the poetry he liked and whatever he was reading. Friends like Brian Gates, who knew Jimmy both in Clearwater and later in Tallahassee, noticed that when he was with Mary, Jimmy was much different from the drunken slacker he usually was. By himself, Jim would show up at dances and act like a tree—really aloof and weird. At parties he'd do stunts like balancing on apartment balconies and pretending to lose his balance. He said he liked to hear girls scream when they thought he was falling. At one party he cut himself doing a knife trick. Taken to the emergency room, he was so drunk and abusive that the doctor walked out before he finished stitching Jimmy up.

But Mary brought out the well-mannered southern gentleman hiding in Jimmy, an unfamiliar role to all who knew him as a compulsive instigator. He told his friends that Mary was someone special, a spiritual person he could talk with for hours. They shared their dreams. He told her he wanted to be a writer. She wanted to be a dancer in the movies, and had an after-school job teaching dance in the local community center. The extent of their intimacy is unknown, and Mary Werbelow has steadfastly refused to comment on their relationship. When Jimmy went to California to see his family later that summer, he told his younger brother that he got laid for the first time in Clearwater.

For the next eighteen months, while he was at Florida State, Jimmy often hitchhiked the 280 miles between Tallahassee and Clearwater to be near Mary Werbelow. Those solitary journeys on hot and dusty Florida two-lane blacktop roads, with his thumb out and his imagination on fire with lust and poetry and Nietzsche and God knows what else—taking chances on redneck truckers, furtive homos, and predatory cruisers—left an indelible psychic scar on Jimmy, whose notebooks began to obsessively feature scrawls and drawings of a lone hitchhiker, an existential traveler, faceless and dangerous, a drifting stranger with violent fantasies, a mystery tramp: the killer on the road.

RETURN TO SENDER

FLORIDA STATE IN THE AUTUMN of 1962 was a second-rate racially segregated education factory with a nationally ranked football team and a reputation as a raunchy party school. Frat-boy R & B was the jam of the day and beer the beverage of choice. While Mick Jagger and Keith Richards—both born the same year as Jimmy—were scuffling in the West London R & B band founded by Brian Jones that was still called the Rollin' Stones, and while Jimmy Hendrix was serving as a paratrooper with the 101st Airborne at Fort Campbell, Kentucky, Jimmy Morrison began his sophomore year at FSU.

Jimmy Morrison moved into a suburban house a mile from campus with his Clearwater friends the Kallivokas brothers and Brian Gates, along with an older student named Bowman who had already been in the army and who took care of the place. Jimmy proceeded to treat his housemates as if they were subhumans unworthy of consideration by the Übermensch. Free of family constraints for the first time, he fell into a pattern of passive-aggressive abuse of those he lived and worked with, which characterized his heroically selfish behavior from then on. He cheated at cards. He guzzled any beer he found in the fridge. He ate the others' food. He didn't put their records back in their sleeves. He borrowed their clean clothes without asking and left them sodden and reeking on the bathroom floor. When their parents sent them money, he intercepted the mail and stole the cash. He borrowed cars and returned them banged up. At Halloween he answered the door in his huge gray West Point cape, and some neighborhood kids claimed he showed them his meat. He played mind games with his victims, testing and probing for weakness and soft spots, and meticulously recorded their reactions in his notebooks. Confronted with being a complete asshole, he just laughed at them.

"Jimmy didn't give a good goddamn," one of them recalled. "But he was really funny. He kept us laughing, even though we were kind of scared of him."

For a while, they put up with him because he was obviously brilliant in a laconic way. His room was a jumble of hundreds of books. With eyes shut tight behind his shades, Jimmy challenged visitors to pick any book and read the first sentence, and he would identify the title and the writer. He was never wrong. He avidly read the popular sociologists of the day, with a special interest in crowd psychology as it related to drama and the theater. Two favorite works Jimmy cited in his notebooks were David Riesman's *The Lonely Crowd,* which explored problems confronting the individual and the threats to personal freedom imposed by mass culture, and Norman O. Brown's *Life Against Death,* an influential 1959 bestseller that attempted to psychoanalyze human history. Jimmy was deeply interested in Cold War–era issues of social control that also appealed to the entire science fiction movement and Beat writers like William S. Burroughs, whose novel *Nova Express* Jimmy also read that year. Elias Canetti's *Crowds and Power* drew him in with its analysis of the performer/audience nexus, and taught him techniques he would deploy in a few years as he famously controlled and manipulated the Doors' young audiences. C. Wright Mills's *The Power Elite* left little illusion about who was in charge of the American republic, and probably doubled Jimmy's deeply ingrained contempt for authority, especially the military. (Arriving drunk at the local draft board to register on his eighteenth birthday in December 1961, he reportedly caused a nasty name-calling scene, and then ran off before the cops arrived.)

Jimmy cultivated and reveled in a bizarre bohemian image amid the square conventionality of WASP-dominated FSU. He had long hair over his forehead before the Beatles arrived. He wore beatnik steel-rimmed glasses with no lenses. He played his Joan Baez album repeatedly, and told friends he was in love with the barefoot folk goddess from faraway Harvard Square. He attended dances and mixers in a stovepipe top hat and offered girls chocolate cigarettes from a silver case. He urinated in public and seemed pleased if people scolded him. When he persuaded some friends to help him test his crowd control theories by disrupting a black revival meeting held under a big tent, he was tackled and beaten up by the angry deacons. He practiced jumping between two cars as they sped down the highway. He arrogantly declined to pay his share of the heating bill during the winter because his grandparents had sent him an electric blanket. He refused to spend the money he got from home on anything but books. He bought one bag of potatoes a week and boiled them when he got hungry. The others had to padlock their food in the kitchen cabinets to keep Jimmy from pilfering.

OCTOBER 1962. The Cuban Missile Crisis coincided with Homecoming Weekend at FSU. With the Western world on the brink of nuclear war, Jimmy started drinking at noon on Friday. Told he'd have to wear a tie to get into the big dance that night, he knotted it repeatedly until it looked ridiculous. Mary Werbelow couldn't come, so Jimmy was going stag. Chris Kallivokas made the mistake of leaving Jimmy alone with his date at their house while he did an errand. When he got back, the glass front door was shattered. Chris's older brother Nick explained that, after Chris had left, the girl had tried to be friendly and told Jim that she liked the knots in his tie.

"You like my *nuts*?" he slurred. "Does that mean you want my *bod*?"

Then he began reciting verses from T. S. Eliot, and bit her on the neck. When she started to cry, Nick (an ex-Marine) grabbed Jimmy and threw him through the glass door. Raving, he ran off by himself. They hadn't seen Jimmy this drunk before, and they all felt bad about it.

Jimmy kept drinking that night and into Saturday. He went to the football game with a pint of Seagram's 7 in his pocket and passed out at halftime. That night, at the big party at the student union, still drunk, he began to bait members of the football team, who had lost that day. The team was called the Seminoles. Jimmy began taunting a bunch of giant linemen, calling them Semi-holes and a bunch of pussies for losing. As his housemates watched in horror, Jimmy climbed on a bench, fished himself out of his pants, and announced he was going to piss on the Semi-holes. Nick Kallivokas dragged him away before the team could kill him. They stuffed Jimmy in a cab and gave the driver their address. When they got home a few hours later, they found Jimmy unconscious and bruised in the front yard. They figured he must have vomited in the cab, so the driver beat him up and left him there.

"It was excessive," Chris later said of Jimmy's drinking. "He'd just go all the way out. We'd never seen anything like this before."

Around this time, Jimmy started picking up on Elvis Presley. Elvis had just completed his career-destroying hitch in the army, and was launched into a secondary career making lame Hollywood musicals. Anytime Elvis came on the radio, Jimmy made everyone in the room or the car hush so he could listen to Elvis's crooning. One night, at the end of Jimmy's first trimester at FSU, he was playing an Elvis record too loud. Asked to turn the hi-fi down, Jimmy refused. He started playing "Return to Sender" over and over again. So, right there, they had a house meeting, voted Jimmy out, and asked him to leave.

KILLER ON THE ROAD

JIMMY DIDN'T GO home to his grandparents' house during the Christmas break. Instead he stayed with the Kallivokas family in Clearwater. The brothers' mom was an aspiring writer, and Jimmy cultivated her with his erudition and charm until he was welcome anytime. Seemingly in no hurry to see his family in California, Jimmy maintained his grades and wrote the required letters home that guaranteed a return flow of cash. When the next trimester began at FSU in January 1963, Jimmy moved his books into an old Airstream caravan parked behind a ramshackle girls' boardinghouse on College Street in the student quarter, halfway between the university gates and the state capitol. The aluminum trailer had a tarpaper roof and an unobstructed view of the girls' rear windows. Soon Jimmy had a telescope and was indulging in nightly voyeurism and making detailed notes on what he saw. His rent was much less than he reported to his parents, and he spent the difference on books, including, according to notebook annotations, *Catch-22,* Kerouac's *The Dharma Bums,* and Wilhelm Reich's *The Function of the Orgasm.* (His copy of Reich's book, with extensive marginalia in his handwriting, survives.)

More interested in his courses now, Jimmy studied drama and theater history in the Speech Department, took some introductory acting classes, and hung around the department's decrepit Conradi Theater. Some of his sketches for a set decoration class survive, showing the imaginative designs that earned him an A for the course. For Tennessee Williams's *Cat on a Hot Tin Roof,* he envisioned a small dot projected on a scrim at the back of the stage; as the play progressed, the dot would grow until, at the end of Act three, it was revealed to be a gigantic projection of the cancer cell that kills Big Daddy. For a psychology course, he wrote a paper on the sexual neuroses of crowds with an extensive bibliography that included Freud, Jung, Aldous Huxley, and George Orwell. The paper presciently discussed the use of music to arouse the sexual energies of a captive audience.

His teachers noticed his restlessness and thought he wasn't challenged enough. The real problem was that Jimmy was obsessed by movies and wanted to study film, but FSU had no such department. One of his professors, who had worked at UCLA, suggested he apply to their Theater Arts Department, which had a film school. Jimmy was intrigued and sent away to Los Angeles for a catalog.

Jimmy didn't need much prodding to begin dreaming of California. His family was already there, and American pop radio was blasting out daily cultural bulletins from Brian Wilson's mythic southern California of surfing, girls, and hot rods. The first three Beach Boys albums released that year (*Surfin' USA, Surfer Girl,* and *Little Deuce Coupe*) contained irresistible siren songs that lured Jimmy west. He later told an interviewer, "The Beach Boys definitely made me want to come back to California."

WHEN THE TERM ENDED in April 1963, Jimmy persuaded Brian Gates to hitch to California with him. Captain Morrison's ship was due into San Diego after a long cruise and Clara wanted the whole family waiting for him dockside. She sent Jimmy money for a plane ticket but he told Gates that he wanted to "feel" his way across America, to be on the road. "The entire trip," Gates told an interviewer, "was a series of the kind of encounters that you'd guess, based on this thing Jim had of getting up peoples' noses."

In New Orleans, their first overnight, he insisted they stay in a cheap flophouse to soak up the Stanley Kowalski atmosphere. In the French Quarter, Jim decided the bars on Bourbon Street were too tame and touristy. "We gotta get to the *fringe*," he told Brian. "Then we gotta get *beyond* the fringe."

Looking for lowlife, Jimmy started talking to the street people and soon they found a quiet side street of gay bars. This was more like it, and they settled into a dark place called the Copper Skillet and ordered beers. Soon Jimmy was talking to an attractive blond girl with big tits and deep southern drawl, and she seemed to really like him. Then her lesbian girlfriend came up to Jimmy and poked him in the chest with a stiletto. He was wearing a jacket, so there was only a puncture and a little blood, and they got out of there fast.

West of New Orleans, hanging out at highway entrances with thumbs out, they were picked up by four people in a rusted Chevrolet and told to get in back. After a few miles, a one-eyed Cajun redneck riding shotgun turned around and announced that they'd just gotten out of prison. Brian almost soiled himself but Jimmy, an experienced hitchhiker, just stared at the guy. Suddenly he pointed a revolver at them. "What we were in prison for, was *murder*," he said, as his companions snickered. The driver produced a bottle of whiskey and ordered the boys to drink, but they refused. There was silence for a while. Then the Cajun turned around again and cleared his throat. "It was people like you that we *coulda* murdered, and gone to prison for." Silence. It was getting dark now, and Brian said that they wanted to get out, so the driver pulled off the road. Brian thought they were done for, but they just told them to get the hell out of the car. Jimmy didn't say anything, and just stuck out his thumb, trying to flag a ride.

The next night in eastern Texas they got a ride from a cousin of Vice President Lyndon Johnson, who insisted they spend the night at the LBJ Ranch in Johnson City. (Johnson was in Washington at the time.) At midnight the following day, they arrived in Juárez, Mexico, where Jimmy played out his B. Traven fantasies when their fleabag hotel turned out to double as a brothel. Jimmy Morrison, nineteen years old, thought he'd captured the heart of the establishment's youngest and prettiest girl, an actual Mexican whore just like in *On the Road,* but he was disappointed when she went off with a well-dressed hombre in his fancy car. Near Phoenix an attractive middle-aged woman picked them up and invited them to her apartment. "There's some things I want you boys to do for me," she purred. Jimmy was game, and told the woman they'd do anything she wanted, but Brian was scared and insisted they stay on the road and head west toward San Diego.

Clara Morrison wouldn't let Jimmy in the house until he got his hair cut. She wasn't happy that he'd brought a friend, and got mad when she found out they had hitchhiked across the country. After a few days at home antagonizing his mother, and with his father's ship delayed, Jimmy and Brian headed up to Los Angeles, where they stayed with Brian's cousins. Jimmy, it appeared to Brian, was in heaven. Jimmy loved the rundown business district of downtown L.A., especially the Mexican neighborhood around Olivera Street near the old Mission, and Pershing Square, where soapbox preachers tried to convert the winos and tramps who congregated there. When one of these orators took a break, Jimmy stole his stepladder, got up, and began preaching a hellfire sermon of his own until the indignant preacher pushed him off. "Jimmy wasn't afraid of anything," Brian said many years later. "I totally enjoyed his love of life and enthusiasm for every kind of bizarre situation that existed."

Captain Morrison arrived home in June, and Brian took Jimmy down to San Diego to meet his ship, the *Bonhomme Richard.* Jimmy and his father hadn't seen each other in two years, and Brian noticed they greeted each other with genuine affection.

Jimmy spent a month with his family in Coronado, vainly trying to convince his parents to let him enroll in the UCLA film school. He begged them, and presented several alternate plans, but Clara Morrison discouraged this idea. Jimmy was being educated for free in Florida, where his family officially resided, and she might not have wanted her younger son, now fourteen, to fall under the baleful influence of an impulsive hellion of an older brother. Finally she shut Jimmy down completely with threats of loss of financial backing, and by June 18, 1963, the deadline to register for classes, Jimmy was back in Florida, unhappily resigned to returning to FSU's summer session in Tallahassee.

Late that month he hitchhiked to New York with a friend, staying at the Sloane House YMCA and visiting Greenwich Village and Carnegie Books on Fifty-seventh Street. There he caught up with the latest issues of *Evergreen Review* and Paul Krassner's satiric paper *The Realist,* which featured obscene comics like the ones Jimmy had drawn in high school.

I T WAS HOT that summer in the metal camper, but Jimmy kept his grades up. For a medieval European history class, he wrote a reportedly brilliant exegesis on Hieronymus Bosch, the mysterious Dutch painter of unspeakably detailed phantasmagorias depicting late medieval life as a hellish maelstrom of human torment. Sparring verbally with the teachers, dominating the classes he liked, he was respected (and feared) for his intellect and beatnik style.

In September 1963, he began his fourth and last trimester at FSU by moving his books to the seedy Cherokee Motel, a former rendezvous for out-of-town state legislators and the local hookers. Jimmy was comfortable in Room 206, liked the decent bed and the maid service, and the Cherokee became the template for the long series of inexpensive motels that he called home for the rest of his days. With Mary Werbelow at his side and consequently on his best behavior (to the undying relief of the apprehensive groom) Jimmy attended Brian's wedding that September. Then he moved his library and himself into an apartment with a small group of older art students and instructors he'd been hanging out with. He told an interviewer later that some opium had found its way to this apartment, his first taste of narcotics, and he'd puked his guts out after getting high.

Mary came up for the weekends when she could. The couple attended a big costume party at FSU that autumn, with Jimmy memorably dressed in a harlequin clown suit, complete with stockings, belled cap, and pointed slippers. He made a point to talk to nobody at the party but Mary.

Later that month, on their way to an FSU football game on September 29, 1963, Jimmy and his friends were carousing in Tallahassee. Some cop cars pulled up, and Jimmy stole an umbrella from a police cruiser. They arrested him, charged him with larceny (a cop's helmet had also vanished in the melee), being drunk and disorderly, and resisting arrest. At the station the cops pushed and slapped him when he compulsively mouthed off, tore the buttons off his shirt, photographed him looking like the bleary, disheveled nineteen-year-old punk that he was. The next day, knowing he was in trouble, Jimmy asked for help from the professor for whom he'd written the brilliant Bosch paper. The teacher got him cleaned up and vouched for him in court, and Jimmy was let off with a fifty-dollar fine. The university, mindful of his good grades, only put him on disciplinary probation.

In October, without telling his mother, Jimmy applied to transfer to the film studies program at the University of California at Los Angeles. He was accepted later that fall, and even assigned advanced placement in the term beginning in January 1964.

That autumn, Jimmy landed the role of Gus in a student production of *The Dumbwaiter,* Harold Pinter's two-character play about a pair of hitmen waiting to murder someone. It was his first public performance since his ukulele jams at the Contemporary two years earlier. Jim quickly turned the rehearsals into anarchic, absurdist experiments in obscene improv, prompted in part by his reading of theater-of-cruelty mage Antonin Artaud. In the mimeographed program, Jimmy was billed as "Stanislas Boleslawski," which conflated the names of Constantin Stanislavski, the Russian actor who created "method acting," and Richard Boleslawski, who had worked in the Moscow Art Theater with Stanislavski before arriving in America to make films.

Waiting for the curtain to rise, the other student actor, Keith Carlson, never knew what Jimmy was going to do. He played scenes and read lines differently every night, sometimes improvising bits of stage business, refusing to repeat himself. The director, who had given Artaud's essays to Jimmy, was kept in a state of suspense. They were all afraid some of the lewd rehearsal material might slip out in live performance. "There was a constant feeling of apprehension," Carlson recalled (anticipating the atmosphere at later Doors shows), "and a feeling that things were on the brink of loss of control. . . . With Jim, we just never knew." A performance photograph of Jimmy, wearing his hair long with muttonchop sideburns, and being berated by Carlson's character, was published in the school paper. Uncharacteristically, he clipped the picture and sent it to his mother.

                                 *   *   *

PRESIDENT JOHN F. KENNEDY was assassinated in Dallas,
Texas, on Friday, November 22. Jimmy watched the news programming at the FSU student center, as numb as everyone else. Two
days later, he watched as the accused assassin, Lee Harvey Oswald, was
murdered on TV by the owner of a Dallas strip joint. In a notebook,
Jimmy noted that Oswald had tried to escape arrest by ducking into a
movie theater, which may have appealed to Jimmy's interior linkage between film and morbidity. From then on, Kennedy's death occupied a
dark corner of the Morrison psyche, making frequent appearances in
notebooks and later lyrics. "Dead president's corpse in the driver's car"
is one of the keystone images from both *Celebration of the Lizard* and the
song excerpted from this long poem, "Not to Touch the Earth."

JIM MORRISON WAS TWENTY YEARS old on December 8, 1963.
Less than a month later, Capitol Records, the Beach Boys' label, would
begin to promote the impending arrival of a new band from England
called the Beatles. Radio stations began playing the first Beatles records,
"Love Me Do," and "I Saw Her Standing There." As if responding to an
occult summons to cheer up depressed America, the Beatles duly arrived in New York early in 1964 with their ninety-second love songs,
long hair, sharp suits, Chelsea boots, and bluff repartee to shake American youth out of its postassassination despondency. After the youthful
Jack Kennedy's brains were blown out in public, American kids were
ready for anything, and they took to the Beatles like dogs on a meat
wagon. The Beatles were soon followed by the Rolling Stones and the
other British Invasion bands, all of whom, like Jimmy Morrison, looked
west to Los Angeles as the new Mecca of rock and roll.
    In December Jimmy left Tallahassee, having told only a few friends
and teachers that he wasn't coming back. Jimmy and Mary had a vague
plan that she would come to Los Angeles when she graduated from high
school in June. They would find an apartment and live together. Jimmy
left his books with his grandparents and flew to California, spending
Christmas with his family in Coronado. He wouldn't return to Florida for

another five years, and when he finally came back it was only to commit professional suicide.

THE DOORS OF PERCEPTION

O N THE SAME NOTEBOOK PAGE on which Jimmy recorded the Kennedy assassination, he wrote the name Aldous Huxley. This was because Huxley, one of the preeminent British authors of the century, died at his home in Los Angeles on the same day Jack Kennedy was murdered. But, unlike the dead president, Aldous Huxley left this life under the influence of a massive dose of LSD-25. By the time Jimmy arrived in Los Angeles six weeks later, he was thoroughly immersed in Huxley's visionary quest for a shortcut to enlightenment, and its natural starting point in southern California. It was no accident that the name of the band Jimmy would start eighteen months later was taken from the legendary book Huxley wrote that alerted the Western world to the new frontiers in the expansion of human consciousness.

After achieving worldwide success with his utopian novel *Brave New World,* Aldous Huxley emigrated to the U.S. and settled in California in the late 1940s. Los Angeles was then a place of endless orange groves, immense ranch lands, and producing oil wells, with a resident film colony in Hollywood and a tiny but determined intellectual and artistic community. Huxley, like many of his fellow British expatriates, was able to see the spiritual and even utopian possibilities of the semi-arid landscape. Its mild year-round climate and fertile valleys, guarded by majestic mountain ranges, provided a dramatic landscape for the restless dreamers who flocked to the southwest shore of the North American continent, the last possible stop on the European migration to the New World. The American movie industry had relocated to Los Angeles from New York in the 1920s, which in turn drew a mass migration of the best-looking people in the country as they tried to pursue their Hollywood-inspired versions of the American Dream. After World War II, the top echelons of the entertainment industry—movies, television, and popular music—became concentrated in Los Angeles. The

1955 opening of the Disneyland amusement park, on an old citrus farm in Orange County, was the final consolidation of California as—and this was heavily promoted by Disney on television—the Land of Make-Believe.

Huxley wrote that Los Angeles was like Venice during the Renaissance—an independent city-state that had funneled the riches and wisdom of Asia to Europe.

In 1953, Huxley and his friend Humphrey Osmond, a British research psychiatrist, began taking mescaline. They were following in the footsteps of the psychologist Havelock Ellis, who in 1898 described the ritual use of mescal, or peyote, by the Indians of the American Southwest. Mescal, a mild hallucinogen taken from certain cactus plants, led to mescaline, a synthetic version of the chemical agent present in peyote. Huxley and Osmond experienced supercharged visual phenomena, peculiar time expansions, and heightened streams of consciousness under mescaline, which led Osmond to coin the word *psychedelic* to describe the effect of hallucinogens on the brain.

In 1954 Huxley published an account of his experiments, *The Doors of Perception,* the first book by an author of Huxley's stature to explore previously unmapped areas of human consciousness. Huxley took the title of his epochal book from the English visionary poet William Blake:

"If the doors of perception were cleansed every thing would appear to man as it is, infinite."

Beat writers had already begun experiments with psychedelic drugs. Poet Gary Snyder had taken peyote while studying Amerindian culture at Reed College in 1948. Allen Ginsberg had tried it in New York in 1959, followed by Kerouac in Big Sur the following year. In 1960 Timothy Leary, a psychologist working at Harvard University, returned from a summer vacation in Mexico with so-called "magic mushrooms" containing the psychotropic agent psilocybin, which he gave to Ginsberg, Kerouac, and Neal Cassady, who been the model for Dean Moriarty in *On the Road.*

In 1964, the year that Jimmy arrived in Los Angeles, Tim Leary published his first book, *The Psychedelic Experience.* The book's subtitle, "A Manual Based on the Tibetan Book of the Dead," pointed to the quasi-religious cast that psychedelic drugs were already acquiring, especially in San Francisco where (still legal) LSD-25 was beginning to be sold on the street. In that year, Leary assumed the mantle of LSD's prophet. "Don't trust anyone over thirty" became his war cry, followed by the hypnotic mantra: "Turn on. Tune in. Drop out." Leary later explained: "'*Turn on*' meant activating your neural and genetic equipment. *Tune in* meant interacting harmoniously with the world around you. *Drop out* meant a voluntary detachment from involuntary commitments like school, the military, and corporate employment."

But dropping out was not yet an option for Jimmy Morrison. With the military draft still hanging over every straight, able-bodied American male, Jimmy knew that the only way to avoid compulsory service was to stay in school. This point was strongly underlined by Jimmy's visit to his father's ship when it docked in Long Beach in January 1964.

Captain Steve Morrison now had the command of the USS *Bonhomme Richard,* one of the navy's premier aircraft carriers. When Jim had first arrived at his mother's house after leaving Florida, she insisted he get a haircut. When his father's ship docked after a tour of the Western Pacific, Jim went aboard in a conservative "Ivy League" outfit of khaki trousers, a buttoned-down dress shirt, and a cardigan sweater with leather patches at the elbows. Captain Morrison took one look at his truculent, slouching son—aspiring Beat poet, Nouvelle Vague film buff, slacker collegiate draft dodger—and ordered him to the ship's barber for another, more military trim. As a navy photographer documented the visit, Captain Morrison ordered his carrier out to sea. Jimmy observed the ship's marines conduct a live-fire exercise, and reluctantly joined in firing at floating targets with an M16 rifle.

THE BLUE BUS

JIMMY MORRISON ARRIVED at UCLA in mid-January 1964, enrolling in the Theater Arts Department as an advanced-placement film major beginning the second half of his junior year. (Whether or not his parents paid his UCLA tuition is unknown. One source indicates that his grandparents helped him financially. Another suggests that he was able to draw on a college fund established by his father when he was born.) Jimmy found a small apartment on Goshen Avenue, near UCLA in Westwood, then still a quiet university village, where he fell into the routines of a bohemian student on the fringes of campus life. To support his book-buying habit, he got a part-time job at Powell Library, the red brick, neo-Moorish colossus across the grassy quad from Royce Hall, UCLA's performance auditorium. Classmates from that time remember him as a pudgy, disheveled kid in beat-up tennis shoes, pushing a cartfull of books to be shelved in the library stacks. UCLA classes changed to the hourly bells in Powell's tower. The bells gave Jimmy Morrison, as he confided to a notebook, the first degree of contentment he had felt in years. He was finally back in California, the only place in which Jimmy felt he really belonged. One night, feeling good, he did his human fly act for some new friends and climbed into the bell tower and threw his clothes to the ground as the chimes struck midnight.

"Film studies" was a new academic field in 1964, and *film student* was considered synonymous with goofball, slacker, draft dodger. UCLA's program was housed in several rusting Quonset huts left over from World War II. Across town, the University of Southern California's film school was in an old stable. But where USC's film school was oriented toward getting local kids technical jobs in the Hollywood movie industry, UCLA's more boho students were interested in current film theory, auteurism, French New Wave cinema, avant-garde movies, and underground and experimental films. At USC the film students read *Variety*. At UCLA they read *Cahiers du Cinéma* and *Film Culture,* published by Jonas Mekas's Anthology Film Archives in New York. When UCLA film students prayed, they faced toward the Cinémathèque Française in Paris. UCLA film school heroes included French New Wavers Jean-Luc Godard and François Truffaut; Norman Mailer and John Cassavetes, who were making starkly literary films away from the Hollywood tradition; Andy Warhol and his transformation of pop art ideas into non-narrative films such as *Empire,* a single eight-hour shot of the Empire State Building in Manhattan; and Stan Brakhage, who treated film stock itself as an artist's canvas, sometimes scratching or painting his negatives to produce abstract expressionist imagery on the screen.

The teachers were an interesting mix of semiretired Hollywood directors like Stanley Kramer and at least one old-school European director. Jimmy was disappointed that Jean Renoir, auteur of *Rules of the*

Game, had just left UCLA, but the arrival of the legendary Josef von Sternberg more than made up for Renoir's absence. Jimmy was able to watch von Sternberg's classic films—*The Blue Angel, The Devil Is a Woman*—along with running commentary in the director's theatrical German accent. (Jim would later say that von Sternberg's last film, *Anatahan,* had the most profound effect on him.) Both Jimmy and his UCLA classmate Ray Manzarek studied with von Sternberg, and Manzarek makes a crucial point when he refers to the German Expressionist roots of the Doors. Jimmy, he says, studied the unsmiling, smoldering body language of Marlene Dietrich, Von Sternberg's greatest star, and would adapt it when posing in his leathers in the early days of the Doors.

UCLA's faculty and students were proud to follow a generally hipper aesthetic than that of Hollywood, which was still selling the 1950s Rat Pack culture of booze and broads and indeed would never really "get" the American sixties at all. It is somewhat ironic that the only classmate of Jimmy's at UCLA who would achieve fame as an "auteur"—a director authorially responsible for the entire film—was Francis Ford Coppola.

Jimmy loved the cultural mix at UCLA, applied himself, and got good grades. He told friends he loved film school because the history of film was only about seventy years old. "Anybody can be an expert," he said. "I love that most about movies." In his spare time he caught the blue bus that took UCLA students out to the beach and the bright lights of Santa Monica Pier. He always had his nose in a book: John Rechy's harrowing gay hustler saga *City of Night,* or Dave Wallis's postapocalypse novel *Only Lovers Left Alive.* Saxophonist Stan Getz's ultrasophisticated "The Girl from Ipanema" was a big hit on the radio, an early taste of the Brazilian bossa nova beat that would begin the Doors' first record. *Another Side of Bob Dylan* hinted at the post-Beat folk-poet's imminent conversion to electric band music. The Beatles were on the rampage with "I Want to Hold Your Hand." And girls were starting to scream at rock and rollers again. Jimmy watched the Beatles' epic first appearance on *The Ed Sullivan Show* in February 1964, along with the rest of America.

The Motion Picture Division of the Theater Arts Department was small, with only a few dozen students, but Jimmy soon made himself the center of a group of existential misfits like himself. Their main hangout was the Lucky U, a Mexican restaurant just off campus that featured a cook named Pancho working in an open kitchen and a big combo plate that chunky, overweight Jimmy liked to wash down with a couple of cold Tecate beers.

Many of Jim's UCLA friends remained near him for the rest of his life. There was Dennis Jakob, known as "the weasel" for his furtive look and scurrying walk. He was as well read as Jimmy and could argue the fine points of Nietzsche far into the night. Movie buff John DeBella was the burly son of a New York cop who bragged that he'd stolen more books than Dennis had read. Phil O'Leno was an obsessive Orson Welles fan who still lived in his attorney father's comfortable home, something that Jimmy teased him about. Paul Ferrara was a cinematographer who knew his way around a 16mm Bolex camera. Alain Ronay had instant cred for being French and for having once met Henri Langlois, founder of the Cinémathèque Française. Frank Lisciandro was an aspiring film editor with a good critical eye and an instant admiration for Jimmy Morrison's weird and addictive charisma.

And then there was Ray Manzarek.

Ray was older than most of the others, being technically a graduate student. Born in 1939, he had been raised in a big Polish-American family in Chicago, where he studied classical piano and listened to blues deejays Al Benson and Big Bill Hill playing the work of the masters—Muddy Waters, Howlin' Wolf, B. B. King, and Little Walter—on the radio. He had graduated from DePauw University as an economics major, served two years in the army, and followed his family to California when they relocated to Manhattan Beach, south of L.A. In 1963 Ray enrolled at UCLA's law school, but dropped out after two weeks, transferring to the film school instead. Ray was something of a star at UCLA because he had an exotically stunning Japanese-American girlfriend, Dorothy Fujikawa, and a working bar band—Rick and the Ravens—with his two brothers.

Ray was also cool because he bucked the faculty and won. As an ardent fan of European directors like Ingmar Bergman and Michelangelo Antonioni, Ray's student film that spring featured a chaste montage of the luscious Fujikawa taking a shower, an innocuous sequence that was still deemed too suggestive by one of the professors, who stupidly ordered it cut from the version to be shown at the semiprestigious Royce Hall screenings of the best work produced by the film students that year.

Ray refused to cut the shower scene, faced down the committee convened to look into the situation, and won the right to show his film uncensored. Everyone at the school was impressed. John DeBella introduced Ray to Jimmy, who would appear in the party sequence of Ray's 1964 student film, *Induction,* more than a year before they started the Doors.

D URING THE EASTER BREAK in 1964, Jimmy and two friends spent a few debauched days along the notorious Avenida de la Revolución in Tijuana. Jimmy enjoyed chatting up the streetwalkers, getting stone drunk on tequila and beer, and running from the packs of roaming dogs when the bars closed at dawn.

Felix Venable was another older graduate student who had a lasting influence on Jimmy. Felix was already thirty-five, a graduate of Berkeley, and a familiar early sixties archetype: the professional student and beatnik. He was slight and bony, with thinning blond hair and a sharp nose jutting out of a haggard face. He was also brilliant and extremely fucked up. Ray Manzarek, who also knew Felix, described him as "a plain, evil-minded fuck." Felix lived in a squalid bungalow along the polluted canals in run-down Venice Beach, where he gobbled speed pills, drank wine, and turned hungry, vulnerable Jimmy Morrison, who couldn't legally buy beer, into an alcoholic.

Everyone at UCLA thought Felix was an asshole. Jimmy Morrison thought he was cool, and adopted him as a mentor because Felix had some Beat wisdom to impart. Felix had followed the disaffected North Beach beatniks who left town when San Francisco became commercialized, and relocated to funky, run-down Venice Beach. Felix knew many of the poets, and mesmerized Jimmy with Beat legends like poet Gregory Corso's exploit of sneaking into Dylan Thomas's hospital room at midnight, and watching him dying in an alcohol coma until the night nurse found him and threw him out. Soon after Jimmy began hanging out with Felix, he began muttering Dylan Thomas quotes: "Whatever is hidden should be made naked. To be stripped of darkness is to be clean." Or, "My poetry is, or should be, useful to me for one reason. It is the record of my individual struggle from darkness toward some measure of light."

Felix might have given Jimmy LSD for the first time, and it is known that the two of them began tripping during weekend excursions to the haunted deserts southeast of Los Angeles. They would drive out to Joshua Tree in the high desert, or to Santa Ana Canyon, where the Indians thought the devil had lived. On one trip to the hidden canyons around Palm Springs, three hours east of L.A., Jimmy had a spectacular, shamanlike experience that flashed him back to the Indian car wreck he had witnessed as a child. Felix might have been the first person Jimmy told about his notion that the souls of one or more Indians entered his "child's fragile eggshell mind" as he watched their owners dying on the road.

Back on Goshen Avenue, Jimmy immersed himself in shaman lore as if he intended to use it to construct a future persona. In tribal cultures, shamans mediate between the tribe and the spirit world, curing the sick and maintaining the equilibrium between the clans. Shamanism had fascinated Western philosophy and psychology since Russian missionaries had first identified Siberian practitioners in the 1700s, and the opening of the American frontier brought the tribal medicine man into American popular culture. In the sixties, with the immense resurgence of interest in spiritual pursuits, shamans and their rituals were seen as glamorous and far-out survivals of the religious practices of preantiquity. By 1964 Timothy Leary was already comparing the psychedelic experience to the shaman's intoxicated journey to the gods and back.

There is speculation that Felix told Jimmy about a former UCLA anthropology student he knew, a serious guy who had done extensive fieldwork in the Sonora Desert of Mexico with a Yaqui Indian *brujo,* or shaman. Jimmy knew someone in the department, and apparently made contact with Carlos Castaneda, whose dissertation would become the 1968 bestseller and counterculture bible *The Teachings of Don Juan: A Yaqui Way of Knowledge.* Poet Michael Ford was also at UCLA at the time and believes Morrison did meet with Castaneda, but no details of the meeting survive. Castaneda, contacted by a researcher fifteen years later, had no memory of meeting Morrison. However, in the summer of 1964, Jimmy began including the Indian shaman riff in his psychic curriculum vitae, for anyone who would listen.

SECRET ALPHABETS

T HE SUMMER OF 1964 was "Freedom Summer" in the American south. College students were being murdered by the Ku Klux Klan while registering black voters in Mississippi. But at UCLA, with its tiny minority of black students, Jimmy Morrison was known for getting crazy drunk and shouting "nigger" around campus, just to provoke the well intentioned. As a conservative southerner, Jimmy seemed to have a racist fear of black people that unfortunately surfaced when alcohol impaired his ability to control himself.

That summer the Beach Boys' "Fun Fun Fun" and "I Get Around" were big jams on the radio, along with the Rolling Stones' sinister, blues-traveling "Tell Me." In southern California the sporty new Ford Mustangs, red Honda motorbikes, and Vespa scooters were cool rides, but Jimmy Morrison was always seen on foot, walking along in his languid southern shamble between his pad and his library job—unless he could convince a girlfriend to drive him.

Living with his mother, brother, and sister in Coronado that summer, he started a new notebook, possibly in July, and wrote the words *Notes on Vision* on the cover. Later published as part of his first book, the jottings and aperçus in this and other spiral-bound notebooks began as an explicit homage to his recent reading of *Illuminations,* the legendary collection of Symbolist prose poems by the French enfant terrible Arthur Rimbaud.

Rimbaud was a perfect lost-poet exemplar for Jim Morrison, as he was for the Beats. The entire Romantic agony of the nineteenth century was summed up in this teenage genius, an instinctive, offhand amateur poet who stopped writing at age nineteen. None of his work was published during his brief lifetime, which ended at age twenty-seven in Ethiopia as he was trading slaves and running guns to a rebel group. In fact it's impossible to overestimate the influence Arthur Rimbaud had on Jim Morrison. Many luminous images from *Illuminations* (the Universal Mind, the feast of friends, the face in the mirror) turn up later in Doors lyrics written by Jim, and he obviously patterned the poetic musings of *The Lords* and *The New Creatures* after Rimbaud's surreal epigrams. Most important of all was Jimmy's uncritical adoption of Rimbaud's famous poetic manifesto, dashed off in a letter to a friend in 1871:

> The first study for a man who wants to be a poet is the knowledge of his entire self. He searches his soul, he inspects it, he tests it, he learns it. As soon as he knows it, he cultivates it. . . . But the soul has to be made monstrous. Imagine a man planting and cultivating warts on his face.
>
> One must, I say, be a *visionary;* make oneself a *visionary.*
>
> The poet makes himself a *visionary* through a long, a prodigious, and rational disordering of *all* the senses. Every form of love, of suffering, of madness; he searches himself, he consumes all the poisons in him, keeping only their quintessences. . . . He arrives at the unknown: and even if, half crazed at the end, he loses the understanding of his visions, he has seen them! Let him be destroyed in his leap by those unnamable, unutterable, and innumerable things: there will come other horrible workers: they will begin at the horizons where he has succumbed.

Reading these lines in the introduction to the New Directions edition of *Illuminations* that he owned (and underlined), Jimmy undertook, consciously or not, to follow Rimbaud's Promethean pronouncement that the true poet was truly the thief of fire. He accepted Rimbaud's challenge and prodigiously and rationally disordered his senses every day for the rest of his life. The initial literary results were highly charged and sometimes breathtaking. The *Notes on Vision* journals brim with a film student's hothouse insights on the nature of seeing, the powers of the eye, the properties of the camera, the new alchemy of cinema, the secrets of the serial voyeur, the sniper's eye, the horror of television and its hold over the world, séances, dead presidents, sleep, prisons, the shaman, mothers, and incest. Many pages recycled film lore and legend, much of it reportedly learned from John DeBella. Jimmy worked on these notebooks almost every day while he was at UCLA, and some of the raw material percolated into the papers on film aesthetics he wrote during his final year at school.

Later in the summer he went back to Mexico with his brother, Andy, and an older family friend who was a retired navy officer. In seedy Ensenada, Jimmy initiated his brother into the world of women and drink, hauling him from bar to bar, talking to all the girls in the street. *"Lions in the street and roaming dogs in heat . . . He went down south and crossed the border, left the chaos and disorder."* Back at home, Jim would get drunk and act up at the navy base's movie theater, mocking military decorum. In August, his mother gladly let him return to UCLA early to get ready for school. He went back to his $1.25-an-hour library job, but got fired by a new supervisor when he couldn't show up on time.

In August 1964, the USS *Bonhomme Richard,* Captain Morrison commanding, was on station in the South China Sea, part of a carrier fleet that included the USS *Ticonderoga* and the USS *Constellation.* After some secret and provocative attacks on North Vietnamese positions by American special forces, the captains of two American destroyers claimed they were attacked by North Vietnamese patrol boats in the Gulf of Tonkin. President Lyndon Johnson ordered retaliatory bombing raids launched from the carriers' decks. A few days later, on August 7, Congress passed the Gulf of Tonkin Resolution, which gave Johnson's government blanket authority to assist the South Vietnamese in their war with the communist North. Though it was hard to envision at the time—many congressmen and senators later claimed they'd been deceived—the United States was about to begin ten years of warfare that would tear the nation apart and result in millions of deaths, ultimate defeat, and national humiliation. And one of the most murderous ironies of the whole era would be that while Jim Morrison was becoming rock music's antiwar spokesman—*"Make a grave for the unknown soldier"*—his father was fighting a futile war against communism on the other side of the world.

I N OCTOBER 1964, the student revolt of the sixties began at Berkeley. UCLA was an apolitical, partying campus, but UC-Berkeley was hot with attitude. A minor spat over censorship in the student commons escalated into civil-rights–style sit-ins and demonstrations that spread to other campuses around America. Mario Savio, the charismatic student leader of the Free Speech Movement, became the first nonshowbiz spokesman for the postwar generation that California beamed out to America, presaging the political turmoil that would prevail at some American universities within four years.

THE SANTA ANA WINDS start blowing across southern California every year as summer turns into fall. Unlike the Pacific winds that usually wash California with ocean air, the Santa Ana winds come from the east, out of the desert, blowing the southern California smog back in the faces of the polluters. Santa Ana winds are associated with bad news and bummers: fire season in the dry hills, earthquakes, street crime, car crashes, drownings, overdoses, chronic headaches, and general malaise. The Indians believed the winds came from Santa Ana Canyon, which Jimmy and Felix Venable visited along with Scorpion Woman Peak and other weird sights around L.A. that autumn. For the next seven years, the Santa Ana winds seemed to have an unsettling effect on Jimmy, as they accompanied a series of yearly crises that happened to him every autumn.

ACCORDING TO NAVY RECORDS, Captain Morrison's ship returned to California in November 1964, but Jimmy decided to spend Christmas with Jeff Morehouse's family in Los Altos, along with some other young guys from scattered navy families who had grown up together. Daily, Jimmy distinguished himself by drinking a big glass of gin for breakfast without appearing to be affected. Jeff's mother, who had known Jimmy as a child, scolded him about this, but Jimmy just laughed his high whinnying chortle and poured himself another. He left a few days later, and Jeff Morehouse never saw him again.

Jimmy Morrison had turned twenty-one on December 8, 1964. It is unsure whether he had any contact with his parents during the holidays, although one source says that he saw his family after Christmas, and may have flown to Florida with them to see his grandparents and Mary Werbelow. What is known for certain is that after December 1964, Jim Morrison never saw his parents again.

CHAPTER THREE

LEARN TO FORGET

The object of life is sensation—to feel that we exist—even though in pain—it is this "craving void" which drives us to Gaming—to Battle—to Travel—to intemperate but keenly felt pursuits of every description whose principal attraction is the agitation inseparable from their accomplishment.

—LORD BYRON

LIVE AT THE WHISKY

NINETEEN SIXTY-FIVE was Year Zero for rock music. It was the pivot of the decade, the real beginning of "the Sixties," when postwar baby-boom culture took over the Western Romantic tradition and turned the volume way up. In England, the Beatles and the Rolling Stones tuned pop music in to the new drug culture. In America, Bob Dylan's heroic songs such as "Like a Rolling Stone" opened the postexistentialist era with their lyrical innovations and chains of flashing imagery. Later in the year Dylan helped invent the rock movement by playing an electric guitar at a folk festival—turning the vulgar instrument into a political statement and making obsolete "the old explanations and mildewed rationalities," as the Beat poet Michael McClure put it.

In 1965 all the elements that made the decade were in place. The Americans began bombing North Vietnam in March, to national and worldwide outrage, engendering a political climate that gradually poisoned the nation. The pacifist civil rights movement was being transformed by its younger activists into a violent struggle for black power. Birth control pills paved the way for the sexual revolution, so-called "free love," and abortion on demand. Marijuana and psychedelic drugs were subverting mainstream America from underground. Eastern religions—"the dharma moving west"—were seeping in via California and London. Assassinations, riot, and rebellion were in the air. The literary novel was behind the curve, and the movies were hopelessly lost, out like the fat kid at dodgeball. Music, fashion, and Pop Art carried the swing in that crucial year, which Jim Morrison later described as "a great visitation of energy." Much of the new pop energy was English or came from the East Coast, but in southern California a handful of young musicians was about to create the new hybrid of quality aesthetics and hype called folk rock. Jim Morrison and the Doors would later ride to fame on the back-wash of this unstoppable wave.

T HE GENESIS OF THIS SCENE—the new Sunset Strip culture—un-cannily coincided with Jimmy Morrison's arrival in Los Angeles. In January 1964 a couple of guys from Chicago opened a nightclub on Sunset Boulevard called the Whisky a Go Go.

The Whisky was a huge departure for L.A. nightlife. Old Hollywood and Rat Pack nightclubs like El Mocambo and Ciro's had mostly peaked by the late 1950s when Frank Sinatra's crew moved their acts to Las Vegas's gambling hotels. In 1963 a club operator and jazz fan named Elmer Valentine, who'd been a cop in Chicago, visited Paris to get inspiration for a new kind of club he wanted to open in Los Angeles. Exploring Paris's jazzy Left Bank club scene, Valentine found the Whiskey a Go Go, Castel, and other new discotheques in full swing, drawing an older, jet-set crowd who liked to dance to Motown and the Beatles and French pop records that were supposed to be for teenagers. Valentine brought this concept—adults dancing to pop songs—back to California, and with some partners opened the Whisky a Go Go in an old Bank of America branch on the corner of Sunset and Clark.

The Whisky was a new sensation from the moment it opened. The headliner was a young Louisiana rocker called Johnny Rivers who Valentine had stolen from Gazzari's, a rival club. Between sets the audi-ence could dance to 45-rpm singles spun by a girl deejay working above the crowd in a glass-walled cage, an innovation inspired by the old bank's weird space limitations. The first deejay hired for the club didn't show up opening night, so the cigarette girl got the job. Patty Brockhurst was wearing a fringed slit skirt, and when she started to dance along to Smokey Robinson, the Shirelles, "It's My Party," "I Want to Hold Your Hand," "He's a Rebel," "Downtown," "What'd I Say?"—the crowd went nuts. Thus was born that icon of the mid-sixties, the go-go girl. Valentine immediately hired two more dancers. One of them, Joanie Labine, designed the official go-go girl uniform: fringed mini-dress, lots of hair, no bra, and short, white high-heel patent leather boots. The discotheque was a new concept in America in 1964 and the club immediately filled with the Sebring-styled younger brothers of the Rat Pack–era swingers and their beehive-coiffed girlfriends.

When the Whisky took off, Sunset Boulevard started to happen again. Veteran scene-makers like record exec Lou Adler and Sonny Bono, who plugged records for Phil Spector, saw adults in coats and ties dancing to rock and roll and realized the audience was broadening. Pop music was thought unsuitable to nightclubs that depended on liquor tabs for profits, but then Johnny Rivers's hit records—covers of Chuck Berry's "Memphis" and "Maybelline," and the album *Live*—made him a viable attraction for the town's swinging young moderns. The Whisky drew turn-away mobs from opening night. The novelty of rock and roll on the Strip plus the sexy lure of the writhing go-go girls attracted movie stars and media attention.

A local Beat artist named Vito Paulekas, who lived with his premature hippie tribe in a redwood hut in Laurel Canyon, started bringing gangs of extremely attractive and scantily clad kids to dance at the Whisky. Vito's dancers had a new kind of dance, whose swinging hips and sinuously seductive arm movements almost mocked the nervous tension of New York dances like the Jerk. One of Vito's troupe was Rory Flynn, daughter of Errol Flynn; when Rory danced at the Whisky in her sheer negligee, the men stopped breathing and the world turned all around her.

Hollywood jammed into the Whisky to get a look. Steve McQueen—the reigning action movie king of Hollywood—installed himself as a regular in his own booth. Natalie Wood. Warren Beatty. Julie Christie. *Life* magazine ran a spread. Jack Paar broadcast *The Tonight Show* from the club. Cary Grant was photographed dancing there. When the Beatles hit L.A., John Lennon and Paul McCartney were chauffeured to the Whisky by Valentine himself, who brought along Whisky regular Jayne Mansfield for the ride. (John started putting her on—"Come off it, loov, they're not real, are they?"—until Jayne let them see them naked.) Elmer Valentine, gruff and lovable, became a local celeb. Jack Nicholson famously quipped that he looked like all seven of the dwarves.

Now new clubs sprouted like mushrooms in the enchanted forest.

Ciro's changed from a restaurant-lounge to a rock and roll club. The Action, the Galaxy, Brave New World, Fred C. Dobbs's, Bido Lito's, the Sea Witch, and Pandora's Box all began showcasing rock acts by 1965, when Elmer Valentine opened his second club, the Trip. Television jumped on the energy with pop shows like ABC's *Shindig* and NBC's *Hullabaloo,* both featuring go-go dancers who became national stars overnight. On the weekend nights younger kids started pouring onto Sunset Boulevard from the San Fernando Valley and the upscale suburbs, hanging out ten deep on the sidewalk and spilling into the Strip, stalling traffic, annoying the cops assigned to move the immense crowds along, creating a frisson of tension and malaise in the usually balmy night air lit by the headlights of purring muscle cars—GTOs and Stingrays—and garish neon from the clubs. There were so many kids you could hardly move from one club to another. The scene on the Strip was sensational, highly sexualized, vividly exhibitionistic, and—magnified by television—it set the tone for the rest of the country.

NOW THE CLUBS NEEDED young musicians to play in them, so the somewhat corny plastic glamour of Sunset Strip reached out to the Los Angeles folk scene for the raw talent that would propel it worldwide. There was plenty of new blood working in the folk clubs, and they began following Bob Dylan into electric ladyland. The Folk Revival of the late 1950s in Boston and New York that had made millionaires of California's Kingston Trio and spawned dozens of folk groups and jug bands was petering out in the wake of younger stars like Joan Baez and Dylan. Greenwich Village folkies Jim McGuinn (the Limelighters) and John Phillips (the Mugwumps) migrated to Los Angeles, where they mingled with local stars at the Troubadour on Santa Monica Boulevard and the Ash Grove on Third Street, Ben Franks on Sunset, and the Golden Vanity, which was out in the Valley. There were dozens of coffeehouses where any ballsy genius could get up and play, including rockabilly painters like Captain Beefheart and teenage slide guitar prodigies like Ry Cooder.

This circuit now began to throw up new bands. Jim McGuinn met David Crosby and Gene Clark, who formed the Jet Set and began to grow their hair like the Beatles and Stones. The Jet Set changed their name to the Byrds and started playing weekends at Ciro's, the frayed lounge on Sunset. The Byrds had once played a rent party for Vito Paulekas when he was in a jam, and now he brought his retinue of Laurel Canyon lovelies over to Ciro's and immediately moved the hip scene away from the suddenly passé Whisky. Those famously luminous nights—the Byrds at Ciro's—brought hip Los Angeles out on the Strip and set them dancing in the streets, dancing on the cars, wild and free-form with flailing arms, buckskin fringe, and long hair; all airborne on Jim McGuinn's twelve-string guitar and Missourian Gene Clark's great songs.

The Byrds' legend was under way, the hot underground flash on both coasts. They got a demo tape to Miles Davis's agent, who got it to Columbia Records in New York. Columbia's new A & R guy, Billy James, had worked with Bob Dylan in New York and interested Dylan in McGuinn's idea of putting some of Dylan's new songs to an electric backup. This became folk rock, blending the tense energy of rock and roll with the social conscience of folk.

The Byrds released their version of Bob Dylan's "Mr. Tambourine Man" in May 1965 and it was an immediate smash, reaching number one on the national charts. The whole Sunset Strip scene just exploded when the Byrds got on the radio. It was like the Strip changed overnight in May 1965. You couldn't drive west on Sunset anymore because it was too crowded, with barefoot kids blowing bubbles and rattling tambourines. "Mr. Tambourine Man" would have been number one forever if the Rolling Stones hadn't released "Satisfaction" a month later.

NAZIS ON TV

JIMMY MORRISON began his last semester at UCLA in January 1965. Mary Werbelow arrived in Los Angeles around that time, but she didn't move in with him, preferring to get her own place. She took classes at L.A. City College and soon got a job as a go-go dancer at Gazzari's on the Strip. This annoyed Jimmy who, like most cool student bohemians, thought the action on Sunset Strip was for teenyboppers and squares. But Mary Werbelow had what it took—big breasts, dark red hair, and (according to Ray Manzarek, who knew her) she knew how to shake that thing. By the end of the year she was billed as "Miss Gazzari's of 1965," much to Jimmy's disgust. His innocent Florida high school sweetheart had been absorbed into the tawdry sleaze of Sunset Strip. They drifted apart. You can't make this stuff up.

At school Jimmy acted like a frustrated artist, thwarted in his dreams. He wanted to make a film about Nietzsche's descent into drooling insanity after seeing a horse beaten in the streets of Turin, but couldn't get it together. His friend Phil O'Leno had made a diagnostic training film for the Psychology Department consisting of a young couple stripping to their underwear and caressing chastely. Jimmy rescued Phil's unused footage and made his own film. "He cut this footage real fast," O'Leno recalled, "so it looked like there was a lot more going on. A *lot* more... But that would be like him, to make a controversy out of something that he could use. He was a mischievous person... It caused quite a furor at the showing. Everyone was screaming at him, especially all the faculty."

In his notebooks Jimmy wrote concentrated poems that described a superhuman elite of elevated beings—"the Lords"—who operated on a higher psychic plane than the rest of humanity, who "saw things as they were." The Lords invisibly imposed a version of social control that seems derived from William S. Burroughs's Nova Mob. These pages also contained caricatures of dozens of fellow students like Alain Ronay, Phil O'Leno, and Dennis Jakob, catching their physical quirks with a few deft lines. Or Ray Manzarek in a jacket and tie, a goofy smile, and a quiff of hair, an arm possessively draped around his ever-present girlfriend, Dorothy Fujikawa, identified by straight black hair, slanting eyes, and a sexy skirt.

Jimmy carried a copy of Rimbaud's *Illuminations* wherever he went and appeared in several student films in his pose as the Human Fly, walking the parapets of tall campus buildings, reading Rimbaud's aperçus aloud like a West Coast version of Truffaut's film hero Antoine Doinel. Jimmy had never been any good with his hands, and had little patience for the mechanics of 16-mm film production, so the technical aspects of things like film splicing eluded him, with the result that his edits and Godard-inspired jump cuts tended to disintegrate in the projector when he tried to show them. Once he got so frustrated in the cinematography lab that he started throwing cans of film and kicking the furniture. No one knew what it was about, but it made a lot of noise.

Jimmy also drank a lot of wine, and had a rep as a roller of perfectly formed, cigarettelike joints. (He preferred coarse yellow wheat-straw rolling papers, or Zig Zag No. 225 rice paper with two leaves glued together. No one understood why Jimmy couldn't splice film but still somehow managed to craft such perfectly tubular reefers.) As the winter rains subsided and the weather grew warm, he hung out with the other film school slackers by the Gypsy Wagon lunch cart near the school, or at the Lucky U Mexican restaurant. Jimmy wrote smutty graffiti on the walls of the toilets. He had these deep-set eyes and would just stand around, doing his Marlon Brando thing, brooding. He was the class method actor. He was also overweight and cultivated a stoned look a lot of the time.

But classmates acknowledge that Morrison was unusually dedicated to learning the obscure byways of film history. Ray Manzarek recalls that Jimmy once hitchhiked 450 miles all night to Berkeley for a one-time-only screening of French existentialist hero Jean Genet's ultrarare homo-erotic prison movie *Un Chant d'Amour*. Only the hippest, most hard-core cinema freaks in L.A. took the trouble to make the scene. "Jim was a very talented and brilliant person," Phil O'Leno said. "But he was a little too young to be wise."

In his notebook Jimmy wrote, "Cure blindness with a whore's spittle."

IN MARCH 1965, the American government began bombing in Vietnam. The military draft was in full swing, sending thousands of Jimmy's generation into the nightmare of Asian jungle combat against a determined peasant guerrilla army. Jimmy spent the spring of 1965 working on his student film, a combination senior thesis and final exam that could make or break his quest for a UCLA degree in cinematography. Mary Werbelow refused to appear in it because 1) her new agent told her not to; 2) the sequence called for a girl wearing only lingerie; 3) she had shown up at Jimmy's place and caught him with another girl. (They had begun making out to the bombastic strains of Carl Orff's *Carmina Burana*—a Morrison fave—playing on Jimmy's little hi-fi.) So a disturbed and angry Jimmy used his cameraman (and featured player)

John DeBella's beautiful blond German girlfriend, Elke, instead. There was no script. "We're just gonna wing it," Jimmy told DeBella.

The untitled original film, essentially just a work print with a sound-track, was first screened at a grading session and kept breaking in the projector, which reportedly embarrassed Colin Young, the film division chairman. It was shown again at the senior screenings held in May 1965 in one of the film school's squalid Quonset huts. Since Jimmy Morrison had a love-him-or-hate-him reputation, the room was packed with students who sat through forty films by wanna-be Truffauts, Chris Markers, and Andy Warhols. Jimmy's film was one of the last shown. About fifty people saw the film, and all would have varying memories of what they saw.

"When the film starts," Jim later said, "the screen is black and you hear noises—a mixture of a record called *Erotica* and a tape of a priest and some children chanting something back and forth from a Catholic catechism-hour on the radio. It sounded like something primitive, out of the jungle." DeBella says there was a fuzzy test pattern film from the *Outer Limits* sci-fi TV show. Then cut to a group of young men (the film crew) smoking and getting ready to screen a presumably pornographic stag film. The film breaks, and the men fill the white screen with crude hand-shadow puppets. Then they throw darts at the *Playboy* centerfolds taped to the walls of Jimmy's apartment on Goshen, over insistent Navajo peyote chanting. A woman is seen from behind, walking down the street and disappearing into an elevator. (This sequence was shot on L.A.'s downtown skid row.) Jimmy is seen taking a cheek-sucking draw on a marijuana joint. As his eyes bulge, he cuts to stock footage of an atomic bomb going off. Then he delivers a huge wink to the camera. (Others recall that this scene started the film.) Cut to a black-and-white wooden console TV with big blond Elke sitting on top of it in bra, panties, garter belt, and black stockings, like a parody of *The Blue Angel* as the shot pans slowly down. Then she straddles the set so the following images seem to come from between her legs. Ray Manzarek, who was there, says Jimmy could be heard shouting over the Stones song that was playing: "Turn the TV on! Turn it on." DeBella's hand reaches in and switches the TV on, then changes the channel to—fortuitously—*Victory at Sea* images of marching Nazi storm troopers taking a salute from Adolf Hitler under flying swastikas. "Leave it on!" Jimmy yells. "It's perfect."

And so on. Porn. Drugs. Television. Nazis. Sex. Music. Irony. The film broke once, then again, to murderous groans from Jimmy's fellow students. Somehow the film got threaded through the projector. There was no plot, no beginning, no middle, no end. The girl licks DeBella's eyeball to purge the filmmaker's eye of the toxic imagery of the TV. Then the TV is turned off and the film ends in a white video line that ends in a black dot.

There was a horrid silence when Jim Morrison's student film was over. The vibe was suddenly chaotic in the steamy screening room, blue with tobacco smoke. No one got it except a few of his friends, and they loved it. Everyone else hated it and said so. Jimmy was perceived by many at UCLA as a hostile guy, talented but untogether, probably disturbed, who liked to provoke and put people on, then put them down. Now some of that negativity bounced back at him hard, in public. Several faculty members announced that it was the worst student film they'd ever seen. The women hated the pictures of naked girls. His advisor, Ed Brokaw, told Jimmy he was disappointed in him. One professor, deeply offended by the Nazi bit, attacked Jim personally, calling him and his film degenerate.

An hour later Jimmy was seen in a phone booth, reportedly tearful, as he told his troubles to someone unknown.

He got a D for his work. He told Ed Brokaw and Colin Young that he was quitting the program, but Young talked him out of it. "Jim just put a lot of things he liked into his film," Ray Manzarek would tell *Eye* magazine three years later. "It didn't have anything to do with anything. Everybody at UCLA hated it, but it was really quite good." A vocal minority defended Jimmy's film as astute, nonlinear cinema. Largely nerds, they all loved seeing Elke in her bra and panties.

"I'd say it was less a film than an *essay* on film," Morrison said later, dryly.

In any case, Jim Morrison graduated from UCLA in June 1965 with a B.S. degree in cinematography. Still bitter, he skipped the graduation exercises and hung out on the beach in Venice instead. His diploma was mailed to Clara Morrison in Coronado. Jim Morrison's legendary, technically incompetent, post-Beat student film—deemed too awful to have a negative cut for the Royce Hall screenings of the year's best—went into the trash with the other subpar wastes of good celluloid, and so is lost to posterity.

LIVE AT THE TURKEY JOINT WEST

BY MAY 1965, there were seismic shifts in the music world as L.A. folk rock suddenly took over AM radio. Sonny Bono and his girl-friend Cherilyn Sarkasian, who were singing backup vocals for Sonny's boss Phil Spector, broke out as Sonny and Cher after massive TV exposure with "I Got You, Babe." Former New Christy Minstrel Barry McGuire hit number one with the nuclear-fear anthem "Eve of Destruction." Neil Young and Stephen Stills formed Buffalo Springfield in the wake of the Byrds. Arthur Lee, the first black mod in America and the brilliant prototype for Jimi Hendrix and Sly Stone, formed Love, the first interracial band on the Strip. John and Michelle Phillips were newly arrived in L.A. with songs like "California Dreamin'" and "Monday, Monday" in their heads, songs that would consolidate L.A.'s claim to be the new generator of American pop.

The Rolling Stones were also in town. Phil Spector convinced England's newest delinquent aristocracy that they should be making their dark, Pop Art records in L.A., an idea validated by 1964 rock masterpieces like "The Last Time" and "It's All Over Now." The Stones were cutting at RCA Studios, arguing over their new song, "Satisfaction." Keith Richards hated it but got outvoted by the rest of the band. It came out in June 1965, a fuzz-toned complaint about girls, soap powder, and cigarettes that knocked the California bands off number one for the rest of the summer.

Jimmy Morrison developed something of a fixation around this time for angel-headed hipster Brian Jones, who had founded the Stones three years earlier. Jimmy Morrison was an ardent fan, as surviving notebooks reveal. They contain numerous references to seeing Jones on television, especially the 1965 *Shindig* broadcast where Brian told the show's host to shut up so that Howlin' Wolf, the hellacious Chicago blues star who was the Stones' special guest, could make his network television debut. With his golden bowl of blond hair reflecting the hot lights of mid-sixties black-and-white TV, Brian Jones gave off a semidivine, cathode-ray aura on television, a shocking and visceral blast of Dionysian energy. Brian Jones's blunt aggression and watchful charisma made a deep impression on America as he shared the front line of the Stones with Mick Jagger.

In L.A. Brian was the most visible of the Stones. While Mick and Keith sat knee to knee at the Hollywood Ambassador Hotel writing their next album, *Aftermath,* Brian Jones got dressed up and made sensational visitations onto the Strip, where he was mobbed on the sidewalks and in the shops and clubs, a numinous exemplar of English pop and Swinging London's saucy glamour. And it wasn't just the street teenies or the Mexican whores he hired who dug him. When not in the studio, Brian was courted by the local post-Beat hepcats. Dennis Hopper, the young actor and Pop Art collector, followed Brian around with his camera. So did motorcycle-riding artist Wallace Berman, who took Brian out to his house in Topanga Canyon for a photo session.

Intelligent, well-spoken, and affable when he wanted to be liked, the notoriously difficult Jones was on his best behavior and obviously dazzled by Hollywood and its azure swimming pools, fin-tailed Cadillacs, and mansions up in the hills above the Strip. Brian moved around L.A. like a young god by night, in a pill-and-booze haze that could turn weird when he got really loaded. Jimmy knew some of the girls who staggered out of Brian's pink poolside bungalow at dawn, carrying lurid tales of sadism, beatings, orgies, and general rough treatment by that insatiable maniac who played guitar for the Rolling Stones.

It's possible that Jimmy Morrison had some kind of encounter with Brian Jones in this period. Four years later, in 1969, one of Jim's major poetic works would be dedicated to Brian, illuminated by detail that could come through personal experience. There is also a May 1965 fan's snapshot of Brian taken at the instrument store Wallach's Music City, where the Stones got some of their gear (including the Gibson fuzz box used on "Satisfaction"). Brian is in a mod collar and a seersucker jacket, surrounded by admiring fans, one of whom looks very much like Jimmy Morrison. Brian Jones was notorious for whispering to people, which drew them closer into his orbit and got them to pay attention to what he was saying. Starting that summer, people around Jimmy got annoyed because he started to whisper all the time, like Brian Jones.

THERE'S NO DOUBT that Ray Manzarek discovered Jim Morrison. Ray originally knew Jimmy though DeBella and O'Leno, and was checking him out as some kind of potential collaborator as early as the winter of 1965. Ray was a semipro musician, making thirty bucks a week in Rick and the Ravens, the South Bay surf band started by his younger brothers, Rick and Jim Manzarek. The Ravens wore electric-blue jackets, ruffled white shirts, and desert boots, and blasted out Dick Dale instrumentals and "Louie Louie" and "Hoochie Coochie Man" at frat parties and—every couple of weeks—at a bar called the Turkey Joint West at Second Street and Broadway in Santa Monica. All the Manzarek brothers had serious musical training, so they were more than competent. Ray had a strong left hand from hours of practicing stride piano, and a relaxed facility on his electric keyboard that allowed him to spice up the solos he took on rock numbers with quotes from Debussy, J.S. Bach, Bill Evans, and Bud Powell.

Rick and the Ravens even had an indie record deal and had released a couple of nowhere singles on World Pacific's Aura sublabel. They almost got on *Shindig,* but the invitation fell through. Introduced as "Screamin' Ray Daniels, the Bearded Blues Shouter" (Ray Daniel Manzarek sported a beatnik goatee), mixing Bach partitas with Otis Spann piano licks, the eldest of the brothers did a Chicago R & B feature in the middle of the surf show that stretched out into a jazz approximation of what the extremely hip Paul Butterfield Blues Band was doing in Chicago—mixing urban R & B with modal sounds from the mysterious East. The Ravens were fun but mediocre. With no original songs and a charisma-challenged lineup, it was a band going nowhere. And Ray was broke.

Ray was an earnest pothead, but he wore straight-looking jackets and a tie, making him seem older and decidedly Ivy League. He was also ambitious and wanted in to the musical energy exploding in Los Angeles. He was also a spiritual seeker who was an early student at Maharishi Mahesh Yogi's Third Street Meditation Center. He was a jazz fan who dug John Coltrane and Thelonious Monk and the MJQ and Brazilian bossa nova and knew you could combine that sophistication with rock and roll the way the folk people had done. Ray saw something totally rock and roll in Jimmy's loutish rebel attitude and, for reasons unknown to his brothers, kept trying to bring Jimmy Morrison into the Ravens' orbit.

But Jimmy had no recognizable musical ability whatsoever. No one had heard him sing yet. He'd forgotten his piano lessons. He was useless on any instrument and had a shaky sense of rhythm. He was also withdrawn and pathologically shy in his non-manic moments. He just looked like a rock and roll star to Ray, who would drop in at Jim's place with Dorothy. It was a nice apartment near the VA hospital at Wilshire and San Vicente, with a wall filled with books and *Playboy* pinups and pictures of the London model Jean Shrimpton. Another wall displayed an enormous Pop Art collage that Jim was working on, composed of hundreds of images clipped from magazines. Jean Shrimpton and Brian Jones were repeatedly featured in this work in progress. Since Jimmy was mysterious about his family, people at UCLA were curious about where he came from and his background. Dorothy Fujikawa thought Jimmy's family must have some money, because of the expensive electric blanket she noticed on his bed.

Ray kept visualizing something, intuiting a latent potential in Jimmy that was waiting for something to happen. Once, when the Ravens were hired to back up Sonny and Cher at a high school dance and one of the guitar players couldn't make it, Ray paid Jimmy twenty-five dollars to just stand there holding an electric guitar. Jimmy strummed an unplugged Fender Strat and glowered and moved around in his feral, faintly unpleasant way. Then, at the end of May, Ray invited a whole bunch of UCLA classmates to a party at the Ravens' gig at Turkey Joint West, and at the midnight hour, when everyone was lubricated, Ray announced: "Ladies and gentlemen, we have a special treat tonight.... Here he is—direct from the UCLA Film Department—*Jim Morrison!*"

Jimmy had never sung onstage before that anyone knew. Ray says that he looked around with his goofy smile. People were clapping. Jimmy did this laugh he had—heh heh heh—and then he jumped on the little stage. Rick Manzarek started playing the "Louie Louie" intro. Suddenly, completely unexpectedly, Jimmy Morrison let out this ungodly, hog-calling rebel yell that landed on the dance floor like a grenade. The place exploded as the drummer rocked the beat and the girls in their shifts and sandals started to shake like pagans. Jimmy and Ray sang it together: "Louie Lou-I, oh baby—we gotta go." People talked about that night for years.

Jimmy loved it and thanked Ray later. He also told Ray he was heading for New York. This gave Ray a sinking feeling. Jimmy told friends that he was going to New York to see about hooking up with underground filmmaker Jonas Mekas, and trying to make poetic alternative films, like that one about Nietzsche and the horse.

I MET THE SPIRIT OF MUSIC

BUT THEN JIMMY CHANGED HIS MIND. When Phil O'Leno and John DeBella invited him on their postgraduation trip to Mexico, Jimmy told Phil he was staying around. "No," Jimmy said. "I think L.A. looks pretty good to me right now. There's energy happening here. I'm not going anywhere."

His family seemed to have cut off whatever financing he was getting, as Jimmy moved out of his apartment. He would never again have a home of his own.

He crashed on classmates' couches for a while. He threw away his shoes and went barefoot all the time. Jimmy's UCLA classmate Dennis Jakob was the resident janitor of a seedy old apartment house on Speedway Avenue, a block away from the Venice Beach boardwalk. In early June 1965, Jimmy moved his books into the basement storage area and began sleeping on the building's roof. He used Dennis's bathroom and kept clean by swimming in the ocean. A girlfriend named Carol Winter also let him stay with her in nearby Ocean Park when it rained. She also fed him now and then, and let him roll his perfect doobies from her stash of Panama Red.

But mostly Jim had just stopped eating. Instead he began taking daily doses of LSD, using the still-legal hallucinogen to raise his consciousness and blot out the psychic trauma of his past. With no money or income, he began fasting and losing weight. He stopped cutting his hair completely. He stopped speaking. He worked feverishly on his notebooks. He spent hours on the roof of the squat gray building, where in better days the old movie comedian W. C. Fields had once once lived, and stared out at the palm trees, the sandy beach, and the Pacific horizon framed between two taller buildings. He saw few people, and to those who knew him it seemed like he was using his languid Venice days to change himself from a college student dependent on his family to a neo-Beat poet of a type that was completely familiar to Venice's older denizens.

THE TOWN OF VENICE had been laid out as a fashionable resort by developer Abbot Kinney in the southern Santa Monica wetlands just before World War I. Kinney built streets and sold house lots along the canals that he dug. He built the Venice Amusement Pier, and on it the Venice Pier Opera House, where in the early 1920s Kid Ory's band played the first New Orleans jazz concert in California. Eventually Kinney overextended himself and went broke trying to re-create an Adriatic port in southern California. Soon oil derricks polluted the canals, and Venice became L.A.'s Japantown and a hotbed of illegal gambling. By the 1940s Venice was full of bingo parlors, elderly pensioners, and clip joints catering to the World War II sailors who flocked to the boardwalk's carny attractions when their ships were in.

Ten years later Venice was faded and run down. Four-room bungalows housed three Mexican families with their kids and chickens. Then old-school beatniks fleeing San Francisco began to settle into Venice's bohemian groove. Former storefronts became painters' studios. Unused lofts turned into Beat pads. When Allen Ginsberg was in town, he read his poetry accompanied by bongo drums at the Gaslight Club. On weekends Venice still drew crowds of freaks and tourists along its carny beachfront, but the rest of the time it was a quietly civilized and inexpensive neighborhood where college students, artists, and Mexicans coexisted in peace and tranquility.

Jimmy loved it. He seemed to take dream-come-true pride in living the poverty-stricken Beat life in Venice. Fueled by large, economy-sized doses of LSD and surviving on oranges and avocados pilfered from the neighbors' backyard trees, he was writing and sketching for hours every day. He carried around Edith Hamilton's best-selling *Mythology* everywhere he went. At night, according to his notebooks, he enjoyed the "threat and power" of watching women prepare for bed from his peeping spot on the roof of Dennis's building. Pages of notebook entries are devoted to the voyeur, and to Peeping Tom as a "dark comedian—pitifully alone." The *Lords* sequence, "The voyeur is masturbator, the mirror his badge, the window his prey," is as autobiographical as anything Jim Morrison ever wrote. When the women pulled the shades or turned off their lights, Jimmy stared at the white California moon.

MEANWHILE, THE KINKS were the stars of the jukebox at Olivia's, the soul food joint Jimmy frequented on the corner of Main and Ocean Park. The saw-toothed guitar on "All Day and All of the Night" had the first adrenalized English power chords that anyone had heard, and it was electric on the Strip. Jimmy Morrison loved the song and its throbbing message of lust. With his brain pulsing in lysergic waves that seemed to echo the phases of the sun and moon, Jimmy continued to transform himself from a pudgy college kid to a hipster godling. Within the space of about six weeks he had lost thirty-five pounds and grown his hair four inches. As his face lost its school cafeteria fleshiness, Jimmy's Celtic cheekbones took pride of place in his visage between intense blue eyes and sensual, Byronic lips. By the beginning of July 1965, Jimmy looked like a classical statue of Alexander the Great.

Sometime in that month of June 1965 he got rid of his old notebooks and journals. With no direction home, as Bob Dylan sang that summer in "Like a Rolling Stone," Jimmy was burdened with boxes full of his adolescent jottings that seemed to weigh him down as he pondered his next moves in a semicomatose state of LSD psychosis. One day in late June he burned some of his notebooks on the roof. Others were tossed in the trash. They represented, he said later, "old ideas I didn't need anymore." He kept only his most recent notebooks that contained the notes on film theory that he'd written at UCLA.

It was a cathartic, emetic act. Jimmy Morrison had burned or discarded the only tangible link to his past. Everything now depended on the destiny he understood the future held for him. Fasting, tripping, living alone in shamanic isolation, shedding his reptilian skins of outdated mentalities, peeping in windows, jerking off, writing and rewriting the lyrics for the rock and roll show that he was hearing in his head, Jimmy Morrison was dying in Venice while Jim Morrison—a new kind of rock god—was busy being born. As soon as he'd rid himself of the received wisdom and Beat quotations—"things that I'd read or heard"—in his discarded journals, the songs that would make him immortal began forming in his head.

Later Jim told *Rolling Stone's* Jerry Hopkins, "There's nothing I can think of that I'd rather have in my possession right now than two or three of those lost notebooks. I wrote in those notebooks night after night. But maybe if I hadn't thrown them away, I'd never have written anything original.... I think if I'd never gotten rid of them, I'd never [have] been free."

H E BEGAN TALKING about starting a band. Taking his cue from *The Doors of Perception,* Jimmy detailed plans to Dennis Jakob about a rock band called "The Doors—Open and Closed." The band would play in the dark, by candlelight. The music would be spooky. He was trying to put melodies to two of his notebook sketches, "I Am Hungry" and "Want"—both now lost. There would be chanting, Indian drums, incense, mixed media, projected films, lots of East-West drones and old blues sounds. Another friend of Jimmy's, Sam Gilman, who had arrived from Florida, also says that early that summer Jimmy was already talking about being in a rock band called the Doors.

Four years later, Jim recalled this period in *Rolling Stone:* "You see, the birth of rock and roll coincided with my adolescence, my coming into awareness. It was a real turn-on, although at the time I could never allow myself to rationally fantasize about ever doing it myself. I guess that all that time I was accumulating inclination and nerve. My subconscious had prepared the whole thing. I didn't think about it. It was just... *thought about.* I never even conceived it. I thought I was going to be a writer or a sociologist, or maybe write plays. I never went to concerts—maybe one or two at most. I saw a few things on TV, but I'd never been a part of it all. But I heard, *in my head,* a whole concert situation, with a band and singing and an audience, a *large* audience. Those first five or six songs I wrote, I was just taking notes at a fantastic rock concert that was going on inside my head. And once I'd written the songs, I had to sing them."

In another interview, he added: "In those days, when I heard a new song, I heard it as an entire performance. Taking place, you know, with the band, the audience, and the singer. Everything. It was like a prediction of the future. It was all there."

"In that year," Jim later wrote, "there was an intense visitation of energy. I left school & went down to the beach to live. I slept on a roof. At night the moon became a woman's face. I met the spirit of music." He wrote the verses and chorus for "Moonlight Drive" on the roof of the apartment building as the sun set over Venice Beach. *Let's swim to the moon...*

By July 1965, the transformation was nearly complete. Starving, brain-fried Jimmy was the Adonis of Venice Beach, wading the shallows half-naked, a verse-writing stoner poetic champion-in-waiting, set down in the far nether reaches of L.A. show business as represented by a nowhere surf band from the 'burbs, Rick and the Ravens.

Out of the froth—that's where Ray Manzarek rediscovered Jim Morrison.

ON THE BEACH

FOR JIMMY, the Rimbaud protocol, the systematic deregulation of the senses, involved tripping every day. Artists have always explored the transcendental worlds exposed by the artificial expansion of normal consciousness. For a Learyite acid head like Jimmy, tripping wasn't about getting high. LSD became a quest for transience itself, cut off from physical life. Walking the beach, Jimmy experienced strange auditory visions, like a psychoprophetic radio show, featuring him singing in front of a rock band. Later he was explicit and adamant about this mental prefiguring of what was going to happen to him, emphasizing that this precognition was something *heard,* not seen. When he wasn't tripping, he could sometimes be found at Felix's seedy bungalow on a stagnant Venice canal, drinking wine and hanging out. Or he and Phil O'Leno would drop acid and freak out along the canals, trying to scare each other. Jim loved to drive Phil's car on acid, winding down the broad L.A. boulevards like Wilshire and Sunset, or prowling through the old downtown business district with its older office buildings, strip joints, and cheap all-day movies.

According to government records, in June 1965, Jimmy received a notice to report to his draft board for a mandatory physical exam prior to induction into the U.S. Army. He went to see a fortune-teller in the Watts ghetto who read his palm, but he refused to tell anyone what she had told him. Jimmy noted the violent race riots going on in Watts at the time, events entered as poems in the notebook he was working in. Then, inexplicably and to the horror of his companions, he began yelling "Nigger" in public, in a Tourette's syndrome of provocation and surreality.

On a brightly hazy day in July 1965, around one in the afternoon, Jimmy was walking in the surf along the beach near Ocean Park when he came across Ray Manzarek sitting on the sandbank above the tideline. Ray now had a master's degree in film studies but no job, and he was dead broke. His girlfriend paid the rent on the apartment they shared above a garage on Fraser Street. Something had to happen for him, and it did.

Ray saw this wading vision—Jimmy Morrison splashing along in the surf, naked except for a pair of ragged cutoffs, about five foot ten, 130 pounds (down from 165!), hair in chestnut ringlets even longer than the silken tresses of the Byrds. Out of the froth, like Aphrodite emerging from the sea on Cyprus. He waved Jimmy over and asked, "What are you doing here, man? I thought you were going to New York City."

Laconic as ever, Jim sat down and told Ray he'd decided to stay in town for a while and try to keep out of trouble. In fact, Jimmy said, he was writing some songs. Ray asked Jimmy to sing something, but he looked away. "Aw, Ray, I don't have much of a voice." Ray reminded Jim that Bob Dylan didn't have much of a voice, either, so Jimmy thought it over for a moment, and decided to have a go. He raised himself up so he was on his knees. He scooped up two handfuls of Venice Beach sand and began to let the grains drift slowly from his fingers as he closed his eyes and began to sing "Moonlight Drive."

Let's swim to the moon, uh huh, let's climb to the tide . . .

He had almost the whole song already, ending in the fatally sexual imagery of *"gonna drown tonight / Going down down down."*

Ray tried to contain himself. "Oh, man—I *love* it. Incredible! Do you have anything else?"

"Yeah . . . I've got a couple of other things." He mentioned "Summer's Almost Gone" and then, taking two more handfuls of sand, began crooning "My Eyes Have Seen You" in a whispery Chet Baker jazz voice. To mark the tempo he drummed on his thighs, getting more intense as the already arranged number built to its climax.

Then he sang "Summer's Almost Gone."

Ray: "I told him, 'Jim, these are the best songs I've ever heard.... With your lyrics, what I can do with the keyboard, playing behind that...Man—we've got to get a band together. *We're gonna make a million dollars.*'"

According to Ray, Jim replied, "Ray, that's exactly what I had in mind." And then a little later, with zero hesitation, Jim announced, "We'll call it the Doors."

"Just the Doors?" Ray asked.

"Just the Doors," Jim said.

R AY WAS TOO SMART to let Jim Morrison out of his sight. He checked out Jim's Grecian profile and realized he'd just stumbled into the next Steve McQueen. He told Jimmy he was taking him in, that he was moving off the roof and into his and Dorothy's apartment on Fraser, effective immediately. Seemingly dumbstruck that someone was actually offering to care for him, Jim could only answer, "Right on, Ray!" And he let out a rebel yell that could be heard up and down the mystical coastline.

So Jimmy packed up his sleeping bag, a few clothes, some books (Fitzgerald, Mailer, Céline, Tennessee Williams's plays), the electric blanket, and his binoculars and moved in with Ray and Dorothy. They gave Jim the bedroom and moved into the living room. In his autobiography, Ray describes this arrangement as blessed by the angel from Truffaut's *Jules and Jim,* which features a ménage à trois. Since Ray is very specific with his other film references in his book, one can only speculate on the sexual politics in the garage flat on Fraser.

Ray had no piano, so after dropping Dorothy at her job he and Jim went on to UCLA to rehearse the new songs in the music building. In addition to the songs Jimmy had sung at the beach, he also had the words and melodies to "I Looked at You" and "End of the Night." "Go Insane" was a little rap about psychosis that echoed a nervous strain in rock and roll culture that produced hit records like Napoleon XIV's "They're Coming to Take Me Away." For the tender narcosis of the romance Jim describes in "Crystal Ship," Ray invented a falling chord structure that gave the tense lyric a sinister, dramatic edge. This went on for about a month, into August. Sometimes in the evenings Jim and Ray went down to the site of the old homosexual "Muscle Beach" exercise area and practiced on the rings and monkey bars until their bodies grew taut. Jimmy now looked like an athlete on a red-figure Attic jar. He was also gobbling acid at Felix's in the canals. Felix was drinking heavily now, and Ray hated him, so when Jimmy wanted to disappear he'd end up at Felix's.

Jim wrote to his father, now stationed in London, telling him that he'd failed to get a job after graduation and of his new plans to start a band with some guys he'd met. According to Jim's brother, his father replied that, after four years of college, and with no musical skills anyone had ever taken notice of, this sounded like "a crock" to him. Jim never wrote to his father again. Andy Morrison told Jerry Hopkins that their father felt bad about this later.

One night Ray asked Jim about his family. Jim said that his parents were dead. Ray was surprised, sympathetic, and he pressed Jim for details—accident, disease, murder? Reluctantly, Jim admitted to Ray that his parents weren't really dead. He would only say that his father was in the navy.

"They just made him an admiral," Ray says Jim told him. "He's in Vietnam." Actually Steve Morrison was now the youngest admiral in the U.S. Navy, and, rather than serving in Vietnam at that moment, was posted to London. "He was real strict," Ray quotes Jim as saying. "He ran the house like he ran his ship."

Ray asked Jim why he told people his parents were dead.

"I just don't want to see them," Jim replied. And then, after a pause: "Ever again."

Ray was shocked. Nothing more was said.

DHARMA BUMS

LATE AUGUST 1965. Ray Manzarek had barefoot Jimmy Morrison in his bedroom watching pop stars lip-sync on *Shindig* and *Hollywood a Go Go,* and Jimmy had these cool songs they were beginning to put together. Ray saw his job as retraining this self-described "writer/sociologist" as a rock singer. They started rehearsing "Break On Through" with

Ray's brothers in the Manzarek family garage in Manhattan Beach while Ray started to look for a drummer. Ray wanted a jazz player, ideally someone who could swing like Max Roach and sizzle like Tony Williams. They informally tried out a couple of guys before Ray reached into his Transcendental Meditation class and came up with a guy who was almost perfect.

Transcendental Meditation was the first of the Asian spiritual cults to invade America in the sixties. Founded in 1957 in India, by Maharishi Mahesh Yogi, as the Spiritual Regeneration Movement, it arrived in Los Angeles in 1960 and spread through the U.S. and Europe until it became identified with the Beatles and eventually mutated into an international corporation. But in 1965 TM was still small, with a faithful cadre of dedicated students. Maharishi taught a practice of deep meditation by means of a personal mantra given to the student by his teacher, a technique based on ancient Vedic scripture orally transmitted to him by his own teacher, Guru Dev. When he established himself in Los Angeles in 1964, the Maharishi's personal charisma and style attracted many young musicians (among them members of the Beach Boys and jazz musician Charles Lloyd) who had found the deep relaxation associated with TM's meditative state a viable alternative to toxic self-medication. By 1968, even the Beatles were singing "Jai Guru Dev."

TM's rise in the California sixties paralleled an increased Western interest in South Asian music. In Los Angeles, Dick Bock's World Pacific Records was augmenting its hip West Coast jazz catalog by recording the great masters of Indian music, Ali Akbar Khan and sitarist Ravi Shankar, when they passed through town. Shankar's blissfully improvised ragas were inspiring his new student George Harrison in England and influencing American bands like Paul Butterfield and the Byrds—young musicians who could see the tonal affinities this soulful music had with the blues. Within a few years raga rock would be the most potent symbol of what pre-Beat philosophers like Alan Watts had foretold: the Dharma Moving West. Given the skewed, demonic relationship the Doors had with the dominant California vibe of the sixties, it was ironic that three of its four members came out of a South Asian spiritual cult.

"We were all seekers after spiritual enlightenment," Ray told a radio interviewer later. "Even Jim in his way."

IT WAS BOCK'S INFLUENCE that led Ray to TM. Ray had recorded for Bock's Aura label and, being a progressive dude, saw the infinite possibilities that trance music like Indian ragas had for the Western audience. After Bock introduced him to TM, Ray started going to a meditation class in the Pacific Palisades, where he received his secret mantra, and met the guy who would be the drummer in the Doors—John Densmore.

John was twenty-one years old and had already dropped out of three California colleges. He was serious, sensitive, tense. He was a Catholic boy whose family was originally from Maine and relocated to the wrong side of the tracks that ran along Olympic Boulevard in West L.A. He was an accomplished drummer in his high school orchestra, an expert time-keeper trusted with the bass drum in the marching band, and had played in various wedding and bar mitzvah groups—including Terry and the Twi-lighters—for years around Los Angeles. He was quick to take offense but no sissy, being used to the aggressive beer-fueled vibe of the frat parties his bands played. His most recent band, the Psychedelic Rangers, re-flected his recent interests in LSD and R & B. John and Ray had estab-lished a rapport over shared jazz heroes—Elvin Jones, who played with Coltrane, and Art Blakey—and so Ray invited John and his three-piece Gretsch drum kit down to his band's next rehearsal in Rick's garage.

Late in August, as the dry Santa Ana winds began to blow in from the east, John Densmore met Jim Morrison for the first time. John drove down to the Manzareks' house in Manhattan Beach, where the Ravens/Doors were rehearsing. Ray was playing an upright piano, Rick was on guitar, and Jim Manzarek was blowing harmonica. "This is Jim the singer," Ray said, introducing John to a barefoot kid lurking in a dark corner, writing in his notebook. Jimmy Morrison was dressed in a dirty tan T-shirt and khakis. Politely, he got up, walked over and said hello to John, then shuffled back to his corner and kept scribbling. John set up his drums and they began to rehearse.

Smart guy, John thought to himself. Jimmy was wearing tinted blue granny glasses. *Corny,* John thought. No eye contact. John began to feel

uptight. Then Jimmy began to sing, looking at the floor, painfully intro-
verted, in a weak voice that could barely carry across a bathroom. He
kept twisting the microphone cord around his arm and wrist, worrying it,
trying to figure out what to do with it. Still no eye contact. The songs—
like the new "End of the Night" and "My Eyes Have Seen You"—sounded
odd, like bummers.

Hmmm, thought John. *I don't know about this.*

When they switched to some Jimmy Reed blues numbers—"Bright
Lights, Big City"—Jimmy seemed to perk up a little as Jim Manzarek
played the classic harp licks. They ran through "Break On Through"
once for John, who immediately knew to enhance the intro by putting a
knock on his snare rim with a sideways stick. Jim barked out his visionary lyric with a sudden baritone intensity that surprised John. As Jimmy
moved around the garage, John couldn't stop looking at him.

"I was uncertain," Densmore told an interviewer three years later.
"Their songs were really far out to me. I didn't understand very much,
but I figured I'm the drummer, not the lyricist."

Later, after the rehearsal, and when Jimmy had vanished, John told
Ray he was interested but wasn't sure about the singer, asking, "How is
this guy going to work up an audience when he's so preoccupied with
the stupid cord?" John agreed to come down for more rehearsals. He
had joined the Doors.

Soon John was totally co-opted, smitten, and driving carless, barefoot
Jimmy around. He even drove Jimmy to his draft board, where Jimmy,
who'd been staying awake on Black Beauties—Nembutal and speed—for
a week, looked the army doc in the eye and told him he thought he had
pronounced homosexual tendencies. The doctor checked the box that
rendered the admiral's son unfit for the military draft. The Lizard King
would not be serving his country in Vietnam.

THE QUEEN OF THE ANGELS SIGHS

ALTHOUGH RICK AND THE RAVENS weren't happening anymore, they had one more single due under their Aura contract.
Ray went to kindly Dick Bock and traded the single sessions for some

studio time, and the Doors—Jimmy, Ray and Jim Manzarek, John Densmore, and a female bass player—cut a six-song acetate demo at World Pacific Studio on Third Street sometime in early September. They set up in a room where Ravi Shankar's group had just finished recording, a studio that had seen sessions by Gerry Mulligan, Chet Baker, Chico Hamilton, and Shelley Manne. In just over three hours, the Doors recorded crude, semicompelling versions of some of the material they'd worked out with Densmore after only three rehearsals. (The first song they recorded, "Indian Summer," was apparently used to test the sound levels, and didn't make it onto the acetate.)

The overall vibe of the demo is prevailing folk-rock, with Ray helping Jim on many of the vocals. Jim's most alluring lyric—"Moonlight Drive"—lopes along to a guitar/harmonica backing track. "My Eyes Have Seen You" got such a heavy echo-chamber sound that it doesn't even sound like Jim singing. "Summer's Almost Gone" was an early ballad mostly informed by Ray's piano chords. "End of the Night," one of the Jim's earliest songs, is a conflation of the existential despair of Louis-Ferdinand Céline's *Journey to the End of the Night* with the fatalistic wisdom of the Doors' main inspirer, William Blake: "*Some are born to sweet delight/Some are born to endless night.*" Jim's seductive invitation to sally forth to "the bright midnight" was heady, surrealist stuff for an L.A. pop group in 1965.

The best song on the 33⅓-rpm microgroove disc was "Hello, I Love You." It had been written late in the summer when Jimmy and Ray had been sitting on a retaining wall along the beach in Venice. "Suddenly a Nubian princess appeared," according to Ray. "She was this black girl, around sixteen, with a perfect figure, perfect breasts, café au lait skin, and a provocative walk. The dusky jewel! I looked at Jim and said, 'Oh, man!'" Jim laughed his redneck whinny: *Hee hee hee hee—eee-ha!* Both of them wanted to say something to her but were too cool to blurt. "A few days later Jim said, 'Hey, remember that girl on the beach? I wrote a song about what I wanted to say to her.'"

The lyrics to "Hello" were set to a blatant rip-off of the Kinks' "All Day and All of the Night." Later, when they cut the track, they stole the drum lick from Cream's "Sunshine of Your Love" as well. There's some serious predestination in "Hello" when Jim asks, "Do you think I'll be the guy/To make the queen of the angels sigh?"

If the queen represented Los Angeles, Jim would be proved right.

The final track on the demo was labeled "Insane." This was actually "Go Insane," Jim's attempt at a witch doctor/twilight zone/nuthouse vibe chanted to a transmitting sci-fi piano/guitar lick. The sinister lyric about "*a little game called Go Insane*" would resurface in *Celebration of the Lizard,* but now it was just a genuinely creepy, half-joking attempt at a novelty record. (The similar but much better "Psychotic Reaction" would be a hot single for the San Jose band Count Five less than a year later.)

The Doors could only afford to press three copies of their demo, and these Ray and Jim began taking around to the record companies in early October 1965. The first place they went was Capitol Records' record-shaped office building on Vine Street in Hollywood. Capitol had the Beatles and the Beach Boys and was the label you wanted to be on in 1965. The Doors couldn't even get into the building. Jimmy put on his best southern gentleman act for the receptionist, but his bare feet kept him in the lobby, waiting hours for A & R guys who never showed up. They were encouraged to leave their demo, but they only had three copies and were afraid to let one go. Ray somehow got an appointment at independent powerhouse Liberty Records, but "Go Insane" got him thrown out of the owner's office.

I N THE LINER NOTES to *December's Children,* the Rolling Stones' rabidly anticipated new album, Stones manager Andrew Oldham referred to the all-powerful head of Dunhill Records in Los Angeles as "Lou Folk-Rock Adler." As the executive producer of the Mamas and the Papas, and the man behind "Eve of Destruction," Adler was the hottest young record executive in California and somehow Jim, Ray, and Dorothy got in to see him at Dunhill and play the Doors demo for him. This was big. But then Adler humiliated them. He dropped the needle on all six songs, track by track, and let them play for a few seconds each. *Nope. Can't use it. Sorry. Next. Nope. Sorry.* He put the record back in its brown paper sleeve and handed it to Ray. "Nothing here I can use," he smiled. Ray was shocked at this rudeness.

Jim Morrison got up and sneered back at Adler: "That's OK, man— we don't wanna be *used,* anyway." Jimmy turned his back on Adler and strolled out of his office without a word. No one treated Lou Folk-Rock Adler like that, especially not some insolent barefoot hippie from fucking Venice. Adler put that one in the bank, and didn't forget it.

Then they were also rejected by Warner Bros., Reprise, Atlantic, RCA, London, and every other label in town.

THE SECRET WEAPON

MEANTIME, with the demo going nowhere, Rick and Jim Manzarek quit the Doors. They didn't get Jimmy at all, wanted to go back to school, and anyway weren't the kind of musicians to jump to the next level in the profession. John Densmore brought over a guitarist named Bill Wolf to audition, but Ray said he didn't fit the image. So John picked up fellow Psychedelic Ranger Robby Krieger at his parents' house and drove him to Santa Monica to audition for the Doors. This is when the Doors' secret weapon joined the band.

John Densmore wasn't sure about Robby Krieger at first. They'd met at the Third Street Meditation Center. Prickly, blue-collar John noticed right off that Robby drove a good car and paid for the gas with a credit card, a rarity in 1965. Robby was shy, quiet, about five nine with wiry long hair. He was one of the twin sons of Stu and Marylyn Krieger, a well-to-do couple who lived in upscale Pacific Palisades, just north of Santa Monica. He took up surfing at fourteen, then started playing blues songs on the family's piano. He and his brother Ron were busted for smoking pot at Palisades High and packed off to Menlo Park, a private school near San Francisco. At sixteen he started playing a friend's guitar, and got a Mexican flamenco guitar a year later. Although he was only nineteen, Robby already had a distinctive, characteristic guitar style that evolved from flamenco lessons with teachers Arnold Lessing and Frank Chin. Instead of using a pick, Robby played with his long fingernails, giving his music an Iberian fluency.

In 1963, the Boston jug band revival was a big part of the folk scene, and at UC/Santa Barbara Robby formed the Back Bay Chamberpot Terriers. After a year, he transferred to UCLA, studying psychology and playing a lot of blues music. After seeing Chuck Berry rock out at the Santa Monica Civic Auditorium, Robby traded in his flamenco guitar for a black Gibson SG electric guitar, with its devilish dual cutaways. He originally planned to play in a jazz group, but decided on rock and roll when the Butterfield band's first record came out in 1964. At the same time he was studying the sitar, the sarod, and other forms of Indian music at the Kinnara Music School, run by Ravi Shankar. Playing with a ready arsenal of riffs from Spain, Bengal, and the Mississippi Delta, Robby Krieger then started jamming with John Densmore from his TM class. They played a couple of blues band gigs as the Psychedelic Rangers. John turned Robby on to LSD, and soon Robby had better acid connections than anyone John knew.

Jimmy had his own amp now and a microphone in the Doors' new rehearsal space, a little house behind the Santa Monica Greyhound bus depot rented by Hank Olguin, a film school friend. Lest the rehearsal proceed in a state of sobriety, Jimmy would announce, "We need some ammunition," and produce one of his yellow wheatstraw joints. A big one.

Robby was in the Doors the minute he started playing bottleneck acoustic slide guitar to the chord changes of "Moonlight Drive." Robby deployed the slithery slide the first time they ran through the song, and Jimmy went ape. He looked up from his notebook and said, "Jesus Christ—where'd you learn to play like that? That's the greatest sound I've ever heard on guitar." He told Robby that he'd never heard a guitar played with a slide before. He said it could be the band's signature—Robby should play that slide on *every song*. Then Jimmy started screaming at cretinous Felix Venable, who was sitting at the kitchen table rolling joints from a dusty pile of Mexican pot and trying to get Jimmy to ditch the boring rehearsal so they could go get a cold one.

On the way back to the Palisades, John asked Robby if he thought Jimmy was too crazy.

"Yeah," Robby answered. "He could also be a star. A *big* star. Don't the two go together sometimes?"

Ray expressed some concern to John about Robby's shyness, the vacant stare while he played, the slightly dazed and confused attitude, but the beautiful, sinuous bottleneck guitar music he had played for them

had won Robby Krieger a place in the Doors. This was a good thing because, aside from Jim, he was the only true artist in the band, and would
write many of the Doors' greatest songs.

DURING ALL THIS Jimmy was living with Ray and Dorothy, but he
was also sleeping around—sometimes on Dennis's roof, or at Felix's, or on Carol Winter's couch, or with some other chick. Friends could
see that Jimmy compartmentalized his life, keeping his circles of friends
separate from, and sometimes unknown to, each other. To some he
spoke only in a kind of hoarse whisper, like Brian Jones. "Jim had a hu-
mongous secret life," his UCLA friend and longtime colleague Paul Ferrara said of him. Often the people who assumed they were closest to him
had little idea of his other shadowy associations. For the rest of his life
Jim maintained a series of bolt-holes, places where he could stash himself and hide from responsibilities and his old lady. Jim Morrison was a
guy who would just disappear.

Jimmy kept up with things in his way. He read magazines like
Newsweek and *Downbeat.* He read and reread Norman Mailer's new
novel *An American Dream,* which was extremely influential on his immediate work. *American Dream* chapters like "A Vision in the Desert" and
"The Lion and the Serpent" soon echoed in Jim's lyrics. The novel's powerful depiction of anal intercourse between the hero and his wife's maid
might have awakened, or validated, Jimmy's own developing erotic
tastes.

He also spent hours at the movies. Godard's new film, *Contempt,* was
shown in Los Angeles that fall, and the film is mentioned in surviving
Morrison notebooks. Considered by some the greatest work of Western
art in any medium since World War II, *Contempt* stars Brigitte Bardot in
a heartbreaking mélange of existential soap opera and movie history,
filmed on the Isle of Capri. Jimmy raved about costar Jack Palance's performance as a predatory American film producer.

He took doses of LSD almost every day, or at least that was what he
told people. He had a huge stash of Owsley Stanley's early product—
"White Lightning" acid that looked like aspirin tablets. So Jimmy was
wildly unpredictable at all times. He'd go out to a café in Venice and

return to Ray's pad with some stranger who was tripping his brains out. Jimmy then tried to mind-fuck the stranger, putting on a Chet Baker side and flipping the light switches on and off until the person had to get up and leave. "I was just testing him," Jimmy told a perplexed Densmore.

Jimmy was starting to scare John, who was driving Jimmy around. John took him one evening to a girl's house in Beverly Hills. Joanna White was one of several attractive UCLA art students who let Jimmy use their bathrooms, sleep on their couches, and borrow their cars. John dropped him off at her apartment and went to get some apple juice. When he returned he found Jim twisting Joanna's arm behind her back in the kitchen, whispering violent threats in her ear while popping open the buttons of her shirt with a carving knife. Jimmy stopped when John walked in. "Just having a little fun," Jimmy said with a smirk, as he released the horrified girl's arm. John left quickly, in shock. The thought—
I'm in a band with a psychotic—ran through Densmore's mind over and over again.

Working with Morrison was traumatic for Densmore from the beginning. He was afraid of Jimmy but later wrote that he knew that this band was his only ticket out of his family. There was also a car-wreck fascination with what this guy might pull next. John Densmore developed a persistent skin rash on his legs when he met Jim, an anxiety dermatitis that only went away when Jim died.

THE DOORS REHEARSED at Hank Olguin's house three times a week for about a month, until the noise got too much for the neighbors and the police arrived and shut down the music. At one low-energy band meeting, the Doors even talked about quitting. Instead they were allowed to set up their gear in the Kriegers' suburban rec room, which had a piano. The fresh air and bourgeois comfort of the Palisades proved good for the Doors as they learned to mesh with themselves. According to Densmore, one day in December Jimmy announced, "We need more material." Everyone, he ordered, should go home and try writing a new song for the next rehearsal. "Use elemental imagery instead of specifics—earth, air, fire, and water."

Two days later, when the Doors got together, Jim asked if anyone had tried to write a new song.

"I wrote one," Robby said. "It came out OK."

"What's it called?" Ray asked.

"'Light My Fire,'" Robby replied.

CHAPEL OF EXTREME EXPERIENCE

FOUR YEARS LATER, Jim told *Rolling Stone*'s Jerry Hopkins: "So what we got was an acetate demo, and we had three copies pressed, right? I took them around, everywhere I could possibly think of. Going to the record companies—I hit most of 'em. Just going in the door and telling the secretary what I wanted. 'The Reception Game.' Sometimes they'd say, 'Leave your number,' . . .

"But then, at Columbia, they became interested. I gave the demo to a girl named Joan Wilson, who worked for the head of talent research and development. She called me a few days later [at Felix's house; the notation *Jim Morrison Ph 384-8489* was scrawled in Jim's handwriting on the demo sleeve] and said he'd like to talk to us. We got a contract with Columbia for six months. . . . Having that contract was kind of an incentive for us to stay together."

No one was more shocked than the Doors when they got a record deal from Columbia Records, the recording arm of the legendary Columbia Broadcasting System and the home of Dylan and the Byrds. But it was also the home of Barbra Streisand, Ray Conniff, and Simon and Garfunkel and seemed a no-chance long-shot to Jim and Ray when they infiltrated Columbia's offices at Sunset and Gower, trying to get their demo played. But then the intensely persuasive, blue-eyed, often barefoot and increasingly godlike Jim Morrison connected with Joan Wilson, secretary to Columbia executive Billy James. Joan got them in to see her boss.

Billy James had been Bob Dylan's Columbia publicist in New York. (James had first broken the story of Dylan's real name being Robert Zimmerman.) Sent to Hollywood to beef up the label's presence there, James worked with the Byrds and helped steer their so-far stellar career. While the Doors were shopping their demo, a photo of James had appeared in *Billboard.* His beatnik goatee gave him instant cred with Jimmy and Ray, so they borrowed Dorothy's yellow VW bug and drove to Columbia. With a mandate to sign new L.A. bands, Billy James liked what he heard in the Doors' demo: a fusion of interesting poetic ideas with blatantly tuneful dreams of pop success. The Doors, he reasoned, could be a perfect example of a subtle transformation that the whole pop scene was undergoing in California.

This transformation was unconsciously evolving through Bob Dylan, who had outraged the sclerotic folk music establishment by appearing at July's Newport Folk Festival playing an electric guitar with members of the Butterfield band. In the autumn of 1965 he began touring with Levon and the Hawks, the Canadian rock and roll group that later became The Band. All that season, Dylan and the Hawks moved around North America playing Dylan's post-Beat/surreal rock music, getting booed in many places when Dylan began playing his new Stones-influenced rock music. A defining moment in that tour happened when Dylan and band played the Community Theater in Berkeley in December, and the stars of the San Francisco poetry scene arrived to do Dylan homage. Allen Ginsberg, Lawrence Ferlinghetti, and Michael McClure were photographed outside the stage door with Dylan, conferring a kind of Beatitude on the Voice of His Generation.

Jimmy didn't go to any of the concerts that Dylan played in L.A. that December, but a girl Jimmy knew went to the Santa Monica Civic Auditorium show, and then was grilled about it afterward by Jimmy in an almost third-degree tone. *What did Dylan wear? What did he sing? What was the band like? Could you hear the words? What were the vibes like? Was everyone high?*

JIMMY ALSO HEARD about the nights at Jim McGuinn's house in Laurel Canyon. Bob Dylan was up there jamming with Allen Ginsberg, who had lately gotten Indian religion and transformed himself into a genial Hindu guru. McGuinn recalled: "San Francisco thought they had cornered hipness and creativity, but it wasn't the whole truth. Hollywood had a bad name for its slickness and superficiality, but there was actually an integrity to some of the stuff that was going on. It was a real kick after the Byrds got to number one with 'Mr. Tambourine Man.' Dylan would come to the house with Allen Ginsberg and we'd all sit around the floor, chanting. He [Ginsberg] didn't sing very well, but he was *really* into it." Hanging with Dylan and the Byrds, chanting sutras with finger cymbals and a little harmonium. Ginsberg conferred Beat-cred on the rock and roll scene, making it OK to be in chilled-out L.A. rather than San Francisco, where the vice cops had just shut down *The Beard,* Michael McClure's surreal play in which Billy the Kid and Jean Harlow hook up in a mythical blue heaven. Bob Dylan did four sold-out concerts in southern California, and no one booed at any of them. "Who digs Los Angeles IS Los Angeles," Ginsberg wrote.

Jimmy and Ginsberg ran into each other around this time, late 1965, at Pickwick Books on Hollywood Boulevard. Jimmy told Allen he was a poet too. Allen, bushy bearded and unusually direct, blatantly cruised Jim, but Jim wasn't interested. Allen told Jimmy that he'd been thrown out of both Cuba and Czechoslovakia that year by communist governments afraid he would spread perversion and dissent.

Billy James called in the Doors for a meeting. (A rumor at Columbia Records in New York put Bob Dylan in James's L.A. office when the Doors' acetate got played. When Dylan heard "Moonlight Drive" with its imagery of swimming and loving to the death, he supposedly told James, "Sign *that* fuckin' band, man.") Jim and Ray went to see Billy James. Ray was stoned and started to giggle when he realized James probably was too. Jim leaned over and murmured, "Shut up, Ray." Densmore says James discussed having his wife manage the band if he signed them to CBS.

Billy James told them he loved their demo but they needed a producer. Then he offered the Doors a no-money option deal from Columbia that gave them six months to write an album's worth of songs good enough to interest one of the label's in-house producers to make a record with them. The four Doors signed this contract in October 1965. Within the band, prompted by Jim, they decided that everything would be split four ways and shared equally.

A record deal with Bob Dylan's label! Temporarily, the Doors were over the moon. Robby even quit the Clouds, the other band he was jamming with.

Unable to bet on the Doors financially, James gave them their unmistakable sound instead. Columbia, he told them, had just bought the English instrument maker Vox, whose U.S. factory was out in the San Fernando Valley. From Vox the Doors got new Super Beatle amplifiers and the famous Vox Continental electric organ that had anchored core British Invasion bands like the Animals and the Dave Clark Five. The black and white keys were reversed on the Continental, and it had two aluminum Z-shaped stands. Mostly it was *loud.* Plugged into a guitar amp and cranked up to 10, the Vox Continental sounded huge. It would give the Doors a churchy-*cum*-carnivalesque sound that made their concerts seem like a doomy chapel of extreme experience.

DESERT VISION

OCTOBER 1965. Ray Manzarek found a new rehearsal room in a beach house at the corner of Northstar and Speedway in Venice, just north of the Marina Channel. It was a classic California surf shack with colored glass in the window panels and a knotty pine interior. The thirty-foot glass front of the house looked directly onto the beach. With their new organ and amplifiers, the Doors could now plug in and begin playing electric rehearsals, like a real rock and roll band. Jimmy would come in with a new song written on a crumpled paper napkin and chant-sing the words while the band helped him figure out the melody and arrangement. "Soul Kitchen" (inspired by Olivia's soul food restaurant) happened that way and emerged in its powerful form during the course of a single evening rehearsal. This was when Ray knew his vision would come true. "I said to Jim, 'This is it. We're gonna make it. We're gonna make great music and people are going to love it.'"

Ray and Dorothy moved into the house's bedroom, and Ray made the other guys in the band split the rent with him. John objected to this, which made Ray describe him later as mean and vindictive.

To Ray's consternation, Jimmy Morrison moved in with Felix Venable and Phil O'Leno in Venice, and proceeded to embark on an exhausting psychedelic binge of LSD, dangerous plant euphorics like belladonna and jimsonweed, plus mass quantities of alcohol. Under Felix's thumb, Jimmy displayed an ugly side Ray had never seen before. Drunk, Jimmy would reel through multiple personae that included Jimbo the racist frat boy, the Dylan Thomas romantic Celt, the village idiot, "Norman Mailer," the bloated biker, the Beat poet, and the southern gent. Ray tried to express some concern when Jimmy told him he was going to stay with Felix, but Jimmy just laughed at him. Soon Jim, Felix, and Phil got so crazy that it affected the band, with Jimmy missing rehearsals because he was tripping, high, drunk, or all three.

But this view of Jim as drugged-out reprobate has to balance with the stark reality of the high quality of work he was producing. The sheer funky coolness of the "Soul Kitchen" lyrics could only have come from a poet comfortably in control of his cadences and imagery. The way that the idea of the "secret alphabet" blended into the admonition "Learn to forget" had an evocative and hypnotic quality that was instantly at the top of rock's lyrical game—as memorable as anything contemporary by the Beatles, Stones, or even Bob Dylan. At the same time he seemed to be a premature acid casualty, Jim Morrison was crafting riveting poetic imagery—the glittering stuff of the Doors' first two albums—that would penetrate his generation's consciousness and echo down through the decades.

Jim finished "Crystal Ship" around that time, according to John Densmore, as he was breaking up with an early girlfriend, possibly Mary Werbelow.

THEY HAD TO MAKE some money now, which meant infiltrating the music clubs on the Strip. As boho film grads, Jimmy and Ray had looked down on this scene, oriented toward squares, tourists, and teenyboppers from the Valley. But they were all broke and the bars were the only source of steady employment for a baby band like the Doors. In early November 1965 they auditioned at the Galaxy and were told to get a bass player or people wouldn't dance. At Bido Lito's, a nonunion rock club on the eastern end of Sunset where new bands could sometimes break in, they were rejected several times for being too weird and not knowing "Satisfaction." Bill Gazzari wouldn't even let Jim into his club to audition because he was barefoot. This went on for a while, Gazzari recalled. "One day Jim said, 'Bill, can we come in now?' I leaned over the counter and he had one shoe on. He didn't have a shoe on the other foot. I said, 'Did you lose a shoe?' Jim said, 'No, I found one so I could get in.'"

Without Jim present, the Doors auditioned a couple of bass players, which made them sound like the Animals, but nobody clicked. The

Doors were already this humidly insular four-piece band that seemingly had no room for another musician in the mix. Then, as the Doors were failing an audition at a club in Westchester where the Turtles were the house band, Ray noticed their stage gear included a Fender-Rhodes keyboard bass sitting on top of a Vox Continental organ, like the one he used. It had thirty-two notes and was played left-handed, boogie-woogie style. Ray remembered: "I switched on the amplifier, played the thing, and realized what it was. I said, 'This is it—we have found our bass player.'"

The next day at Wallach's Music City, they learned they had nowhere near the $250 price of the keyboard bass. But three days later Robby walked into the sunroom of the beach house with a brand new keyboard bass, still in its box. Stu Krieger had written a check and told his son that if they made "Light My Fire" a hit record, the Doors wouldn't have to pay him back.

The first rehearsal with the bass was epochal. John started playing with a little more snap with a bass line under him, and Jim grabbed the single maraca he liked to shake and danced around the room like a spastic dervish. The Doors had never sounded so good before. "We're ready to take on the *Stones* now," Ray announced to the band with typical grandiosity. Both John and Robby had been jamming with other bands all this time, and Ray now asked them to quit and devote their full energies to the Doors. "And I did, finally," Densmore says. "I could see that Jim was really special."

The Doors played several gigs around town that fall, including frat parties, a wedding, and a dance at a union hall. Ray still did most of the singing, with Jimmy's back turned to the audience as he faced his band in a four-squared circle while he slowly grew accustomed to performing music. "Gloria," "Money," and Bo Diddley's "Who Do You Love?" were huge jams for the early Doors. On December 10, the Doors played as an augmented quartet at UCLA film school's Royce Hall screenings of the previous year's best student films. They set up offstage and provided a live soundtrack as Ray Manzarek's *Who I Am and Where I Live* was shown. Ray played flute, Robby played guitar, and Jimmy, John Densmore, and assorted girlfriends played drums, rattles, and tambourines. (Felix Venable's short film *Les Anges Dormants* was also screened.)

On New Year's Eve they played at the home of some friends of the

Kriegers', where they took requests for popular songs of the day. Asked to play "Ticket to Ride" and "Satisfaction," Jimmy asked if the guests thought the Doors were a jukebox. Someone gave him a quarter, which he threw high in the air, caught in his mouth, and swallowed.

A ROUND THIS TIME, EXALTED by permanent intoxication, Jim Morrison resurrected his childhood experience on the New Mexico highway. He told many of his friends of his notion that Indian spirits had somehow entered his soul. He spoke of finding a shaman he could ask about this. In January 1966, right after the new year, Jimmy decided to follow Carlos Castaneda's trail to the Sonora Desert in Mexico to find some Indian shamans and eat peyote. To prepare for the trip, Jim and Felix dropped acid and freaked out on the Fox Hills golf course. (They called Carol Winter at dawn to come and pick them up.) Then they borrowed Phil's brother's old car and set off for the desert. In suburban Hawthorne, an already tripping Jimmy saw a beautiful girl on the sidewalk and jumped out of the car to kiss her. A cop car pulled up. The girl turned out to be only fourteen. Jimmy called the cop an asshole and dared him to make an arrest. When the cop declined, Jimmy in typically provocative mode called him a chickenshit.

They never got to Mexico. They made it out to Needles, on the California-Arizona line, where they settled into a motel room. There Jimmy performed a wordless little ritual. He took a check out of his wallet, set it on fire as his friends watched, and let it burn down to his fingertips. He didn't say what the check was, but Phil assumed it was the last check he had received from his parents.

The next day, they dropped some Sandoz acid that Felix had, and walked into the desert hills. Jim and Felix disappeared together down an arroyo, where Phil lost them. When they returned from their trippy hike, many hours later, Phil was gone, having driven away by himself.

No one really knows what happened next, except that Jimmy and Felix returned to Venice with cuts, bruises, and black eyes, having been brutally beaten up during their trip home. Some say they were hitchhiking and were assaulted by rednecks who picked them up. Felix told a friend of Jimmy's that cops had done it. Ray thinks some Chicano low-riders did the long-hair stomp on them in a bar. Felix got the worst beating, but

Jimmy was cut up and disheveled when he showed up at the beach house. He seemed dazed, and really out of it. Ray suggested he could use a haircut. Suddenly Jimmy screamed at Ray—"NO ONE TELLS ME WHAT TO DO!"—and ran out of the house, slamming the door behind him.

When Jimmy and Felix returned, half dead, without Phil O'Leno, people asked where he was. Jimmy drawled, "Well, man, we like, uh, *killed* him in Mexico, you know—and we buried him in a dry wash." Some friend of Phil's took this seriously, and it got back to O'Leno's attorney father, who filed a missing person report and had Jimmy arrested on a battery charge in Inglewood on January 23, 1966.

Carol Winter bailed Jimmy out, and the matter was dropped when Phil turned up intact a few days later.

BOOK II

JIM
MORRISON

CHAPTER FOUR

BACK DOOR MAN

Talent does whatever it wants to. Genius does only what it can.

—EUGÈNE DELACROIX

BAND FROM VENICE

IN EARLY MARCH 1966, at the height of the nightly teenage rave on the Sunset Strip, the Doors landed an audition at a dank bar on Sunset called the London Fog. The owner, Jesse James, who said he was the great-grandson of the famous Missouri outlaw, told Jim and Ray that he'd let them play when he heard they had a recording contract. The deal was that if they drew a crowd they could be the London Fog's new house band. A few days before the gig, they contacted all their friends from UCLA and implored them to come to the Fog.

The Fog was basically a dive bar. It was the former Unicorn coffeehouse, located between Hamburger Hamlet and the Galaxy, about fifty yards down Sunset from the Whisky. It was long and narrow with the ambience of a subway car, with a long bar and a small, strangely shaped, unusually tall stage wedged into the end of the room. In a cheesy attempt at a swinging London vibe, British music papers and magazines were glued to the walls. Between the house band's sets, Rhonda Lane, the ample, bosomy go-go girl, gyrated to English records above the heads of the regulars, who, because teenagers weren't allowed into dive bars, consisted mainly of older guys, sailors, barflies, out-of-town businessmen, and the occasional hooker.

But on the night when the Doors auditioned, the London Fog was packed with the band's friends. They played their best songs—"Hello, I Love You" and "Light My Fire"—and padded the show with competent

R & B covers like "Little Red Rooster" and British hits like "Gloria." The vibe was groovy and the bar did great business. James asked them to stay and play a second set. The customers appeared to love the Doors so much that they were immediately hired as the Fog's new, nonunion house band: four sets a night, from nine at night until two in the morning, for four nights a week (which later increased to six). They played for five dollars each on weeknights, ten on the weekends. It was a shitty deal, and they rarely got all the money they'd earned, but the London Fog gig turned the Doors into a professional rock band within ten weeks.

The next night the Doors arrived at the London Fog for their first night's work. The owner had spread a banner across the front of the club: THE DOORS—BAND FROM VENICE. No one showed up. The place was empty all night. Jesse James couldn't figure this out until someone clued him in that the Doors' college pals weren't coming back.

B UT THE DOORS MADE the most of it, especially Jim Morrison. At the London Fog he began to turn from a writer into a musician, progressing from a back-to-the-audience singer into the beginnings of a performer. He played his maraca and tried to grunt out blues licks on harmonica.

The band evolved too. Robby Krieger brought Willie Dixon's classic blues boast "Back Door Man" to the band (via John Hammond Jr.'s recording), and John Densmore gave it a rocked-up tom-tom tribal drive that turned it into a showstopper. Dorothy Fujikawa suggested they try "The Alabama Song," from Bertolt Brecht and Kurt Weill's 1927 German opera *The Rise and Fall of the City of Mahagonny*. The song sounded great with rock drumming, and "Show me the way to the next whiskey bar" was a funny and ironic indication of where the Doors really wanted to be—just down the street at the Whisky a Go Go, where Love and Buffalo Springfield were the hottest bands on Sunset Strip.

Love—black and white hippies playing early acid rock—worked at the Whisky five nights a week, and crowds lined up around the block to see the biggest act on the Strip. Front man Arthur Lee was a striking black mod with processed hair, flowing silk scarves, and a Carnaby Street wardrobe. His multiracial band played a weird mixture of punkish soul, psychedelic English blues, cocktail jazz, and pseudo-Mexican music with slightly sinister and insinuating lyrics. Love had a reputation for chaotic shows, but they also had great songs like "Seven and Seven Is," and a recording deal with Elektra Records. They had taken up where the Byrds' primal burst of energy had left off, and they carried the swing on the Strip until supplanted by the Doors a few months later.

Between sets at the Fog, John Densmore used to walk down to the Whisky—whose cover charge he couldn't afford—and watch from the front door as Love played to a full house amid adulatory abandon. "I really wanted to be in Love," Densmore said later. "They were really making it. But no—I was in the demon Doors."

R AY AND DOROTHY were still living at the band's rehearsal space, the bottom floor of an isolated beach house south of Washington Boulevard. The Doors were each paying a share of the two-hundred-dollar-a-month rent. There was some growing resentment about this arrangement, so Jim decided to pick at it, like a scab. One morning at dawn Jim and Robby showed up at the house, peaking on acid, with two young Fog hookers in tow. According to Densmore, Jim began mocking Ray and Dorothy's noisy lovemaking—he'd heard it plenty at the Santa Monica house when they lived together—and then began abusing Ray's treasured record collection, ripping the LPs from their jackets and tossing them around the long room like they were Frisbees.

Ray emerged from his sleeping area as Jim was grinding *Kind of Blue* beneath his boot heel. When Ray saw the broken platters and the stupid look on Jim's face, he just walked back in the bedroom and closed the screen behind him.

T HE DOORS BEGAN TO BUILD a little fan base on the Strip, and there were hip people who had stumbled into the Fog by mistake who were now ardently supporting the new band from Venice. Jim was still taking the stage in his street clothes—khaki trousers and long-sleeved pullovers—but he was starting to turn around and actually look at his audience for the first time. Singing hard blues songs and screaming out snatches of verse every night began to strengthen Jim's neck muscles and vocal cords, and his voice changed from a wispy drawl to a deeper, emotionally rich baritone that could really put a song lyric across.

To stretch out their four sets a night without repeating themselves, the Doors were also developing as a jazzy, improvising, bossa-inflected jam band. "The End" had begun as a three-minute love ballad and now stretched into a twelve-minute Indian raga. "Light My Fire" could go for a quarter of an hour with Jim ad-libbing surreal poetic riffs in the mid-section. "When the Music's Over" was born at the Fog to kill another fifteen minutes. (Jim had actually heard Jesse James tell the bartender one night, "When the music's over, turn out the lights.")

They also had a couple of different sequences they called "Latin Bullshit #1" and "LBS #2" that were instrumental jams based on jazz arrangements by Gil Evans and John Coltrane's "Afro Blue." These could run half a set at the end of the night in front of the usually empty house.

As the band got tighter, Jim stopped playing harmonica. He also started his first bit of stage business with a black silk scarf during the jazz solos, wrapping the fabric around his head or draping it over the microphone stand. Felix Venable introduced Jim to poppers around this time, amyl nitrate capsules used to revive heart patients. They provided a whiff of ammonia and a half-minute out-of-body experience. Jim liked to crack them open under the noses of the musicians during their "Light My Fire" solos. Sometimes, when stuck for a lyric while he was improvising, he'd crack a popper under his nose. Jim's eyes rolled up into his head and he'd collapse over the keyboard. Ray just kept playing until Jim regained consciousness and the set would go on.

Some nights there were only a few people in the Fog. The place was dirty and the air blue with cigarette smoke. Jesse James stiffed them on their pay, but they liked him because he fed them for free and they could see the joint was losing money.

O N NIGHTS the Doors weren't working the Fog, they played other area gigs, like the Van Nuys Teen Center in the Valley. They also played a private party at Moonfire Ranch in Topanga Canyon. Moonfire was owned by Lewis Beech Marvin III, an heir to the Green Stamps supermarket premium fortune (and a good friend of pop artist Andy Warhol). Marvin had built a big round house on his ranch, and hired the

Doors to entertain there several times that year. Jim loved wild and dramatic Topanga Canyon, which was still undeveloped and felt like Old California with its craggy landscape and itinerant population of "creek rats," who looked like the denizens of an old mining camp.

Lewis Marvin was involved with social causes, such as a campaign to ban war toys in the face of the increasingly horrendous situation in Vietnam. That year, 1966, Robert McNamara, secretary of defense, was describing the massive American troop deployment as a defense of the South Vietnamese against invasion by the North, which he implied was just a proxy for the Communist Chinese. In Washington, mad-dog senator Strom Thurmond was backing nuclear arms to end the war. General Curtis LeMay, chief of staff of the armed forces, was urging America to "bomb North Vietnam back to the Stone Age." On American campuses, antiwar professors were beginning the "teach-ins" that would evolve into a full-blown antiwar movement the following year.

The Doors played a benefit for the war toys protest on April 23, 1966, in Will Rogers State Park.

PEOPLE WHO HEARD the Doors' original material were impressed by songs like "Crystal Ship," with its dark, brilliantly romantic vision of love and narcosis. Robby Krieger wrote "Love Me Two Times" and the band developed it into a stunning display of repetitive firepower. Jim shouted, *"She gets—she gets—she gets—Hiiiiigh"* at the climax of "Break On Through," and the room felt like it would explode. The Doors got asked a lot if they had a record out, and began to wonder why they were saying no. The Doors thought they were ready. Once, driving around town, Jim asked John Densmore if he thought the Doors could be as big as the Rolling Stones. John thought Jim was kidding, but when he looked over at Jim, he realized it wasn't a joke.

But nothing was happening with Columbia. Someone had shown up at the Fog one night and introduced himself as their producer, but they never heard from him again. John Densmore went to see Billy James that spring and, while waiting for him, noticed "the Doors" at the top of Columbia's list of bands to be dropped. So they asked for their immediate release. James pointed out they had a month to go on their contract and would get a little cash if they stuck it out, but Jim felt something could happen with another label, and James let them go. A few months later Billy James left Columbia for Elektra Records, and so he ended up working with the Doors anyway.

SHE GETS HIGH

SUNSET STRIP'S CHRONICLERS generally agree that the spring of 1966 was the high point of the whole scene. Love was at the Whisky; Iron Butterfly at the Galaxy. Rhinoceros was at Thee Experience. The Doors at the London Fog. Musician Jimmy Greenspoon (from Three Dog Night) remembers, "Late night, after the shows, we'd hang out at Cantor's Deli on Fairfax—every freak and band in town, Zappa's people, all the groupies, the Byrds, the Seeds, the Turtles, Buffalo Springfield, Kaleidoscope, the Daily Flash, the Sons of Adam. If Phil Spector or Brian Wilson came in, they'd get a standing ovation.

"Morrison stood out in all this because he was so fucking handsome. And, if he wanted to, he could get very loud. Even then Jim was already attracting the budding little dark poet chicks, the little lost waifs with big eyes and secret smiles."

About a month into the Doors' gig as house band at the London Fog, an extremely beautiful and alluring redheaded girl walked into the Fog late one night, and sat down to listen to the band. Her name was Pamela Courson. She was nineteen years old, and it was here that she became, inextricably, part of Jim Morrison's legend.

PAM COURSON WAS STUNNING. She was petite, about five foot two inches, with beautiful auburn hair ironed straight and parted in the middle, a slim and small-breasted figure, and an Orange County smile accentuated by perfect white teeth and haughty Celtic cheekbones. (The Château de Courson is about thirty miles southwest of Paris.) Pam had milky, almost translucent skin, lightly sprinkled with cinnamon-colored freckles, and the softest and most soulfully expressive green eyes. She was a glorious American archetype, the living image of Brian Wilson's mythic California Girl, with the aura of a hippie princess or an ethereal wood sprite. Her clothes were *au fait*, ahead of the times: minis and shifts in exotic fabrics with tribal embroidery or Op Art chevrons, worn with sandals or high boots. Her physical delicacy and outward fragility, and her seeming vulnerability that demanded care and protection from any man who would be with her, belied Pamela Courson's steely will, a rebel attitude, profoundly disturbed psyche, and dominating personality that would earn her many enemies in the Doors' orbit as she bonded irrevocably with Jim Morrison and then tried in vain to run his life.

John Densmore saw her first. She came into the club one night while prowling the Strip with a girlfriend. After the Doors' first set, John sat down at her table and chatted her up. Jim went to the bar and drank a beer. Next set: Jim had to coax John back on the stage with "John? Where the fuck are yew? Get yoah ass up here, boy!" When John looked for Pam at closing time, she was gone. But two days later, she and her girlfriend were back! John went back to work on her, but at closing time, once again, she was gone.

Apparently Pam and Jim encountered each other at a midweek party at UCLA a few days later. She was radiant, laughing, and seemingly with another guy. Jim circled around her, looking for an angle, but Pam wouldn't make eye contact. According to Jim's friend January Jansen, who later made his leather stage clothes, "He saw her there across the room and wanted to meet her, so he asked around until he found a friend of hers who could arrange a proper introduction." They chatted for a while, and she told him she was taking art classes at Los Angeles Community College. He asked for her number, but something distracted her and she didn't give it to him.

The following weekend, in early April 1966, Pam Courson came to the London Fog both nights. On Saturday night, while John Densmore and Pam were talking in one of the Fog's booths, Jim Morrison made his move and sat down with them. There was talk of mutual friends, astrology, acid, and real estate. Ray later tried to accurately describe this encounter: "Once their eyes combined, their psyches did a caduceus up the staff of Mercury and their souls sprouted wings. They were mated. Olympian. Cosmic."

John Densmore knew enough to move on.

After the set, Jim and Pam went to Cantor's. Frank Zappa was there, and they sat with his Laurel Canyon entourage for a while. Jim Morrison later told one of his girlfriends that when Pamela finally took him home at dawn, it was the first time he'd ever really made love. A few nights later, they went on their first date, to see French director Claude Lelouch's hit film, *A Man and a Woman.* Pam loved the movie's soft-focus romanticism, which sent Jim off on a tirade about the bogus use of music to manipulate the emotions of the viewer.

PAMELA SUSAN COURSON IS ONE of the more enigmatic figures of the American sixties. As the Old Lady of the biggest rock star in Los Angeles she would carve out her own legend of romance, high style, and excess that rivaled Jim's for recklessness and danger. Those who really knew the couple understood that she was stronger than he, that he would give her anything she wanted, and that she knew all his secrets, especially the ones that could ruin him in an instant. She acted out the role of rock star wife to the max, calling herself Mrs. Morrison, wearing a wedding ring, and burning through his money as if he owned a bank. He never married her, he often cheated on her (and she on him), but he *always* came back to her. He wrote about her, dedicated his poetry to her, and left her everything in the end.

Jim Morrison loved Pamela Courson to death.

She was born in Weed, California, on December 22, 1946, in the shadow of Mount Shasta (much made of this by Jim), a notorious spiritual power spot famous for occult and paranormal phenomena. Her father, Columbus "Corky" Courson, who'd brought the family to California from Texas, had been a naval officer like Jim's. He then pursued a career in teaching that took the family to Orange County, the hotbed of suburban conservatism just south of Los Angeles. To make ends meet, he moonlighted at Disneyland when the massive theme park opened in Anaheim in 1955.

Friends who knew Pamela and her sister Judy as children recall her as a reclusive little girl from a family that didn't mix much with the neighbors. Pam was cute but truculent; she quit the Brownies because she hated the drab brown uniforms. She did well in school until junior high, when school records indicate her family was contacted about her constant truancy.

She hated high school too. She was turning into a beauty, with a nymphet's figure and long straight hair like the Beatles' girlfriends. At Orange High, where her father was now principal, she was considered smart, cynical, wry, and somewhat mysterious. After school she disappeared, and told friends that she went home to design clothes. On weekends she sneaked out to catch the surf bands in nearby Balboa.

When she was sixteen, her grades nosedived, and she began to get a reputation as a fast girl, a wild child, a beatnik weirdo. Given her father's position, this was anathema in the far-right political atmosphere of Orange County, which in 1964 was hard-core Goldwater country. (Some say Pamela was hounded out of high school by squares who persecuted her.) She didn't return to Orange High for her senior year, and enrolled in Capistrano High instead. She dropped out that spring and "ran away" to Los Angeles, where she and a girlfriend got a cheap apartment below Sunset in West Hollywood.

By the time she and Jim met, Pam already had a track record on the Strip, although many of the stories still told about her are impossible to verify. She is said to have worked as a go-go dancer in the clubs, and to have been a semi-pro party girl at the type of parties that turned into orgies. Slender and waiflike, weighing under a hundred pounds, she had an electric, star-quality presence that could kill all conversation when she walked into a room. Pamela was coveted as an old lady by many of the musicians on the scene, and it has long been rumored (and denied) that Neil Young wrote his epochal rock song "Cinnamon Girl" about her.

When she met Jim, she already had a couple of boyfriends, who remained on the scene even after she started living with Jim. Two of them became fatefully involved in his life (and death) as well. Tom Baker was a slim, dark-haired, blue-eyed young actor who later swore that he had introduced the star-crossed couple to each other. He and Jim became close friends and drinking buddies despite (or perhaps because of) their mutual lust for Pam. Then there was Jean de Breteuil, a twenty-year-old French aristocrat nominally studying at UCLA. He was really just a playboy and classy dope dealer: His hashish and opium supposedly came from a Moroccan chauffeur attached to the French consulate in L.A. The de Breteuil family owned all the French language newspapers in North Africa. When his father had died a few years earlier, Jean inherited his title of Comte de Breteuil, so he was an actual French count whose lineage went back seven hundred years. (Pamela adored having a boy-friend she often described, snootily, as "real French royalty.") Unlike Tom Baker, Count de Breteuil remained very close to Pam, even after she and Jim got together, especially when the count started supplying her with much harder drugs than hash.

Once Jim and Pamela started going together, she often came to the London Fog. One night there were only three people in the joint, this young redheaded girl and two drunks. The Doors came out and played their last set as if the Rolling Stones were in the house. Jim roared like a lion with a hard-on, and crooned like Bing Crosby from hell. The band was transcendentally hot. It was probably one of the great Doors shows, played with relentless existential urgency, and no one but Pam was listening.

Like most nights, Jim insisted they walk home afterward. Pam asked Jim why he'd bothered to put out so much soul-force when no one was there. Pam later told a friend (Paul Rothchild) that Jim looked at her and drawled, "Baby, you never know when you're doing your last set."

In May 1966, Jim and a friend of his were drinking at the Phone Booth, a bar on Santa Monica Boulevard. Jim was making notes in a spiral notebook and the friend asked what he was writing. "I got this little girl now," Jim said. "She's wonderful."

There was a silence while Jim took a pull at his second scotch on the rocks.

"She's *trouble*," he whispered.

WARHOL IN HOLLYWOOD

JIM HAD OTHER GIRLFRIENDS, too, so he and Pamela danced around each other for a while. He went home with Rhonda the go-go girl some nights. He was sleeping with one of the dancers on *Shindig*. He was rear-ending a girl named Connie, one of Vito's dancers. A Strip-scene girl named Gay Blair took him home, told him he was the worst lay she'd ever had, and he threw a lamp at her. Then Jim pinned her onto her bed, ripped her clothes off, and spit all over her face until she cried. Afterward, he dragged her into the shower and then took her out to Barney's Beanery for a late snack. He had an affair, and then a long friendship, with Pamela Zarubica, the groupie immortalized by Frank Zappa as Suzy Creamcheese. She was working at the Whisky while studying English Lit at Pepperdine University in Malibu. She later told Jerry Hopkins: "It was wonderful. *Period.* He didn't know much about what was going on, and neither did I. And he was so fucking puritanical. And he copped to it too. He admitted it!"

Eve Babitz was another of the brazen hussies Jim attracted:

"I met Jim in early 1966, when he'd just lost the weight and wore a suit made of grey suede, lashed together at the seams with lanyards, and no shirt. He was so cute that no woman was safe. He was just twenty-two. He had the freshness and humility of someone who had been fat all his life and was now suddenly a morning glory.

"I met Jim and propositioned him in three minutes, even before he opened his mouth to sing at the London Fog. 'Take me home,' I demurely offered when we were introduced. 'You're not really going to stay here playing, are you?'

" 'Uh,' he replied, 'we don't play. We *work.*' "

The next night Eve came back to the Fog in a miniskirt so short her undies showed. On her first date with Jim, she told him her father was playing the violin that night in a symphony orchestra in Pasadena. Jim insisted she drive him there, and pouted when she wanted to leave at the intermission.

"Being in bed with Jim was like being in bed with Michelangelo's [statue of] David, only with blue eyes. His skin was so white, his muscles were so pure, he was so innocent."

I N EARLY MAY 1966, the Doors were told that the Fog was bleeding money and would probably close. Jim started flirting with Ronnie Haran, a chic and sexy twenty-something blonde who helped book bands and did promotion at the Whisky. He'd been after her to come see the Doors, but no one could really be bothered to deal with the Fog and the loser-outcast bands that played there. But she promised she would stop by.

The Doors also played at Night Flight, a sporadic after-hours cabaret at the tiny Warner Playhouse in Hollywood. The band alternated with exotic dancer Claudette from two to four a.m., two or three nights a week. Claudette took Jim home, too, which was a room at the famous Tropicana Motel, beloved of Hollywood hopefuls, starstruck tourists, and the local demimonde. (There was no water in the swimming pool.) Jim started living there, too, when he had the money.

JESSE JAMES GAVE THE DOORS two weeks' notice on Friday, May 6, but fired them the next night when Jim provoked a brawl between two drunks and Joey the bouncer, which brought the cops around and caused some minor damage. But Ronnie Haran had come to the early show and loved the band. "I knew Jim Morrison had major star quality the minute he started singing," she later recalled. "The poetry of the words; I'd never heard lyrics like that. . . . They [the Doors] needed more polish, but the sound was already there."

She went back to her bosses at the Whisky and told them they had to hire the Doors. She got her girlfriends to call up Elmer Valentine and ask for the Doors. So on Monday, May 9, the Doors played an audition set—"Break On Through," "Light My Fire," "Crystal Ship"—and Valentine immediately hired them as the fabled club's house band at almost five hundred dollars a week. (Densmore, in his memoir, claimed they were hired sight unseen.)

Jim told Ronnie that they wanted a few days to think about it. Then the Doors disappeared for a couple of weeks.

"The Whisky was for Hollywood swingers," Ray later said. "When we were at UCLA, it was the antithesis of everything artistic that we could imagine. Everyone derided it. It was slick, and Hollywood and Sunset Strip—a rock and roll version of the Rat Pack. . . . And then we wind up being the house band there. How ironic."

The Doors kept playing Night Flight—long, long passages of "Latin Bullshit #1," and Jim didn't always show up—and also at a couple of nights at Brave New World in Hollywood. Ronnie Haran couldn't find them to tell them to show up for work. She didn't have a contact number and the London Fog had closed down. She heard that Jim was sleeping under a beach pier in Venice. None of them had a phone and there was no manager. Finally Jim called her and said the Doors wanted to do it—and by the way did she want to cook him dinner?

So Jim moved in with Ronnie for a month, and she started managing the Doors. The Whisky was a union shop, so she got the Doors into the musicians' union. She bought Jim new clothes—shirts and trousers—at an army-navy surplus store. "He didn't have a pot to piss in," she recalled. She booked the gigs and got the Doors their first publicity. Ronnie Haran was their Big Break.

While he was staying with her, Jim smoked up all her grass. He rolled thick, thumb-sized stubbies, and fired them up, one after another, until the entire stash was consumed. Other guys she knew didn't act like this.

MAY 1966. Andy Warhol and his troupe arrived in L.A. and blew Jim Morrison's mind. He ended up blowing theirs as well.

Andy Warhol was the most famous artist in America. Arriving in New York from Pittsburgh ten years earlier, he had first made his name as a successful commercial artist. In the 1950s the New York art scene was dominated by the Abstract Expressionist painters—a bunch of macho, brawling drunks like Jackson Pollock and Willem de Kooning. But in 1960 the so-called Pop artists began turning away from introspective abstraction, and appropriated the blatant imagery of print advertising and comic strips. Pop artists like Jasper Johns and Roy Lichtenstein produced quotidian images anyone could recognize—flags, cartoon panels, Coke bottles—an exaltation of the commercial art that the Beat-influenced abstract artists hated.

Andy Warhol's first show of his soup can paintings in Los Angeles in 1962 was an instant sensation. Warhol copied national icons—Jackie Kennedy, Marilyn Monroe, Brillo boxes, Green Stamps—and made them seem radical, hyperreal, and beautiful. "Once you 'got' Pop," Warhol wrote, "you could never see a sign the same way again. Once you 'thought' Pop, you could never see America the same way again."

Pop artists like Warhol were different. Their undeclared manifesto was that the post–Abstract Expressionist sensibility would be homosexual or sexually ambivalent, not hypermasculine. Beginning in 1965, Pop Art's gay (or "camp") bias began to seep into pop culture, influencing the Rolling Stones' fabulous run of mid-sixties hit singles from "Satisfaction" through "Have You Seen Your Mother, Baby, Standing in the Shadow" and echoing down through the Velvet Underground, David Bowie, and the disco movement of the 1970s.

Having conquered the art world, Warhol began making movies in 1963. Epic productions like *Sleep* and *Empire* did things with cinematic time and audience attention span that no one had ever done before, and soon were de rigueur viewing at film schools like UCLA. Then, taking cheap porno movies as his model, Warhol and his associate Paul Morrissey began using a 16-mm Bolex camera to document the faux-glamorous lost moths drawn to Warhol's bright flame as they destroyed themselves acting out their sexual fantasies at the Factory, his studio on East Forty-seventh Street. Warhol "superstars" like Edie Sedgwick, Viva, and Ultra Violet became heroines of the burgeoning sixties "underground" culture. Warhol's technique in movies like *Chelsea Girls*—long raps lasting a whole reel, without cuts—established a new grammar of film, in much the same way Bob Dylan's flashing imagery was changing pop music.

Warhol wanted to tap into the new energy of pop music somehow. He was frustrated by his edgy contacts with Dylan and the Stones, who had kept him at arm's length. In early 1966, someone suggested to Warhol that he put together some kind of club act. All Andy had to do was show up every night for a few minutes, creating an instant scene, and everyone would make money. Warhol said yeah, right, but there had to be a rock band involved.

Then a friend of Warhol's found the Velvet Underground, a local band playing in the Village, fronted by two young musicians named Lou Reed and John Cale. Warhol's people rented a hall called the Dom, on St. Marks Place in the East Village, and they began putting on a "mixed media" show: a throbbing rock band accompanied by strobe lights and projections from Warhol's underground films—*Eat*, *Vinyl*, and the so-called "screen tests" of Factory regulars and visitors. It packed the Dom every night. After a few of these, Warhol and Morrissey decided that Lou Reed couldn't carry the show by himself, so for a dash of dark glamour they brought in a German actress who had been introduced to the Factory by Brian Jones.

Nico.

Her name was Christa Paffgen, and she was twenty-seven years old. She was big—about five ten—and blond, with a young son and a deep, smoky voice. Warhol wrote that she sang like an IBM computer with a

German accent. Born in Budapest, she was already an international star-let, having appeared in Federico Fellini's *La Dolce Vita.* Singing motion-less onstage, she had a remote and icy presence that seemed to complement the Velvet Underground's primitive, monotonous drone. Reed and Cale hated her and resented having her in the band, but they followed Morrissey's orders and began to write for her, producing beau-tiful songs that limned the vivid, conflicted, emotional currents of 1966: "I'll Be Your Mirror," "All Tomorrow's Parties," and "Femme Fatale."

When the Velvets played at the legendary Factory parties, they were joined by Gerard Malanga, Warhol's young art assistant and protégé. As the music pulsated in the dark, crowded, smoky loft, Malanga got up and danced with the band, assuming the role of "lead singer" by moving to the music with various props, such as long-handled flashlights and knives. Then sexy Factory chick Mary Woronov, a lithe brunette who knew how to move, started to dance with him, which evolved into a sadomasochistic routine where Malanga pretended to beat Mary with a bullwhip. Malanga began performing in a two-piece black leather suit, writhing and cracking his whip as the Velvets conjured a sweaty Dionysian ritual in midtown Manhattan. Soon Andy's art clients—New York society figures and jet-setters from Europe—flocked to the Factory for this druggy rite of underground music and sex, over which Warhol presided like a platinum-wigged vizier.

This was the package show that Andy Warhol marketed as "The Ex-ploding Plastic Inevitable" in March 1966. It was an electric, avant-garde carnival of trendy mixed media: rock band, S & M dancers, psychedelic light show, underground movies, slides, fashion-forward style, illicit drugs, and superstars. Nothing in contemporary American culture radi-ated more heat than this. Hollywood was in an excited buzz about it that spring because Elmer Valentine had booked Warhol's show into his newest and hippest club, the Trip.

The Exploding Plastic Inevitable's debut in Los Angeles was part of a full-scale assault on Californian culture, timed to coincide with Warhol's second one-man show (of helium-filled Mylar balloons titled "Silver Clouds") at the Ferus Gallery. The EPI was booked through May 18, with Warhol movies playing daily at the Trip, beginning at four o'clock in the afternoon.

The Trip was tiny and chic. "Flip out. Skip out. Trip out." It had been the Crescendo, a jazz club, and still had a taste of that ambience. Jim Morrison was there on the EPI's jammed opening night, along with the entire Hollywood hipoisie: Warren Beatty, Julie Christie, Natalie Wood, Dennis Hopper, Peter Fonda, Jane Fonda and Roger Vadim, Jack Nicholson, John and Michelle Phillips. As the Velvets throbbed and Nico droned her dirgelike songs while the strobes and the projections flickered, Gerard Malanga got up in his full S-M leather suit and performed his whip dance, to the max. Jim Morrison, probably tripping his brains out, dug the whole scene and immediately realized that he could do for a leather suit what the talent-challenged Malanga couldn't.

But Andy Warhol's stage show didn't go over in Los Angeles like it did in New York. The Strip didn't really appreciate the Factory's jittery Manhattan aesthetics, having already experienced Ken Kesey's organic, bacchanalian Acid Tests—compared to which Warhol's show seemed contrived and emotionally dead. The *Los Angeles Times* quoted Cher on the Warhol experience: "It will replace nothing, except maybe suicide." Frank Zappa, whose band, the Mothers of Invention, was opening for the EPI, was openly contemptuous of the New Yorkers' uptight, fake psychedelia, which owed more to speed and barbiturates than LSD-25. Zappa wanted to quit after the crowded opening night. Valentine wanted to substitute the Doors, but at the time Ronnie Haran couldn't find them.

Then, after only two or three nights, the vice squad cops shut down the Trip, alleging noise violations and dope dealers openly operating in the club. The EPI's gig was canceled, but the damage was done. Jim Morrison had already picked up on the fetishistic possibilities of Gerard Malanga's leathers and starkly theatrical presentation. Then he stole Nico too.

Warhol and his fourteen-member troupe were staying at the Tropicana. When the gig was canceled, Andy rented the Castle, a sprawling hillside concrete bunker on Glendower Avenue in suburban Los Feliz. The big house was subleased by film actor John Philip Law, who made it available to visiting bands. (A previous tenant had been Bob Dylan.) With their next gig in San Francisco starting on May 27, there was plenty of free time for the nervous New Yorkers. Nico and Edie Sedgwick (whose place as Warhol's muse Nico was usurping) were both in residence at the Castle, competing for attention and drugs.

Jim Morrison was a frequent visitor, lurking around for whatever action the troupe might provide. Jim was introduced to Warhol, who suggested he appear in one of their screen tests, but this never took place. Jim told friends who asked, "What's Andy like?" that Warhol never finished his sentences. Warhol acolyte Dotson Rader later claimed that Edie gave Jim a blow job, but others swear this didn't happen. Others on the scene have vivid memories of Jim and Nico balancing naked by moonlight on the castle's highest parapets, in the throes of lysergic ecstasy. By the time the Warholites left town, Jim was trying to find a pair of vinyl trousers for himself, and Nico had fallen madly in love with him.

SHOW ME THE WAY

THE DOORS BEGAN their epochal gig at the Whisky a Go Go, at 8901 Sunset Boulevard, on Monday, May 23, 1966. Coheadlining were Captain Beefheart and the Magic Band (with a young Ry Cooder on guitar) and the hot new group, Buffalo Springfield.

For the next three and a half months, the Doors got an education in Classic Rockology by opening for some of the best groups in pop music. In the process they would turn into a fire-breathing rock band, land a recording contract with one of the better labels in the industry, and begin to build a notorious reputation as a noirish, artistically valid band fronted by a potential superstar and godhead-in-waiting.

It was slow going at first, and the Whisky's reputation as a squares-only mob operation didn't help. In Hollywood the Trip, the Ash Grove, and the Troubadour were considered hip clubs, while the Whisky had an uncool vibe, out-of-town owners, Mafia-grade bouncers, and a swinger clientele in jackets, ties, and beehive hairdos. Besides, in 1966 the whole go-go/discotheque thing was *so* 1964.

When the Doors first appeared at the Whisky, some people mistook Ray Manzarek for John Sebastian, whose cheerful pop tunes with the Lovin' Spoonful ("Do You Believe in Magic?") were holding their own on the radio with new Beatles songs like "Penny Lane." Jim Morrison was visibly nervous in his first few shows. Some of the Whisky's swingers thought Jim's piercing screams and his Beat poetry shtick were hokey and pretentious, and that he embarrassed himself and the club.

But Captain Beefheart—the painter Don van Vliet—liked the Doors, and so did his patron Frank Zappa. If any L.A. band had a claim to artistic integrity, it was the Mothers of Invention, composed of actual musicians and led by Zappa, who lived in Laurel Canyon with his wife and extended hippie family. The Mothers' first album, *No Commercial Potential,* was released that summer as a savagely antipop satire. Though intrinsically cynical, Zappa connected with what Jim Morrison was trying to do. Zappa actively talked up the Doors and even discussed signing them to the record label he was planning.

The other band on the bill was Buffalo Springfield, only a few months old and still unknown beyond the Strip. But this band's meteoric career quickly eclipsed the Doors'. Neil Young and Stephen Stills were recognized as superstars early on, and the band was signed to Atlantic Records. (Jim Morrison particularly loved "Mr. Soul," buckskin-clad Neil Young's long-form, trance-rocking guitar groove.) By July, less than ten months old, Buffalo Springfield would open for the *Aftermath*-era Rolling Stones at the Hollywood Bowl. A few months later, they became the official voice of the Strip when Stills's "For What It's Worth" hit the charts and the radio, alerting a national audience to the brutal police suppression of the Sunset Strip riots that would cause much bitterness that fall.

On the last weekend in May, the Doors opened for Love, about to release the superb single "Little Red Book" on Elektra Records. It was the first time Arthur Lee had seen Jim Morrison, and he was impressed. Lee invited Jim up to his house in the Hollywood Hills, which Jim began using as one of his hideaways. The next time he spoke to Elektra's president, Arthur Lee told Jac Holzman about this new band, the Doors, that was going to be the biggest thing on the Strip one day.

B UT THE DOORS SETTLED IN QUICKLY, with Jim performing in a t-shirt and white Lee Rider jeans, singing with his back to the audience for twenty minutes at a stretch and banging a woodblock with a drumstick in the instrumental passages. The Doors played two basic hour-long sets per night. Starting around nine o'clock, when hardly anyone was in the club, they opened with "Break On Through," Jim closing his eyes as he emphasized the *cunt* in "*I found an island in your heart, country in your eyes.*" Then, varying the set lists on different nights, they progressed through "Take It as It Comes," "Moonlight Drive," "Twentieth Century Fox" (beloved of Vito Paulekas' writhing harem of long-haired, barely dressed dancing girls), "I Looked at You," "Close to You" (with Ray singing), "Money," "Little Red Rooster" (a showcase for Robby's slide guitar), "Unhappy Girl," and "When the Music's Over."

While the headliners performed and the house was cleared for the next show, the Doors had something to eat and got stoned. Jim would sit with Pamela; if she wasn't around, he flirted and made dates with other girls after the show. Pam once walked in while Jim had his hand up Suzy Creamcheese's miniskirt, and her friends had to drag Suzy away before a wild-eyed Pamela could stab her with a pair of scissors.

Jim often performed the Doors' second set with his eyes shut tight, as if he were in a shamanic trance. "The Alabama Song" often came first, with Jim singing in a decadent Lotte Lenya accent—*"Ah-la-bah-mah."* Then "My Eyes Have Seen You," "Summer's Almost Gone," and a long, jazz-inflected "Light My Fire." Vito's dancers hated "Crystal Ship," which was so slow they couldn't move to it. Then the Doors tore into "Gloria," with Jim's gutter-mouthed improvisations about getting a schoolgirl to go down on him. *"Hey, little girl, howdja like to suck my mama?"*

Jim's dirty mouth irritated Elmer Valentine and Phil Tanzini, the Whisky's manager, and instigated a constantly fluctuating current of stress between the band and the club. Sometimes, in the middle of a song, Jim would look over at Valentine and yell, "FUCK YOU, ELMER!" Or he'd started cursing a blue streak just to annoy Tanzini, who threatened to fire the band if Morrison kept it up. But Jim found he could get away with being outrageous because Valentine saw the Doors bringing in customers. (Jim also used Valentine's house above Sunset as a place to hide when he didn't want Pamela or the band to find him.)

"Gloria" ended in a big jam, so the band slowed down for "The End of the Night." The finale, "Soul Kitchen," indicating that the clock said it was time to go, now, ended the set on a rousing note. The encore was always "The End," then still a good-bye love song with a flamenco guitar interlude, over which Jim extemporized stream-of-consciousness imagery or recited verse he had memorized. The uptempo "ride the snake" section, with Jim chanting *"Fuck fuck fuck"* into the microphone, gave the dancers such an extended workout that some of the Whisky's headlining bands were reluctant to follow the Doors as the summer of 1966 progressed.

Soon word began to filter out that the Doors, this new band at the Whisky, had to be seen to be believed. A new generation of kids—high schoolers from Beverly Hills, the Valley, Orange County—began jamming the intersection of Sunset and Clark on weekend evenings, spilling into the street, blocking traffic, trying to get in to see the Doors. Some nights Jim would seem very shy, even fearful, onstage—especially if he was tripping. But after two weeks at the Whisky, he started to turn around and connect with the audience.

"It took me a while," Jim told *Rolling Stone* in 1971, "to realize that this thing—performing rock and roll songs—was really about a theater trip. That's when I understood what was going on."

O N JUNE 2, Van Morrison arrived at the Whisky with his band, Them, for a two week engagement. Them was a tough R & B band from Belfast who'd had hit records in Britain and America with "Gloria" and "Here Comes the Night." The Doors watched stinko-drunk Van Morrison doing berserk white Irish soul routines as Them slammed through long versions of "Baby Please Don't Go" and "Boom Boom" and "Mystic Eyes." The Whisky hadn't seen a rock and roll passion this crazed before. Van worked the microphone stand like a madman, swinging it aloft and singing into it upside down before smashing it on the stage in a frenzy of Virgo anger and R & B conviction.

The two Morrisons, Van and Jim, hit it off, got drunk together a couple of times, wondered if they were related. Each band liked the other, so on Them's last night, June 18, after the last set, the Doors set up their gear alongside Them and both bands jammed Wilson Pickett's "In the Midnight Hour." After half an hour, they waded into "Gloria," with Van and Jim trading verses and singing the G-L-O-R-I-A chorus together. Union rules prohibited the club from recording the show, so the historic jam was lost, but photographs show Jim (in black) and Van (in a shaggy hairdo) singing rapturously as the two drummers burned away behind them.

This proved to be Them's only American tour, with the Doors also opening for the group on two subsequent L.A. area dates. After Them returned to England, Van Morrison left the band and moved to Boston, then on to Woodstock, and eventually to California. For years, he told interviewers that one of the highlights of his brilliant career was the night Them jammed with the Doors at the Whisky.

HALFWAY THROUGH JULY, word about Jim Morrison's carnal séances at the Whisky began to spread via Sunset Strip's jungle telegraph. *The Daily Bruin,* UCLA's student paper, published a positive review, describing Jim as "a gaunt, hollow Ariel from hell...screaming terraced flights of poetry and music." Then the all-powerful *Los Angeles Times* weighed in when the Doors opened for the Turtles at the Whisky on Saturday, July 16. The Turtles had hit the national charts with a folk-rock version of Bob Dylan's "It Ain't Me Babe." Critic Pete Johnson devoted his last paragraph to the opening act:

> Sharing the bill are the Doors, a hungry-looking quartet with an interesting original sound, but with what is probably the worst stage appearance of any rock and roll group in captivity. The lead singer emotes with his eyes closed, the electric pianist hunches over his instrument as if reading mysteries from the keyboard, the guitarist drifts around the stage randomly, and the drummer seems lost in a separate world.

Jim took this review to heart. He began closing his eyes in the dressing room, enclosing himself in a private reverie from which he would emerge to emote onstage. For a while, the other guys in the band took turns leading Jim downstairs to perform, as if he were blind.

THE NEXT BIG THING

JULY 1966. The Doors getting better every night at the Whisky. At the same time, their sets tended to drag when the band took long pauses between songs while they argued about what to play next. They opened for the Seeds, Gene Clark (who had quit the Byrds because he was afraid to fly), the Chambers Brothers, Love (rampaging, at the height of their considerable powers), the Locos (Mexico's top band), and Johnny Rivers that month.

Now the Doors had their own following, something rare for an unsigned band. Young kids would leave the club after their set, before the headliners came on. Jim had some frisky new stage business with his mike stand, which he'd rub against his crotch until he got visibly hard in his tight velvet pants, worn without briefs, working himself into a pagan ritual he described, tongue half-in-cheek, as his way of "invoking the muse." "Back Door Man," with its obvious connotations of anal intercourse, was torridly sexual, delivered by Jim with a stoned leer that could barely contain his rapturous smile as he contemplated the barely dressed young girls dancing at the edge of the stage. The most brazen of these bosomy, miniskirted, heavily mascaraed eighteen-year-old chicks could reach up and rub Jim's impressive bulge—if his redheaded girlfriend wasn't around. (Jim dressed to the left.) It made him half smile, eyes closed, when the girls touched him in public like that.

But those who knew Jim understood that he was no animal. Much of the time he was polite, extremely funny in a dry, southern style, and an intellectual who read as much as he could. Jim Morrison at this stage of his life was an amalgam of differing personae, often shifting, dependent on the stimuli provided by the people he hung around with. He was, like so many young rock stars, a great bunch of guys.

Later that month, the Doors played some of their first shows outside of L.A., opening for Them (and the Count Five) in Oxnard and Santa Barbara. They also played a club called the Fifth Estate in Phoenix. It was around this time, according to Ray Manzarek, that Jim told him, with deep conviction, that they had to get rid of John Densmore.

According to Ray, Jim didn't dig John Densmore at all. Jim thought John was a downer. Jim considered John uptight and abrasive. John complained a lot, and hated the band's total dependence on Jim's chaotic charisma. He challenged Jim on his bullshit, and it got under Jim's skin.

Ray, in his memoir, quotes Jim Morrison to this effect. "We've *got* to get rid of the drummer.... I can't stand him as a human being.... We've got to fire him." Ray claimed that he talked Jim into keeping Densmore as an indispensable component of the Doors' run for the rainbow. "All right, all right," Jim supposedly said. "But I'm not gonna like it."

A UGUST 1966. The Rolling Stones were in Los Angeles. "Paint It Black" was blasting enigmatically on the radio. The new Stones album, *Aftermath,* was a dark, sensational masterpiece, dripping with zeitgeist and flaunting an unprecedented misogyny in songs like "Stupid Girl" and "Under My Thumb." Their long blues jam, "Going Home," cracked open the standard album format with its jamming, twelve-minute span. By night, Brian Jones and his stunning girlfriend, Anita Pallenberg, moved through Sunset Strip clubs like deities, their hair dyed the same shade of canary blond. Along with Bill Wyman, they visited the Whisky and caught the Doors' set. Anita Pallenberg later recalled: "Brian really liked the Doors. He sat there and paid attention to them. But then we left, and we didn't meet Jim."

Sometimes, late at night, flying on star-quality "Purple Haze" LSD, Brian Jones would cruise the clubs by himself, blowing his harmonica with whatever band would let him sit in. Carousing with girls he picked up, Brian cut a glamorous, out-of-control swath across Hollywood. One night, Jim Morrison and some friends were drinking at the Phone Booth, a strip joint in West Hollywood, when Brian Jones and two girls came in at three in the morning. When a drunk started hassling him about his hair, Brian suddenly smashed his wineglass on the bar and slashed the drunk's cheek to the bone. Blood began spurting everywhere as Brian was hustled out of the Phone Booth, then out of town, before the cops could ask questions.

Jim Morrison was impressed.

S UMMER 1966, and the Doors had arrived. Jim Morrison was *the* new sex symbol on the Sunset Strip. (He was having a torrid affair with Joan Blakely, a twenty-year-old waitress who let him do her from behind, and bragged about it to her friends.) The Doors, it was said, had it all: decent chops, artistic integrity, good songs, and a ballsy singer. Everyone on the scene said they were the Next Big Thing. Frank Zappa continued to talk up the Doors, and wanted to produce them. Elite producer Terry Melcher, who had worked with the Beach Boys, the Byrds, and Paul Revere and the Raiders, and who now had a label deal with the Turtles' management, wanted to produce the Doors. Jack Goode, Sonny and Cher's manager, was interested.

On the other hand, no one was making any actual, serious, concrete offers to the band. The Doors were a buzz without a deal. Other bands had started big, peaked in the clubs, and died without a trace. It was a touch-and-go thing at best. So the Doors kept working at the Whisky, waiting until a decent offer came along.

On August 3, 1966, the comedian Lenny Bruce overdosed on heroin in his Sunset Plaza Drive apartment. Bruce had been the cutting edge of American comedy in the posthipster, prehippie early sixties. He was an acerbic, shpritzing social critic who had been persecuted for the alleged profanity in his act. Bruce had been convicted of public obscenity in New York two years previously. Since then, Bruce had obsessively recounted his legal problems in his act and in print, becoming a gadfly critic of outmoded bourgeois morality. The cops hated him, and gleefully gave their grisly photographs of the death scene—Bruce had collapsed on the toilet, with his arm tied off—to the press.

Lenny Bruce's death bothered Jim. It bothered everyone. On Sunday, August 7, David Crosby, the Byrds' protean rhythm guitarist and co-creator of their brilliant new album *Younger Than Yesterday,* dropped acid with some friends and wound up at the Whisky to see the Chambers Brothers. The Doors opened the show, as usual. But an agitated Jim Morrison, also blasted on LSD, stopped the Doors' act in the middle of "Back Door Man," jumped down into the audience, and lurched over to Crosby's table. Jim pointed to Crosby, who was wearing dark granny glasses, and began shouting that the time was over when people could hide behind their shades. "WAKE UP!" Jim screamed in Crosby's face, before regaining the stage and continuing the Doors' set. It was an astonishingly gauche act of disrespect for local rock royalty, and it shook David Crosby up so much he remembered it in his memoirs thirty years later.

The following week, Jim Morrison attended a memorial wake for Lenny Bruce at his grave, way out in the western San Fernando Valley. A hundred people listened as Phil Spector riffed on how great Lenny was. Dennis Hopper stood up and said that Lenny wouldn't have wanted everyone to be in tears... "so let's have fun!" Some of Frank Zappa's seminaked girl entourage started dancing. Other mourners fired up joints and sat on the grass.

Within a few years, Jim Morrison would also be fighting politically influenced obscenity charges. And, like Lenny Bruce, he would lose his legal case, and face the bitter end of his hard-won career.

ELEKTRA COMPLEX

WHEN JIM MORRISON began giving press interviews a few months later, he was already nostalgic for the Doors' regular gig at the Whisky, and especially for the creative charge that it gave the band. "Our most interesting songs develop over a period of time, playing night after night in clubs," Jim said in early 1967. "We'll start out with a basic song, and then the music settles into a...hypnotic river of sound. That leaves me free—to do anything that comes into my head—at the time. It's the part of the performance I enjoy the most. I pick up vibrations from the music—and what's coming from the audience—and then I follow it wherever it goes. Music puts me into that...state of mind... with its hypnotic qualities. Then I'm free—to let my subconscious play it out, wherever it goes. The music gives me a kind of security, and makes it a lot easier to express myself."

BY AUGUST 1966, Jim Morrison and the Doors were in the third month of their residency at the Whisky, taking advantage of a superb opportunity to rehearse and workshop their own material in a club that tolerated Jim Morrison's excesses as long as the cash registers kept ringing. The Sunset Strip kids had picked up on Jim's dangerous vibe, his dead-eyed stare into the spotlight, his psychological approach to his lyrics, his boner-charged stage act, and his dirty mouth. Elmer Valentine later said: "[Jim] was kind of ahead of his time on certain things, like swearing."

When Jim was late, drunk, or unruly, he could still charm the Whisky's bosses with his decadent charm. When comanager Mario Magliori screamed at Jim for missing a set, Jim would grab Mario's head and kiss him on the lips. "I *tried* to get rid of them, more than once," Elmer Valentine said. "But then, I'd get all these phone calls from customers—people I liked. 'When's that horny motherfucker coming back?' The phones were incredible, for just a second group. What could I do? The Doors pulled people into the club, every night."

O N AUGUST 10, 1966, the Doors, opening for Love at the Whisky, played their usual first set. During the intermission, around eleven o'clock, a tall, conservatively dressed New Yorker walked into the club. This was Jac Holzman, the president of Elektra Records, just off an American Airlines 707 from New York. Holzman had dropped in at the Whisky to see Love, his label's only foothold on Sunset Strip. Afterward, Holzman went backstage to say hello to Arthur Lee, who took Holzman's arm as he was leaving and rasped: "Stick around for the *Doors,* man."

The Doors, having been alerted by Arthur Lee that Holzman was in the audience, played a boring, self-destructive show. Jim seemed to actually hide behind the other musicians during their set. They were so dull that Holzman thought Ray Manzarek's baroque-influenced keyboard stylings were what the Doors were about. "Morrison," Holzman said later, "made no impression whatsoever." The Elektra chief thought the lead singer seemed tentative and reclusive, and he left before they finished. But Ronnie Haran chased him onto the sidewalk and pointed out the long line of young kids waiting to get into the next show. Ronnie made Holzman promise to come back the next night.

Intrigued by a band that didn't seem to care, Holzman returned to the Whisky, but he still didn't get the Doors. Arthur Lee told Holzman that he was missing something. "You got to look at this group with a different pair of eyes in your head," Lee told him.

Jac Holzman, in a 1991 memoir, said he kept coming back to the Whisky for five straight nights. On August 13, the Doors played "The Alabama Song" and Jac Holzman finally got it. These L.A. guys were doing Brecht! They were entertaining teenage girls with a forty-year-old song from the Weimar Republic. It was totally hip—rock and roll and cabaret. Later Holzman would describe the "austerity, cleanliness, and simplicity" of what he heard in the Doors that night: "Morrison really moved out front, and on 'The Alabama Song' and 'The End,' it all came together."

During "The End," as he'd been doing for a couple of weeks, Jim began chanting *"Fuck-fuck-fuck"* during the instrumental vamp, spitting the guttural curses into the mike so it functioned like another component of the rhythm section. The kids loved it, as the tension built—*fuck fuck fuck*—and Vito's dancers swayed and shimmied like pagans.

The next day Jac Holzman called New Jersey and told his star producer to get on a plane to Los Angeles. Jac Holzman wanted to sign the Doors, and he needed Paul Rothchild to tell him whether or not he was crazy.

JAC HOLZMAN WAS a Park Avenue doctor's son, whose obsession with early high-fidelity recording gear led him to start an independent record company, with only a tape recorder and a motor scooter, in 1950. Interested in classical music and ethnographic recordings, Holzman named his company Elektra Records, after the Greek demigoddess who had killed her mother in revenge for murdering her father, Agamemnon. In 1955, Holzman's recording of Israeli folk songs by actor Theodore Bikel was a hit album for Elektra. This allowed Holzman to jump on the folk music revival, and he began challenging established labels Vanguard and Folkways with older, tie-wearing folk singers like Bikel and Oscar Brand Jr., who could get on television. Then Judy Collins, from Colorado, was signed to Elektra. She sold a ton of records as a more commercial alternative to Vanguard's folk queen, Joan Baez. By 1963 Elektra Records had become a mainstream independent label.

Two of Holzman's signings gave Elektra considerable street cred. The legendary album *Blues Rags and Hollers* by Koerner, Ray & Glover— early Bob Dylan associates from Minnesota—was the coolest and hardest-rocking record of the whole folk revival. And, in 1965, Elektra released *The Paul Butterfield Blues Band,* a virtuosic album by the integrated Chicago group that was the only American band with the chops to challenge the Rolling Stones as champion R & B preservationists. Butterfield's new album, *East-West,* paired R & B with lucid raga inflections. It was extremely hip—the dharma moving west, and landing at Dixie's Midnight Lounge.

Then Jac Holzman signed Love, and Arthur Lee was given almost unlimited opportunities to pursue his singular, ambiguous, and often sinister sonic dreams. Later on, people in the record business would say that the Doors and Elektra were also a perfect match. They said that Jim Morrison's band could not have thrived on any other label that then existed.

Elektra staff producer Paul Rothchild arrived in Los Angeles on the afternoon of August 15 and checked into the Chateau Marmont Hotel. He had dinner with Jac Holzman that evening and later went with his boss to see this new band at the Whisky. After checking in with Arthur Lee—Rothchild had produced Love's first album—the two New York executives settled into a private booth to watch the Doors' first set.

It was awful. The Doors sucked. Jim kept his back to the audience, except when he spent painfully long intervals talking to the chicks in front of the stage. Jim seemed to be trying to get one of them to meet him in the alley behind the club after the band's set. Rothchild and Holzman looked at each other. "Let's stay for the next set," Paul said.

Years later, Paul Rothchild recalled: "Knowing that the record company *always* gets to hear the bad sets, and reminding myself that I had just flown across the continent to see them, I stayed—and heard one of the greatest sets I'd ever heard—*in my life,* from any band. . . . That night, it was like a microcosm of the Doors to come: the best, and the worst, it would get."

After the Doors' set, Rothchild and Holzman went backstage to talk to the band. Or, more accurately, to talk to Ray, since Jim was otherwise engaged (with a long-haired redhead), and the other two—Krieger and Densmore—mostly just listened.

Someone had told the band that the president of Elektra Records wanted to see them. This was a huge deal, because the Doors really wanted to be Love. Jac Holzman stepped into the tiny dressing room. He was six three, with horn-rimmed glasses. He was a little geeky, but well spoken, an Industry Heavy, obviously intelligent and somewhat classy— unlike the knuckle-dragging, pinky-ring-wearing morons from the L.A. music business. Holzman told the Doors, as sincerely as possible, how much he liked the band.

Jac Holzman was exactly the kind of male authority figure that Jim lived to torment. But if Holzman was a little officious, somewhat pompous, he'd also had the brains to bring along one of the champion shmoozers of the sixties with him.

Paul Rothchild was a veteran New York scene-maker. He was both a serious musician and a master of the Hang. Paul was thirty years old, a fiercely intelligent hipster from the streets of Brooklyn, and he knew how to talk the talk to musicians, how to prod and inspire them. Rothchild told Ray flat-out that he dug the band and wanted to produce them. He'd done Butterfield, and he'd done Love, and now he wanted to do the Doors.

Then Jac Holzman offered the Doors a recording contract. Jim Morrison was now outside the club with some girls, balancing on a concrete wall. But he came in to hear what Holzman was offering: five thousand dollars for three albums, guaranteed, against a five percent royalty, with Elektra keeping twenty-five percent of the publishing. (Holzman would later claim this was a generous offer to an unproven band in 1966.) Ray told Holzman and Rothchild that they needed some time to think about the offer and decide what to do.

Jac Holzman went back to New York with a tape of the Doors' acetate demo. He played the tape for his six-year-old son Adam (who, twenty years later, would be playing keyboards in Miles Davis's band). Right away Adam Holzman picked up on "Hello I Love You." Jac Holzman knew he had to have this band on his label.

The Doors didn't really need to think about it either. The Whisky thing was getting old after three months. No other record company had offered them anything real. Elektra was one of the great record labels in America. They already had enough good songs for the first two albums. Their fate was sealed.

THE DOORS HAD BEEN making $135 a week each at the Whisky, so Jim Morrison was semiliving in a comfortable nine-dollar-a-night room at the Tropicana Motel. Sometimes he stayed with Pamela, who told her friends that he read poetry to her aloud, until she fell asleep. Her friend Mirandi Babitz, sister of Eve, remembered that when Jim got his first paycheck from the Whisky, Pamela was so thrilled that she insisted they blow it all on a celebratory dinner. Now, after Holzman's offer was on the table, Jim told her that if this record deal went down she could find them a little place in Laurel Canyon, where the cool people lived. They could live together, like she wanted.

Meanwhile Ray was scurrying around, trying to get help. The Doors had a deal now but no management and no lawyer. He went for advice to Billy James, who told him to sign with Elektra. (Billy James would join Elektra's new L.A. office shortly afterward.) Ronnie Haran suggested her lawyer represent them, but this didn't work out, and Ronnie stopped working with the Doors. As Jim was moving his stuff out of her apartment, he told her, "I'm gonna be dead in two years."

Then Stu Krieger found Max Fink, a well-connected, cigar-chomping Beverly Hills attorney seemingly sent to the Doors by central casting. Max Fink began negotiating with Elektra on the Doors' behalf. On August 20, the Doors signed a preliminary contract with Elektra that would let them cut a record while the real contract was being negotiated. Max Fink then put Jac Holzman through several months of agony wondering whether the Doors would ever sign the final contract (which indeed didn't happen until November 1966).

Max Fink was a smart guy and a competent lawyer, and he did all right by Jim Morrison in the end. Jim ran to the savvy, no-nonsense Fink whenever he got in real trouble, and the lawyer took care of Jim's interests his own way, sometimes using strong-arm tactics when called for. Max Fink even got Jim Morrison to trust him enough to reveal some of his most intimate secrets.

THE KILLER AWOKE

JIM MORRISON LOOKED UP "Elektra" in the copy of Edith Hamilton's mythology book he was carrying around. In one of his notebooks he noted that Electra was the daughter of King Agamemnon, who was murdered by his wife when he returned victorious from Troy. Electra and her brother avenged him by killing her mother, Clytemnestra, and her lover. Jim asked a friend who taught psychology at UCLA about the so-called Electra complex, and learned that it described a daughter falling in love with her father. There was some discussion about the relationship of this with the Oedipus complex, named for Sophocles' classical Greek tragedy *Oedipus Rex,* in which the protagonist fulfills a hereditary curse by killing his father and marrying his mother. Jim told the friend, who later became a prominent psychoanalyst in San Francisco, that he wanted to look into this a little more.

THE PROSPECT OF A RECORDING CONTRACT for the Doors, and the fact that the group's dream of actually *making it* might come true after a year of starving and paying dues, seemed to completely unhinge Jim Morrison. "He was going crazy," Ronnie Haran said, "and taking acid every day. He was obsessed with death, never did anything in moderation." At a party in Westwood, Jim's UCLA classmate Richard Blackburn asked him about the recording deal that was the talk of the Strip. "And he, in a drug haze, looked over at me and for an instant the haze was gone, and with a real tiredness [he] said, 'It'll happen, man.' I waited for some elaboration, but he had already unplugged from the immediate."

Jim was also mumbling to himself as he walked from his motel to the Whisky in those hot summer evenings. "Fuck the mother," he kept chanting in a low voice: "Kill the father. Fuck the mother—kill the father. Fuck the mother kill the father. Fuckthemotherkillthefather."

It was his new and obscene Oedipal mantra, and Jim was really working it, babbling away and as usual overdoing it in his no-limits style until people close to him thought he was really losing it this time.

"I used to have this magic formula," Jim recalled later, "like, to break into the subconscious. I would lay there and say over and over, 'Fuck the mother, kill the father, fuck the mother, kill the father.' You can really get into your head just repeating that slogan over and over. That mantra can never become meaningless. It's too basic and can never become just words, 'cause as long as you're saying it, you can never be unconscious."

ON SUNDAY, August 21, at the end of a tumultuous week that had seen his band land its crucial, career-establishing record deal, Jim didn't show up for the Doors' gig at the Whisky opening for Love. The band played the first set without him, with Ray singing and the group stretching out "Latin Bullshit #2" and some fake Coltrane jams as much as they could. Afterward Phil Tanzini collared Ray in the backstage stairwell and told him their contract stipulated a quartet, and if Morrison didn't play that night the Doors wouldn't get paid.

So John and Ray drove down the street to the Tropicana. The room clerk said that Jim was in a different room because he'd set fire to his bed the night before. The Doors knocked on Jim's door. No answer. John started pounding and Ray called out, "Jim! Wake up, man. We got a gig. C'mon, man, you missed the first set. We know you're in there."

After an eternity, Jim opened the door. He was wearing his underpants and a pair of hand-tooled cowboy boots. He didn't smell good. He looked at them with the million-mile gaze of a tripping medicine man. Slowly, he opened his mouth.

"Ten . . . thousand . . . mikes."

The other guys looked at each other. Five hundred micrograms of LSD-25 was a higher-than-average dose. Jim—if he was telling the truth—was on another planet.

"Come on, Jim. We gotta get back to the club or we don't get paid."

"Hey, man—I can't go on, you know? Can you do it without me? I'll dig you later." He sat down on the bed, dazed, and opened the drawer of the night table, which revealed some purple vials of liquid LSD. "You want some?" he asked, and fell back on the bed.

They had to take his boots off to get his jeans on. It took another ten minutes to get the boots back on. Jim was doing the Dean Moriarty laugh and yelling about fucking his mother and killing his father. They finally loaded him into John's VW bus and drove back to the Whisky. "He was humming like a generator," Ray recalled. "You could feel the energy coming off him."

Jim seemed to revive a little in the dressing room. He drank a couple of beers, which got him to a familiar place, headwise. He asked a waitress for a blow job. She laughed at him and he laughed with her. He looked good enough to be able to perform the second set, but his blue eyes were still on fire from the lysergic volcanoes exploding right behind his face.

The Doors took the stage. Jim mumbled his way through with his back to the audience, which began to get bored and restless. Three songs into the show, Jim thought he saw Jac Holzman, his new "father," in the audience. He wanted to kill him. He wanted to kill his own father, the admiral, as well. Jim turned to Ray and called for "The End." This was weird. "The End" closed their set and they had another forty minutes to do, but Jim was determined.

* * *

T HE DOORS HAD BEEN FINISHING sets with "The End" since
the early days at the London Fog. The guys in the band generally
believed that Jim had originally written it about breaking up with Mary
Werbelow. "It started as a simple good-bye song," Jim told an interviewer. "Just the first verse and the chorus. As we did it each night we
discovered a peculiar feeling—a long, flowing, easy beat; that strange guitar tuning that sounds vaguely eastern or Indian. It was a form that
everyone brought something to."

Through nightly repetition at the Fog and the Whisky, "The End"
had elongated into a fifteen-minute set finale. After running through the
vivid imagery he had been developing for a year—the weird scenes inside the gold mine; the blue bus; riding the snake (Jim's allusion for the
saw-toothed back end of an acid trip); and all the insane children—Jim
would extemporize snatches of Beat poetry and perfectly memorized
verse by his fave bards. Densmore kept up an ambient drum rhythm
while Robby finger-picked his guitar in a raga style, bending his notes
and tracing Bengali/Andalusian arabesques of East-West fusion. Words
and music built to a molten climax, crash-landed in a vortex of feedback and random chords, and finished in a postcoital, whispered invocation of laughter and soft lies, and "the nights we tried to die." The
Doors would then walk off, to astonished applause. They never played
encores.

Paul Rothchild: "It was one of their newer numbers at that point, and
so 'The End' was always a changing piece. Jim used it as an open-ended
canvas for his poetic bits and pieces and fragments and little couplets
and things that he just wanted to say. It was a completely fluid song that
changed all the time. If he saw a chick he liked in the audience, he'd
start riffing on her, and she became part of 'The End' that night. It was a
changeling song until Jim came up with the new ending and we
recorded it. After that, it never changed again."

That night the Doors started playing "The End" and ran through the
familiar verses as Robby Krieger played his flamenco licks so Jim could
freestyle on top.

Jim just stood there, eyes closed. "Something just clicked," he said
later. "Just then, at that moment, I realized what the whole song was

about—what it had all been leading to." As the band kept up its steady sonic cushion, playing better than they had before, the Whisky became quiet. People stopped talking. The cash register was still. Waitresses stopped taking drink orders. There was a hypnotic anticipation of something in the smoky atmosphere. Finally, lit by a single spotlight in the dark room, the ceremony began.

"The killer awoke before dawn. He put his boots on."

The guitar ambled down a goat path in southern Spain.

"He took a face from the ancient gallery, and he—walked on down the hall."

Ray Manzarek looked at Densmore, then at Robby. They'd never heard this rap before.

Jim then sang about visiting the room where his sister lived. And then he paid a visit to his brother. And then he walked on down the hall.

The guitar now rumbled darkly, in a reverie of disturbance.

When Jim arrived at the door to his parents' room, he told his father that he wanted to kill him.

Ray: "At this point, I realized. I *saw* it. The whole room did. I thought, *My God! He's doing Oedipus Rex!* And then I thought, *My God! I know what's coming next.*"

Jim pulled the microphone up to his lips, raised his right boot onto the base of the mike stand to steady himself, paused, looked to his right, and sang out:

"Mother? I want to . . . *FUCK YOU MAMA FUCK YOU MAMA FUCK YOU MAMA ALL NIGHT LONG—FUCK YOU ALL NIGHT LONG—FUCK YOU ALL NIGHT LONG—WAAAUUUGGGHHH!!!"*

And Jim Morrison let out an ungodly shriek of primal sin that penetrated to the marrow of those present that night. The band erupted into a crazed, out-for-blood frenzy, and the audience, which had been mesmerized by this drama, began to shake in a furious free-form dance. Jim stood at the side of the little stage, chanting *"Kill—fuck—kill—fuck"* while the band did its thing, and then prepared to finish the number.

"This . . . is . . . the . . . end," Jim sang, and the Doors left the stage.

There was no applause, and a strange hush settled over the room.

Meanwhile, Phil Tanzini was furiously dialing Elmer Valentine's house in the hills above Sunset. "Elmer! We've got this crazy fucking Morrison here and he's singing about fucking his mother! That's right—FUCKING HIS GODDAMN MOTHER! We could get closed down for this shit. What are you gonna do?"

"Pull him off the fuckin' stage," Valentine growled, "and break one of his fuckin' legs."

After the show, the Doors were cooling off backstage. Phil Tanzini ran up the stairs and started yelling. "You *filthy* motherfuckers! You guys have the dirtiest mouths I ever heard in my life! Morrison—you can't say that shit about your mother! 'Mother, I want to fuck you.' Are you *shitting* me? What kind of fuckin' *pervert* are you? You are *sick*! And you are fucking fired as of right now."

"OK, Phil," Jim grinned. "But can we still have a bar tab?"

Tanzini stormed back down the stairs.

"Hey, Phil," Ray called out after him. "Didn't you ever hear of *Oedipus Rex*?"

THE DOORS KEPT PLAYING clubs around L.A., but they had an album to cut now and never again had the relative artistic luxury of a long-term residency like the one at the Whisky. The midnight hour had passed, and after the halcyon summer of 1966 the Doors had to morph into something else to survive. Two years later, blown away by the impossibility of trying to create new music in a sterile recording studio, Jim Morrison fondly recalled the good old days on the Sunset Strip:

"I just remember that some of the best musical trips we took were in clubs. There's nothing more fun than to play music to an audience. You can improvise at rehearsals, but it's kind of a dead atmosphere. There's no audience feedback. There's no tension, really, because in a club with a small audience . . . you're free to do anything. You feel an . . . *obligation* to be good, so you can't get completely loose. There are people watching. . . . I can put in a full day's work, go home and take a shower, change clothes, then play two or three sets at the Whisky, man . . . and *I love it*. I love it the way an athlete loves to run, to keep in shape."

THE FIFTH DOOR

JIM MORRISON DEVELOPED an instant—if sometimes grudging—respect for the Doors' new producer when the band began working on its first album at Sunset Sound Recording Studios in September 1966, about three weeks after being fired from the Whisky.

Paul A. Rothchild at thirty-one was already a certified Industry Heavy and a wise, rabbi-looking pothead with impeccable hipster credentials. Rothchild was a classically trained musician, raised in New Jersey, whose mother had sung with the Metropolitan Opera. As a teenager he had studied conducting with Bruno Walter, and later followed the folk music revival to Cambridge, Massachusetts, where Joan Baez was singing barefoot for Harvard students at the famous Club 47, where Bob Dylan played some of his first shows outside of New York. Rothchild's hustle and intellect landed him on the board of Club 47, and he went on to produce his first record, with the bluegrass-revivalist Charles River Valley Boys. He also worked as a record salesman to support his wife and kids, and developed an aware image that made him the folk music producer of choice. He talked a lot, cemented his musical friendships with excellent reefer scored from jazz musicians, and generally came on like someone who knew all the answers.

After the artistic breakthroughs of Bob Dylan and the Beatles in 1963 and 1964, Rothchild naturally turned to rock music. He discovered Paul Butterfield's band and produced them for Elektra. His production of the difficult Arthur Lee's first album with Love was unusually sympathetic. Rothchild had two of the best "ears" in the business, great hang-out talent, and the intellectually charged rap of a hepcat crossed with a professor.

He also rolled an impressive joint. Jac Holzman: "It defined Paul's hipness, rolling joints in front of artists—two thirds the diameter of a cigarette and perfectly tubular—works of folk art." This impressed Jim Morrison, who was also known for his joint-crafting skills. Rothchild had old-school viper style; he carried his dope and paraphernalia in compartmentalized sections of one of the narrow attaché cases fashionable in the day. But he had also been busted for marijuana possession when a mysterious trunk full of pot was delivered to his house in New Jersey, followed quickly by the cops. Rothchild denied the pot was his, and swore to Jac Holzman and others that someone, possibly a disgruntled musician he'd worked with, had set him up. Paul Rothchild had served seven months of a two-year prison sentence in New Jersey before being paroled in early 1966.

He was still out on parole when Holzman assigned him to produce the Doors' album. Rothchild was initially reluctant, having seen their lead singer's gonzo behavior and having immediately understood its deeply disturbing implications. But Holzman called in the favors Rothchild owed him for Elektra's steadfast support during his prison term, and Rothchild finally capitulated, telling Holzman, "Well, if you put it *that* way . . ."

Holzman had to testify in court as to Rothchild's character and the progress of his rehabilitation before Paul could fly to Los Angeles in September to begin production of *The Doors* at Sunset Sound. This four-track studio, built by a Walt Disney executive, was where most of the music for Disney's soundtracks and albums was recorded. Sunset Sound's owner, Tutti Camaratta, assigned a recently hired nineteen-year-old engineer named Bruce Botnick to the band's sessions, thus putting in place the basic six-man team that together would create the darkly lit, subterranean sound that defined the legendary Doors.

PAUL ROTHCHILD HAD an instinctive precognition of how to handle Jim Morrison and the Doors. Rothchild was a martinet in the studio, a dictator who took no shit from generally clueless, contractually obligated young musicians. He also had major street cred. "We saw the name Paul Rothchild on a Paul Butterfield record," Robby Krieger said. "We *loved* that record. Plus, the guy had just gotten out of jail, so we figured he couldn't be all that bad."

His outlaw status carried serious weight with Jim Morrison, but Rothchild also had a larger-than-life personality that was hard to argue with. "He was the only guy who could intimidate all the Doors," according to their roadie (and later manager) Bill Siddons. "He could yell and scream in a very specific way. He was a very well-equipped negotiator and fighter. He was so detailed that whatever he went into, he knew every molecule in the structure of it. He had a very Germanic feel to him. He could always put you in your place. He was 'the leader.' He was 'the producer.'"

Ray Manzarek: "Paul was the hippest, coolest, most intelligent producer on the planet. Paul was *us.* Paul was a head. Paul knew his Bach, Mingus and Monk, Sabicas, Jim Kweskin Jug Band, Arthur Rimbaud, and Federico Fellini.... Jim and Paul hit it off immediately." So controlling and precise was Paul Rothchild that he managed to cut the Doors' brilliant first album in a little over a week in late August 1966.

D URING THE DAY at Sunset Sound, Mickey Mouse cartoons were voiced and scored. The Doors came in at night and stunk up the studio with clouds of pot and tobacco. They began work in the large open space of Studio A and cut "Moonlight Drive" first. The songs, honed by five months in the clubs, came fast and furious. They were cut in the deeply influential wake of the Rolling Stones' *Aftermath,* a blatantly sadomasochistic masterpiece widely acknowledged as a creative breakthrough for its tone of dark, bluesy negativity. *The Doors* would prove to be another somber masterpiece in the same general mood.

The sessions went smoothly, and Jim, his long hair now hanging below his shoulders, seemed to be having a good time. He laughed as he and the others stamped their boots on the studio floor to get what Rothchild called "that very Nazi sound" used for the rhythm track of "Twentieth Century Fox," Jim's clever and loving portrait of Pamela Courson. "I Looked at You" and "End of the Night" were both from the band's earliest days. Rothchild used the band's popsy concert arrangement of the former, while Robby Krieger grafted a liquid psychedelic blues guitar solo onto the art-rock ambience of the latter, Jim's existential tribute to the notorious Céline. "Take It as It Comes," with Manzarek's cheesy organ solo, was a very close approximation of the Doors' live club sound. Jim later said he wrote the song for Maharishi Mahesh Yogi, but in Jim's worldview, the meditative intent of TM was subverted by his directive to "specialize in having fun."

Everything went well until the "Light My Fire" sessions, which took place during a late season pennant race between the Los Angeles Dodgers and the San Francisco Giants. The legendary Sandy Koufax (who owned the Tropicana Motel, where Jim was staying) was pitching for the Dodgers in the final game of the series, and avid baseball fan

Bruce Botnick took the liberty of hiding a portable television set in a corner of the studio, which was the only place the set's antennas could receive a decent picture. The sound was off, and only someone sitting in the control room could see the screen.

They were working on the "Light My Fire" solos. Session musician Larry Knechtel, brought in by Rothchild, played bass to give the band a funkier bottom than it usually had. It was A-minor to F-sharp minor, what Ray later called "a Sonny and Cher song." John was playing in a mix of Latin groove and "hard rock four" time. (The song was wholly Robby's except for Jim's second verse, which rhymed "no time to wallow in the mire" with "funeral pyre.") For the recording, Manzarek and Krieger grafted together jazz-structured solo riffs from recent John Coltrane records: *Coltrane Time, Olé Coltrane,* and "My Favorite Things." For the introduction, Ray remembered his Bach lessons and created a baroque circle of fifths that could have been played on a clavichord.

While they were trying these out at the "Fire" session, Jim was dancing around the studio, moving to the music, restless and trying to concentrate on the groove. In the corner of his eye, he saw a slight reflective glint on the window of the control booth and noticed that the engineer seemed to be focused on it. Jim walked over to the corner and looked at the TV. A change suddenly came over him like a dark cloud moving across the prairie. Jim freaked out. He picked up the TV, yanked the cord out of the wall, took two steps back, and tried to throw the set through the thick studio window.

The set bounced off the heavy glass and crashed to the floor. Stunned silence.

After a glowering pause, Jim drawled, "No fuckin' TVs in the recording studio—*ever.*"

The others just shrugged this off and kept on working.

The next night, Jim and Pam drove with some friends to the notorious bend in the road in Cholame, California, where James Dean had fatally wrecked his Porsche in 1957. Jim made this pilgrimage because he wanted to see the spot where Dean had died, but he was disappointed to learn that his idol had actually expired in a nearby hospital a few hours after the crash.

DOES ANYBODY UNDERSTAND ME?

A S THE DOORS' sessions progressed, "Soul Kitchen" got its organ intro, secret alphabets, and neon grooves. The slow shuffle of "Crystal Ship" was balanced with a tender piano interlude. "Alabama Song" became a cross between an oom-pah beer garden band and a decadent Weimar carousel. The zitherlike carnival music on the track was overdubbed by Ray on a Marxaphone, a sort of autoharp often used on the Disney sessions. Jim also changed the lyrics of the song by dropping the sarcastic verse that began "Show us the way to the next little dollar."

"Back Door Man" was the hardest rock on the record, and would become a critical Doors performance piece: the sonic cushion over which Jim ranted, improvised, and declaimed onstage for the next four years. Everything about the recording meshed with the rough-trade sexuality of Jim's stage demeanor: the primal tom-tom rhythm, the no-limits blues style, the grunts and vocal cries that ended in an ear-piercing scream. It was the most elementally evil of Doors songs, and carried sinister echoes of illicit, down-and-dirty sex that stayed forever with anyone who heard it. Jim reconfigured his version of "Back Door Man," using only two of the five verses written in 1952 (as "Back Door Friend") by Willie Dixon, the in-house arranger and bassist at Chess Records in Chicago. Howlin' Wolf later cut "Back Door Man," which was later covered by John Hammond Jr., whose version was brought to the Doors by Robby. Jim Morrison supplied his own twist, with lubricious insinuating rants and a mocking, contemptuous sneer in the song's chicken-eating narrative. Jim Morrison, the song implied with an evil grin, was the guy who was going to put a giant pair of horns on America's young men by fucking their girlfriends up the ass.

Productionwise, Paul Rothchild deliberately distanced Jim from the analog immediacy of the band's music. The voice of the Doors sounded far away from the listener when "Break On Through" exploded out of the speakers, giving the vocals a mythic, haunting quality. To bring this great, epochal rock song into play, John Densmore turned to Brazilian rhythm, slightly rocking up the brushy drum intro to the bossa classic "Desafinado" as recorded by Stan Getz two years earlier. They speeded up the number halfway through, so by the time Jim got into the intense counting of week-to-week, day-to-day, and hour-to-hour, the number was an urgent telegram. Soon "Break On Through" (in slightly censored form) would take its place as one of the greatest album openers in the history of rock.

JIM WENT A LITTLE MAD when they tried to cut "The End." The first night he had taken LSD and they failed to get a magical version of the Doors' dramatic show closer. On the second night, Jim had disappeared before the session started, and someone found him in Blessed Sacrament, the big Catholic church just across Sunset. Jim brought back a prayer book and started tearing out pages one by one, mumbling to himself. Bruce Botnick turned up the monitor in the control booth, and heard Jim chanting: "Kill the father, fuck the mother." He assumed that this was part of "The End," which he hadn't heard before they recorded it. He noticed that occasionally Jim referred to some handwritten lyrics that were jammed into the back pocket of his dungarees.

On the second night, Rothchild recalled, "We were in the middle of recording 'The End.' The lights had been dimmed and candles were burning right next to Jim, whose back was to the control room. The only other illumination came from the lights on the VU meters. The studio was very dark. We had it kind of choreographed. Sometimes Jim was leading the band. Or when the band was full-out cranking, we couldn't have Jim in the room, so we had him in the vocal booth, and he'd be running back and forth between the booth and the [vocal] mike Bruce had set up out there.

"It was totally hypnotic. There were four other people in the control room at the time. When the take was over, we realized that the tape was still running. Bruce, the engineer, was completely immersed in this take—we all were. We all felt like the Muse had visited the studio that time, and all of us were the audience. The machines knew what to do!"

In the cataclysmic raga and white-noise band section that followed the song's primal scene, Jim scatted out percussive *kills* and *fucks* like a talking drum; these were mixed way down and suppressed on the album, but were transcendent in the studio—the Doors in full cry, immortalizing themselves in their moment.

Rothchild: "We were halfway through and I got chills, top to bottom.

I said, 'Bruce, do you know what's happening out there? This is history, right at this moment. This is why we came here. *This is it.*' At the end of the take I was as drained as anyone in the room."

It was a moment that neither Rothchild nor Botnick ever forgot. Then Rothchild asked for another take.

It didn't happen. Jim was in a full-blown manic episode now, although no one recognized the situation. "He was on this Oedipus complex trip," Robby Krieger said later. " 'Fuck the mother, kill the father.' He would just rant on like that, for *hours*. When we finally got him in to record ['The End'], he did it great. Then we decided he was too high to continue the session, so we closed up and left."

The night was young, though, and the moon was full in Scorpio. Two hours later, peaking on acid and alcohol, Jim the human fly vaulted over the chain-link fence surrounding Sunset Sound and broke into the studio. Storming into the room where they had just finished "The End," Jim sat down, took off his boots, and lit a joint. He looked around awhile, and then grabbed a big copper fire extinguisher off the wall and let fly, soaking the studio, the equipment and the instruments—even the harpsichord!—with chemical foam.

Paul Rothchild jumped the wall and dragged him out of there. But Jim had left his boots behind.

The next morning, Bruce Botnick got a phone call from an apoplectic Tutti Camaratta. "Get down here! What the hell is going on?"

Jim's boots were found, covered in foam, although he claimed to have no memory of the incident. In fact, he just laughed when asked about it. To John Densmore, Jim avowed incredulity. "Did I do that?"

Jac Holzman mollified Tutti with a check, and someone cleaned up the mess Jim had made. Camaratta suggested to Holzman, a valued client, that the five thousand dollars he was spending to record the Doors was a waste of Elektra's good money. Holzman thanked him for his sage advice, and tried not to worry. (As of this writing, the Doors' album sales, in all formats, is above fifty million units and climbing.)

A FEW MONTHS LATER, as *The Doors* was released, Rothchild deployed his vintage 1967 hip-speak to explain just what "The End" was really about. He was Elektra's village explainer, and his remarks were published in the early rock journal *Crawdaddy,* which was partially subsidized by Elektra.

Rothchild: "At one point during the recording session [Jim] was very emotionally moved, and he was wondering, and he was tearful . . . and he shouted in the studio: 'DOES ANYONE UNDERSTAND ME?' And I said, 'Yes, I do.' Right there we got into a long discussion about just what does this mean—kill the father, fuck the mother—which Jim kept saying over and over—and essentially it boils down to just this:

" 'Kill the father' means kill all of those things in yourself which are instilled in you and are not of yourself. They are not of your own. They are alien concepts which are not yours. They must die. Those are the things that must die. The psychedelic revolution.

" 'Fuck the mother' is very basic. And it means, get back to the essence. What is the reality? Fuck the mother is, very basically, Mother: mother-birth, real, *very real,* you can touch it, you can grab it, you can feel it. It's nature, it's real, it can't lie to you.

"So what he says at the end of the Oedipus section, which is essentially the same thing as the classic [*Oedipus Rex*] says: kill the alien concepts, get back to reality, which is precisely what the song is about. The End. The end of alien concepts, the beginning of personal concepts. Get to reality, get to your own reality, get to your own in-touch-with-yourself situation."

JAMES PHOENIX

J IM MORRISON'S OWN SITUATION was changing in the autumn of 1966 as he partially moved into his redheaded girlfriend's funky one-bedroom apartment in a ramshackle green house in Laurel Canyon.

Everyone in the music scene was living in Laurel Canyon now: Zappa and his entourage; most of the Byrds; Mamas and Papas; Billy James, Steve Stills from Buffalo Springfield. (Neil Young had moved into an old ranch house in Topanga Canyon, even farther away from the Hollywood scene.) Laurel had been the first of the canyons in the hills above Hollywood to be settled, when hunters and early movie people started building camps and cabins up there around 1915. Fifty years later, it was thickly settled with quirky houses, a few Spanish Colonial villas, and a cool reputation limned by Joni Mitchell's song "Ladies of the Canyon."

The apartment Pam found was at 1414 Rothdell Trail, just behind the Canyon Country Store, where David Crosby bought his rolling papers. Jim paid the seventy-dollar monthly rent. The apartment had a second floor balcony, where Jim liked to hang out with a beer, watching the parade of freaks passing through the little marketplace, and making notes about life on Love Street, where the creatures meet.

Two guys from the band Three Dog Night lived upstairs. Downstairs was Pam's friend Mirandi Babitz, sister of the not-shy groupie Eve, and Mirandi's boyfriend, Clem. Mirandi was into clothes—she measured the inseam of Jim's leg for his first vinyl trousers—and was then starting one of the first boutiques in Los Angeles so she could sell her own designs and other hip threads in the new peacock styles radiating from London. Pamela Courson, also heavily into fashion, watched Mirandi carefully, and secretly planned to open her own boutique as soon as Jim's band money started coming in.

Jimmy and Pamela had been together (more or less) for about six months when he moved some clothes, his books, and his electric blanket into her apartment. This is also when they began fighting a lot—epic battles over infidelity, lack of consideration, and other issues that burst through their doorway and out into the street. At least once a week Pam would explode in fury, throw open the bedroom window, and dump Jim's clothes and books into the street, screaming curses and bloody murder as the laundry and literature flew. Mirandi Babitz ascribed some of Pam's chronic unhappiness to sexual incompatibility between the two lovers. Jim, Babitz claimed, preferred anal intercourse, while Pamela, who was tiny and rail thin, was less than thrilled taking Jim's reputedly prodigious reproductive organ into her rectum.

Mirandi Babitz: "I know their sex life was weird. He tied her up all the time, and sometimes he was really brutal with her. It was okay with her up to a point, but then he would always go over the line. . . . He really preferred women from the backside. Pam was pissed off about that, but she stuck with it. It was part of the reason she was always snarling at him.

"One time when we were living in the apartment with them, she got pissed off at him because she thought he was running around with someone else, so she took his favorite vest that he liked to wear onstage and wrote FAGGOT on the back of it with a Magic Marker. Then she cut up a bunch of his clothes and left for a day."

Jim loved fighting with Pamela, who was overcontrolling, quick-witted, and gave as good as she got. She threw plates, crockery, knives, and frying pans at him, but he just laughed. When they went out at night, Pam thought nothing of hauling off and punching Jim in the face with her tiny fist if she thought he was getting too close to another chick. They taunted each other, tried to scare and startle each other, starved together, dared each other to be more outrageous. They dropped acid together and then got B_{12} shots at UCLA Medical Center to help them come down. Pam was the only woman who knew how to taunt Jim, and this could make him really crazy. After one of their fights, he would go into the Hollywood clubs and lash out at some unsuspecting girl who couldn't defend herself. He belted Suzy Creamcheese at the Whisky one night and was roughly thrown out. He slapped Pam Miller another night at Bido Lito's. He kept a motel room in various places around West Hollywood, but most nights he could be seen hitching up Laurel Canyon Boulevard to sleep with Pamela Courson.

Their bond was intractable and would seemingly remain so through multiple cycles of abuse and redemption. Ray Manzarek, who knew them well in this period, later said: "They were like the same person, you know? They were the opposite sides of the same coin, the same person as a male and as a female...They were perfect for each other." Through the years, Manzarek would overromanticize Jim and Pamela's cosmic-soul-mate legend, but his feelings about these two glittering misfits' suitability for each other has never wavered.

THE DOORS PLAYED A FEW TIMES around L.A. in September and October, while Paul Rothchild worked on their album in New York. They played with Sky Saxon's band, the Seeds, at Bido Lito's in Hollywood and some private parties with John Kay's hard-rocking Sparrow. Jim suggested to Kay that he change the band's name to Steppenwolf, with fateful results.

Jim was thinking about changing his own name as well. As the poet of action that Rimbaud had foreseen, he had big, even revolutionary plans, and he realized that some of them could negatively impact his father's sacred naval career when his provocations got serious and events moved beyond his control. Ray Manzarek says that Jim talked about calling himself "James Phoenix" on the Doors album jacket, and considered trying out the new name and persona when the Doors played their first shows in New York. James Phoenix—a mythical bird rising from the smoldering ashes of outmoded bourgeois consciousness. James Phoenix—herald of the Aquarian Age. But then Jim was persuaded to keep his own name, and sadly to insist to the media that he was an orphan.

On October 31, Halloween, the Doors flew to New York and registered at the Henry Hudson Hotel on West Fifty-seventh Street. Elektra was so hot to promote the Doors—even months before their record was released—that Paul Rothchild had arranged a month's residency for the band at Ondine, arguably the hippest venue in 1966 Manhattan, on East Fifty-seventh Street under the Queensboro Bridge. That first night in New York, the Doors attended a grotesque Halloween costume party at the club, attended by Ondine's usual crowd of Warholites, jet-setters, and drag queens. Otis Redding's "Knock On Wood" was the club's current hot record. At the end of the night Jim Morrison disappeared with the lovely black groupie Devon Wilson, an Ondine regular and future muse of Jimi Hendrix, causing tongues to wag among the uptown amphetamine crowd.

The next night, November 1, the Doors got to see the Jerk performed on its home turf for the first time when they opened their gig at Ondine. Unlike the spacy, undulating dancers they played for at home, the New York crowd did a different bop—nervous, jumpy dances like the Frug, the Monkey, the Watusi, the Shing-a-ling. "They didn't know trance dancing," Manzarek observed. "They didn't know psychedelic." The Doors were shit-hot from the moment they lurched into mojo-heavy "Backdoor Man" to start their set. The Mothers of Invention had played New York two weeks earlier, and Frank Zappa had talked up the Doors in radio interviews. Billie Winters, Ondine's extremely hip deejay, had already met the Doors in L.A. and was spreading word among Manhattan's children of the night that the Second Coming was nigh. And Elektra Records, home of Love and the Butterfield Band, was plugging the Doors as the Next Big Thing, the American Rolling Stones, with Jim as California's answer to Mick Jagger. Consequently there was a huge rush to see Jim Morrison in the first days of the Ondine gig. The smallish, nautically themed club sold out every night, and there were long lines to get in.

Andy Warhol came the second night with his entourage. Outside it was raw Manhattan November, but during the Doors' second set, Ondine's basement ambience turned into a Hopi sweat lodge as Jim turned in one of his most shamanic early performances. The band played as if for their lives, with the staggering drama of "The End" climaxing in mass orgasm at the end of the evening. Afterward, Jim reconnected with Nico. Paul Morrissey, who had taken over production of Warhol's films, agreed with Andy that they simply had to get Jim Morrison to star in their next project, whose working title was *Fuck*.

The alternative press loved the Doors, and reviews were ecstatic. *Village Voice* columnist Howard Smith called Jim the most important American sex symbol to appear since James Dean. Richard Goldstein, the first rock critic ("an English major with a boner for rock"), wrote that the Doors' lead singer "could act every position in the *Kama Sutra* with his lips alone." Photographers fought each other to get good camera position. Linda Eastman, later to marry Paul McCartney, shot several rolls at Ondine and noted Jim's ferocious concentration and his habit of cupping his hand behind his ear so he could hear his vocals over the din of the band.

Warhol's protégé, Gerard Malanga, hated the Doors, and for good reason. "He stole my look," Malanga wailed after he, too, had made the scene at Ondine, and his fellow Warholites could only shake their heads and agree that, yes, Jim Morrison in his vinyl pants and serpentine theatrics had appropriated Gerard's underground poète maudit gestalt and then ratcheted it up to the next level. It was generally agreed that if Malanga had any musical talent he would have been there first, and Jim might have seemed redundant. But Malanga's talents lay in visual arts—silk screens and photography—and he could never have written anything even approaching "My Eyes Have Seen You" or "Crystal Ship." So Gerard sulked and began writing poetry while Warhol and Morrissey obsessed over trying to get Jim to star in their new movie.

The Doors spent their afternoons helping Paul Rothchild mix their record in a small studio Holzman had built in Elektra's midtown office. The label had hoped to have the record out for Christmas, but it was delayed until January 1967 to give Rothchild more time. Rothchild created the final mix of "The End" by fusing the first session's first half with the incendiary second half from the next night. Rothchild and Holzman had already decided that "Break On Through" was the obvious first single.

In an uncomfortable meeting with the band, Holzman told them that Elektra felt it necessary to censor the word *high* from the song's exultant proclamation: "*She gets . . . she gets . . . she gets. . . . hiiiigh.*" Radio wouldn't play such a blatant drug reference, Holzman told the Doors, and when Rothchild backed up his boss, the band had to cave.

Elektra kept the Doors busy that November. They bought new suits in Greenwich Village (after Ondine's owner said their L.A. clothes were unhip), and new boots from the Chelsea Cobbler. Jim burned a hole in his suit jacket with a cigarette and then threw it in the trash. Danny Fields, Elektra's hip young publicist, began churning out articles for the teen music magazines that were the only print outlets for rock star stories. Since Fields was gay, his articles such as "My Dream Date with Jim Morrison" captured something of the adolescent yearnings of the readers of pulp mags like *Datebook* and *Hit Parader*.

And then there was Gloria Stavers, the thirty-something former model who was the editor of *Sixteen*, the biggest of the teenage magazines. Stavers was a tough cookie, who had fought her way out of rural poverty and established herself as a force in the music business. She had been Lenny Bruce's girlfriend and confidante, and enjoyed exercising her power over the young rockers who craved her immense audience. Gloria Stavers could make (or break) careers with cover stories and photo spreads in her magazine. She liked to shoot her own photo sessions in her apartment, which if truly successful ended up in her bed. This in turn guaranteed continuing monthly coverage in *Sixteen* and a clear shot at national stardom. (The most blatant example of this, repeatedly pointed out to the Doors, was the case of Peter Noone, the cherubic lead singer of Herman's Hermits, the second wave teenybopper British Invasion group. Stavers's seduction of Noone resulted in multiple *Sixteen* covers for the Hermits, who finished 1966 by outselling both the Beatles and the Stones that year.)

All four Doors arrived at Stavers's apartment and were dutifully photographed by her. Then Danny Fields herded Ray, Robby, and John out the door so that Gloria could work with Jim alone. She opened a fresh bottle of wine. She mussed Jim's long hair a bit, rapping to him, teasing him. She took out a comb to style his hair, but he grabbed it and threw it out the open window. "Get that comb away from me," he snarled. Soon Jim's shirt was off. Then he started going through her closet, trying on necklaces and fur coats. She shot him pouting like a sex kitten, and posing against her brick walls like a Greek hero. She told him about her trip with Lenny Bruce, and showed him how to stay thin and sexy by throwing up the food he'd eaten. At dawn they tumbled into bed. She lubricated herself with melted butter and let Jim do what he liked best. A couple months later, when *The Doors* was released, *Sixteen* published a fawning, breathless cover story under the headline: "Morrison Is Magic!"

CALLING SIGNALS

NOVEMBER 1966. Jim Morrison on the loose in New York. He saw every movie in town, often late in the afternoon. *The Tenth Victim. Modesty Blaise.* On foot, he haunted the used bookstores on Fourth Avenue, buying Genet, Brecht, Mailer, and LeRoi Jones. He was reading William Burroughs's new novel *The Soft Machine.* He was extremely welcome at Warhol's midtown studio, the Factory, where he scored pills from the regulars and star-quality blow jobs from Nico in a bathroom covered in aluminum foil.

Andy Warhol, lisping like a girl, literally begged Jim to be allowed to film him having sex with Nico. (Nico apparently thought this was an OK idea.) "Fuck no, Andy," Jim laughed. Then Warhol begged to be allowed to just watch, while the big German woman expertly fellated Jim. "Fuck no, Andy." Jim, however, did agree (verbally) to appear in *Fuck* when production began early in 1967. Warhol's film *Chelsea Girls* was at that moment the hottest thing in the American underground, and Warhol and Morrissey tried to convince Jim (who knew better) that it was the highest honor the New York avant-garde could bestow to be asked to star in Andy's next production. The script, such as it was, called for unprecedented full-frontal nudity from its male lead. One of the film's actors, already cast, was Valerie Solanis.

Jim told Warhol and Morrissey he would be there when production started on *Fuck* in L.A. after the new year. Then he thought better of it, or was talked out of it by the Doors' management. Without warning, Jim sent his drinking buddy, actor Tom Baker, to the shoot instead. Warhol and Morrisey were surprised, but used Baker anyway in what became *I, A Man,* one of Warhol's better movies.

I N 1966, THE FILMED PROMO CLIP—forerunner of the music video—began to be deployed by record companies eager to get their product on television. Both the Beatles and Rolling Stones began regular production of film clips to accompany their new singles that year, as Canadian media philosopher Marshall McLuhan was forecasting—with huge attendant publicity—the birth of the global village and the conquest of the mass media over actual substance. Jac Holzman, not wanting to be left out of the action, decided to produce a film clip of the Doors performing "Break On Through."

Elektra executive Mark Abramson produced the clip. Shot in color on a stark black set lit by club lights, the clip featured mostly Jim's face and features—the blue eyes, pillowy lips, and long hair of a beautiful new rock star. This was offset with glimpses of Ray Manzarek looking professorial in his tweed jacket, blue shirt, and rep tie. The three-minute clip, edited with dissolves and jump cuts, presented the Doors as the antithesis of a sunny California pop group and tried to position the band alongside the scowling, antisocial Rolling Stones of such dark albums as *December's Children* and *Aftermath.* The "Break On Through" clip captured some of the proselytizing psychedelic fever of the Doors' first single, but with no regular outlet for this new medium, the clip would only rarely be broadcast when the album came out the following year.

On November 15, 1966, the band signed their contract with Elektra Records. Flashbulbs popped, leather-jacketed Jim appeared with smiling execs in eight-by-ten glossies sent to *Billboard* and *Cashbox.* The Elektra deal called for seven albums over the next five years. The Doors also signed with their new management team, two bit players on the fringes of the music business in Los Angeles, who, their label hoped, might be able to control Jim Morrison's wild streak.

The way the record business worked (and still works) is that the recording companies preferred to have relationships with talent managers who could ensure that their artists showed up as scheduled at the studio and at concerts. The record guys sent the royalty checks to the management company, who in turn doled (or didn't dole) the money out to the guys in the band. The Doors' new managers had been hastily chosen at the last minute by a committee of sleazo Whisky insiders and attorney Max Fink (who was new to the music business). Salvatore Bonafede was an old-school East Coast music guy who had worked with Italian-American pop stars like Dion and the Belmonts. Asher Dann was a swinging Beverly Hills real estate agent and Whisky regular who, it was naively believed, could handle the unpredictable, trouble-prone Jim Morrison.

"Sal and Ash" were a problem from day one. They had no experience breaking in a new band, and immediately tried to get the Doors out of the Elektra deal, and so were hated by everyone at the band's label. Jac Holzman called them "the antithesis of class." Sal and Ash would last only about a year, and the Doors never would have proper management for the rest of their career.

P AUL ROTHCHILD INVITED THE BAND to his house in New Jersey for Thanksgiving dinner. Jim got drunk and came on to Paul's wife, whispering intimately in her ear and fondling her beautiful hair. Paul pretended not to care, but the conservative Densmore was appalled. Later, when their producer drove them back to Manhattan, Jim started pulling Rothchild's long hair until the car swerved sickeningly in the Holland Tunnel and Paul told Jim loudly to cool it. Then Jim started in on Ray, trying to tear his hair out, which Manzarek tolerated until they got back to the hotel. Once there, Jim got naked and stepped out onto the ledge outside his window, a dozen stories above the traffic on Fifty-seventh Street. He screamed curses and verses into the freezing ether for an hour, until the others finally persuaded him to return to the overheated hotel room, where Jim put a lampshade on his head, took a long, loud, boozy piss on the carpet, and passed out.

T HE DOORS FLEW BACK TO L.A. in early December and found the scene on Sunset Strip much changed from when they'd left. It was in the aftermath of the riots and police suppression that convulsed the teen scene on the Strip while the Doors were away, and feelings were still running high. It had started when kids spilling out of Pandora's Box stopped traffic to protest an arrest of one of their own. Using the techniques of the civil rights movement, hundreds of kids spontaneously sat down in Sunset Boulevard and the cops used dogs and tear gas to disperse them. This turned into several nights of rioting and increasing police brutality that outraged the bands that depended on the Strip's kids for their livelihoods. Steve Stills's acerbic take on these events, "For What It's Worth," would within weeks become Buffalo Springfield's first hit single.

The Doors played the Sea Witch, one of the better L.A. clubs, on two weekends that month. They got an earful from the groupies and scene makers who had seen innocent kids gassed, beaten, and badgered by the heavy-handed riot cops who had restored order to the sidewalks of Sunset. Hearing these stories late at night at the gig, and at Cantor's Deli, made Jim's antiauthoritarian blood boil. He told Paul Rothchild he was crushed that the Doors had missed the party.

On December 8, 1966, Jim celebrated his twenty-third birthday with Pamela Courson at home, in Laurel Canyon. She was wearing a wedding ring now, and had begun to call herself Mrs. Morrison. They borrowed a car and went for an early evening ride along Mulholland Drive, which wound westward through the dry Hollywood Hills. Pam, in one of her goofy, dangerous moods, kept trying to grab the steering wheel from Jim and run the car off the road and onto the gravel edges of the steep cliffs, just for kicks.

A ROUND THIS TIME ELEKTRA BEGAN to assemble its campaign to promote the Doors. Prior to the photo shoot that made him a legend, Jim was taken to star hairdresser Jay Sebring's salon on Fairfax Avenue in West Hollywood to have his hair cut. Sebring was *the* barber to the stars, having invented a new style of cutting and sculpting long hair with little Italian blow-dryers. It was a cool operation, with sexy, barefoot starlets handling the shampoo chores. Sebring's clientele included Steve McQueen, Warren Beatty, Paul Newman, and Peter Fonda. He was a consummate Hollywood swinger, and drove a racy AC Cobra Ford Mustang that he parked outside the salon. Jim Morrison coveted this car from the minute he saw it.

Sebring styled Jim's long and unruly mane of brown locks into a tousled coiffure that resembled the marble bust of Alexander the Great then displayed at the Getty Museum in Malibu. Photographer Joel Brodsky took the famous black-and-white pictures that presented Jim Morrison as a bare-chested incarnation of classical Aryan manhood: a hypnotically gazing Adonis with a circlet of love beads around his neck. Later on, when Jim had radically changed his appearance and repudiated the persona depicted in Brodsky's pictures, Elektra executives joked that Jim Morrison had only actually looked that good for about twenty minutes. When the photos were released, in January 1967, the joke around Hollywood was that Jim Morrison looked like he'd been invented on the telephone by two fags.

Then there were the press releases and artist bios. These were assembled by Elektra secretary Sue Helms and edited by Billy James and geared to the pre–*Rolling Stone* teen mags in the form of personal-fave lists and dopey questionnaires. The bios of The Other Three were the usual boring, fan-driven boilerplate (although Densmore referred to his bandmates as "these creeps"); but Jim Morrison's bio was unlike anything the press had ever seen before.

Jim had been reading his McLuhan and understood, as he later put it, that the interview was an art form that should be prepared like any other art. Jim's term for this was "calling signals," echoing the football quarterback's audible commands to his teammates at the line of scrimmage. Beginning with his first Elektra bio, Jim Morrison launched his campaign to spread chaos and anarchy through American youth culture via poetry and rock music. Jim Morrison's bio ran perversely against the cheery tone of hippie media sprouting out of California, and identified Jim as a dark, challenging, mysterious, and provocative rebel and seeker:

FULL REAL NAME: James Douglas Morrison
BIRTH DATE AND PLACE: December 8, 1943, Melbourne,
    Florida
PERSONAL DATA: 5'11" [enhanced by about an inch and a half],
    145 lbs., brown hair, blue-gray eyes
FAMILY INFO: Dead
HOME INFO: Laurel Canyon, L.A.—nice at night

SCHOOLS ATTENDED: St. Petersburg Junior College, Florida
State U., UCLA
INSTRUMENTS PLAYED/PART SUNG: lead voice
FAVORITE SINGING GROUPS: Beach Boys, Kinks, Love
INDIVIDUAL SINGERS: Sinatra, Presley
ACTOR AND ACTRESS: Jack Palance [psychotic villain in late-
period Hollywood westerns, and craven American movie pro-
ducer in Godard's *Contempt*], Sarah Miles [slatternly British
actress in Joseph Losey's *The Servant*].
TV SHOWS: news
COLORS: turquoise
FOODS: meat
HOBBIES: horse races
SPORTS: swimming
WHAT DO YOU LOOK FOR IN A GIRL: hair, eyes, voice, talk
WHAT DO YOU LIKE TO DO ON A DATE: talk
PLANS/AMBITIONS: make films

The Elektra bio continued with Jim's artistic manifesto:

You could say it's an accident that I'm ideally suited for the
work I am doing. It's the feeling of a bowstring being pulled
back for 22 years, and suddenly being let go.

I am primarily an American; second, a Californian; third, a
Los Angeles resident.

I've always been attracted to ideas that were about revolt
against authority. I like ideas about the breaking away or over-
throwing of established order. I am interested in anything about
revolt, disorder, chaos—especially activity that seems to have no
meaning. It seems to me to be the road toward freedom. Exter-
nal revolt is a way to bring about internal freedom. Rather than
starting inside, I start outside—reach the mental through the
physical.

I am a Sagittarian—if astrology has anything to do with it—
the Centaur—the Archer—the Hunter. But the main thing is that
we are the Doors.

We are from the West / The whole thing is like an invitation to the
West.
The Sunset   This is the end
The night   The sea
    The world we suggest is of a new wild west.   A sensuous evil
       world.
    Strange and haunting, the path of the sun, you know?
    Toward the end.   At least for our first album
    We're all centered around the end of the zodiac.
    The Pacific / violence and peace / the way between young
       and the old.

Jim Morrison's anarchic screed wasn't lightly released by Elektra. According to John Densmore, old pro Billy James, while working on the Doors' bios, muttered under his breath: "Too much power in Jim's hands could be *very* dangerous." Two years later, Jim told interviewer Jerry Hopkins that the claim that his parents were dead was "a joke."

JIM MORRISON AND PAMELA COURSON spent the Christmas holidays together in a motel room in the desert town of Palm Springs. During the days they explored the palm-lined secret canyons where the Agua Caliente Indian tribes had lived in oasislike splendor amid the searing heat of the desert. At night, Jim read Ezra Pound's *Cantos* to her by candlelight.

On New Year's Eve, the Doors played a private party in Montecito, a Santa Barbara suburb. Now it was fateful 1967. Soon *The Doors* would be released, and Jim Morrison's private life would be over, forever.

CHAPTER FIVE

THE WARLOCK
OF ROCK

*The effect was, accordingly, electric; his fame had not to
wait for any of the ordinary gradations, but seemed to
spring up, like the palace of a fairy tale, in a night.*

—THOMAS MOORE, ON LORD BYRON

GET IT ON

JIM MORRISON WAS HAVING TROUBLE sleeping. He kept dreaming, he told his girlfriend Pamela, about napalm—the flaming jellied gasoline that Americans were dropping on Vietnamese villages. In the recurring dream, he couldn't rub the stuff off as it burned through his flesh. The Vietnamese couldn't either. Jim began drinking more, he said, to help him fall asleep at night.

In January 1967, the Vietnamese communists, noting the contradictions and dissent in the policies of their American enemy, began a counterescalation of their own. Viet Cong and North Vietnamese army units began probing American defenses in preparation for the major offensives that would happen later. America's intervention in the civil war in Vietnam was turning into a bloody slaughter, televised nightly. Napalm turned the jungle into wasteland. VC dead were displayed like trophies as they were dragged from their caves. Young marines torched reed-thatched villages with their Zippo lighters. It was disgusting, grotesque, and very un-American. Jim Morrison numbly watched this brutality and violence unfold on the TV in his motel room, and then took notes.

President Johnson ordered more American soldiers, most of them teenaged draftees, into combat in Vietnam. As the war got hotter, and as more of these kids came home in body bags, America began to writhe in bitterness and turmoil. The underground art movements of 1966 became the counterculture of 1967, as a great mass of the postwar generation turned away from the corporate mainstream in disgust. The Doors' first album became part of this, released around the same time as strong debut records by Buffalo Springfield, Eric Clapton's band Cream, the Jefferson Airplane, and other San Francisco bands.

Jim liked *Surrealistic Pillow,* the Airplane's record, and the Doors would often appear with them over the next two years. The Airplane was a leading band of the San Francisco Sound, a cohesive movement of about a dozen bands that played the city's electric ballroom circuit in front of throbbing psychedelic light shows, pounding out acid-soaked hard rock whose message was implicitly antiwar. By contrast, the Doors weren't part of any movement or grouping of L.A. bands, such as the Byrds and Springfield, whose members came out of commercial folk music. The Doors were jazzers, Coltrane fans, and their singer was a post-Beat poet.

The Doors were unique unto themselves, a democratic band. At Jim's insistence, all the money and writing credits were split equally among the four musicians, and all decisions concerning the group had to be unanimous. Through most of 1967 the Doors would use this outsider unity to drive their fast and furious rise to national fame on the strength of their powerful music, dark vision, and charismatic singer. Jim Morrison was about to blow America's mind during an action-packed year of hard work, constant travel, chaos, and adventure.

JIM HATED TELEVISION with all the passion of a film student, but he was still fascinated by its power to instantly communicate to millions. On New Year's Day, as their first 45-rpm single "Break On Through" was released, Jim made his broadcast debut on *Shebang!,* a local L.A. teen dance show produced by *American Bandstand*'s Dick Clark and hosted by disc jockey Casey Kasem. Miming lamely to a tape of "Break On Through," the Doors looked like bored collegian mods, and Jim hardly bothered to dramatize the song. But Elektra's marketing people were plugging the Doors hard, and the band felt obligated to cooperate. They were photographed in the scaffolding of the huge new Doors billboard that dominated the section of Sunset Boulevard near La Cienega. This was the first time a record company had sprung for one of these giant outdoor ads, which usually featured movies or cigarettes, and signaled (to the record industry) Elektra's unusually strong commitment to a new group. The billboard (which also signified that Elektra itself was now a major player in the music biz) magnified Guy Webster's cover shot from *The Doors*, and proclaimed:

BREAK ON THROUGH
WITH AN
ELECTRIFYING ALBUM

Jim and Pam first saw the billboard the night it was unveiled, spotlit in the early winter evening. Stunned and then bemused at seeing himself magnified like a demigod above the legendary Sunset Strip, Jim didn't say another word all night.

J IM WAS STILL LIVING part-time with the tourists, hookers, and Hollywood hopefuls at the rowdy Tropicana Motel, but he spent many nights in Pam's candlelit apartment in the ramshackle green house in Laurel Canyon. He liked to get up around two in the afternoon, scratch himself, and get a beer if there were any in the fridge. Then he'd put on his acetate copy of the as-yet unreleased *The Doors,* and play it as loud as the neighbors could take it. The first time he did this, it attracted the surprised attention of naked-except-for-panties Pamela Miller, one of Frank and Gail Zappa's brazen teenaged babysitters, who was staying next door with a friend named Sandy.

Miss Pamela recalled: "I'd seen the Doors a hundred times by then, and I really wanted to get to know Jim, because I'd never seen such blatant sexuality onstage before. And I was really surprised to hear this music coming out of this green shack behind the Country Store, because I knew the Doors had recorded an album, but it hadn't been released yet. So I slipped on my little purple dress and walked barefoot down the stone steps between our houses to see what ultrahip neighbor had an advance pressing of the Doors record. I tiptoed up on the old wooden porch and peeked in the window of the room that 'Crystal Ship' was coming from. I stifled a scream as my eyes adjusted to the dark and Jim Morrison came into focus, in the flesh, his hair mussed up and wearing nothing but a pair of black pants. Oh . . . my . . . God!

"I was so flustered—I ran back to the pad where I was staying and tried to figure out what to do. A little earlier, I'd been given a quart bottle of a tranquilizer called Trimar by the bass player of Iron Butterfly, who had a day job working in a hospital. This stuff was used to block labor pains, and even a little bit poured on a handkerchief and inhaled made me feel like Alice falling down the rabbit hole. Maybe this would be a good way to meet one of my sex idols.

"I grabbed the Trimar and negotiated the steps, got up on the porch and bravely knocked on the door. When Jim answered, I smiled and introduced myself. 'Whatcha got there?' he asked, nodding at the bottle of clear liquid I was holding.

"When I next came to my senses, I was executing a perfect backbend on Jim's tattered Oriental carpet, and my purple velvet minidress was over my head. I don't remember if I was wearing panties—maybe not. And suddenly there was his redheaded girlfriend, glaring at me with a look of pure hatred in her pretty eyes. I looked over at Jim: he had backed into a dark corner of the room, about to enjoy what he figured would be one of Pam's jealous tantrums. He was murmuring to her, *'Get it on . . . Get it on . . . Get it on.'*

"It was one of those classic 'uh-oh' moments. I stood up and offered the redhead a shot of the Trimar, but she just turned her back and told me I'd better leave. I went back up to Sandy's pad. Just as I got in the door I heard Pam screaming: 'Don't you *dare* go up there, Jim Morrison. Don't you dare!' But he was already at the door, smiling shyly, extremely interested in another blast of the Trimar.

"Social niceties forgotten, we spent the rest of the afternoon and evening sniffing the stuff, sitting on the floor, laughing at everything and getting to know each other. I ran out of the stuff early the next morning, and Jim wished us a pleasant good-night and politely thanked Sandy for her hospitality. What a gentleman. I was disappointed that he made no attempt to lay a hand on me, but now that we were friends I had high hopes for the future—as long as that redhead wasn't around."

The Doors was a masterpiece album, with "Break On Through" one of the hardest rocking album openers ever, but at first the record didn't catch on. "Break On Through" didn't fit the popsy, jingle-oriented format of Top Forty radio, dominated by good-time bands like the Lovin' Spoonful and Motown records, and Elektra had trouble getting the record played beyond KRLA in Los Angeles, where deejay Dave Diamond seemed to play it every ten minutes. ("Break On Through" wouldn't even break through the Hot Hundred, only reaching number 106.) *The Doors* struggled on the album charts as well. It wasn't an easy sell: This was an unusually brilliant first album, with a dark, organic vision and enough hard rock tracks ("Soul Kitchen," "Twentieth Century Fox," and "Back Door Man") to back up the Doors' claim that they were no insipid art-rock group.

And then there was "The End," which closed the album the way it closed the band's show. The recorded version of "The End" was immediately compared to the Rolling Stones' "Goin' Home," the long-form piece that had closed *Aftermath*, released a few months earlier. Critics immediately understood that "The End"—with its mystical journey and murderous sexual furor—was one of the most complex and interesting works of art anyone in this generation had yet released.

But for all that, the audience for this music was limited mostly to college kids at the time. Rock music's infrastructure wasn't yet in place. The new American FM stations programming "free-form radio," which began playing album tracks as an antidote to the AM Top Forty, were still confined to progressive cities like San Francisco and Boston and a few college towns. The rock press was in its infancy, with only the *Village Voice* in New York and the new *Rolling Stone* in San Francisco writing seriously about rock music. If *The Doors* was slow to find its place in the emerging counterculture, it was only because it was actually helping to create the culture while trying to infiltrate it at the same instant.

Jim Morrison was extremely interested when an Elektra promo man mentioned to him that the American military had ordered an unusually large shipment of *The Doors*, to be sold at the post exchanges in Vietnam. It was a signal of the future.

THE HUMAN BE-IN

ON THURSDAY, January 5, 1967, the Doors drove up to San Francisco to play two weekends at the Fillmore Auditorium. Bill Graham, the Fillmore's famous impresario, had booked the Doors unheard, after seeing Jim Morrison's publicity photo. Joel Brodsky had made Jim look like a Greek god, and Graham bought into it. Graham worshipped

Mick Jagger, the epitome of the savvy rock star, and often told associates he wanted to find the American Rolling Stones. Maybe this was it. (Jac Holzman later claimed he had to plead with Graham to book the Doors, for scale wages that barely covered their plane tickets.)

San Francisco was the place where Jim's childhood had been the happiest, and he had someone drive him over to the Morrisons' old house in Alameda. San Francisco in 1967 seemed to be reinventing American civilization as an Aquarian community with a cohesive new culture. The city had new ideas about art, poetry, music, philosophy, communal housing, organic food, LSD, and other drugs. Free community services like health care and meals were provided by millenarian groups like the Diggers. Bands like the Dead and the Airplane lived together in old Victorian houses. The Haight-Ashbury hippies, the Berkeley radicals, and the Black Panther party in Oakland were all bent on new worlds, and new ways of living in them. The music scene was becoming famous with its light shows, tribal dancers, and magical, transpersonal agenda.

At the Fillmore, opening for the Young Rascals and Sopwith Camel, the Doors premiered a new show with the dramatic "When the Music's Over," and then crashed straight into "Break On Through." Robby's flamenco solo "Spanish Caravan" in the second set was followed by a long blues jam on "Crawling King Snake." The band was well received and Bill Graham told the Doors they could play the Fillmore whenever they wanted.

But Jim vanished the following weekend. The Doors were again on the bill at the Fillmore, appearing with the Grateful Dead and Chicago bluesman Junior Wells's band. On Friday night, as showtime approached, the Doors' road crew—Robby's brother Ron and teenage Long Beach surfer Bill Siddons—was dispatched to try and find him, but Jim never showed up for the gig. The Fillmore was in a tough black neighborhood, and some worried Jim had been mugged by local gangs. Furious, Bill Graham had to offer refunds to the Doors' fans.

The next day, Jim walked into Graham's office above the Fillmore marquee and apologized sheepishly, saying he'd been with a girl in Sacramento, had gotten drunk, and sat through three screenings of *Casablanca*. Graham, somewhat charmed by Jim's sober sincerity, courtly deference, and devastating eyes, managed to stifle his eruptive temper. Graham had a kind of worshipful crush on Jim. "He was *it* for me," Bill later said. "He had *that* face, and he had *that* voice, and he wrote *those* songs. And no underwear! *Very* powerful statement." The Doors played their best for Bill Graham that night. During Robby's flamenco solo, when the strings seemed to turn to *kif* smoke, Jim fell to his knees to watch Robby's fingers as they flew across his red Gibson guitar.

Elektra promo man Steve Harris later claimed that in San Francisco Jim tried to enlist him in a death hoax publicity stunt. "He took me aside and said, 'I've got a great idea. Let's tell everyone I'm *dead.*' And I said, '*Great* idea, Jim, except that nobody knows who you are yet.'"

Jim Morrison was impatient for fame, as if he instinctively knew his time was short. "Jim never thought we were big enough," Robby Krieger said. "He thought we should be at least as big as the Stones. It *never* happened fast enough for him. He kept saying, like, 'Why isn't it *faster*? Look at the Beatles, man—*swoosh,* straight up!'"

ON A BRIGHT WINTER SATURDAY, January 14, Jim and his crew joined thirty thousand Bay Area freaks at the idyllic "Great Human Be-In" held at Golden Gate Park. This festival, billed as the Gathering of the Tribes, jump-started what became the "Summer of Love" and united different sectors of the counterculture for the first time, bringing flower children into contact with the antiwar people, the poets, and the bikers—members of the Hell's Angels, who famously provided what little security was needed by the placid throng.

Jim stayed near the stage and saw many of the major local bands— the Dead, the Airplane, Country Joe and the Fish, the Charlatans, Quicksilver Messenger Service. Dizzy Gillespie led a big jazz band, and between acts the city's champion poets held the huge crowd spellbound. Allen Ginsberg chanted mantras and sang, "Peace in America, peace in Vietnam." Gary Snyder, Lawrence Ferlinghetti, and Lenore Kandel declaimed. Timothy Leary read his psychedelic prayers. Alan Watts spoke about Zen. Michael McClure performed his spiky blank verse. Jim and some others dropped acid and wondered among the flower children on a trippy day that proved to be the prototype for the massive rock festivals that were to dominate pop culture later in the decade.

Jim was impressed, and inspired. "The city is looking for a ritual to join its fragments," he told an interviewer soon after this. "The Doors are looking for such a ritual too—a sort of electric wedding."

ON JANUARY 18, 1967, Jim flew to New York. The next night the Doors began their second residency at Ondine. Wearing a striped shirt and rumpled jeans, Jim launched into "When the Music's Over" for a packed house unfamiliar with the song because it wasn't on the album. The hip crowd stopped dancing and listened raptly to the first ecology rock song—*"What have you done to the earth?"*—that ended in the apocalyptic scream for salvation and release. Ninety minutes later, after a stupendous, unusually uptempo set and during the volcanic climax of "The End," Jim launched himself upward in a contortion of incestuous rage—and smashed his head on the club's very low ceiling. For five seconds he seemed dazed, and then he collapsed. The girls in front thought it was part of the show. But then Ray noticed Jim looked funny, so the roadies dragged him off the stage, and he managed to recover in the dressing room—later scoring a revivifying blow job from an attractive Warholite of whose actual sex no one in New York was certain.

One night Tandy Martin showed up at Ondine, having heard the buzz about the Doors. She hadn't seen Jim since he graduated from high school. Now married to the poetry editor of the underground weekly *The East Village Other*, Tandy had reached Jim on the phone, and he promised to leave her name at the door. He didn't, and she had to pay her way in: four dollars, with a five-dollar drink minimum. When she found Jim in the club, he smiled blankly and looked right through her, telling her he had a business meeting with some people in the VIP area, and that he'd catch up with her later. He didn't. She left the club after the last set, feeling very strange.

This second Ondine gig began the Doors' love affair with the underground press. In the *Village Voice* the influential music critic Richard Goldstein rhapsodized about the mystery and drama surrounding Jim Morrison, the Doors' walking phallic symbol. The fanzine *Crawdaddy* praised the Doors for their energy, zeal, and what editor Paul Williams identified as an authentic passion sadly lacking in the other American bands of the day. (Jim paid close attention to this, and also asked the staff at Elektra's New York office to let him have all his fan mail, which he pored over in total fascination. Jim personally answered letters that piqued his interest.)

Between sets, an unusually attentive Andy Warhol was whispering to Jim and cajoling in his passive-aggressive manner, still trying to get Jim to get naked on camera. Warhol lackey Eric Emerson found girls to spend the night with Jim at the Albert Hotel, on Tenth Street and Fifth Avenue. A few days later, Jim brought along Tandy Martin as his date to dinner with Jac Holzman and his family at Holzman's rosewood-paneled apartment on West Twelfth Street, and seemed to enjoy amusing Holzman's son, Adam. Jim chose to get along with Jac Holzman, whose regal bearing and industry mystique earned a measure of respect that Jim accorded few others.

AFTER TEN DAYS in New York, the Doors were back at Gazzarri's on the Strip. On February 11, 1967, Jim was arrested for public intoxication after taunting cops outside the Whisky. Then the Doors played two nights at the new Whisky franchise in San Francisco, which featured topless go-go girls. People who were around Jim every day began to notice that he was taking LSD much less, and starting to drink a lot more.

All this time, he was writing down the songs he heard in his head—*People are strange, when you're a stranger*—that became the raw material of *Strange Days.*

Then, on February 18, it was back to the Hullabaloo on Sunset and Vine, which during the swing era had been the Moulin Rouge. That night, Jim once again intersected with lovely Pam Miller, who was still (sort of) a virgin, but definitely hot to trot.

As a nascent rock courtesan, soon to be a founder of the notorious Zappa-affiliated groupie clique the GTOs (Girls Together Outrageously), Miss Pamela had recently learned about sound checks, and had arrived at the club's back door around four o'clock. She could hear the Doors testing their equipment and sound levels inside. Wearing a black-and-white-striped bell-bottomed ensemble of her own design, clutching her replenished glass jug of Trimar, she waited expectantly, hoping Jim Morrison might arrive, without his redheaded girlfriend. Sure enough, Jim showed up at five, scooped up Miss Pamela, took her backstage, and began what used to be known as "heavy petting," alternated with liberal doses of Trimar. "I melted in his mouth like honey," she later wrote. "My whole body became sticky liquid, and his fingers on my face pushed holes through my cheeks like they were on fire and left gaping holes where more honey gushed out."

Someone called Jim to the stage, and Pam sat there awhile, trying to come to her senses, while Jim did his vocal sound check.

When Jim returned, he took Miss Pamela's hand and led her up a rickety ladder to a dark loft in the rafters above the club floor. Old spotlights rusted in the corner. Jim took Miss Pam's raggedy muskrat jacket, spread it on the floor, and started in on her. "Jim, honey, I'm still a virgin," she managed to gasp.

"What a face he had," she later said. "One of God's greatest gifts to rock and roll was that guy's face. And there he was, right above me, his lips parted and his eyes closed, going in and out of focus. . . ."

Then, through their mutual Trimar fog, somewhere far below them, they heard the opening bars of "When the Music's Over." Jim sat up. "Hey—*shit!*—I'm on!" He laughed, and zipped down the ladder as if it were a fire pole. Miss Pam followed him and suddenly found herself onstage with the Doors before a packed Hullabaloo as Jim let out the psychotic scream that began the song. Someone reached over and yanked her off the stage, and she watched Jim go full throttle into a perfectly pitched club set.

Afterward, at two in the morning, Jim drove her around Hollywood in her dented Oldsmobile. She cuddled up next to him, like they were going steady. She says he told her his whole rock star persona was just an act, and that he wanted to be known as a poet. He said the Trimar was "hurting our heads," and on their way to get something to eat at Tiny Naylor's on La Brea, he pulled the car over and threw the Trimar bottle out the window. "Now we won't be tempted," he told her. They ate date nut bread and fresh orange juice as the sun rose over the hills, and then cruised over to a cheap motel where Jim was staying because, he said, he was fighting with his girlfriend. Miss Pamela: "After some more necking, he climbed from behind the wheel and said, 'I really want to see you again, darlin'. Come here and see me, or call me—anytime.'

"But when I called, he had checked out. What a drag."

THE MATRIX TAPES

THE DOORS WORKED REGULARLY around L.A. in February 1967, playing mostly at Gazzarri's and the Hullabaloo. On February 22 they played a benefit in the Valley with the Byrds and Buffalo Springfield to raise money for a group working to resolve the tensions between the police and the kids on the Strip. Long-haired kids on their way to the show in Woodland Hills were harassed and arrested by the cops, duly noted by Jim Morrison in sarcastic, antiauthoritarian remarks from the stage.

One of the shows at Gazzarri's drew praise from the *Los Angeles Times,* the first time the band was mentioned in the mainstream press. Noting the "vibrant" band's dramatic impact on the packed house of dancing kids, the writer elicited a quote from Jim that their music was "primitive and personal."

In March the Doors relocated to San Francisco, where they stayed in a cheap motel. At the Avalon Ballroom, playing with Country Joe and Sparrow, Jim led the Doors through some of the earliest public performances of "Moonlight Drive," the haunting song Jim had first sung to Ray on the beach in Venice. The song now had a semi-improv midsection known as "You got fishes for your friends." Jim was also playing harmonica on "Back Door Man," but with no musical talent to rely on, he could only manage a series of off-tempo bleats and squawks as he tried to play along with the guitar. The show was taped by the Avalon, providing the Doors' earliest known concert recordings that survive.

They stayed in Frisco after the gig to play five nights at the Matrix, the small music club part-owned by Airplane singer Marty Balin. The Matrix was licensed for only a hundred, so the Doors' shows there in early March 1967 were relatively low key. Jim and the band used the club and the progressive vibes of the city to work out new material and indeed a new sound. The Doors had been together for almost a year and a half, and Jim, in conversation with Ray, felt they needed another, more bluesy direction. (Jim was also influenced by having recently seen Canned Heat, the L.A. blues-rock band founded a year earlier by record collectors Bob Hite and Al Wilson. Canned Heat played potent, updated versions of old Skip James Delta blues songs, and Jim loved their nonaura of street clothes, beards, and total commitment to a pure representation of old blues material.)

At the Matrix the Doors tried some new stuff, the way they had workshopped their songs at the Whisky a year before. So their laconic sets were sprinkled with slack R & B jams, with lyrics ad-libbed by Jim. He adapted vocal riffs from Lee Dorsey's "Get Out of My Life Woman" and interpolated an original lyric, "The Devil Is a Woman," whose title recalls one of von Sternberg's greatest films. With Jim spinning his own ideas into old songs, they churned through "King Bee," "King Snake," "Who Do You Love?" (uptempo, with slithery guitar and a poignant aside, crooned by Jim: "Do you love him? Do you love him? *Do you?*").

There's little doubt Jim knew that, while he was out of town, his woman was fucking his drinking buddy Tom Baker back at the green house in Laurel Canyon. Pam would've made sure Jim heard about it, because she was obviously paying him back for something he'd done to her. This was a deliberately public affair on her part, flaunted on the Strip, with semilewd public displays of affection, and it provoked much comment in L.A. groupie circles. "Get out of my life, woman," the song went. "You don't love me no more."

Jim was no saint either. The band was evicted from their motel when Jim was caught sneaking a (very) underage girl out his room, where she had spent the night giving Jim a leisurely bath, in which he fell asleep.

JIM BEGAN PREMIERING NEW SONGS at the Matrix, and changing others inside out, with newly written poems and illuminations. The great "People Are Strange," written by Jim on a Laurel Canyon hilltop near the house John and Robby shared, was first performed there. "Unhappy Girl" was given a loving and vengeful reading. The surviving tapes of these shows document Jim inserting new poetic "routines" in the middle of set pieces. "When the Music's Over" was bisected by two of these, "Who Scared You?" and "Everything Will Be Reported. (At night your dreams will be recorded.)" The molten climax of "The End" was prolonged with two pieces Jim repeated several times that spring: "Fall Down Now, Strange Gods Are Approaching" and—just after he kills his father:

"*Can you stand by and watch the pictures burn? Grab these ashes for your face. Keep the incense burning pure. The flames eat higher on the walls. This is the end of all we're fond of—all those times that matter.*" The drummer dropped a bomb. "*Mother? I want to . . .*"

JIM STAYED ON THE ROAD during Pamela's wild fling as the Doors flew east for their third stint as house band at Ondine for three weeks in March 1967. By all accounts Jim was raging and hellacious, delivering blistering performances that began with "Back Door Man" before exploding into "Break On Through." These were some of the Doors' finest club shows, and they needed to be because Elektra was now bringing the press to hear them. Jim Morrison, raw with conflicting emotions about his old lady and his friend, screamed in jealous rage and blue murder. No one in New York had ever seen anything quite like it.

The press went for it, big time. The trade magazines—*Cash Box, Billboard, Record World*—rhapsodized. Richard Goldstein made critical love to Jim in the *Village Voice,* calling his material "literate, concise, and terrifying." The Doors, Goldstein wrote, "are worshipped, envied, and bandied about like the Real Thing. The word is out—the Doors will floor you." Andy Warhol was there almost every night at the beginning, still hoping to get Jim to star in his new film.

Jim seemed visibly upset, and was drinking a lot. He ran up a huge liquor tab at Ondine. He was sexually rapacious, trying to fuck everyone who came his way. In his memoir *POPism,* Warhol described Jim getting jerked off at the bar at Ondine by young girls while firing down screwdrivers and downers. There were many nights that Warhol's people had to carry out Jim of the club and get him back to the pad on West Fortyfifth Street where he was staying. There was also an often-repeated story that a carousing Jim Morrison, stinko drunk and tripping, tried to batter down Jac Holzman's apartment door at four in the morning, while the label boss and his family cowered inside. People who claim to have been there say that Jim then puked in the building's elevator. But Holzman insists this never happened, and couldn't have, because a drunken Jim Morrison would *never* have gotten past a night-shift New York doorman.

Jim spent a lot of time on the phone, talking to Pam, which made him crazier. It was probably in this climate that—when the Doors management insisted he not appear nude onscreen—Jim sent Tom Baker in his place to the set of *Fuck* as a kind of cosmic joke on Warhol, Baker, and himself.

LITTLE RED SILK HEART

IN APRIL 1967 THE DOORS played all over California every weekend, trying to pull off their rock theatrics in Legion halls, hockey rinks, and fairgrounds from Fresno to Merced. On April 9 they played the L.A. version of the Cheetah on the Santa Monica Pier with the Jefferson Airplane. The band had been away for a month, so it was like a homecoming for the Doors fans, who packed the 3,800-seat club. It was the Doors' first big indoor crowd, so Jim premiered a new piece of stage business, balancing on the lip of the stage as if it were a tightrope while the band played the solos of "Light My Fire." Jim got the same thrill from this as he got from his human-fly exploits on apartment balconies and roofs of tall buildings. The crowd had its stress level ratcheted up as they wondered whether Jim would fall. He did, losing his balance during the guitar solo and tumbling about eight feet, but the fall was broken by the surprised teenage girls he landed on.

JIM RECONCILED WITH PAMELA COURSON. They were careful to be seen around town together, and acted very lovey-dovey. They swore mutual love and trust in her dark little pad, and he bought her a bunch of stuff she wanted, mostly clothes and guns (she was collecting Luger pistols). She embroidered a scarlet silk heart on the bottom of her jeans, just over her anus, which the local gossips interpreted as a public statement of what her old man had in mind when they were alone together.

Pam reveled in her persona as Jim Morrison's old lady, once again calling herself Mrs. Morrison. She was getting stronger now that she had Jim by the balls. She was arrogant, fearless, daunting in private, shy in public, daring, and funny around people she knew well. She was spending Jim's money and enjoying it. She was rumored to be dabbling in heroin provided by her sometime boyfriend—"a *real* French count," Pam insisted, though few actually believed it.

Meanwhile, Jim was brooding, and seemed very down. He was quiet to the point of being morose. To Mirandi Babitz, who was making him a pair of vinyl jeans and had to measure the inseam of his leg, Jim said he thought he was ugly, and could never live up to his publicity photos. Babitz thought Jim Morrison was clinically depressed.

Jim didn't take Pamela to screenwriter Gavin Lambert's big party for Andy Warhol in Santa Monica Canyon. It was a Young Hollywood crowd, with oddball musician Tiny Tim performing for movie stars Warren Beatty, Julie Christie, and Tuesday Weld (whom Warhol was dying to meet). Jim met director Roman Polanski and his stoned starlet wife, Sharon Tate. Janis Joplin—the hot, gravel-voiced singer of Big Brother and the Holding Company—was there, too, dressed in handmade crushed velvet clothes and peacock feathers, holding her trademark bottle of Southern Comfort.

Jim sat down next to Janis and threw his arm around her. He was drinking scotch. Jim asked Janis about herself, and she blurted a few phrases about her troubled high school years in Texas, where she had been mocked and shunned because her family wasn't well off. After an hour, and after many more drinks and some pills, just as Janis was laughing a little too raucously at something Jim had said, he grabbed her by her hair and suddenly forced her face down into his crotch.

It was an awful moment. People near them backed off. Furious at this humiliation, Janis hit Jim in the face and walked away, calling him an asshole over her shoulder. "I *know* I'm an asshole," he said to her back.

Later, as she was leaving, an even drunker Jim stopped her car in the driveway and tried to speak to her. Witnesses said she rolled down her window and, when Jim bent down to apologize, she smashed her Southern Comfort bottle over his head before driving off, cursing him.

Much later, after everyone else had left the party, they had to put an incoherent Jim Morrison in a cab.

* * *

APRIL 1967. The Doors played the psychedelic Avalon Ballroom in San Francisco with the Steve Miller Band, then a gig at Taft High in the San Fernando Valley. They did shows at the Kaleidoscope, a new Sunset Strip rock club where Ciro's had been. At an April 29 gig with the Grateful Dead in Santa Barbara, the Dead's sound engineer and acid alchemist Owsley Stanley III (the father of so-called "designer drugs") presented Jim Morrison with a bag filled with tabs of artisanal "Purple Haze" LSD-25.

This was a meaningful gesture, the Dead being a closed society that rarely bothered to acknowledge nonmembers. But Jim was almost through with acid, and gave most of Owsley's stuff to whoever was backstage later in the night.

MEANWHILE *THE DOORS* WAS STALLED, midcharts. Radio people told Elektra they needed a Top Forty version of "Light My Fire," so Paul Rothchild cut tape at Sunset Sound, surgically removing five minutes of tedious instrumental solos and dumbing down Robby Krieger's melodic plea for transcendence to an AM-friendly two minutes and fifty seconds. The Doors heard this at a listening session and had no objection.

Elektra released the "Light My Fire" single, with "Crystal Ship" on the flip side, on May 1, 1967. It was the perfect record for the summer of 1967, the epochal Summer of Love, and launched the Doors into a stratospheric orbit that not even a visionary like Jim Morrison could have foreseen.

Around this time, Jim began to seriously wonder about what he was doing. "Here's what disturbed me," he later told Jerry Hopkins. "I went to a movie one night in Westwood [Arthur Penn's *Bonnie and Clyde*], and then I was in a bookstore, or some shop where they sell pottery and calendars and gadgets, you know? And a very attractive, intelligent— intelligent in the sense of aware and open—girl thought she recognized me, and she came to say hello. And she was asking me about this partic- ular song ['The End']. She was just out for a little stroll with a nurse, on leave just for an hour or so from the UCLA Neuropsychiatric Unit. She lived there, and was just out for a walk. Apparently she had been a student at UCLA and freaked on heavy drugs or something, and either committed herself, or someone picked up on her and put her there. Anyway, she said that that song was really a favorite of a lot of kids in her ward.

"At first I thought: 'Oh, man . . .' and this was after I talked with her for a while, telling her ['The End'] could mean a lot of things, kind of a maze, or a puzzle to think about. Everybody should relate to their own situation. *I didn't realize people took songs so seriously.* And it made me wonder—if I ought to consider the consequences. And that's kind of ridiculous, because . . . you don't think of the consequences [when writing songs], and you can't."

The Doors began recording their second album with Paul Rothchild and engineer Bruce Botnick at Sunset Sound in May 1967. They worked on "People Are Strange" and a new version of "When the Music's Over." Poet Michael McClure, deeply impressed by the visionary poetics of the Doors' album, visited during the sessions and exchanged phone numbers with Jim. The Doors then went back on the road, only returning to the studio later in the summer after it had upgraded to eight tracks from four. Jim and Pamela went to see the L.A. production of McClure's play *The Beard,* in which Dennis Hopper, as Billy the Kid, tore off Jean Harlow's panties and pretended to pleasure her with his mouth—in heaven. Unlike in San Francisco, the local vice squad didn't intervene.

Jimi Hendrix's *Are You Experienced* was the hot music of the moment. A notebook of Jim's records the titles of movies that he probably saw: *Blow-Up, The Graduate, Point Blank, The Battle of Algiers.* The same journal, quoting Marshall McLuhan's best-selling tract *The Medium Is the Massage,* notes: "Use the medium as a narrative device."

In May, the Doors played the Whisky for six nights, their first appearance in the club since they'd been fired as its house band eight months earlier. They were supposed to open for the Byrds, but the great band was now in disarray and Jim McGuinn canceled. (Buffalo Springfield was booked instead.) Jim Morrison, wearing a new black leather suit on opening night, seemed loaded to the gills, distracted and baked. During the instrumentals he leaned hard on his mike stand, like it was his life support. He only seemed to come to life when it was time for one of his deeply anguished screams.

The Doors played the Whisky for the last time on May 21, 1967. "Light My Fire" was everywhere on the radio now, climbing the charts, a huge national hit. Soon the Doors would be too big to play any more club-sized venues in California. It was a whole new era.

A LIFE FORCE BLOODY BUT SERENE

IAN WHITCOMB WAS A BRITISH INVASION has-been at twenty-six. He had one hit record in America, "You Turn Me On," a breathy pop song with a sexy stutter that was a big jam at gay parties and went Top Ten in 1965—and then: nothing. But he relocated to L.A. because it was where the action was, and a real Brit could get on the pop TV shows. He put himself under the mentorship of George Sherlock, who'd supposedly been the model for the Rolling Stones' "Under Assistant West Coast Promo Man," and waited for something good to happen. Nothing ever did.

In the summer of 1967 Whitcomb woke up in his cheap motel. He had just been home to England, and now he was asking himself why he was back in hell. Still in his pajamas, he grabbed a book and waddled over to the nearby Copper Skillet, an all-night coffee shop at Sunset and Gower. He took a stool at the counter, ordered breakfast, and opened his book. A minute later, someone said, in a hoarse, faintly southern voice: "I can quote the whole of that poem you're readin'."

It was Jim, in full leathers, with bushy muttonchop whiskers growing down his cheeks. Whitcomb had seen him in the magazines, and of course knew that he currently ruled radio. Jim was recognizable, but looked slept-in, exhausted, and very used. "The eyes let him down," Whitcomb remembered. "Beyond the broodiness, they were empty. He looked like a hero from *Classics Illustrated*." Jim was eating an open-faced meat-loaf sandwich, and also had a book open. He was, Whitcomb observed, not inattentive to the stares of some of the male patrons, in a neighborhood with a sizable gay population.

Whitcomb: "Beyond the boy hustler appearance, I could sense good breeding. He was holding his knife and fork in the British manner, and his voice was polite and assured. And I could see that sure sign of civilization: an open book." Jim was reading Nietzsche's *The Romantic Anxiety*.

Too hip to try pop chat on Jim Morrison, Whitcomb ventured: "It's a pompous title, but I've always been fascinated by late Victorian sexuality."

"Me too," Jim said. "You want me to prove I'm not bullshitting you?"

"Come again?"

"Want me to recite that poem?"

"Fire away, old bean." And, to Whitcomb's muted astonishment, up-and-coming rock star Jim Morrison closed his eyes and perfectly chanted Piers Brighton's morbid 1897 poem:

> *A sturdy lad of seventeen summers hung*
> *From an old oak in his death among*
> *The hollyhocks and oleanders his frame*
> *Though arrow-pierced took on a purple flame*
> *That fitted him so natural in this scene*
> *He seemed a life force bloody and serene*

Two cruising middle-aged men checked them out, these two young guys in fetish leathers and pajamas.

"They like you," Whitcomb teased.

"No, they like *you*," Jim said. Then he shrugged. "I guess they like us both."

Whitcomb then went for broke. He was decidedly over, and Jim was the Next Big Thing. "Tell me, how do you do it?" he asked Jim. He didn't think Jim knew who he was.

"I never dug Gerry and the Pacemakers," Jim drawled. And then: "Do what?"

"How do you stay an intellectual—and still be a hit with the kids?"

Jim thought for a minute, and looked at his now-cold meat loaf before answering.

"I saw you on *Shindig* and *Lloyd Thaxton* [a syndicated TV show], and you were like—*goofing off*, telling the audience that rock and roll was a big joke. You were too comic. You have to be *tragic*, man. Western civilization is fucking going down the tubes, and we don't even need an earthquake to finish it. We're performing music for the final dance of death and . . . Aw, shit. You know what? Truth lies beyond the grave. C'mon, I'll get the check."

*   *   *

IN JUNE 1967, the Beatles released *Sgt. Pepper's Lonely Hearts Club Band,* a "concept album." This wasn't just a random collection of tunes, but a unified program of related pieces by a rock group pretending to be an old-fashioned music hall band giving a concert. *Sgt. Pepper* was a numinous mass-cult artifact that brought psychedelia into the mainstream and took over Western youth culture that summer. The Beatles' album ruled the charts—until it was knocked off by the Doors, later in the Summer of Love.

The rip-roaring Doors were now at the top of their form. Before another trip to San Francisco and New York, they played the Hullabaloo on June 8. When the club's revolving stage wheeled the Doors out, the audience—mostly girls—began screaming and firing off their flash Instamatics. White light, white heat: Jim moaned a disgusting grunt to open "Back Door Man" and the chicks jammed up to the stage like wriggling fish. Jim got himself hard with the mike stand, and the girls in front moaned like they were in heat.

Halfway through a supercharged performance, Jim tripped on a wire and fell down. The girls thought it was part of "Break On Through" and screamed louder. Jim got up and started smashing the mike stand down hard on the stage floor. Then he knocked it down and stomped on it until it bent. Up again like a fallen enemy, then down with more savage kicks. The girls should have been scared, but they just looked on in utterly dazed wonderment. The club had to find a new microphone and stand so Jim could finish the show.

The next night, the Doors were back at the Fillmore, mother of all electric ballrooms, closing the show for the first time. (Opening were singer Richie Havens and the Jim Kweskin Jug Band.) Jim was late, and arrived drunk. Bill Graham yelled at Jim, who ignored him, which enraged Graham even more. During the "Light My Fire" solos, Jim began to twirl his microphone at the end of its cord, like an electric lariat, coming perilously close to the heads of the audience, which was riveted in suspense at the danger. Graham charged toward the stage to make Jim stop, just as Jim "accidentally" let go. The mike smashed Graham in the head, raising an ugly bruise and the already elevated temperature of Graham's ego.

Jim Morrison's high school yearbook picture, spring 1961. (ARCHIVE OF ROCK)

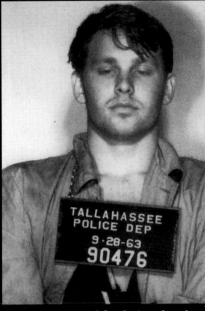

Jim was arrested for being drunk and disorderly while at Florida State University, September 1963. (ARCHIVE OF ROCK)

Jim acting onstage in Harold Pinter's *The Dumbwaiter,* at Florida State, autumn 1963. (ARCHIVE OF ROCK)

The Doors model new Mod outfits in New York, November 1966.
(MICHAEL OCHS ARCHIVE)

Early Doors publicity photo, Los Angeles 1966.
(MICHAEL OCHS ARCHIVE)

The Doors rock Steve Paul's Scene, New York 1967.
(DON PAULSEN / MICHAEL OCHS ARCHIVE)

Both photographs: Jim Morrison at full throttle at the Crosstown Bus, Boston, July 1967. (PETER SIMON)

Jim and friends on Sunset Strip, spring 1967. (MICHAEL OCHS ARCHIVE)

Legendary chanteuse Nico, with whom Jim enjoyed a tempestuous affair during the summer of 1967.
(MICHAEL OCHS ARCHIVE)

POLICE DEPT
NEW HAVEN CONN
23750

Jim Morrison was arrested onstage for giving an obscene performance in New Haven, Connecticut, in December 1967. (ARCHIVE OF ROCK)

Jim Morrison began performing in a leather suit in mid-1967.
(DON PAULSEN / MICHAEL OCHS ARCHIVE)

The Doors toured Europe in the fall of 1968. Here they tape a TV show outdoors in Frankfurt, Germany. (MICHAEL MONTFORT / MICHAEL OCHS ARCHIVE)

Jim urging the crowd up to the stage in Stockholm, Sweden.
(MICHAEL OCHS ARCHIVE)

Jim Morrison and Pamela Courson, summer 1968.
(EDMUND TESKE / MICHAEL OCHS ARCHIVE)

Jim Morrison after one of his violent stage dives, Frankfurt, 1968.
(MICHAEL MONTFORT / MICHAEL OCHS ARCHIVE)

After the show, Graham threw everyone else out of the band's dressing room and began to howl at Jim: *"ARE YOU OUT OF YOUR FUCKING MIND?"* The adrenaline and sweat of a good Doors show usually sobered Jim up, and so he apologized to Graham with a show of sincerity that couldn't quite hide an annoying delinquent's smirk. "Yeah, you're right, you know? I got to be more careful. Wow... you know?"

A week later in San Francisco, Ray Manzarek put the stick of incense he lit to start every Doors show in the holder atop his organ. John Densmore tested his drums, and Robby Krieger splashed some Iberian electric guitar chords on the ten thousand freaks packed into the Mount Tamalpais Outdoor Theater. When Jim Morrison strolled onstage in a T-shirt, black vinyl trousers, sharp-toed boots, and long curls, the crowd let out a shattering roar. The Doors tore into "When the Music's Over" amid general rapture.

Jim usually hated performing in the daylight, but this afternoon show was part of pioneering FM radio station KRFC's "Fantasy Faire and Magic Festival," a two-day outdoor party, showcasing more than twenty acts, including Moby Grape, Canned Heat (whose set was watched by Jim), the 13th Floor Elevators, the Airplane, the reconstituted Byrds, Tim Buckley, Smokey Robinson and the Miracles, Tim Hardin, and many others. Hell's Angels sat next to hippies and Berkeley fraternity guys as Jim worked hard to put the Doors' midnight trance over on a sunny afternoon. He displayed his shaman's dance during the solos, and amused the crowd by climbing the flagpoles on either side of the stage. By the climax of "The End," Jim had the audience hypnotized. The cheering and applause they rained on the Doors when Jim released them from his spell seemed equal parts genuine gratitude and relief.

The Mount Tamalpais concerts would have been remembered today as the first big rock festival if they hadn't been eclipsed by the Monterey Pop Festival the following weekend. This was a sore point for the Doors, because while they were in San Francisco the Monterey lineup was still fluid and the subject of frantic lobbying by managers who wanted their bands to appear alongside Jimi Hendrix, the Who, Ravi Shankar, Otis Redding, and other major international stars. Brian Jones would be introducing Hendrix. Everyone would be there—except the Doors, who were shut out because Lou "Folk Rock" Adler, one of the organizers, had a long memory of being dissed by Jim Morrison after rejecting their demo two years before.

Elektra and the Doors' clueless managers frantically worked the phones, almost begging, reminding everyone that "Light My Fire" was about to go to number one. They were told, flat out, that *no way* was that drama-queen punk Jim Morrison playing Monterey.

So the Doors flew east instead, and played some of the defining shows of their entire career.

EROTIC POLITICIANS

IN EARLY JUNE 1967, the Doors boarded a night flight to New York, where they made their bones with a series of blistering performances that stunned everyone lucky enough to see them.

The first of these took place on Sunday night, June 11, at the Village Theater on Second Avenue (which became the Fillmore East after Bill Graham bought the old Lower East Side vaudeville house later that year). WOR-FM was celebrating its first anniversary of programming free-form album cuts with a cavalcade of acts including the Blues Project, the Chambers Brothers, and Janis Ian. The audience went nuts when Jim strolled onstage, and the sound was cranked so high for this important showcase that the walls of the old theater actually shook. Jim pulled out all the stops—the neo-Artaud rock theater, the shaman's hop, his most mellifluous baritone croon on "I Can't See Your Face," the blood-boiling screams. Richard Goldstein wrote, "His hand cupped pillowlike over his ear, Morrison's pudgy cherub face curls into a bristling lip. He stands like a creature out of Kenneth Anger, then sidles up to the mike, curls around its head, and belts."

When the faulty microphone began feeding back during "People Are Strange," Jim started twisting it so the static became a percussion track. After a stunning performance of "The End," with Jim dancing in dervish whorls while the band burned in Arabic modes behind him, the tough New York crowd gave the Doors a standing ovation. A few even yelled *Bravo,* like they'd been to the opera.

The Doors kept up their offensive the next night, the first of an extended run at Steve Paul's Scene that would last through most of June 1967. The Scene was a basement club at Forty-sixth Street and Eighth Avenue, an underground warren that catered to Manhattan's nascent rock elite and visiting English stars like Paul McCartney and Brian Jones. Jimi Hendrix often arrived late with his guitar and jammed all night. Beginning June 12, the Scene was packed with new Doors fans excited by the incredible buzz from the Village Theater concert.

The Doors bore down. They played really loud, and seemed to speed up their show, playing "Light My Fire" much faster than on the record. "Soul Kitchen" and "Back Door Man" cooked with rhythmic white mojo. During the "Back Door Man" interlude, Jim began improvising lines that developed into "Five to One," and whispered an eyes-closed reverie (later known as "Coda Queen") about being seduced by a young girl in Florida, after school, when her parents weren't home. *"I didn't want to do it,"* he repeated, night after night.

PAMELA COURSON FLEW TO NEW YORK, and stayed with Jim and the band at a hotel on West Fifty-seventh Street. Jim at this time—early summer 1967—was writing the beginnings of the long poem that became "Celebration of the Lizard," which he described as a cross between a theater piece and an electric ritual, developed with a sense of irony.

The Doors' shows in New York that month helped establish and validate the new rock music movement. Rock was different from rock and roll. Rock was virtuosic and adult, as opposed to popsy and teenaged. Rock and roll was apolitical and fun, while rock was "heavy" and often political, creating vistas of psychic energy that carried beyond the music itself, and into radical politics and art. The Doors' California base was still provincial in terms of mass communications, so before the Doors came to New York that June, no one in the national media had ever seen a rock singer like Jim Morrison offer a furious response to environmental pollution, such as in the "What have they done to the earth?" section of "When the Music's Over"—then still unreleased on record, but a crucial element of the band's live presentation. Jim Morrison's ecology rock made a deep impression.

The Doors also arrived in New York in time to reenergize the relatively small group of tastemakers who could promote their favorites into national attractions. Steve Paul, Gloria Stavers, Danny Fields, and Lillian Roxon were the core of the crucial promoters, publicists, editors, and writers who invented "Rock" as a media phenomenon, and they all liked the Doors. (These cynical New Yorkers also tended to dislike the sanctimonious San Francisco bands.) Key New York FM radio personalities like Rosco Mercer, Jonathan Schwartz, and Murray the K started adding Doors' album tracks to their playlists. And the Doors virtually begat rock criticism by bringing intelligence and depth to a scene dominated by often mindless psychedelia.

The rock pantheon—Dylan, Beatles, Stones, Beach Boys—had been static for two years. The Doors' new "rock theater," which now brought classical drama into play, opened new literary possibilities for the small but influential group writing professionally about pop. *Life* magazine's skeptical jazz critic, Albert Goldman, was so jazzed by the Doors that he switched from covering jazz to writing about pop, and praised Jim to the skies in the early issues of *New York* magazine. Jim virtually owned Richard Goldstein and Paul Williams, the two principal rock critics, who wrote about the Doors' lead singer as if he were a combination of Lord Byron and Sophocles. (These and other key critics had received, with their acetate test pressings of *The Doors,* little wooden boxes filled with hashish, courtesy of Elektra.) Critics Mike Jahn and Michael Lydon were unusually friendly to the Doors in the *New York Times.*

As soon as quote factory Jim Morrison began giving interviews, "think pieces" about the Doors and Rock Theater began appearing in the press, garlanded with poetic epigrams that were carefully strung together by Jim like love beads.

"We're really politicians. You could call us *erotic* politicians."

"We're primarily a rock and roll band, a blues band, just a band—but that's not all. A Doors concert is a public meeting called by us for a special kind of dramatic discussion and entertainment. When we perform, we're participating in the creation of a world, and we celebrate that creation with the audience. It becomes the sculpture of bodies in action. That's the political part, but our power is sexual. We make concerts sexual politics. The sex starts with me, then moves out to include the charmed circle of musicians onstage. The music we make goes out to the audience and interacts with them. They go home and interact with their reality, then I get it all back by interacting with that reality. So the whole sex thing works out to be one big ball of fire."

"I offer images. I conjure memories of... freedom. But we can only open doors; we can't drag people through."

"Our work, our performing, is a striving for metamorphosis. It's like a purification ritual, in the alchemical sense. First, you have to have the period of disorder, chaos; returning to a primeval disaster region. Out of that, you purify the elements, and find a new seed of life, which transforms *all* life, *all* matter, *all* personality—until, finally, hopefully, you emerge and marry all those dualisms and opposites. Then you're not talking about good and evil anymore, but about something unified and pure."

Jim could even make sense when he was dead drunk. Thoroughly loaded, Jim slurred his words in what was supposed to be a major interview with a nervous, intimidated Richard Goldstein. "See, the shaman... he was a man who would intoxicate himself. See, he was probably already an... ah... *unusual* individual. And, he would put himself into a trance by dancing, whirling around, drinking, taking drugs—however. Then he would go on a mental trip and... ah... describe his journey for the rest of the tribe."

Everyone who read this understood what Jim was saying: that the Doors were more than just an act, more than just a rock band. Jim was calling signals, and the wide receivers of the nascent rock culture definitely caught the ball.

Asked two years later about the marketing of "erotic politicians" and other, almost copywritten quotes, Jim recalled: "I was aware of the national media while growing up. They were always around the house, so I started reading them. And so I became aware of their style, their approach to reality. When I got into the music field, I was interested in securing a place in that world, and so I was 'tuning keys'—and I just instinctively knew how to do it. They look for catchy phrases, and quotes they can use for captions, something to base an article on, to give it an immediate response. [Erotic politicians] is the kind of term that does mean something, but it's impossible to explain. If I tried to explain what it means to me, it would lose all its force as a catchword."

* * *

J IM WAS USUALLY LATE for Doors gigs, but he thought Steve Paul's "Noo Yawk" showbiz act was so funny, he told Densmore, that he often arrived early at the Scene just to hear Steve rap.

The Scene was a club where Jim felt he could hang tight, but loose. Jimi Hendrix came to see the Doors on June 14, on his way to make pyroguitar history at Monterey a few days later. Actor Paul Newman met with Jim about writing a song for a movie he was directing called *Rachel, Rachel.* (It didn't work out.) Tiny Tim, a tragically weird ukulele player (real name: Herbert Khaury) who frequently performed on Johnny Carson's *Tonight* show, often opened for the Doors at the Scene, and was even offered the chance to cover "People Are Strange" by Jim himself. (This also didn't work out.) One night a drunken Jim started up his microphone lariat trick during "Light My Fire." On one pass, he missed his drummer's head by an inch. Doors comanager Asher Dann grabbed Jim to make him stop, and Jim punched him in the face, drawing blood. They both ended up in a pile on the floor, and the show was over for the night.

"Light My Fire" was now huge, on the radio dial every minute. When the Doors asked for tickets to see the Butterfield Band play in Central Park, they were advised to come in separately, so they wouldn't be mobbed. (They made a point to come in as a group to see what happened, but they were unmolested.) Jim was now isolating himself from the band a bit more, taking long, solitary walks around the empty streets of lower Manhattan. One night Paul Rothchild and Elektra publicist Danny Fields took Jim out to a late dinner in the fabled back room of Max's Kansas City on Park Avenue South, the ground zero of Manhattan's downtown hipoisie. "Light My Fire" played incessantly on Max's jukebox, but no one—artists, models, musicians, dealers, industry heavies— bothered to look at Jim as he sauntered by in his leather trousers. (One could see this Manhattan cliché "rough trade" look on Christopher Street in the West Village any night of the week.) Friends of Paul's and Danny's came over to the table, but Jim refused to speak to anyone at Max's all night, a laconic pose that might have belied any reservations he had about the pace of his fame.

* * *

ANOTHER NIGHT the band and some friends were eating in Chinatown amid lots of beer and laughter. Suddenly Jim stopped eating and smiled moronically at Robby Krieger, who was chomping away, noisily, at the other end of the table.

"Jim, what are you doing?" Pamela asked.

"Everybody stop what you're doing," Jim said, "and smile at Robby." A minute passed, everyone smiling.

Pam: "Jim, *why* are we doing this?"

"I want to see . . . if he stops chewing . . . *with his mouth open,* and then smiles back at us—with his mouth open."

Krieger didn't care about being needled by Jim. He'd written "Light My Fire," and had already been told that Jim hated him for it, would never forgive him. Robby smiled back with his mouth open and full of half-chewed food. Everyone laughed. Jim just shook his head, because he had a thing about table manners.

Everyone noticed Jim wasn't happy when his old lady was around. With "Light My Fire" now in the top ten, all she could talk about was Jim buying her a house. She whined a lot, demanded all his attention, was pathologically shy in public, and even started putting down the band as being beneath Jim Morrison's true vocation as a poet and film-maker. No one could quite believe this, and there was general relief when Pamela Courson went back to L.A. in the middle of the month. Steve Paul closed the Scene during the weekend of the Monterey Festival, so Jim tried to call on his friend Nico for some large-scale Teutonic companionship, only to be told Nico was in Monterey, on the arm of Brian Jones. So Jim was depressed, and drinking much more than usual, when the Doors drove out to Long Island to play the Action House on Friday, June 16.

The Action House was a depressing dance club in Long Beach. They got there at four and went on at eight. Jim quickly downed a dozen shots of V.O. at the bar, and kept drinking until the show. The Doors' set then ended early when Bill Siddons (who'd been working as a roadie between semesters at Cal State before recently being hired full-time as the Doors' nineteen-year-old "scared to death" road manager) dragged Jim offstage as he was trying to unzip his tight vinyl pants in the throbbing heat of the crowded, sweltering club. Backstage John Densmore announced he was quitting the band—"I can't do this! I'm going home! I don't wanna do this shit anymore." No one took him seriously. The Doors was all he had. They were all in thrall to Jim, trapped in what Dr. Freud had famously termed "hostile dependency." They were fucked, and they all knew it.

The next day, Saturday, Jim started drinking in the late afternoon and was in a stupor by showtime. As the Doors swung into "Back Door Man," which sometimes could revive Jim when he was shitfaced, he started burping into the mike. Jim then swooned in an alcoholic coma, and had to be helped offstage. It was the shortest Doors performance on record. Bill Siddons later asked the bartender how many shots Jim had drunk before going on. Twenty-six, he was told. The old Action House record had been twenty one.

The next day, the three Doors loaded their gear in a rented VW minibus and prepared to drive to Philadelphia for that night's gig. They couldn't quite wake Jim, who had passed out in the leathers he'd been wearing at the Action House. So they walked him to the van, laid him across the organ and the amplifiers, and let him lapse back into a coma. He only woke up when the crew at Town Hall in Philadelphia opened the van's back door to outload the band's instruments. But Jim was stone brilliant that night. The small auditorium on North Market Street had only sold about a hundred tickets, but the Doors cranked out a loud, sweaty show. The finale of "The End" was so intense that the audience sat stunned in their seats for half an hour after the Doors walked off, buzzing and exhausted by the spiritual "public meeting" they'd been part of. You never knew what to expect when Jim Morrison was performing.

ACROSS THE COUNTRY, in the California desert near Palm Springs, Frank Sinatra was furious. Years later, Sinatra's valet reported that Frank would get seriously annoyed every time "Light My Fire" came on the radio that summer, because he thought that Jim Morrison's silken crooning was a blatant rip-off of his style. "We ought to let that guy have an accident," Frank is supposed to have said.

SUMMER OF LOVE

WHEN THE DOORS GOT BACK TO NEW YORK, they had to endure tales of Monterey from those just returned. The Who had dominated. Hendrix was God. Otis Redding stole the show from the white boys. The Doors consoled themselves: Cream and Traffic hadn't been invited either. (Nor, two years later, would the Doors be booked at Woodstock, amid fears that Jim Morrison would take his pants off. As it turned out, half the audience was naked anyway.)

The Doors played the Scene every night between June 19 and July 1, with Jim turning in passionate and deeply affecting performances. (Howlin' Wolf shared the bill with them one night, much to their shock and awe.) The band was playing fast, hard rock, with "Light My Fire" burning with jazzy fever. Jim was seeing a pretty dressmaker, a little older than him, whose shop was in the East Village. They went to the movies and to dinner a few times. Jim didn't talk a lot, and always had his nose in a book. She says they didn't even make love that much, because it was hot in her railroad flat on Fourth Street near Avenue A. Jim gave her some cash to help with her rent, because things were a little slow for her in that early summer of 1967.

On June 30, before their nightly Scene gig, the Doors saw the Charles Lloyd Quartet, with Keith Jarrett on keyboards, perform in Central Park. This was the first jazz group to sell a million copies of an album (*Forest Flower*), and even Jim, not normally a jazz lover, sat entranced by the band's ethereal interplay.

Steve Paul loved the Doors. They worked hard, had drawn the biggest crowd in the Scene's history, and best of all Jim gave Paul the respect he craved. (The Scene was outrageously muscled and shaken down by various Mafia factions throughout its existence). Paul threw the band an after-hours party at the end of their stint at the Scene, locking the place at three in the morning and breaking out a case of warm champagne.

Jim, in a corner with Nico, found a condom, blew it just to bursting and let it go. It landed across the room in the champagne glass of Ingrid Superstar, about to replace Nico in the Warhol firmament, just as Nico had usurped Edie Sedgwick's role as Warhol's platinum muse the year before. Jim later brought Nico to the band's hotel, the seedy Great Northern. Densmore later wrote, "I'd never heard such crashing around. It sounded like they were beating the shit out of each other. I was worried, but never dared to ask what happened."

JULY 1967. With Jim Morrison's profile rising ever higher as "Light My Fire" grappled past "Up, Up and Away" and "Windy" toward the thin-air summit of the American charts, the Doors exhausted themselves traveling constantly, playing all over southern Cal and all along the West Coast. The Beatles' *Sgt. Pepper* still ruled, but "Fire" was outselling their new single "With a Little Help From My Friends." In a Beatlesque scene of fan mania, the Doors were mobbed by teenaged girls for the first time in San Diego after a performance of "The End" caused wild cheering in Balboa Stadium. In Santa Clara, Jim began slipping the "Names of the Kingdom" section of "Celebration of the Lizard" into the improv slot in "Back Door Man." He also inserted, for the first of many times, a surreal dream sequence called "Stop the Car, I'm Getting Out" into the "The End." Late in the band's set, he built drama with "Get together one more time," which he would develop as part of "Five to One."

Oakland. San Jose. Sacramento. Anaheim—often with the Jefferson Airplane. Grace Slick kept making sketches of Jim. "The West is the best," he sang in a voice rubbed hoarse by screaming. After the set's first few songs, he often broke character and chatted and rapped with the young kids in front, sometimes exchanging snotty insults with hecklers: "Oh, *yeah*? Why'd you come, then?" "Have you taken a good *shit* lately?" (This always got a laugh.) "Why don't you *jump up my ass*?"

If the kids in front got really stupid with him, he flicked lit cigarettes into the crowd.

THE DOORS made their national television debut on July 22 with an appearance on a weekly summer edition of *American Bandstand,* broadcast in color on ABC. Jim had watched the old daily program all through high school, when Chubby Checker and Frankie Avalon were all the rage. The cameras lingered on Jim, dressed in black with long sideburns along his cheeks, while the Doors mimed their way through a limpid "Crystal Ship." Then Dick Clark appeared and interviewed Jim.

CLARK: People seem to think you come from San Francisco. Is that right?

JIM: Uh, no. We actually got together in L.A. But we do play in San Francisco a lot.

CLARK: That must be why you have that association. Why is so much happening in San Francisco?

JIM: The West is the best.

CLARK: What about the new album, what's it gonna be called?

JIM: I think it's called *Strange Days.*

CLARK: All right, fair enough. . . . We'll do the thing that set the whole music business on fire. Ladies and gentlemen, again—the Doors!

Jim Morrison lip-synched for all he was worth, closing his eyes, emoting, acting a little, while his bandmates in the background looked bored and amateurish. Almost nobody saw the summer *Bandstand* show, which was broadcast at one-thirty on a Saturday afternoon back east, but it would help the Doors get ready for the rigors of playing live on *Ed Sullivan* two months later.

THE DOORS PLAYED two of their best shows ever in Seattle on July 23 and 24. They performed a lot of unreleased *Strange Days* material amid an atmosphere of total and adulatory reverence. (Even the tune-up was greeted with hushed awe on both nights.) Jim never went out of character, and brought forth new "Lizard" sections to rapturous applause. Future comic novelist Tom Robbins, reporting for the underground weekly *Helix,* was one of the young Seattleites who staggered home from Eagles Auditorium, stoned and dazed, after the Doors' first appearance.

Robbins outdid himself: "The Doors. Their style is early cunnilingual, late patricidal, lunchtime in the Everglades, Black Forest blood sausage on electrified bread, Jean Genet up a totem pole, artists at the barricades, Edgar Allan Poe drowning in his birdbath, Massacre of the Innocents, tarantella of the satyrs, L.A. pagans drawing down the moon. . . . Jim Morrison is an electrifying combination of angel in grace and dog in heat.... The Doors are musical carnivores in a land of musical vegetarians.... The Doors scream into the darkened auditorium what all of us in the underground are whispering more softly in our hearts: We want the world and we want it ... NOW!"

Jim Morrison shouting "*Try to set the night on fire!*"—the sound of sedition—wafted across America on fifty-thousand-watt AM stations as "Light My Fire" went to number one in the third week of July, 1967. (Jac Holzman: "Elektra's first—*my* first—number-one single.") The Doors had been together for two years.

On the last weekend of the month, they were back at the Fillmore. Jim arrived at the gig with an explorer's pith helmet, painted in Day-Glo whorls and stenciled "Morrison Special," which he presented to Bill Graham to apologize for having nearly brained him with the microphone back in June. Someone stole the helmet from Graham's office a week later.

STUD IN BLACK LEATHER

D URING THE SUMMER of 1967, the Doors, prodded by Jim, decided to make a documentary rock and roll film. Amazed by the nightly scenes of fan mayhem and rapture that unfolded in front of them, the band realized these Bosch-like images had to be documented. So the Doors got a couple of 16-mm Bolex cameras and hired Paul Ferrara, a UCLA classmate of Jim's, as cameraman on the film crew that would accompany the Doors as they made their plutonian way through America during the next year. The footage of Jim bathing with friends in a California river and climbing among rocks dates from around this time.

This is also when Jim ordered a black leather suit from his friend January Jansen, a drinking buddy who tailored expensive hippie duds. "I made a lot of his stage clothes," Jansen told Frank Lisciandro in an interview years later. "He said he wanted something in leather, but didn't like what was available. He said it looked like linoleum." Jim also had a leather suit made for him by Mirandi Babitz, with a flyless sailor front on the trousers. This butch leather look would define Jim Morrison's public image for the next year, until he abandoned it late in 1968.

IN AUGUST 1967, between Doors gigs on both coasts, Jim Morrison left Pamela Courson and plunged into a passionate resumption of his affair with Nico. The bombshell German avant-garde sultana was staying at John Philip Law's concrete "Castle" in Los Feliz while trying to write songs for her first solo album on Elektra Records. She was also one of the stars of Warhol's film *Chelsea Girls,* about to make its Los Angeles debut.

Jim loved Nico's sultry Berlin accent and cold, rock-operatic Wagnerian aura, and he deeply respected her connection to Federico Fellini. She also let Jim do what he wanted to her. She was two inches taller than Jim, even broader in the shoulders. He told her she was the first woman who'd borne a child that he'd ever made love with. When she sat on his face, which was her thing, it almost drowned Jim in labia and fur, or so he told a friend. Nico was physically strong, was a little older than Jim, was probably even crazier. She was also extremely intelligent, and still bore a slight black eye that Brian Jones had given her when he'd smacked her at Monterey. Jim insisted that Nico tell him everything that Brian had ever said to her. Nico insisted that Jim teach her how to write a song.

Nico's friends said later that she really gave her heart to Jim. She loved him with a lionesslike intensity that frightened even her. He drove her, with the car radio blaring "Light My Fire" and Aretha Franklin's "Respect," out to some of his desert haunts—the Indian canyons around Palm Springs, Joshua Tree National Monument, Death Valley—where they took acid trips together a couple of times. When he told her about the girls he'd loved in the past, Nico dyed her trademark straight blond hair a lustrous pale red.

"He had this fetish for *shanties* with red hair," Nico remembered. "You know—Irish shanties." (Nico had an endearing way with English slang; *shanty* was her word for "chick.") "He was the first man I was in love with. I was so in love with Jim, that I made my own hair red, after a while. I wanted to please his taste. It was silly, no? Like a teenager or something." When Jim saw this, Nico said later, it made him cry. She asked him to propose marriage to her. He laughed so hard he fell off his chair, so she hit him.

"We hit each other because we were drunk and we enjoyed the

sensation," she said. "But we made love in the gentle way, you know? It was the opposite to Brian [Jones]. I thought of Jim Morrison as my brother, so I hoped that we would grow together."

Nico remembered they watched the TV news together in the evenings. The Black Panther party in Oakland was parading their rifles and shotguns in public. (Of the five thousand Panthers, twenty-eight would be killed by the police, and sixty-five wounded. The Panthers served more than two hundred thousand free breakfasts to hungry black schoolchildren.) The Vietnam body count escalated in a roar of helicopters, atrocities, and bullshit propaganda. America was hell, Jim explained to Nico. There would be hell to pay, soon enough. Strange days were coming.

The lyrics the two lovers worked on became part of Nico's superb 1968 album *The Marble Index,* whose song titles have an undeniable echo of her collaboration with Jim Morrison—"Lawn of Dawns," "Frozen Warnings," "Evening of Light." Nico was unsure of herself, as she'd always sung the songs of others and was writing in English, a foreign language to her. "Jim gave me permission to become a writer," she said later. "He said to me, 'I give you permission to write your poems and compose your songs.' My soul brother believed I could do it. I had his authority. His song ['Light My Fire'] was the most popular song in America!"

Jim never mentioned Nico in his extant notebooks, but late that month he was often seen with her at the Castle, sometimes balancing—naked—on the parapet above the pool during the hot summer nights. Downstairs, other castle residents—Dennis Hopper, Peter Fonda, screenwriter Terry Southern—were snorting mass quantities of dentist-quality cocaine and writing the early drafts of the screenplay that would become *Easy Rider.* This ultrahip, post-Beat clique regarded Jim Morrison as a parvenu punk because of his notoriety and his narcissism, his outré leather trousers, the put-on shyness. They were also annoyed that he was fucking the lubricious Nico. But at least one of the hipster adepts hanging around the castle, poet/playwright Michael McClure, who was also working on a novel about a cocaine dealer, took the trouble to talk to Jim. This meant a lot to Morrison, who invited McClure to visit the studio when the Doors started recording again.

So Jim and Nico went at it tooth and nail, fornicating like tigers and battering each other black and blue. Pam didn't see Jim for a month, but she knew where he was, and who he was fucking, and she didn't take this public payback and humiliation lying down. Actually, she *did* take it lying down. She had a fling with a friend of Jim's. Pamela also let it slip to the local gossips, but not to breathe *one word,* but she was having an affair with John Philip Law. This was a huge deal since Law—Jane Fonda's costar in Roger Vadim's 1967 comic sci-fi movie *Barbarella*— was considered an A-list sexual conquest. Law later vehemently denied any sexual liaison with Pamela Courson, describing his relationship with her as only a few dinner dates—he knew Pam through her sister, Judy— and as a ploy to get Jim Morrison's attention.

Jim Morrison's torrid affair with Nico lasted a few weeks longer, and then petered out in exhaustion. Jim went back to Pamela, as he always did. Nico dyed her hair an even darker shade of red.

A MID ALL THIS, the Doors flew east early in the month. Jim got so drunk and loud in the first-class section that the pilot had to speak to him. At this, Jim bolted upright, to attention. "Yes, sir!" Jim snapped. He saluted, sat down, and passed out. Densmore: "Sometimes it felt like I was trapped on an airplane with a lunatic."

On August 9, they played the Hampton Beach Casino in New Hampshire, a stupendous recital that left its audience breathless and disbelieving of what they had seen—Jim Morrison in full, Oedipal, anarchic fury. For the next two nights, the Doors played the Crosstown Bus, a new Boston club that was closed down by the cops immediately after the Doors' tumultuous shows, during which Jim guzzled Southern Comfort onstage and emoted like Prince Hamlet with a hard-on. (In the afternoon, between gigs, Jim sat in quiet Harvard Yard in Cambridge, minded by Elektra exec Steve Harris, and revised "Celebration of the Lizard" in a big gray ledger.) Then on to New York, where on Saturday, August 12, the Doors played the first of many debacle concerts that would damage the band's career.

Paul Simon knew a fellow poet when he heard one, and besides the Doors were number one. Jac Holzman told Simon the Doors were going to be the biggest band in America. This is why the Doors were personally chosen by Simon, already a sharp music biz veteran, to open Simon and Garfunkel's big "homecoming" show at Forest Hills Tennis Stadium in Queens. In 1967 Paul Simon and Art Garfunkel were chart-topping folk-rockers whose "Mrs. Robinson" had anchored the soundtrack to the year's biggest movie, *The Graduate.* They actually were from Queens, and so it was a hometown crowd—and a notoriously tough audience. Forest Hills had booed Bob Dylan when he "went electric" two summers before. Only a couple of months earlier, they had booed the Jimi Hendrix Experience off the stage when they had dared opened for the Monkees, a band that only existed on TV.

Jim Morrison was in a truculent mood when he got to Forest Hills, refusing to make eye contact with anyone or sign copies of the album. He was rude to Paul Simon when he tried to chat up the Doors backstage, where chaos reigned because the Doors' gear was late and Bill Siddons was scrambling for drums, amps, and an organ while ten thousand people waited to hear them. The tension was thick, and Jim was drinking. Then it was time to go on.

"Ladies and gentlemen: from Los Angeles, California—THE DOORS!" There was some applause, then silence. As the Doors tuned up, Jim glared out into the crowd, annoyed at having to perform in summer evening twilight. "This is the end!" he shouted as the band dashed into "Break On Through." Mild Applause. "Back Door Man." Scattered clapping, as the crowd was getting impatient for S & G's "Feelin' Groovy" and other precious harmony ditties. "Light My Fire" was still number one, and the Doors took it hard and sharp, so the audience picked up a bit. After a sinister production of "The End" was met by a mass exodus to the bathrooms, Jim raged out, purging himself of hatred and fear, slamming the mike stand down and screaming pure murder for more than a minute during the last cataclysm. Then Jim bowed and said thank you, and the band walked off—completely demoralized.

"We were in hell," Ray said later. "It was an awful gig. Jim said it was the worst audience he ever faced."

Later in the evening, Simon chided the audience for their reaction to the Doors, saying the music business was rough enough on new musicians. By then the Doors were already back at their midtown hotel, with Jim drinking to blackout at the Blarney Stone, an Irish bar next door.

*   *   *

ELEKTRA EXECUTIVES were ecstatic when "Light My Fire" stayed at number one for the third week in a row. The following night they threw a party for the Doors in the wine cellar of the Delmonico Hotel on Park Avenue, where the band was awarded a gold record and a Hot Hundred number one plaque from *Billboard*. All the band's New York friends and the press and radio people were invited. Jim arrived, to total astonishment, in a white shirt and black tie under his full leather suit. He was sober, freshly shaved, and looked incredible with brown ringlets of long hair falling about his chiseled cheekbones and over his shoulders. For once he looked like his eight-by-ten glossies. All the woman stopped talking when he walked into the party. Flashbulbs popped for the trades and the tabloids; the entire Elektra staff and every deejay in Manhattan had to have their pictures taken with Jim.

Jim joined Andy Warhol and his entourage in a large semicircular banquette at the back of the room, surrounded by racks containing the hotel's wine collection. Andy was in his wispy, faux-naïf persona, and gave Jim a big package, wrapped in pink ribbon, to commemorate the occasion. "Well, um ... *thanks*, Andy," Jim said, in a put-on "manly" baritone, as he took the gift out of the box. It was a reproduction of an antique French telephone, with a Moderne headpiece and a "gold" rotary dial. It was hideous. Jim laughed. "It's just what ... I always wanted."

"You can talk to *God* on it," Warhol whispered to Jim, as the Warholites broke into titters and applause.

Jim started downing rounds of Courvoisier, got loaded and loud. When he saw Jac Holzman sneak out of the party, followed by other Elektra execs, Jim took over as host, demanding the waiters bring more food for the guests, plus a corkscrew and wineglasses for himself. He proceeded to uncork bottles of the house's most expensive wines, pouring for his friends as the Doors' album played loud and the room filled up with raucous laughter and reefer fumes. Soon Jim was walking on the tables, knocking over glasses and crockery, grabbing even better wines higher up in the racks—until the hotel's general manager called the police, who arrived in five minutes and rudely threw everyone out.

Later that night, as a summer rain soaked the streets, Jim was driven downtown in a limo with Warhol, Danny Fields, Robby Krieger, and his new girlfriend, Lynn Veres (a dancer from Jersey who had been seeing Jim earlier in the year). They were headed to Jac Holzman's apartment to listen to the Doors' new tracks. At a red light in the East Village, Jim rolled down the limo's electric window and beckoned over a derelict hippie. "Hey, man, this is for *you*," Jim said, as he handed over the vulgar phone in it's pink-ribboned box. Warhol didn't say a thing, and looked away. As the light changed and the limo sped away, Jim Morrison just closed his eyes and smiled.

WAKE UP!

ON AUGUST 18, 1967, the Doors played a roller rink in Alexandria, Virginia, where Jim had gone to high school. (They topped a bill of a dozen local bands.) By this time, Jim's mother had been trying to contact him through his record company for several months, but her calls were never returned. Jim's younger brother, Andy, would later say that their father, Admiral Morrison, showed no overt emotion when Andy played him his firstborn son's Oedipal ravings for the first time.

Right after this the Doors went back into the studio, Sunset Sound having been upgraded to eight-track recording capability. It was a time of increasing pressure, stress, and anxiety in the Doors' charmed circle. The advance order for *Strange Days* was five hundred thousand, the biggest in the label's history. Producer Paul Rothchild was back at the board in his black porkpie hat, with the tightly rolled joints and compartmentalized stash. He now had to produce a follow-up to "Light My Fire," and so far a nervous Elektra did not hear an obvious hit single among the tracks they had. Jim Morrison and Robby Krieger were under extraordinary pressure to come up with great songs. They kept hearing that a "flat" Doors album could kill their career, but these two space cadets were only coming up with uneasy songs about the eerie strangeness of America in 1967—the old, free republic dying in pain; an undercurrent of moral queasiness about everything; the rot underlying the structure of American existence; a free-floating fear of psychic earthquakes in a suicidal dreamscape of drugs and sex.

Working in *Sgt. Pepper's* awesome wake was another challenge that

Rothchild tried to meet by using the new, machinelike sounds of the early music synthesizers and samplers. He also insisted the Doors work with a bass guitar to cushion some of the new songs, and brought in Doug Lubahn, who played bass with label-mates Clear Light, to get more swing out of the band on hard-rocking numbers like "Love Me Two Times." (The Doors recorded with bass from then on.) The music they eventually produced, *Strange Days*, was easily the best album of their career, and lives on today as one of the great artifacts of the rock movement. But *Strange Days* also proved to be the Doors' worst-selling album, a commercial setback relative to the wild success of *The Doors*. The new music was too edgy, the lyrics too creepy, the ambience too uncomfortable, for this sad and wistful masterpiece to have succeeded the way it needed to in late 1967. The album's lack of acceptance had a profoundly negative impact upon Jim Morrison.

He wasn't well known for handling stress well, and he started really hitting the bottle during the *Strange Days* sessions in September and October. Paul Rothchild recalled: "You never knew. You just *never knew!* Was he going to be Dr. Jekyll, or was he going to be Mr. Hyde? Was it gonna be the calm, erudite scholar, or the crazed kamikaze pilot drunk? Jim, man. He'd push every one of your buttons to see what you'd do with it."

TWO OF THE EARLIEST finished tracks were "People Are Strange" and "Unhappy Girl." The former was written by Jim after he'd turned up depressed at Robby's place in Laurel Canyon and they'd walked up Appian Way to a lookout view over Hollywood, the whole city laid out in front of them. Robby had walked down by himself, leaving Jim with his notebook out. Half an hour later, Jim came back with the verse and the basic melody. "Unhappy Girl," with its prison imagery, backward piano track, and guitars "treated" by Paul Beaver, Elektra's resident Moog synthesizer expert, would be the single's B-side when the label released "People Are Strange" as the Doors' third single in mid-September.

The recording sessions continued between the band's weekend gigs over the next two months. "My Eyes Have Seen You" was revived from the band's original demo, speeded up, and given a reading that recalled the Stones' "Let's Spend the Night Together" with distorted piano and furious acid guitar as Jim decried the television skies. Jim's lyrics took on a new, emotionally raw tone on the title track, "Strange Days," with the song's paranoid dislocation underlined by a distorted, machinelike vocal hissing about confusion and flight. "Moonlight Drive" was the same romantic death-trip Jim had sung on the beach to Ray in 1965, updated with Moog-synth washes and a freaky guitar solo.

"When the Music's Over," a concert showpiece for almost a year, received its final five-episode arrangement, starting with Ray's organ intro based on Herbie Hancock's hit record "Watermelon Man." The episodes included: 1. "Turn out the light/Dance on fire" in a droning duel of raga guitars; 2. "Cancel my subscription," a negation of faith amid surreal imagery (the face in the mirror, the feast of friends [Jim consuming those around him], and the scream of the butterfly, which Densmore said came from the title of a porno movie); 3. "What have they done to the earth?"—a beatnik duet for voice and drums that ends with the epochal proclamation "We want the world and we want it . . . NOW!" 4. "Persian Night," a climactic band explosion in which the singer *renews* his subscription to the Resurrection and, in acute spiritual turmoil, calls on Jesus by name for salvation; 5. Return to the main themes, softer and mystical, ending in an operatic crash with an abrupt, thunderclap stop. It was, and remains, one of the Doors' great masterworks, and more than filled the "epic" slot at the end of the album, previously occupied by "The End." Jim insisted the band record it live, so the final take was postponed to the end of the sessions.

O N THE WEEKENDS, the Doors played shows. In Asbury Park, New Jersey, on September 2, Jim, in full black leather, performed the "Wake Up" section of "Celebration of the Lizard" for the first time to an audience that included the eighteen-year-old Bruce Springsteen. Jim's demonic shriek—"WAKE UP"—out of a dead silence startled Fort Worth, Texas, the next night, after short sets by the Box Tops, the McCoys, and the Electric Prunes. "Wake Up" was pure theater of cruelty, jolting the stoned audiences out of their muzzy torpor and into red-alert receptiveness. As Jim got more practiced at this, and as he worked with much larger crowds, some of his college readings of Canetti and Riesman came back to him, and he began to taunt and play with the crowds, learning what he could (and couldn't) do with the denim-clad votaries who had paid as much as six and seven dollars to do him homage.

The Vagrants and the red-hot, integrated Chambers Brothers band opened for the headlining Doors the next night at the Village Theater in Manhattan. Elektra had every important critic, publicist, teen mag editor, and radio deejay in New York present for the ten-thirty show. The band started with "When the Music's Over," and Jim caught the hem of the theater's curtain as it rose. On cue he let go, landed on his feet, and produced the savage scream that opened the vocal part of the song. The audience rose to its feet and stayed there for the next hour. Albert Goldman, covering the show for *Life*, and not one given to hyperbole, called it "an incredible moment." For many of the music pros there that night, it was one of the defining moments of their lives.

The Doors went right into "Horse Latitudes" before a long rendition of "The End," with Jim on his knees during the *Oedipus Rex* part, whispering the lines in a sinister, intensely theatrical manner. Jim then precisely timed a leaping vault into the air as the band exploded, before collapsing into an abject posture of postcoital remorse. As the band then vamped, he twirled the mike in an electric shaman's ritual. The Doors finished the night with a fast, intense "Light My Fire." The cheering lasted ten full minutes and there was no further encore.

ONE NIGHT JIM WAS lying down in his New York hotel room. Elektra promo man Steve Harris and Paul Rothchild were hanging out with him. Jim was very drunk. He reached into his leather pants and pulled out a piece of napkin, on which were scribbled the lyrics to a new song, "The Unknown Soldier." He handed the scrap of paper to Paul. Then he lay back down on the bed, grabbed the wastebasket, and vomited his guts out. Then he passed out and began to snore.

THE COVER OF THE NEW ALBUM became an issue when the band informed the label that they didn't want the album title or the name of the band on the sleeve. "I hated the cover of our first album," Jim told writer John Carpenter of the *L.A. Free Press*. "I said, 'I don't want to be on this cover. Put a chick on it. Let's have a dandelion, or a design.' And because of the title, everyone agreed, 'cause that's where we were at. That's what was happening. It was right."

Jim told Elektra's art director, Bill Harvey, that he envisioned the band sitting in a room surrounded by a pack of thirty dogs. Harvey asked why, and Jim informed him that it was because *dog* was *god* spelled backward. As a compromise the band settled on some kind of carny tableau. "You know," Jim told Harvey. "Like *La Strada*. Dali. A bunch of Fellini freaks."

This was what Joel Brodsky captured on a late summer morning in a private "Old New York" mews, Sniffen Court, off East Thirty-sixth Street. A midget, two acrobats, a juggler, and a strongman cavorted. A taxi driver became the trumpeter. A chic fashion model, Zazel Wild, wore a flowing silk caftan, the only vivid color in a bleakly gray image, as she contemplated giving the scary midget a tip. There was an old Doors poster on the wall under a banner announcing *Strange Days*. The sinister, surreal vibe of the wraparound album sleeve was unusually sophisticated for a pop album, and an apposite representation of the shocking, lurid carnival of dread to be found within.

Bill Harvey was surprised and relieved when the Doors signed off on it.

YELLING "FIRE" IN A CROWDED COUNTRY

SEPTEMBER 1967. As the easterly Santa Ana winds blew the desert dust, pollution, and old bad vibes back into southern California, the Doors recorded "You're Lost, Little Girl," the first song Robby Krieger ever wrote. The basic track was simple, but Krieger couldn't get the guitar solo right, so Rothchild cleared the studio, lit some candles, turned off the lights, and got Krieger stoned on good hashish. Robby then got it on the first take. Rothchild tried to conjure the same atmosphere when it was time for Jim to sing. He told Jim he wanted it like the way Frank Sinatra, who was then breaking up with his much-younger wife Mia Farrow, might do it. Paul suggested they hire a hooker to give Jim head while he was cutting the vocal. They brought in a girl to fellate

Jim, but Elektra exec David Anderle claimed Jim could neither sing under those conditions, nor even get hard. In John Densmore's version of this session, Pamela Courson, who had begun visiting the studio, took off her dress and slipped into the vocal booth as Rothchild killed the lights. Jim got halfway through the song and then stopped. "We heard rustling noises. Who knows what went on in there?...We went with a later take."

A few nights later the Jefferson Airplane called. They wanted to visit the sessions. They came in as Jim was declaiming the drowning sequence of "Horse Latitudes," set to a dangerous vortex of extreme musique concrète and electronic noise. *"...IN MUTE NOSTRIL AGONY...CAREFULLY REFINED...AND SEALED OVERRRR."* The studio was completely dark except for the instrument lights. A feast of friends, including Pamela and Alain Ronay from UCLA film school, shrieked in the background after "Awkward instant." Grace Slick, a hardened rock veteran, went back to San Francisco and told everyone the Doors had scared the living shit out of them.

The night that the Doors, at Jim's urging, were going to record "When the Music's Over" live, with no overdubs, he didn't show. At three in the morning he called Robby: "We're in trouble here," Jim whispered. "You better come over." Robby drove down the hill to Pam's, where she and Jim were freaking out on a large dose of acid. Jim wanted Robby to drive them to Griffith Park, where they could try to cool out. Jim started to walk out the door, but Robby suggested that he first put on his pants. At dawn, when Robby dropped the now subdued couple off at home, he reminded Jim to come to the studio at noon.

Jim didn't show. Runners were sent to Jim's nearby haunts—Barney's Beanery and the Palms, a bar on Santa Monica Boulevard—but he wasn't around. Jim and Pamela had taken acid again, according to Densmore, and wandered over to the house John shared with Robby nearby in Laurel Canyon. Densmore claimed that Jim thought it would be really funny to empty his bursting bladder into John's bed, and let flow.

The Doors waited at Sunset Sound until two-thirty in the morning, but Jim never showed. So they cut "When the Music's Over" without him, with Ray singing lead. When Jim did come in, on time the next day, Densmore was confrontational, demanding to know where he'd been. "I had some...um...personal business."

"Like what?" Krieger asked.

"Well, I'm not gonna tell you, because ... it's personal."

Densmore started to get uptight, but Rothchild intervened. "Hey—let's do something." Jim wanted them to record again, live, but the band refused, having gotten a good take the night before. Jim bitched that if he had to sing in overdub mode, he wouldn't know where to come in. Ray said he would cue him. Jim Morrison nailed "When the Music's Over"—perhaps the Doors' career-defining statement—on the second take.

O N SEPTEMBER 14, 1967, the Doors and the Jefferson Airplane taped a TV appearance for the CBC in Toronto. After the Airplane did "White Rabbit," Jim roared into "Wake Up!" and then played a sweet version of "The End" with the mother-fucking part left out, reportedly the band's idea. That same night they played in the suburbs of Cleveland, only drawing five hundred people in a two-thousand-capacity tent. "We've never been to the Midwest before," Jim told the Cleveland *Plain Dealer.* "We don't know what to expect." When he ambled onstage that evening and saw all the empty seats, he put his right boot on the base of the mike stand, raised the mike, belched out a vulgar beer burp, laughed, and drawled: "Well ... since there's no requests ..." The band blasted into "Soul Kitchen" and played a ferocious short show that featured Jim Morrison in full cry: wild dancing, heroic leaps, artful crooning, and hell-mouth screams.

The Doors then spent a windy fall day on a chaotic New York TV location, making a video sequence of "People Are Strange" for broadcast on Murray the K's local show. Jim was singing with a live mike to a prerecorded track, and Murray kept flubbing his introduction, causing many retakes. Finally Jim got annoyed, telling the aging disk jockey that if he kept him waiting any longer, "I'm gonna rap you in the nose."

Not many guys in new bands said that to Murray the K.

S EPTEMBER 17, 1967. Fifteen years before MTV, Ed Sullivan's Sunday night variety show was the only live broadcast venue for popular music, all other such shows being pretaped. Sullivan had launched Elvis Presley's national career in 1956, and done the same for the Beatles in 1964. Nine months earlier, in January 1967, the puritanical Sullivan had successfully censored the Rolling Stones, forcing Mick Jagger to change the lyrics "Let's spend the night together" to "Let's spend some time together." Ed Sullivan was able to do this, the Doors were reminded by their newly hired publicist Derek Taylor, a suave Londoner who'd worked with the Beatles, because he had the only live gig on television that could pull in up to seventy million viewers. Any act that crossed Sullivan was never booked on the show again. The Doors agreed to do *The Ed Sullivan Show,* but only if their own guys, Rothchild and Botnick, could run the soundboard during their two songs.

Ed Sullivan, meet the Lizard King.

Sullivan met Jim Morrison that Sunday afternoon, when Ed dropped by the band's dressing room after rehearsal. The band was laughing at Robby, who was doing his Three Stooges imitation, running in a circle while lying on the floor. Sullivan looked at them for a moment, and said (according to Densmore): "You boys look great when you smile! Do that tonight—you're too *serious.*" Then Ed moved down the hall to see the other acts on the program that night—Yul Brynner, Steve and Eydie, Rodney Dangerfield, the Skating Epsteins. The Doors were still goofing on Sullivan's famous uptightness when his son-in-law, Bob Precht—the show's producer—knocked and walked in. Precht had successfully forced the great Mick Jagger to censor himself, and now he targeted Jim Morrison, explaining in a genial manner that the phrase *Girl, you couldn't get much higher* would be seen as a drug reference and would get them in trouble with "Standards and Practices"—the CBS network's censor. Precht told Jim that he couldn't say *higher* on network television, and asked Jim to change the lyric for the broadcast.

"Fuck you," Jim murmured. Shocked silence.

Precht: "What did you say?"

Jim: "What do you want to change it to?" After some embarrassed glances between the band over some of Precht's suggestions, Ray Manzarek assured Precht that they would cooperate.

They couldn't believe this lame bullshit. Jim was angry as he changed into a Byronic white shirt and his leather suit, threatening to substitute "Let's Spend the Night Together," or just start cursing a blue streak during the broadcast. No one knew what would happen, least of all the other Doors. Of course no one felt they could talk to Jim about something like this. "We all sensed rage," Densmore later wrote, "and a possible explosion too near the surface to mess with, in dealing with Jim."

Ed Sullivan introduced the Doors with his lip curling slightly, in evident distaste. The Doors performed "People Are Strange" during the show's first segment, with Jim looking unusually dead eyed, and struggling to sing in tune. Few singers could risk looking as drunk and dissolute as Jim did on that broacast, and the cuffs of his white shirt were soiled. In the last segment, they did their sololess version of "Light My Fire," and of course Jim sang the word "higher" *twice,* not with any unusual emphasis, but exactly the way he'd sung it a hundred times before. At the finale, hot and sweaty under the blazing TV lights, Ray called out to him, "Come on!" and Jim made eye contact with the camera and really let loose, sending Morrison scream-energy out to a Middle America unprepared to hear anything so painfully acute.

As the song crashed to a halt, there were screams and applause from the audience, and Jim assumed his most Marlene-esque pose, with his legs crossed and the mike held behind his shoulders, like a javelin about to be thrown. Grim-faced Ed Sullivan, who had famously shaken hands with Elvis, the Beatles, and the Stones, stayed at the side of the stage and applauded mildly. An angry Bob Precht whined about the Doors' breaking their promise to him. Ray told him it was an accident, that Jim—in the excitement of being on *Ed Sullivan!*—had simply forgotten.

"We were going to book you for six more shows," Precht told them. "Mr. Sullivan *liked* you boys. *Six more shows*—you know what that would have meant to your career?"

Jim didn't give a shit. "Hey, man," he said, stopping Precht with a glare. "*So what?* We just *did* Ed Sullivan."

Indeed, Jim's Morrison's performance had been the sexiest, most provocative thing on American television since Elvis Presley's debut on Sullivan's show, eleven years earlier. It was a deliberate provocation, like yelling "Fire!" in a crowded country. And there's little doubt that, wherever he was, in Memphis or Los Angeles, Elvis Presley also watched Jim Morrison's leather-clad Sunday-night broadcast. A year later, making his own legendary 1968 television comeback, Elvis wore a black leather suit that was a close copy of what Jim had worn that night.

The Doors never appeared on Ed Sullivan's show again.

VIET CONG ROCK

IN THE LAST MONTHS OF 1967, Jim Morrison refined and extended his stage presence as the Doors played in high school gyms and college field houses, drawing bigger and bigger crowds every night. They played famous Staples High School in Westport, Connecticut, in the wake of the Yardbirds and Cream. At Brown University on September 22, after a performance described as brilliant by the school paper, Jim smashed the annoying light show's screen, which had been bathing him all night in throbbing oily whorls, with his mike stand.

The next night, at SUNY in Stony Brook, on Long Island, Jim baited an overenthusiastic audience (which had been warmed up by singer Tim Buckley) by experimenting with long passages of silence to heighten the inherent tension of the performance. Many simply got bored and walked out. Others got impatient and yelled, "Louder." This made Jim, hunkering down on his knees with his eyes closed, wait even longer. Trying to sense the exact moment when the crowd would explode, Jim would flash back into "Back Door Man" or "The End." The school paper described the show as "Viet Cong rock" and a broken black mass. Backstage afterward, Jim told Gloria Stavers: "You have to *have* them. They can't have you. And if you *don't* have them, you have to stop and *get* them. That's what was happening tonight. I mean, can you dig it?"

On Saturday night, September 30 at the Family Dog in Denver, the Doors took the stage after Lothar and the Hand People and Captain Beefheart. The band was rocking hard, with Jim at his black leather best, playing to the braless chicks in the front row. He performed the second half of "The End" hanging, upside down, from a guardrail at the front of the stage, looking like a Goya torture victim under a single spotlight.

OCTOBER 1967 SAW THE DOORS' final days in the rock clubs, and they were played out during another week at Steve Paul's Scene in New York. The basement club was so jammed with Doors fans that no one could even move. Jim sang with his right hand cupped over his ear, the only way he could hear himself singing over the din.

On October 6, the gym at Cal State was packed and seething with anticipation. The giant room erupted when Jim strode out in his leathers and went right into the sonic boom of "Soul Kitchen." He moved around the stage like a cougar, urging on the band, screaming at them. "Yeah! Louder! *Play it!* More of that, Robby!" Then he'd thrash back to the mike in time "to reinstate pure human horror in the black air of the auditorium," according to UCLA's *Daily Bruin.*

On October 8, the Doors played the last night of the Oklahoma State Fair in Tulsa. Jim had been obsessively writing and reworking "Celebration of the Lizard," his new and hotly anticipated rock theater piece that was planned to take up the whole second side of the third Doors album, and in Tulsa he performed the "Wake Up" section in its nearly complete form, leading into "Light My Fire." They also experimented with lighting, using only red, blue, and amber spots. At one point Jim somehow connected with a young guy in the fourth row of Tulsa Civic Assembly Auditorium during "Back Door Man."

"You out there," he pointed, laughing his evil backdoor stage cackle, "You are alone. You want to dance.... AND NO ONE CAN HELP YOU!" Later, people who heard the tape of the Tulsa show realized that although Jim was speaking to one guy, he also meant the whole audience, his whole generation. Jim was the madman dancing in the hills, the eyes staring from the edge of the forest. It wasn't enough that his audience paid to see him. He wanted them to go out and *do* something.

On October 11, Cadillac limousines ferried the Doors from Manhattan to Danbury High in Connecticut. The band's film crew rode with Jim and Albert Goldman as the writer interviewed Jim for *New York* magazine. But Jim had been boozing with Tom Baker all day, and nothing much came of their talk. Baker introduced the Doors after the school's starchy female principal warned the customers to stay in their seats. The audience was terrible; many had come to see the Four Seasons, who had canceled. This annoyed Jim, who kept lunging at them with his mike, which he then smashed to pieces in a blind fury after reciting three (only semicoherent) sections of "Lizard" during "The End." (As of 1998, the dents Jim made on the stage at Danbury High were still visible.)

On October 12, the Surf Nantasket, on the beach south of Boston, got a killer show for a packed house. The next night, in Baltimore, the band played their entire first album, and Jim tried some stage business with a red silk scarf during "The End," before collapsing and lying still on the stage for several minutes as the band played on. The audience didn't know if it was part of the act, because Jim looked genuinely unconscious. But he then got up, started spinning, and finished the song with his shaman dance. The applause was so long and loud that the band came back and played "When the Music's Over," from their still unreleased album, as an encore.

It was homecoming weekend at Susquehanna University in western Pennsylvania when the Doors came to town on October 14. It was a field house show, and the band played well to an audience that just didn't get it, so Jim mouthed off, insulted some sorority girls, and got his rocks off on a long version of "Who Do You Love?" The next day they flew to California to play a show in Berkeley, then back to New York the day after that to play Steve Paul's Scene. Their bookings were so badly scheduled that the Doors sometimes flew between coasts twice a week, but playing shows was their only source of ready cash. So they all fought exhaustion and slept when they could, trying to ignore the flocks of teenage girls knocking on their motel room doors.

The first time John Densmore's new girlfriend, Julia Brose, saw Jim Morrison, in an airport in the Midwest, he was passed out, drunk, and had been stashed under a bench against a wall. Bill Siddons had blocked the bench off with two trash cans, so Jim couldn't escape if he came to.

"There he is," Densmore told her with contempt. "That's our famous lead singer."

O CTOBER 20, 1967, was homecoming weekend at the University of Michigan in Ann Arbor, near Detroit. Jim Morrison was so drunk that there was a mutiny onstage. As they were tuning up, Jim blearily realized they were playing to a crowd of fraternity types who had no clue who the Doors were. So Jim started cursing the kids, asking if they wanted to hear "Louie Louie," or what. Ray got two guys to escort Jim off the stage and told the crowd they'd be back when Jim felt better. In the dressing room Jim recovered a bit and fired up a cigar. The others came in and just stared at him. Being the Doors, no one said anything at all.

When Jim finished smoking, they went back on. Jim started singing in a high, squeaky voice that sounded (to a Detroit kid named Jimmy Osterberg who was there that night) like the cartoon character Betty Boop. Jim kept this up, infuriating the crowd and his own band. There was booing, catcalls, and stuff got thrown onstage. Jim refused to play "Light My Fire."

Hundreds walked out, followed by embarrassed Densmore and disgusted Krieger before the show was over. Then Jim chanted some John Lee Hooker riffs and ad-libbed the doggerel lines to "Maggie M'Gill" as Ray gamely comped along with him—until the football players and their dates began to throw cups of fruit punch at them.

Jimmy Osterberg was deeply moved by this anarchic, contemptuous rock show. Almost immediately he founded his own band, the Psychedelic Stooges, and eventually changed his name to Iggy Pop.

T HE DOORS FLEW to Colorado College the next day, then back east to Williams College in Massachusetts the day after that. The band's film crew captured some prophetic (and unconsciously metaphoric) dialogue as Jim, Ray, and Robby were drinking Michelob beer and playing poker in the motel before the show. Jim wanted to fold rather than throw another quarter into the pot.

RAY: "We need you to stay in the game."
ROBBY: "We all want to suck you dry."
JIM: "Well, the thing is . . . *I don't like the game.*"

And he laughed his teasing whinny at the others, and the reel ran out. They were talking about the card game, but they could have been discussing the band itself.

The Williams school paper captured the drama and hair-raising anxiety of the Doors that night almost perfectly: "Morrison dislodged the microphone and staggered blindly across the stage as the lyrics and screams which are 'The End' poured out of his mouth, malevolent, satanic, electric, and on fire. Then he stumbled and fell in front of a towering amplifier and sobbed to himself. The guitarist nudged him with the neck of his guitar. He got up on his knees and stretched out his arms in an attitude of worship toward the cold amplifier. . . . The audience didn't know whether to applaud or not. The guitarist unplugged the electric cord that makes his instrument play, the organist stepped off and left, the drummer threw his sticks to the ground in contempt and disgust, and Morrison had disappeared through the velvet curtain without a wave or a smile."

They flew back to L.A. the next day. No one spoke. After five days of rest, Jim recovered, and over the next six weeks the Doors played well up and down the West Coast, where Jim felt most comfortable and accepted. He was living at Pamela's place again and working on "Celebration of the Lizard," trying to make it ring with a master poet's cadences as the showpiece of the next album. He had begun a surrealistic screenplay about a hitchhiking killer roaming the American desert. He was also writing sequences for a new song that would also be a theater piece, guaranteed to be controversial, concerning a soldier in Vietnam who deserts and is executed by a firing squad. Jim had been moved by the photographs of his literary heroes (Allen Ginsberg, William Burroughs, Norman Mailer, Terry Southern, and Jean Genet) in the front ranks of the marchers who attempted a quixotic levitation of the Pentagon during the massive antiwar march on Washington earlier that month. Jim now intended to make some sort of strong statement of his own. "The Unknown Soldier," which the Doors would preview in San Francisco in November, was the angriest protest song of the entire Vietnam era, and certainly one of the most effective.

Jim was also now the subject of continuous rumor and gossip in Los Angeles. He disappeared for days at a time when the band wasn't working, and was said to be variously holed up with some gay friends at a ranch in Topanga Canyon, or hiding from Pamela with a secret fifteen-year-old girlfriend with whom he shared a motel love nest. Jim Morrison knew how to hide and compartmentalize his friends, and didn't really care who sucked his dick as long as *someone* was sucking it. Jim Morrison kept everyone guessing.

ON OCTOBER 27 at California Polytechnic State University, a tight-packed mob of squirming girls crowded the stage, waiting for the Doors. Onstage were sixteen metal-gray Acoustic amps in four stacks of four, red eyed and buzzing; a bent and battered chrome mike stand; a black-and-red Vox organ with a silver-colored Fender bass keyboard on top; and a burgundy Gibson SG guitar. A heavy smell of reefer smoke hung in almost total darkness. The girls stopped squirming as the band materialized and tuned up. "Ladies and gentlemen, please welcome the Doors!" The scary carnival organ began "When the Music's Over" as Jim ambled up to the mike and turned himself into a queasy blur of terror, a twisting phantom in black leather with bulging corpse eyes—dancing, fainting away, collapsing into lifelessness before leaping up like a marlin. He flicked lit cigarettes at the front row girls, exciting them with suggestive gestures and sex talk. After twenty-five minutes the band walked off. The audience didn't realize there was another set, and many left the building. The whole band attended the homecoming bonfire rally afterward. Jim Morrison chatted with the students who recognized him, and seemed to enjoy himself.

Strange Days was released that fall, more surreal than fashionably psychedelic, but its tense, experimental ambience and downbeat messages of loss and elusive human connections failed to capture the huge audience of the Doors' first record. The album would only reach a respectable number four on the charts. Nevertheless, *Strange Days* still stands as the Doors' singular masterpiece, their only truly great album, and an accurate depiction of warped 1967, when the generations ground against each other, the social progress of the "Great Society" dissolved in rancor and hatred, and America seemed on the brink of civil conflict.

Time and *Newsweek* reviewed the album. *Time* called the Doors "the black priests of the Great Society" and Jim "the Dionysius of rock." Not even the Rolling Stones had gotten this kind of attention. Critics subjected *Strange Days* to unprecedented scrutiny and identified its themes: the alienated unfamiliarity of the nervous times; the unredeemable loss of a little girl, an unhappy girl, who can be neither satisfied or consoled; the equation of ocular vision and love, where "my eyes have seen you" and "I can't see your face." Jim's romantic scenarios described visionary quests amid dark, brooding, existential dread. (In a contemporary notebook, he wrote: "You may enjoy life from afar. You may look at things but not taste them. You may caress the mother only with the eyes.") "When the Music's Over" glibly canceled the Resurrection and then, in howling agony, asked Jesus for salvation. The cheesy Doors organ sound, treated with primitive synthesizers, gave everyone the creeps (and still does). No wonder *Strange Days* didn't sell: It was a brilliant work of art, and a total bummer.

"The Beatles and the Stones are for blowing your mind," wrote the underground *L.A. Free Press*. "The Doors are for afterward, when your mind is already gone. It's like screeching your fingernails on the blackboard."

IN THE TOWN OF NEW HAVEN

"**T**HE UNKNOWN SOLDIER," the Doors' heroic antiwar anthem, came to life at the Fillmore Auditorium in San Francisco on November 16, 1967, when the Doors opened for the British band Procol Harum. "Soldier" was a blatant provocation. As American soldiers in the Mekong Delta, the Iron Triangle, and a mountainous wilderness called Khe Sanh came under increasing pressure from the communist insurgency in Vietnam, "The Unknown Soldier" described the experience of seeing the violence of the war on television, and the death of an unknown soldier, *any* soldier sent into the fog of war at the behest of old men with an ideology to defend. (Later the Doors would develop the song's performance into a sketch involving a mock execution.) The San Francisco audience received the public premiere of "The Unknown Soldier" with subdued wonder. This was a serious piece of antiwar agitprop, a work of art that commanded immediate attention among the generation for whom it was intended. No band other than the Doors could have produced a song (and then a film) so devastating, so violent, so impossibly dead-on.

(This was also the Doors' last show at the Fillmore in San Francisco. That weekend, they also played the Winterland Ballroom for the final time. The Doors were outgrowing the electric ballroom circuit, and would soon pioneer the playing of rock concerts in large-scale sports arenas.)

Back in L.A., Jim quarreled with Pamela, whose experiments with heroin were now more frequent. He moved into another motel and really hit the bottle, drinking daily with the guys in the film crew, especially Paul Ferrara and Babe Hill. Babe was a bearded, burly, blond biker-type, who Ferrara had brought in to hold the boom microphone at the chaotic Doors shows they were filming. Babe Hill quickly became a valued confidant of Jim's, often doubling as a bodyguard.

The following weekend, the Doors flew east for a three-night stand, with the Nitty Gritty Dirt Band opening. At Hunter College in Manhattan on Friday night, Jim seemed visibly fatigued and weird. Despite looking like a drunken god in black leather, Jim phoned in a disappointing show (in front of an audience heavy with New York media people) that only came alive with the still-evolving execution skit of "The Unknown Soldier." (Al Aronowitz, writing in the *New York Times:* "On Morrison's face was the look of someone who knows he is too beautiful to ever enjoy true love.") At the party later, Jim accidentally spilled his drink on a girl reporter, who had asked him if he'd been stoned on stage that night.

"Man, I'm stoned *all the time*," Jim laughed, and everyone laughed with him.

The Doors' road crew spent the next afternoon fending off the advances of Jim Morrison's mother. The Morrisons were living near Washington again, and Clara Morrison had been trying to contact Jim with an invitation to Thanksgiving dinner, but Jim ignored her messages and refused to return her calls. She left several messages that she and Jim's brother, Andy, would attend that evening's show in the ballroom of the Washington Hilton. Jim told Bill Siddons that his mother was to be accommodated with tickets, but Jim also ordered that she be kept far away from him. "I just don't want to see them," he said. Rich Linnel, a young promoter who would soon start working with the Doors, was deputized to keep Clara and Andy in a hotel room until the Doors were safely onstage. John Densmore later described Clara (who was obviously frustrated at being stonewalled) as being aggressive and demanding. Biographer Jerry Hopkins, who got his information from Siddons, described Jim recognizing and staring at his mother, who'd been given seats in the front row, as he performed a searing version of the Oedipal section of "The End." After the show, Jim was whisked out of the ballroom and disappeared. He would never see his mother—or speak to her—again.

The Doors' touring weekends were now forming a pattern. Jim sucked on Friday night. Saturday night was a little better. On a Sunday, like in Hartford on November 26, they absolutely killed. As the show began, the band vamped on "Soul Kitchen" for five minutes, waiting for Jim. When he finally strolled out, the cheering was so loud and vehement that he asked for quiet. Suddenly the room went still—validating Ray's often-stated admiration of Jim's astonishing crowd-control abilities.

Jim began the story of Olivia's soul food joint in Venice Beach, and the room exploded as the big audience sang along on the chorus. Every song received long, sincere ovations. "Morrison was shooting high for musical achievement," reported the *Hartford Times*. "He was working hard with all his soul and his heart."

The Doors flew back to L.A. the next day. The guys in the Nitty Gritty Dirt Band told the *Hartford Courant* that playing with the ego-tripping, always-late Doors had been a big fucking drag. "The Doors like to play games with their audience—it's scary."

CANNED HEAT, Jim's favorite blues band, opened for the Doors at Cal State Long Beach on December 1, 1967. Jim fell off the stage after telling Mother what he wanted in "The End." The kids figured it was part of the act and applauded. Police stopped the Portland, Oregon, show on December 3 when Jim leapt off the stage during "Light My Fire" and started shouting about how the cops had the guns, but *we* had the power. Chaos and confusion ensued in Memorial Coliseum. The house lights came up. The cops told Jim to get back on the stage, but Jim started rapping with the crowd, on mike, and the police pulled the plug.

Then the Doors flew east for another of their hairy weekends. In Troy, New York, they were largely ignored by an apathetic and distracted frat crowd at Rensselaer Polytechnic. "Break On Through," "Alabama Song," "When the Music's Over"—nothing worked. During the interlude of "Back Door Man," Jim recited the lyrics of the new "Five to One" with its triumphant boast—"They got the guns, but we got the numbers"—but no one cared. After an hour, Jim got bored and yelled, "If this is Troy, I'm with the fuckin' Greeks!" The Doors walked off.

It was Jim's twenty-fourth birthday, and he was mad as hell.

THE NEXT DAY they drove to New Haven. Jim Morrison was sullen and cranky, still bothered by his defeat in Troy. It had been another shitty birthday, and now the vibes in New Haven were deadly. The cops were uptight because the Black Panthers had come to town and were actively pursuing claims of police brutality. Several days earlier, the cops had violently broken up an antiwar rally near Yale, beating and arresting demonstrators. Even the local papers complained about police brutality in what had once been a quiet college town.

The concert was in a hockey rink, the New Haven Arena, and was sponsored by the fraternities at New Haven College. Bill Siddons got some help setting up the gear from Vince Treanor, an organ builder from Andover, Massachusetts, and four friends who'd seen the great performance at Hampton Beach at the end of the summer and had come to New Haven to see the band again. Also in New Haven to document the show was a team from *Life* magazine, including Tim Page, a combat photographer just returned from Vietnam (later the model for Dennis Hopper's gonzo hippie in *Apocalypse Now*). Page invited his friend Mike Zwerin, the *Village Voice*'s jazz critic, along for the ride. Both would be arrested with Jim that night.

Jim went out to dinner with some people before the eight-thirty show. A girl, a student at Southern Connecticut State College, asked Jim for his autograph, and he invited her to the show. Later, backstage, Jim and the girl disappeared into the shower room, and were just getting acquainted, talking and kissing, when a New Haven police officer walked in. (The girl's boyfriend was looking for her, and had asked the stage door cops for help.) The officer didn't know who Jim was, and rudely told them to get lost. Jim invited the cop to jump up his ass. What? "Eat me, asshole. Go fuck yourself." In an instant, the cop unhooked a can of chemical Mace and sprayed Jim right between the eyes. Blinded and tormented, like Oedipus at Colonus, Jim burst out of the shower and ran down the hall, shouting blue murder with tears streaming from his bloodshot eyes.

Mike Zwerin: "It was crowded backstage, and then it got much worse. Someone told the band, 'The pigs just Maced your lead singer!' People were outraged, and there was pushing and shoving. Tim Page was taking pictures and got jostled by the cops. The Doors' manager, who looked about sixteen, took Jim into the bathroom and was trying to rinse out his eyes." Lieutenant Kelly of the New Haven police barged into the scene, a crusty old Irish cop—Sterling Hayden in *The Godfather*—and said he wanted to arrest Jim immediately. The band's agent, Dick Loren, warned him that the two thousand college kids out front would likely riot if the show didn't go on. Eventually the police figured out they had brutalized the star of the show, and the offending cop was brought in to apologize to Jim. The police assumed that everything was squared away—"No hard feelings, right Jim?"—but Morrison said nothing, only smiled blearily, and asked for a beer.

The show started an hour late. "Ladies and gentlemen—from Los Angeles, California—the Doors!" Four songs into the set, during "Back Door Man," Jim stepped out of character and started rapping: "I wanna tell you a little story, something that happened here . . . just a little while ago, right here in New Haven." Densmore kept up the heavy tom-tom rhythm. ". . . We weren't doing anything, just standing there talking, and this little man came in . . . a little man in a little blue suit and a little blue cap, and he reached down behind him, and brought out this little black can and he sprayed it in my eyes. . . . I was blind for about thirty minutes, man."

Mike Zwerin: "Jim basically incorporated the narrative of what happened into the show. He told the whole story in detail, speaking in a low-key southern accent: the dinner, the girl, they were in the shower room together, and this cop started hassling them. He imitated the cop's dumb-ass voice, which pissed the hell out of the police guarding the edge of the stage. When he told the crowd that the cops had Maced him, there were loud protests. A few of the girls in front started to curse the officers, calling them pigs and scumbags. It was a hairy situation, and the cops were furious."

Jim went right into "When the Music's Over." At the climax, he screamed, "WE WANT THE WHOLE FUCKING WORLD, AND WE WANT IT . . . NOW." When he heard Jim's unnerving scream, and saw the crowd surge toward the stage in various states of rapture, Lieutenant Kelly ordered the house lights up. Then he strode onstage. He tapped Jim on the shoulder and said, "You've gone too far this time, young man." Ray got up, walked over, and whispered something in Jim's ear. Jim ignored him and yelled to the angry audience. "Do y'all wanna hear some more?" And, "Turn off the lights! *Turn the fuckin' lights off.*" He offered Kelly the microphone and provocatively drawled, "C'mon, man. Say your thing. Go ahead."

But two other cops grabbed Jim by each arm and marched him off the stage. Bill Siddons, in a white Cossack shirt, tried to intervene, but Jim said, "Cool it, Bill. They have to do this. It's what's happening." Vince Treanor followed them down the back stairs and witnessed the two cops punching Jim hard around the lower back and kidneys, really working him over. When they got to the loading dock behind the building, the cops knocked Jim to the ground, kicked him in the legs, and banged the top of his head on the roof of the squad car. Jim took all this without a word.

Treanor ran back upstairs. The Doors were milling around. Bill Siddons looked stunned. "Go to the jail," the older and wiser Treanor told him. "Get down there as fast as you can. Do what you can do. We'll take care of the stage."

Mike Zwerin: "The cops were horrible. They cleared the hall quickly, so there would be a nice little riot outside." Sirens. Police reinforcements. The kids got mad, with little girls cursing out the pigs. Tim Page, fresh from Vietnamese landing zones and firefights, was rattling off his Nikons when the cops arrested him, too, along with Zwerin and a *Life* researcher who was taking notes.

As about thirty people gathered outside the station, the police booked Jim, took mug shots, taunted him for his extra-long hair, charged him with obscenity and resisting arrest, and released him on $1,500 bond. (The arrest report described Jim as a self-employed singer, six feet tall—he was actually five nine—and 145 pounds. He listed his address as 8721 Sunset Boulevard, his managers' office. Closest living relative: "None.") Zwerin and the others were charged with disturbing the peace. "Which was bullshit," Zwerin said. "We had to come back to New Haven a couple of months later, and the charges were thrown out." The cops had also maced some of the kids who'd marched over from the arena to protest at the police station.

The arrests of Jim Morrison and the *Life* staffers in New Haven was national news the next morning. The *New York Times* covered it as the first arrest of a rock singer onstage, during a performance, recalling the harassment of Lenny Bruce and other gadfly artists. The story made the newsweeklies. Tim Page's images of an astounded Jim Morrison, pilloried onstage by uniformed policemen, were published in *Life* a few months later. Soon the mainstream press concluded that Jim Morrison and the Doors were trouble. Their agency reported the first slight drop in the band's bookings since "Light My Fire" had been number one, earlier in the year.

BLACK PRIESTS OF THE GREAT SOCIETY

EVEN THE ROAD-HARDENED DOORS were shaken by the Battle of New Haven. Jim's body was covered in bruises, according to one of his teenage girlfriends who liked to wash Jim in the bath. Jim ached all over. He saw a doctor, who told Jim that nothing was broken but that he had to rest. Instead Jim went on a major alcohol binge, cruising his preferred saloons with the guys from the film crew. The next Friday night, Jim Morrison didn't even show in Sacramento, and the Doors had to cancel. He was at the airport in L.A., drunk, but then disappeared. The next night, the Doors' sound system failed in San Bernardino, and the band walked off after Jim delivered an "acoustic" version of "Horse Latitudes" that filled Swing Auditorium with strange, disembodied poetics.

The band's faltering management consulted with Siddons, and hired superefficient Vince Treanor to fly out to California and try to fix the gear. When Treanor arrived in San Francisco a few days later to start work with the group, Jim didn't know who he was and threw him out of the band's dressing room. Slender and rock-charismatic with long brown hair, Treanor became the Doors' indispensable equipment manager—and still looked like "Jim Morrison" long after the real one had grown a beard, put on weight, and looked more like Canned Heat's Bob "The Bear" Hite.

BY THE END OF THE YEAR, the money started coming in. Splitting their sales and publishing royalties four ways, Ray says they each got about fifty thousand dollars. (The biggest loss was Robby's, who'd written their hit record.) After "Light My Fire" had gone to number one, Jac Holzman told the Doors they could have anything they wanted as a gift. Ray and Robby got tape decks. John got a horse. Jim got a dark blue Ford Mustang Shelby GT 500, an even hotter car than the sizzling AC Cobra that stylist Jay Sebring drove. This souped-up Mustang hot rod had incredible pickup and an evil, low-slung profile that appealed to Jim. It was christened "the Blue Lady," reportedly by crony/soundman Babe Hill, after the whore-of-Babylon character in Jim's evolving hitchhiker screenplay.

The Mustang really hauled ass. Jim Morrison was the scourge of winding Mulholland Drive. Everyone in Hollywood and the canyons knew it was his ride. He liked to drive it, full bore, up rugged Topanga Canyon Boulevard from the Pacific Coast Highway, through the great gorge over the mountains to the 101 freeway, and back to Laurel Canyon or West Hollywood.

Drunk.

O N DECEMBER 21, 1967, the winter solstice, a bright and warm day in subtropic Los Angeles, Jim Morrison and Pamela Courson witnessed the marriage of Ray Manzarek and Dorothy Fujikawa at Los Angeles City Hall. Then they walked over to the old mission neighborhood nearby, and had a big Mexican lunch under the veranda of one of the restaurants on Olivera Street. When a little band of mariachi musicians came over to serenade, Jim lifted his margarita and toasted the couple: "To the newlyweds—may you dance, forever!" Pamela raised her glass and whispered, "Forever."

Later that night, there was a fight at Pam's place when she told Jim she needed to get married, and he callously told her that the record company said it would be bad for his image. When Jim woke up (or came to) the next morning, Pam was gone. Before she left, she scrawled the word FAGGOT in red lipstick on the bedroom mirror.

T HE DOORS PLAYED TWO NIGHTS at the cavernous Shrine Auditorium in L.A. On the first night, Jim grabbed a spotlight during the jazz solos, trying to work out awkward movement problems. Jim had to figure out what to do, how to project, as the band now moved into really large rooms. No one in 1967 knew what a rock singer was supposed to do with himself in an arena show. There were no video screens, no choreographers, no lighting directors, no sound engineers, no stylists or wardrobe people, and the PA systems were still primitive. Arena rock concerts were invented at the same time they were being hastily improvised by the Doors in 1967.

Robby Krieger: "Sometimes [Jim] would fall on the stage and writhe like a snake. I knew he didn't really mean all that stuff, but I knew he felt he had to *push himself,* to do more and more, as the crowds got bigger. I just felt sorry for him."

There was an awkward instant. Jim burned his hands on the hot light. Then a stagehand showed Jim how to hold the spot, and he spent some time picking out faces. At least it gave Jim something to do while Robby played the "Eleanor Rigby" hook during eleven boring minutes of "Light My Fire"—a song Jim was learning to loathe the more he had to sing it. The next night, some kids who couldn't get in started throwing bottles at the cops, who then raided the Shrine and stopped the show.

Just before Christmas, the Doors taped two songs for *The Jonathan Winters Show* on CBS, mostly because they thought comedian Winters was extremely funny. Jim, stone-drunk, sang in dark sunglasses, and "Moonlight Drive" went well. But at the end of "Light My Fire," Jim got tangled in a chicken-wire stage prop and muffed the end of the song. The director assured them that another take was unnecessary. Densmore later wrote that they were all embarrassed for Jim; too embarrassed, as usual, to actually say anything about it to him.

T HE DOORS FINISHED 1967 at Winterland, in San Francisco, where Jim Morrison seemed to come alive again. Otis Redding, who Jim had idolized, had been booked to headline, but he'd died in a plane crash on December 10, and Chuck Berry subbed instead when the Doors were bumped by Bill Graham to the top of the bill. January Jansen made Jim a new black velvet shirt with gray cobras twining up the left sleeve. Backstage Jim asked Jansen to get him a dozen red roses—"Not romance red. Blood red"—for a tribute he wanted to make to Redding. (Jansen also says he intercepted megadoses of LSD and STP intended for Jim from Owsley Stanley, so that Jim could perform straight.) That night Jim appeared with a dozen long-stemmed roses and handed them out to the youngest girls in the front row. Then he sang: *"Poor Otis, dead and gone, left me here to sing this song, pretty little girl with the red dress on, poor Otis, dead and gone,"* and the band slid into "When the Music's Over."

The first show on December 26 was filled with poetry and ad-libs, due in part to the presence of Michael McClure in the audience. The new and hideous demonic peal of laughter began "Back Door Man." "Break On Through" was intercut with Jim riffing, "Come on baby, *be my man, be my man,* you understand—yeahhhh." He put his whole body into a suggestive posture during Muddy Waters's "I'm a Man" and seemed to gaze longingly at a handsome guy in the crowd.

The next night at Winterland, a TV set was wheeled onstage during the Doors set so the band could see themselves on the *Jonathan Winters Show.* They stopped playing "Back Door Man" when their song came on (there were no home VCRs as yet). The audience watched the Doors watching themselves on TV. They finished the song when their bit was done, and Ray walked over and turned the TV off.

The next night was their last ever at Winterland. All the girls cried at a stunning, beautifully sung version of "You're Lost, Little Girl." "Love Me Two Times" was killer hard rock, played with discipline and real heat. As a prelude to "Light My Fire" Jim deployed an anguished variation on his recitation "Wake Up."

The encore was "The Unknown Soldier," and with this Jim Morrison blew them away. The execution scene was now a skit where Densmore rolled the drums, Jim stood at attention with his arms behind his back, Robby pointed his guitar like a rifle, and Ray raised his arm in a quasi-fascist salute. When he brought it down, Densmore hit a shattering rim shot and Jim dropped to the stage like he'd been kicked in the scrotum or gut-shot, point-blank. It was the Doors' last great bit of rock theater, and it brought the house down, and would for the next year.

Pamela Courson went to Colorado with the band on December 29, where they played at the Family Dog through New Year's Eve. While in Denver, she obtained a Colorado marriage license. She filled it out for both of them, but the license was neither notarized nor filed, and as far as is known the couple never married. To placate his girlfriend, to get her off his back, Jim agreed to her demands that he back her in a high-fashion boutique she wanted to open in West Hollywood, and he instructed the Doors' new accountant to give Pamela Courson access to his money.

CHAPTER SIX

SUNKEN CONTINENTS

Poetry will no longer accompany action but will lead it. These poets are going to exist!

—ARTHUR RIMBAUD

Jim was a wild guy. He lived his life on the edge, all the time. Jim had a burning fire inside of him. He was testing life, all the time.

—ROBBY KRIEGER

He who is a legend in his own time, is ruled by that legend.

—VICTOR HUGO

UP AGAINST THE WALL, MOTHERFUCKER

NO ONE WHO LIVED THROUGH 1968 has yet been able to adequately explain what happened that terrible year. Wars ravaged Southeast Asia and the Middle East. America was in turmoil and unrest, not between regions as in the past, but between generations. In April the civil rights activist Martin Luther King was assassinated and American cities erupted in race riots. Two months later, Robert Kennedy was gunned down by a Palestinian assassin after winning the California presidential primary as an antiwar candidate. Many members of the Black Panther Party were killed or wounded by the police. European capitals were rocked by a radical coalition of students and workers. One came close to toppling the French government in May. Soviet Russia sent tanks to crush Czech rebels. "Black and white the news is read: television children fed." Violence. Atrocities. Repression. Napalm. Genocide. It was a year that, over and over again, felt like the end of the world.

Apocalypse, *now.*

American youth responded to this in various ways. Radical students, furious and powerless, shouted "Up against the wall, motherfucker" at their teachers and the cops. Student organizations split off into militant groups, some of whom carried out bombings and sabotage. There was a huge surge of interest in gurus from the East and occult oracles like the tarot and the *I Ching.* These were witchy times, especially in southern California. Out in Topanga, and even farther out, near Death Valley, frustrated songwriter Charles Manson and his band of hippie desert rats were fucking their brains out and preaching bloody murder. *Heavy* was the operative word in the youth vocabulary that year. Heavy metal. Heavy friends. Industry heavies. "She's so . . . heavy." The whole hippie giggle turned heavy in the face of grim reality. Men threw off the peacock clothes of 1967, grew beards, tried to look like rural carpenters. The commune movement began, with groups of alienated youth seeking solace on old farms, away from an America they disavowed.

And who was the archrebel of 1968? The American baby boom generation, the largest population bulge in American history, now embraced "Jim Morrison" as the saw-toothed, skin-clad personification of its rebellion. In the press he was described as "the mystery poet of psychic liberation" and "a daring acid evangelist." There is no little irony in the fact that an admiral's brilliant and troubled son was thrown up by the counterculture to demand, "We want the world, and we want it—now."

In January 1968 the Doors were the biggest band in America. No one else could touch them for talent and mystique. Jim Morrison was faced with writing their next album, which definitely had to be a heavy masterpiece that perfectly captured the intensity of the burning days through which people were living and dying. Elektra Records was a corporation now, pumped up by Doors dollars, and the pressure on Jim became unbearable.

Jim responded to this creative challenge by becoming a major alcoholic, alienating almost everyone with whom he came in contact, disgracing himself in public, getting blackmailed by street hustlers, ruining concerts with drunken antics, dooming his band, and wrecking his career as a rock star.

It was probably the best he could do, under the circumstances.

There were other pressures on Jim as well. Sometime around the turn of the year, the Doors' hapless managers tried to separate Jim from the group. They took Jim out to lunch and told him that splitting the publishing royalties to his songs with the group would cost him millions by the time he was an old man. They told Jim that he could make much more money by going out as a solo act, with hired musicians. It was a shrewd gamble on their part. They knew Jim was disaffected, and it could have worked. Janis Joplin was said to be quitting Big Brother, and many great bands were breaking up—Cream, Traffic, Lovin' Spoonful, the Byrds (again), Buffalo Springfield—as star musicians joined each other in newly configured "supergroups." Jim disliked John Densmore so much, according to Ray, that he'd wanted to fire him back in 1967. The other Doors were "heads"—pot smokers—who didn't hang out with Jim in the bars he frequented. Jim couldn't take the Doors anywhere. They didn't drink. Ray was pompous and boring. Robby chewed with his mouth open. Densmore complained all the time. Jim now arrived at the gigs separately, and with his own entourage, and left the same way after the show. The atmosphere in the Doors' dressing rooms had become unusually sullen and morose. The Doors before a show looked like a combat platoon before an assault, wondering who would die that day.

(The feelings were mutual, by the way. Densmore despised Jim's lunacy and monumental selfishness, and was generally terrified of having to depend on someone he thought was crazy. Robby, Densmore claims, also grew to dislike Jim "intensely," and began to think of his future with the Doors as a day-to-day thing.)

So Jim was ripe for the plucking. It could be The Jim Morrison Show! He later said that another record company offered him bribes—a house in Beverly Hills, a Rolls, a quarter-million-dollar signing bonus—to let their lawyers break the Elektra contract and sign with them. But Jim just laughed at them. The Doors had a pact, signed in blood, and he meant to honor it. Anyway, Jim probably knew that he had already written his best stuff, his finest work. No one could top the first two Doors albums.

At the next Doors gig, Jim offhandedly mentioned to the others what Sal and Ash had suggested. The next morning, Robby Krieger went to Jac Holzman. The Elektra chief, immensely relieved to be rid of people he considered incompetent, advanced the band fifty thousand dollars to buy their managers out.

Then, in an act of willful contempt for the business and themselves, the Doors appointed Bill Siddons, their twenty-year-old roadie, to manage them—the biggest rock band in America.

ROBBY: "How would you like to be our manager?"
BILL: "What's a manager do?"
ROBBY: "Well, just answer the phones, and then we'll have a meeting and decide what to do."

The Doors said years later that they thought all the manager did was work the phones and supervise the bookings. No one could quite believe it, but Jac Holzman let it go through because Siddons would be easy to control, and he was like Jim Morrison's son. Besides, no one else besides Bill could tell Jim what to do.

Bill Siddons: "Jim always did what he wanted, not what other people wanted. He could see through any of us, whatever game we were trying to play. He could read anybody he was talking to. He only provoked people that he knew could fuck with him. He was fearless in a lot of ways. He had zero regard for his own well-being, no respect for authority, and usually he would take extra steps to provoke it. He could dominate me any time he needed to, but he knew that I came to him with what the reality was. I couldn't make him do anything, but he would respond to me because he knew I was telling him the truth. He'd be like, 'I don't want to embarrass the kid.' So he'd go along. He was always the father figure, and I was the son who knew better. That's how it worked."

I N THE FIRST FEW MONTHS OF 1968, Jim Morrison's daily world was consolidated into a few square blocks of West Hollywood, a neighborhood of art galleries, antique shops, and designers (including Rudi Gernreich, whose topless bathing suits were a current fashion scandal). Bill Siddons found an office at 8512 Santa Monica Boulevard, a ramshackle duplex that had been an antique shop. The main room served as the band's hangout and rehearsal space, while the upstairs was used as an office by Siddons and the staff. Jim insisted on having his own desk, where he read his fan mail and made calls. Around the corner, at 962 North La Cienega, Elektra was building its state-of-the-art recording studio, soon to be one of the best in the country. Pamela Courson moved herself and her golden retriever, Sage, to a one-bedroom apartment (No. 2) on the second floor of 8216 Norton Avenue, three blocks to the east, between Harper and Fountain. Later in the year, she opened her new boutique, Themis, across the street from Elektra at 947 North La Cienega, in the Clear Thoughts Building, where rock manager David Geffen had his office. Jim later had his film production office upstairs in this building as well.

Early in 1968, Jim also took semipermanent possession of Room 32 in the Alta Cienega Motel, at the intersection of Santa Monica and North La Cienega. This inexpensive, well-kept, and clean motel was basically Jim's home for the next three years. Nearby were Jim's favorite bars: the Palms, Barney's Beanery, the topless Phone Booth, and its sister saloon, the Extension. Conveniently across the street from the Doors' workshop was Monaco Liquors, where Jim had an account. He could often be seen eating at the sidewalk café of the Garden District restaurant, farther south on La Cienega.

This was Jim Morrison's neighborhood. Within a small, six-square-block area, he had his band, his two offices, his record label, his woman and her shop, his motel hideaway, his friendly bartenders, the strippers who worked at the Phone Booth, his favorite greasy spoons, his liquor store, and everything he needed. In that year, Jim Morrison, the biggest rock star in America, could often be seen walking around West Hollywood, or idling at the Garden District, dressed like marmoreal rough trade in his full leathers, totally unprotected, vulnerable, and seemingly comfortable in his familiar neighborhood.

J IM HAD TO WRITE NOW, had to churn out some hit records, and he turned to alcohol for inspiration. He basically gave up LSD and became an alcoholic, a boozehound, a sometimes pathetic drunk who, if someone didn't take him home, passed out in the bushes while he was pissing. Everyone around him was totally horrified as Jim began an epic drinking binge that would imprison one of America's best young poets in a pagan stupor for the next three and a half years. In 1968 smoking pot was cool, cocaine was just beginning to be fashionable in the music and movie communities, and heroin preoccupied the few who needed the ultimate high. Getting drunk (not just drunk, but shit-faced), falling down, passing out, slapping women, getting tossed out of clubs on the Strip, vomiting in the street—was *so* uncool, *so* unhip, that no one could believe it. The other Doors—meditating potheads who sipped organic apple juice at recording sessions—and obsessive joint-rolling producer Paul Rothchild were all mortified.

Paul Rothchild later theorized that Jim's drinking disorder was compounded by a possible enzyme deficiency whose symptoms seem to align with the drastic personality changes Jim went through after an afternoon of drinking. Jim could put away two dozen shots of whiskey and a couple of six packs of beer without showing it. But then one more drink could suddenly turn him into a stumbling, psychotic drunk, shouting "Nigger!" in the streets, pissing in public, and disgracing himself. It was a scandal, and no one had the faintest idea what to do about it.

Several of their friends have said that Pam Courson was extremely upset about all this, and insisted that Jim see a psychiatrist. Pamela's father later said that Jim did visit a therapist to please her after, as he put it, "something bad had happened." Jim reportedly consulted someone for a couple of weeks, and then didn't go back, at which point the intrigued therapist began calling Jim, and called every day for a week until Jim told him to cool it. (The therapist has never been identified.) Jim told Pam that the doctor had asked him a lot of questions, and that the sessions had gone "pretty good." That was it.

Columbus Courson later said, "Of course, knowing Jim, you never know whether he's putting you on or not. I can just see him . . . sitting there with the psychiatrist, really giving this guy the biggest trip in the world."

VIVA LAS VEGAS!

JIM MORRISON'S DISSIPATION WAS KEPT SECRET; unknown to the masses of rock fans who idolized him. To them, Jim was still a ballsy god with a literary bent and a bulge in his crotch, the Back Door Man, the studly, cop-baiting rocker whose interviews, then just beginning to be widely published beyond the underground and alternative press, revealed him as thoughtful, articulate, and sometimes profound:

"I find that music liberates my imagination. When I sing my songs in public, yes, that's a dramatic act, but not acting as in theater, but a social act—real action."

Another interview: "Music is so erotic. One of its functions is a purgation of emotion, which we see every night when we play. To call our music 'orgasmic' means we can move people to a kind of emotional orgasm through music and words. A concert only clicks when the musicians and the audience reach a kind of united experience. For me, it is stirring, satisfying to know that the various boundaries which separate people from other people are lowered for the space of one hour."

And, from a taped interview: "We appeal to the same basic, human needs as classical tragedy or, you know, southern blues. Think of it as a séance in an environment which has become hostile to life, cold, restrictive. People feel they're dying in a bad landscape. So they gather together in a séance to invoke, palliate, and drive away the dead spirits through chanting, singing, dancing, music. They [the shamans] try to cure an illness, to restore harmony to the world."

Jim was also very funny. When he was comfortable and with friends he would laugh and joke about everything. If he was in one of his bars and someone kidded him about "The End," Jim said, "Oh, yeah? Hey, man—come on. I don't want to fuck my mother." Pause. "I wanna fuck *your* mother." Bar fights started this way. Jim almost got brained by a stool thrown at him by an enraged customer who came after him at the Whisky one night. The bouncers held the guy down until Jim and the two girlfriends he was with could get out of the joint.

B Y JANUARY 1968, Jim Morrison rarely bought records, but he went out and got Bob Dylan's new album, *John Wesley Harding,* a suite of visionary songs cut in Nashville with local musicians. Jim listened repeatedly to "All Along the Watchtower" and "I Dreamed I Saw St. Augustine" in Pamela's second-story flat on Norton Avenue, up a flight of red-tiled exterior steps from a small courtyard off the street, behind a hedge of oleander and cactus. Jim had his books there, displayed in plastic milk crates against a wall. Jim liked to read in an overstuffed lounge chair, covered in hideous purple shag, while Pamela cooked supper. Candles burned day and night.

Elektra publicist Diane Gardiner lived downstairs, and remembered that Jim and Pamela's fights would course up and down this red-tiled staircase, like the swashbuckling swordfights in old Errol Flynn movies. She'd be screaming, "You'll get yours, Jim Morrison!" He'd yell back, "You'll get yours, baby, and I'll get mine." Soon Jim's books and clothes would fly out the window, piling up in the courtyard below.

Jim loved the new Dylan album, and even copied some of the lyrics—evidently from memory, since there are discrepancies—into one of the notebooks he was working in.

Early that month, the Doors filmed a new promo clip for their next single, "The Unknown Soldier." Shot in grainy, underground newsreel style by Mark Abramson and intercut with stock footage of Vietnam war scenes and hippies lolling in the grass, *The Unknown Soldier* film began with a family gathering around the breakfast table, then depicted the four Doors walking barefoot on Venice Beach. Three of the musicians carry Indian instruments: tablas and a sitar. As the song's story of graves and executions unfolds, Dorothy Manzarek binds a Christlike Jim—unshaven, long stringy hair, dirty fleece jacket, drunk looking—to a pier piling with orange ropes, along with a bouquet of flowers. More images flash—Viet Cong corpses, Zippoed huts, artillery firing—before the fatal shot rings out and Jim spews horrid blood from his mouth from four different angles. Blood drips on the flowers as Jim collapses, held grotesquely in place by the ropes. The other musicians play a raga at Jim's dead feet during the extravagant emotion of "It's all over—war is over," and then walk away down the beach, carrying their instruments. (The unintentional subtext of this was the three Doors "killing" Jim with their tedious meditation and Indian spirituality.) *The Unknown Soldier* was edited in January, and made its debut in New York the following month. But the film was considered too violent for general broadcast, and was shown only on public TV stations in Boston and San Francisco.

O N THE WEEKEND OF JANUARY 19/20, 1968, after three weeks off, the Doors resumed their concert career at the Carousel Theater in West Covina, near L.A. The first night Jim was great, energized by the thrilling music, collapsing onstage and then leaping back to the mike, directly on cue. The following night, at the same place, he was so drunk he had to hang on to the microphone stand all night.

During the week that followed, Jim began to codify the six sections of his epic poem "Celebration of the Lizard," which was supposed to fill one or both sides of the next Doors album. The band was having a hard time trying to knit the sections together in a cohesive, playable way. Jim was also working on another long poem, "Texas Radio," based on the cadences of the Bible preachers he used to listen to in high school. He also presented his new "Orange County Suite" to the band, a group of short poems dedicated to Pamela. They hated it.

Jim was also hanging out with novelist Robert Gover, author of the 1961 cult novel *One Hundred Dollar Misunderstanding.* Gover had been given the plum assignment of profiling Jim for the Sunday magazine of the *New York Times,* and they'd had lunch together in New York the last time Jim was there. Jim had been quiet and distracted during the meal as his managers ("two sharpies," Gover remembered) blabbed away. Afterward, Jim had taken Gover for a walk in the park, and told him the managers were about to be fired. Jim looked at Gover and murmured, "See, I'm really a poet." He pulled out a notebook and began to read aloud. "There was something about each poem that made me want to hear it again," Gover later wrote. "That's when I met the widely read, philosophical, poetic Jim Morrison."

After that meeting, Jim began dropping in at Gover's apartment on the beach in Malibu, studying the writer's collection of occult books, and pulling stunts like swinging from the balcony railings. Jim would show up at four a.m. and raid the refrigerator. He repeatedly asked Gover how he could get his poems published. One night he tore *Strange Days* off Gover's stereo and smashed it to bits with his boots, cursing wildly. (The next time he showed up, Jim brought a mint copy of the album and offered to autograph it.) Some days he would turn up, light a joint, and invite Gover to walk down the beach. At sundown, Gover's girlfriend would cook supper. As they were about to sit down, Jim would mutter, "Ah...I left a chick...y'know...sitting in the car." The girl, Jim's latest pickup, usually very young, would be invited in for dinner.

The *Times* took Gover off the story when he and his editor couldn't agree on an angle, but Jim kept coming around to Gover's place. One stoned night they decided to take a road trip to Las Vegas, then still a barbarous Mafia gambling town in the desert wasteland between Death Valley and Paradise Valley in Nevada. Gover had lived there for a while, and had often sung its praises to Jim as America's material concentration camp. Jim wanted to drive Gover's huge piece of Detroit iron, an Olds 98, to Vegas, and said that Pamela wanted to come along. But, just before they left, Jim and Pam had a tremendous row. (A woman close to

Pamela believes that Jim might have passed on a case of gonorrhea to Pamela, and she was livid with rage.) So Jim went to Vegas with Gover and his girlfriend as a threesome.

JANUARY 29, 1968. Jim drove into the desert all day, morose, and they arrived in Vegas around sundown. They met some of Gover's friends, among them a black guy named Don Chaney and his lady, and went to dinner, then on to a strip club called the Pussycat a' Go Go.

Jim was in his tight leather pants, tipsy on wine and pot, part of an interracial long-haired group in redneck Las Vegas. He proceeded to provoke a disaster in one of his best-documented flip-outs. As he got out of the car at the strip club, he bummed a cigarette from Gover and smoked it cupped in his hand, like he was hiding a joint. The guard at the club's entrance hassled Jim, and Jim gave him some attitude back. "Whyn't you jump up mah ass?"

Suddenly the guard was swinging a billy club, smashing Jim in the head with three quick shots. Shocked, Jim reeled back and started bleeding. The guard knocked down one of Gover's other friends, who tried to intervene. The black man—Chaney—started yelling for the cops. In all this chaos, Jim never said a word, leaning against the wall with a bloody face. The Vegas cops drove up and bent an agitated Jim over the hood of their patrol car. Jim started in on them: "You chicken-shit pigs. Assholes. Fuckin' stupid redneck bastards. I'm gonna have your fuckin' badges, and you're gonna be back collecting garbage again." The cops arrested Jim and Robert Gover and threw them in the back of their squad car.

Gover later wrote: "It wasn't just our momentary plight that aroused these invisible avenging angel/demons. It was also the temper of the times, the war in Vietnam, the plight of millions all over the planet unjustly harmed by such uniformed nitwits as these. Morrison thought and felt in planetary terms, and his mind had an uncanny way of reaching back in time, as though he was the reincarnation of a pagan priest who'd been burned at the stake during the Inquisition and was here to avenge that wrong, and all the others. When manhandled by the emperor's troops, he would rather be killed than humbled. In the heart and soul of Jim Morrison, there was an uncontrollable rage against injustice."

At the station house, the police sergeant took one look at their shoulder-length hair and called for a strip search, a ritual humiliation inflicted on hippies. Then the cops sprayed them with roach powder. They made Jim and Gover bend over, spread their cheeks, and sprayed them with "a final blast up the ass." This brought chuckles from the cops on duty that night. Jim and Robert Gover were charged with public intoxication and disturbing the peace.

"By the time we'd been booked, fingerprinted, thrown into the holding tank, James Douglas Morrison was no longer present," Gover wrote. "His eyes were out of focus and he was panting like a fire-breathing dragon. That's when he climbed the bars of our extra-high cell [and started] yelling, 'Hey, Bob—aren't these fucking pigs *the ugliest MOTHERFUCKERS you ever saw?*' and other such endearments, delivered in that resonant voice and clear diction that was his trademark as a singer. There was no point in reminding him that that the police in Las Vegas had the extralegal power to kill you. Whatever force had gained control of him didn't care for his physical safety, or mine."

The cops who arrested them stopped by, said they got off duty at midnight and would see them "in private" when they were sprung. Gover was terrified.

Gover's girlfriend bailed them out at eleven-thirty. They fled the police station and went to retrieve the Olds in the Pussycat parking lot. Jim got behind the wheel and decided to drive down the wrong side of the street. Chaney grabbed the wheel, forced Jim to the side of the road, and Gover took over. Jim was laughing like a maniac. They went to the Moulin Rouge, where Jim decided to sit in with the jazz combo. He let out one of his insane "Back Door Man" screams and the musicians just stopped playing. At this point Chaney, who was built like a linebacker, grabbed Jim and told him he would die that night if he didn't behave himself. They ended up at a friend's apartment, listening to Doors records. Chaney bluntly told Jim he wasn't impressed by this "jive-ass shit" he was hearing.

Jim drove the Olds back to L.A. the next day, took Gover and his old lady to dinner, and then to the Whisky, where he delivered an in-depth analysis of how the Doors had gradually, methodically, developed their music there, refining it in response to a familiar, discerning audience. Jim complained that now they had to write new songs cold, in the studio. Now he had to emote to thousands of screaming teenagers in hockey arenas, kids who had no fucking idea what was going on. He said he was bored. They dropped Jim off at the Alta Cienega Motel and went home to Malibu. Robert Gover didn't have much more to do with Jim after that.

The Nevada charges were dropped as soon as Jim's lawyer obtained the police report. Jim Morrison never went back to Las Vegas. This wouldn't be the last time that one of his patented flip-outs was triggered by the aftermath of a fight with the indomitable Pamela Courson.

BALLROOM DAYS ARE OVER

THERE WAS BY THEN, the early months of 1968, serious interest in Jim Morrison in certain movie circles. Not in the hippest of movie circles—Fonda, Hopper, and Terry Southern, writing their cocaine movie over at the Castle, thought that Jim was a punk—but in old-school Hollywood production circles. The children of the L.A. studio execs were hot for the Doors and told their dads about this guy in leather pants and no underwear doing poetry at rock shows. *Vogue* magazine ran a fashion-style portrait of Jim that validated him as a mainstream face. Memos about the Doors started to fly around Universal City and even Paris. The trade papers announced that Universal Studios had offered the Doors half a million to appear in a film featuring the band. Two of France's best directors, Jacques Demy and his companion, Agnès Varda, were in L.A. and actively trying to interest Jim in working with them. Michael McClure was prodding MGM executives about having Jim star in a movie version of his play *The Beard.*

One evening in January, screenwriter John Gregory Dunne arrived at TTG Recording Studios on Sunset and Highland Avenue, where the Doors were working on their third album. Dunne was producing a new movie, *Panic in Needle Park,* and wanted to speak to Jim about starring in it with Tom Baker. Dunne brought along his wife, Joan Didion, and spent the evening like everyone else, waiting for Jim Morrison to show up.

Didion wanted to interview Jim for the *Saturday Evening Post.* She noted the "uneasy symbiosis" of the studio ambience, as the other three

Doors and bassist Doug Lubahn worked on Robby's flamenco track "Spanish Caravan." She noted the cold tile floor, the harsh lights, the ennui of waiting, the boring dialogue:

RAY: "You think Morrison's gonna come back? So we can do some vocals."
No one answers.
Finally, ROTHCHILD: "I hope so."
RAY: "So do I."

"The Doors interest me," she later wrote. "They have nothing in common with the gentle Beatles.... Their music insists that love is sex and sex is death and therein lives salvation. The Doors are the Norman Mailers of the Top 40, missionaries of apocalyptic sex."

The head missionary finally arrived, Didion observed, wearing black vinyl pants. He was drunk. A slutty-looking teenager trailed behind him. (Didion failed to mention these last two.) No one spoke to him. He sank into a couch and closed his eyes. Another hour passed in silence and studio frittering. Finally she recorded this scintillating dialogue:

JIM (whispering to Ray): "It's an hour out to West Covina. I was thinking, maybe we should spend the night out there after we play."
RAY: "Why?"
JIM: "Instead of coming back."
RAY: "We were planning to come back."
JIM: "Well, I was thinking, we could rehearse out there. There's a Holiday Inn next door."
RAY: "We could do that. Or we could rehearse Sunday, in town."
JIM: "Will the place [the Doors' new office] be ready to rehearse Sunday?"
Ray looked at Jim for a while, and said, "No."

It's possible that Joan Didion had never attended a recording session, and was expecting to be entertained. Maybe Jim picked up on this. There was no way he was going to do her interview.

Didion just put down the facts. "Morrison sits down on the leather couch again and leans back. He lights a match. He studies the flame for a while, and very slowly, very deliberately, lowers it to the fly of his black vinyl pants. Manzarek watches him. There is the sense that no one is going to leave this room, ever. It will be some weeks before the Doors finish recording this album."

BUT JIM WASN'T COMPLETELY OUT OF IT. He was too smart to appear in Dunne's depressing junkie movie. Instead he contacted Demy and Varda and befriended them. Jim was flattered by their attention, and invited them to dinner. Jacques Demy had made *The Umbrellas of Cherbourg* and was currently enjoying another hit with *Young Girls of Rochefort* starring Catherine Deneuve. Agnès Varda was already a legend for her 1962 masterpiece *Cleo from Five to Seven*, and had made recent radical films about Vietnam and the Black Panthers. (Jim would appear as an extra in Varda's California film, *Lions Love*, made late that year.)

Also at this time Jim also wrote to critic Wallace Fowlie at Duke University, to compliment him on a new edition of Rimbaud's poetry that Fowlie had edited:

> *Dear Wallace Fowlie:*
> *Just wanted to say thanks for the Rimbaud translation. I needed it because I don't read French that easily. I am a rock singer and your book travels around with me.*
> [Under the signature is a postscript:] *That Picasso drawing of Rimbaud on the cover is* <u>great.</u>

FEBRUARY 10, 1968. The Doors played the Berkeley Community Theater. Iron Butterfly opened: their heavy metal jam "In-A-Gadda-Da-Vida" was on its way to number one. Jim scrapped the normal Doors set and led the band in a live performance of "Celebration of the Lizard." Ill-advisedly, Jim deployed his harmonica just after the "Not to Touch the Earth" segment. Again, some of the musical transitions proved difficult for the group, and press reviews of the show expressed astonishment that Jim Morrison would stiff his fans and recite poetry all evening. (They did do the obligatory "Light My Fire" at the end of the show.)

Jim drove back to L.A. the next morning with his crew—Jan Jansen, Paul Ferrara, and Babe Hill. He had his notebook out—he was supposed to be writing lyrics—and intently watched the California landscape go by on California Route 1, down through Big Sur. They were talking about the smaller places the Doors had played in, and someone said to Jim, "Your ballroom days are over, baby." He wrote this down. Later, going by San Simeon, William Randolph Hearst's palatial house, Jim wrote the "The mansion is warm at the top of the hill" verse in his notebook, which was soon incorporated into "Not to Touch the Earth" in "Celebration." Every time they stopped—to eat, to pee, to get gas, Jim found a pay phone and called Pamela to read her the latest lines he'd written. Jim's friends rolled their eyes every time he called, and kidded him about being pussy whipped. Jim just laughed and kept scrawling.

That night they visited a friend of Jansen's who lived in a trailer. "Crystal Ship" came on the radio and Jim's mood changed. Jansen thought he was embarrassed. "Why are they playing this, now?" Jim asked.

"And he turned," Jansen recalled, "turned around and went into this *spasm*. He was the classic Jekyll and Hyde. As he did, the trailer rocked off its blocks and it tipped over with us inside. It was an interesting evening."

The next day Jim made Babe Hill, who was driving, stop at every gas station and diner so he could call Pamela and continue to read the stuff he'd scrawled in his notebook to her.

EARLY ON THE EVENING OF FEBRUARY 15, Jim Morrison turned up unexpectedly at Jac Holzman's front door in L.A. with a haphazardly wrapped present for his son, Adam, who turned ten years old that day. The present was a kalimba, an African thumb piano, and Jim spent the next two hours sitting crossed legged on the floor with the musically inclined boy, teaching him how to play it.

JIM'S DRINKING WAS GETTING WORSE. He got thrown out of the Whisky again. He was banned from the Troubadour. He crashed his car. He crashed the rental car. He lost his license. He slapped girls in the face at the Whisky, the Troubadour, Ben Frank's. He'd dump Pamela and disappear in a car with some people to get fucked up. He threw up on people, yelled obscenities and racial slurs, ran across busy intersections dodging cars, pissed in front of people. The local hipsters in L.A. felt extremely let down by this, and hated him for embarrassing himself in public. His fellow artists and musicians found him excruciating, and avoided hanging out with him. His reputation as a cool renegade and an arrogant outsider derived from the fact that no one wanted him around when he was drunk. If Jim came in the front door, the cool people—Gram Parsons, Dennis Hopper, Taj Mahal, Michael Butler, Jack Nicholson—slipped out the back door. Jim was also gaining weight, and a second chin was now faintly noticeable on what had been classically beautiful features. Local groupies like Eve Babitz, who once wanted to fuck him, now wanted to kill him.

THE DOORS hated Jim for bringing his sleazy friends to the recording sessions. This drove them nuts. Jim would arrive drunk with musicians Wes (Densmore: "long blond hair, Charles Manson vibes") and Freddie ("male groupie leech"), who Densmore suspected of giving Jim blow jobs. Teenage girls who accosted Jim outside the studio were allowed upstairs by him only if they agreed to take off all their clothes and follow him in naked. One evening Jim came in with Wes and Freddie and a very pretty hippie girl (long rumored to have been one of Manson's sex slaves) with whom they were apparently engaged in a prolonged, ongoing orgy of anal intercourse. Densmore: "It was amusing when Jim's buddies pulled up Mrs. Manson's skirt in the vocal booth and encouraged any comers to have themselves off in her ass, but it was also disgusting and pathetic. She was clearly in a drunken, downer stupor."

Paul Rothchild was spending a lot of his energy throwing Jim's entourage out of the studio. He had to talk the appalled Densmore out of quitting the band. One night, after Jim had passed out drunk in the vocal booth, Rothchild told the Doors that they were witnessing "a special psychological experience." According to Densmore, Rothchild urged them to get as much on tape of Jim as humanly possible, because he didn't feel that Jim was going to be around much longer.

Robby Krieger: "There was a *lot* of Jim getting drunk, bringing drunken friends into the studio, and Paul throwing them out. Scenes. Heavy pill-taking. Stuff. That was rock and roll to its fullest." Densmore wanted Ray to do something, to stop the madness. In the drummer's mind it was Ray's band. But Ray was afraid, and never said a word to Jim that anyone else heard.

Finally Paul Rothchild put his foot down. In a meeting that included Jac Holzman, Rothchild insisted the label hire a "minder" for Jim, someone to make sure that he stayed sober enough to participate in the recording sessions, and actually get to them on time. Since this job description—baby-sitting rock stars—fit very few people, Rothchild suggested they hire the legendary Bobby Neuwirth to look after Jim. Neuwirth definitely had the credentials, a musician/artist/hipster/mascot who had helped dope-addled Bob Dylan survive two international tours in 1965 and 1966 and had worked with Janis Joplin, whose solo record Rothchild was about to produce. With Dylan in seclusion in Woodstock following a motorcycle accident, Neuwirth was available.

Since Jim was too proud and clever to agree to being baby-sat, it was put to him that Neuwirth, an aspiring filmmaker, would hang out with his Super-8 movie camera while he was making a documentary about the Doors. Jim pretended to buy this ridiculous pretext because Neuwirth was one of the few people who could match (and even out-point) Jim on matters of erudition, hipness, and wit. So, trying to accommodate his long-suffering label, Jim agreed to let Neuwirth look after him.

Neuwirth moved into the Landmark, a quiet hotel on Franklin Avenue. Cannonball Adderly's band was living there, along with the Ice Capades skaters and a lot of magicians. Jim started hanging out, late at night, waking everyone up doing perfect swan dives into the pool at three in the morning.

Neuwirth: "It was a matter of trying to keep him interested in making a record—a lot of cajoling. Jim knew I represented the record company, that I was there to bounce ideas around him. He didn't want to be tricked into anything. He was his own man and he knew what he was doing. Even when he gave the impression of being out of control, he pretty much knew what was up.... There were a lot of times when he pretended to be more out of control than he was. He had a method behind all of it, he had a great sense of his own image, and he played it up. A real scamp!"

* * *

FEBRUARY 1968. One morning America woke up, turned on breakfast television and watched in awe as a barefoot peasant militia battered American troops and took over the major cities of South Vietnam. This was the fabled "Tet" (Lunar New Year) Offensive, when the Viet Cong almost overran the South Vietnamese army and their American allies. South Vietnam was saved only after bloody pitched battles. (Famous quote: "We had to destroy the village in order to save it.") From that moment on, the great mass of Americans knew the Vietnam conflict was lost. The war dragged on for seven more years, at enormous and disgraceful cost to American lives.

The Doors, to their credit, did their best to stop the carnage. They had been performing "The Unknown Soldier," their acute and furious protest song, for the past several months. Their "Soldier" promo clip—meant to be broadcast, immediately banned for its violence and amateurish production values—was shown at Doors concerts beginning the following month. The audiences were stunned, and a few even realized they had seen one of the most intense antiwar statements that Americans had ever committed to film.

It was around then, according to the (heavily censored) Federal Bureau of Investigation files on the Doors, that a group of radio executives in the South sent letters to FBI director J. Edgar Hoover suggesting that the Doors were disseminating enemy propaganda and damaging civilian morale with their obscene performances and antiwar messages.

One night in the studio, Jim got Densmore to play a basic, primitive 4/4 beat—tribal, mindless rock—and began chanting, *"Five to one, baby, one in five—no one here gets out alive."* Ray and Robby fell in, and Jim began improvising some of the lyrics he'd been doing in the previous year's shows. *They got the guns, but we got the numbers.... We're takin' over ... C'mon!... Your ballroom days are over ... Get together, one more time.*

Later Densmore asked Jim what *five to one* meant.

"John, that's for me to know," Jim said, as he closed the bathroom door, "and for you to find out."

Densmore then asked Rothchild, who told him he didn't know either, but thought it forecast what would be the ratio of young to old in America in 1975. People close to Jim and Pamela said that the heroin Pam was buying was cut five to one. (In this view, the *"trading your hours for a handful of dimes"* lines, which were interpreted as anti-panhandler remarks, actually referred to dime, or ten-dollar, bags of street heroin.)

When Jim came back later to do the "Five to One" vocal, he was drunk and stoned on downers. With him was the famous groupie Sable, wearing a microminiskirt that revealed a livid bruise on her thigh. When Ray asked her about it, she slurred through her Quaalude fog: "Jim hit me on the leg with a fucking board, man."

Then, in a spellbinding emotional spasm, Jim blurted out "Five to One," one of the most intense and hellacious performances ever caught on tape, complete with the surreal and sickening narrative about leaving his woman and "going out in a car with these people and getting fuuuuucked uuuuuppp"—as if he was staring deep into the mouth of hell itself.

CELEBRATION OF THE LIZARD

A LOT WAS RIDING ON *The Celebration of the Lizard.* It was the working title of the third Doors album (as was also *American Nights,* a title written on the cover of Jim's big ledger notebook.) Jim wanted the album jacket printed in pseudosnakeskin, the title embossed in gold foil. "Celebration" was actually a collection of poems and lyrics compiled over the past three years, woven into an outlaw ballad about the epic journey of the Lizard King and his young companions across an empty and monumental desert. The classically cadenced "Lions in the street and roaming dogs in heat" stanza opened what Jim was calling a "theater composition." The Lizard King leaves the body of his mother rotting in the summer ground and begins the journey. He wakes in a green hotel with an oozing reptilian creature groaning beside him. The stanza ends with the invocation:

Is everybody in? The ceremony is about to begin.

Then "Wake up!"—a stanza of lines Jim had performed many times onstage. The snake appears again in a dream. There are visions in bathroom mirrors. *"I can't live thru each slow century of her moving."* Blood, hissing snakes of rain. Then into "Little Game," rewritten from the Doors' earliest demo recording. *This is the game called "go insane."* Musically it was a pop ditty strewn among more jazzy and portentous arrangements.

"There's been a slaughter here" culminates the next stanza, known as "The Hill Dwellers" for its depiction of a quiet sleeping suburbia threatened by creeping evil, which lusts after their *"daughters, smug / With semen eyes in their nipples."*

"Not to Touch the Earth" continues the Lizard King's journey. He's on the road—*Run, run, run*—and a glimpse is given of true horror: *"Dead president's corpse in the driver's car."* The minister's daughter falls in love with the snake. Screaming now, the Lizard King evokes the sun and the moon and calls burning fire on the planet.

The journey is almost over. "The Names of the Kingdom" calls forth desert cities—Carson, Springfield, Phoenix. *"Let the serpent sing."* Then, in a whisper, Jim echoes, *"I am the Lizard King. I can do anything."* In a softer voice, he relates how he dwelt in the palace of exile for seven years, sporting with the girls of the island.

> *Now I have come again*
> *To the land of the fair, & the strong, & the wise*
>
> *Brothers & sisters of the pale forest*
> *O Children of Night*
> *Who among you will run with the hunt?*
>
> *Now Night arrives with her purple legion*
> *Retire now to your tents & to your dreams*
> *Tomorrow we enter the town of my birth*
> *I want to be ready.*

"Celebration" was clearly an important poem (and still stands as Jim Morrison's major poetic opus). Its imagery and cadences imagined a preliterate, oral-tribal world. (The psychic landscape of the poem was derived in part from Dave Wallis's influential sci-fi novel *Only Lovers Left Alive.*) A year later, Jim explained: "The central image of 'The Celebration' is a band of youths who leave the city and venture into the desert.

Each night, after eating, they tell stories and sing around a fire. Perhaps ... they dance. Y'know?—for pleasure, to enhance the group spirit."

Jim later called the poems "an invocation of the dark forces," but then admitted that, like everything he wrote, its grandiose imagery wasn't meant to be taken so seriously. "It's like when you play the villain in a western, it doesn't mean that that's *you*. It was supposed to be *ironic*. I mean, come *on*."

But the American sixties were actually the last time that such personal passions could be ardently displayed without the ironic detachment and self-consciousness that shaped experience later in the century. The sixties counterculture, Jim included, honored the natural world by declaring nature sacred. The pitiless desert, the fetishization of the lizard, represented a cosmos much bigger than the petty concerns of human beings, mere permutations of the carbon atom. "Celebration" cast Jim Morrison as a bardic singer of neo-epics, a playful worker of language, an innovator of poetical forms responding to the conditions of his time.

The problem was, this theater composition called "Celebration of the Lizard" refused to hang together in the recording studio. They cut a thirty-six-minute version, then one that lasted only twenty-four minutes. The young musicians in the Doors were incapable of realizing musical forms that matched the energy and complexity of Jim's lyrics. This was only one of several contributing factors making its author totally nuts. Another was Paul Rothchild, whose obsessive style was aggravated by the high-test marijuana from the Mexican states of Michoacán and Guerrero that he was now smoking. Stupendously baked, Paul would force the band to repeat "Hello, I Love You" forty or fifty times, robbing the Doors' creative process of any and all spontaneity in his manic quest for the perfect take. Gone were the loose, swinging rhythms of the Doors' first album. Influenced by Cream and Hendrix, Rothchild was trying to produce a more manufactured, artificial sound that could guarantee the radio hits his Elektra colleagues were demanding in the wake of *Strange Days'* relative failure.

The Doors felt they had to cooperate. Their new lawyer, Abe Somer, had recently negotiated a higher royalty rate for them, and, incredibly, had gotten back Elektra's twenty-five-percent stake in the Doors' crucial song publishing rights from Jac Holzman, who had been enriched by the

Doors' success and felt it was the right thing to do. (This publishing rights reversion would cost Holzman millions over the decades that followed, but it earned him the almost total loyalty of the Doors.)

MARCH 1968. The Doors broke from recording and went back on the road in the Northeast on their legendary spring '68 tour, when they performed some of their greatest shows with such fervor that on some nights it seemed like they were playing the stars from the sky. Postadolescent manager Bill Siddons survived a coup attempt by gear guy Vince Treanor, who was instead appointed the Doors' road manager and given a raise. Opening many of these shows was Linda Ronstadt, a big-voiced young rock singer ("Different Drum") from Tucson, and her band, the Stone Poneys.

Jim was in New York by March 7. That night he went to Steve Paul's Scene, where Jimi Hendrix liked to jam, after hours, with whatever musicians were in the house. Hendrix recorded some of these sessions on an Ampex open reel tape recorder that his roadies lugged into the Scene and set up. That night Hendrix was taping a performance of his blues "Red House," with members of the Young Rascals. Sexy photographer Linda Eastman was taking pictures.

On bootleg copies of Hendrix's tape, one can hear stinko-drunk Jim Morrison, who had crawled on the stage, suddenly bellowing for attention. He embraced Hendrix's knees, and slurred out what seem to be the words "I wanna suck your cock. Hey, man, just lemme suck it." Jim then got woozily up, and blurted some smutty lyrics to Hendrix's incendiary blues licks. Jimi was irritated by this unwanted intrusion, and made head gestures to his crew to get Morrison off the stage. After Jim ran out of steam (according to musician Paul Caruso, who was playing harmonica with Hendrix that night), he staggered back down and blundered into a table, spilling several drinks into the lap of Janis Joplin, who'd been sitting there digging Hendrix. Janis got up, wiped the beer off her velvet trousers and yelled, "Ah wouldn't care, if the crazy motherfucker could only sing!" Some witnesses, who swear they were there that night, say that Jimi, Jim, and Janis ended up in a brawl on the floor, but there's no documentary evidence on the tape—or on Linda McCartney's archived contact sheet—to support this oft-repeated legend, or even the notion that any rock star was rolling on the floor that night, other than Jim Morrison.

SUNKEN CONTINENTS

O N MARCH 7, 1968, a mysterious item flashed over the tickers of United Press International, an American news wire service: JIM MORRISON DIES...MORE LATER. The UPI retracted the story the following day, after it had run on countless radio stations as a bulletin. Jim was more affected by this morbid hoax than he let on. He reportedly told his friends, "I don't mind. I'm dead already." His girlfriends, turning over tarot cards, casting amateur horoscopes, and tossing *I Ching* coins in candlelit motel rooms, told Jim this was some kind of warning. He just laughed at them like he always did.

A couple of weeks later, Joan Didion's hatchet job on the Doors, "Waiting for Morrison," was published in the *Saturday Evening Post,* then an American institution and one of its largest-circulation magazines. Portrayed as a narcissistic asshole presiding over a psychotic, deadly recording session, Jim was wounded, but tried to remain objective.

"Yeah, I read it," he told the *L.A. Free Press* a few months later. "You know, I knew she was gonna do it that way.... These chicks, these journalists, if you don't really come on to them, they feel neglected, you know? She ended up doing a number. It was written good, though. You really felt like you were there."

On the other hand, the new glossy magazine *Eye* did a sympathetic, widely read profile of Jim written by Digby Diehl, the *Los Angeles Times'* film critic. Diehl had been hanging out with Jim and saw what was behind his raunchy stage persona: "Jim would work himself into these frenzies. I'd arrive with him, sit backstage, and watch him, in an hour or so, drink or toke himself into the performer who went onstage. Often he would arrive as the shy poet, and then become that wild, theatrical, sexual figure."

In his article Diehl picked up on the Lewis Carroll poem about "James Morrison" and his neglectful mother, and tried to put forward Jim as a mystic incarnation of "forces that rarely see the light of day."

"I think there's a whole region of images and feelings inside us that rarely are given outlet in daily life," Jim told Diehl. "And when they do come out, they can take perverse forms. It's the dark side. The more civilized we get on the surface, the more the other forces make their plea. Think of [the Doors] as a séance in an environment that has become hostile to life—cold, restrictive. People feel they're dying in a bad landscape. So we gather them together in a séance in order to invoke, palliate, and drive away the dead. Through chanting, dancing, singing and music, we try to cure that illness, to bring harmony back to the world.

"Sometimes I look at the history of rock and roll like the origin of Greek drama, which started out on the threshing floor in the crucial harvest season, and was originally a tribe of worshippers, dancing and singing. Then, one day, a possessed person jumped out of the crowd and started imitating a god. At first it was pure song and movement. As cities developed, more people became dedicated to making money, but they had to keep contact with nature somehow, so they had actors do it for them. I think rock serves the same function. . . ."

In the long run, Jim Morrison and his music outlasted the *Saturday Evening Post, Life, Eye, Crawdaddy,* and all the critics who either hailed him as a god, or mistook him for a fool.

THE TOUR STARTED IN MARCH 1968 at Colgate University's hockey rink in upstate New York. Jim's microphone, much damaged from ill use, failed. When it was finally made to work, the Doors' premiered "Not to Touch the Earth" from "Celebration" and played "The Unknown Soldier" in full skit form, with Jim's gut-shot "execution" drawing screams from the girls.

After a gig in Rochester, the band was late for the first of two shows at the Back Bay Theater in Boston on March 17. During the long delay, a screen was lowered and *The Unknown Soldier* film had its concert debut. Elektra had released "The Unknown Soldier" as a prealbum single to coincide with the tour, but its incendiary, possibly seditious content had earned it a nationwide radio ban. Only the college radio stations played it consistently. The Boston audience, mostly college students, responded to the film's radical politics with a standing ovation and demanded that it be shown a second time. When the band finally arrived, Jim strode out in leather pants, a navy pea coat with the collar turned up, and a funky straw hat covering the longest hair he would ever have. The band played great, but Jim phoned in the show, even delivering "Light My Fire" in a mock Boston accent.

But Jim was on fire for the second show. The scream that began "When the Music's Over" scared the hardened Boston cops guarding the pitch-black stage, lit only by a single spot on the delirious singer. Halfway through "Back Door Man" Jim started in on the unreleased "Five to One," drawing more cheers from the hypnotized audience. "The End" contained four poetic beatitudes—"Ensenada," "The Holy Shay," "Accident," and "Across the Sea"—and culminated in a shattering performance that had the thousands who saw it buzzing for months.

The next weekend, March 22 and 23, the Doors played four shows in two nights at Bill Graham's new Fillmore East. Graham had brought the Joshua Light Show from San Francisco, and Elektra Records' art-rock bands Ars Nova and Chrome Syrcus opened for the Doors.

Serious Doors aficionados think these defining Fillmore East performances were the best the band ever gave. They had been playing in New York since 1966, had built a loyal following, had the media firmly behind them, had two albums in the top five, and now were seen as the living incarnation of rock. The anticipation for these shows in New York in March 1968 verged on the rabid. The ten thousand five-dollar tickets sold out in an hour and were scalped for as much as fifty dollars a piece.

Three Doors came out first and began playing. Ray was in a cream-colored pinstriped suit, Robby in all black, and John in an unforgivable scarlet ensemble. Jim, when he finally appeared, as the tension built and the music reached a psychic peak, was in his leather pants and a maroon shirt under the heavy pea coat; a brown, broad-brimmed leather hat was pulled low over his eyes. Wild cheering began the moment he stepped on the stage and put his right boot on the mike stand to steady himself, while he raised the mike to his lips.

All four sets began with "When the Music's Over"—drawn out for maximum religious effect in the packed, smoky, blacked-out theater. They played "Break On Through.," "Alabama Song," and "Back Door Man"/"Five to One" in a stunning sequence of lust and threat. Then "You're Lost." After "Love Me Two Times," Jim assumed the role of a pompous film professor, advising his class that they were to pay close attention to the following screening because there would be a quiz on the material. A screen came down and *The Unknown Soldier* was run, again drawing prolonged applause as the band took the stage and played the new song, just released as a single and already the subject of a ban on Top Forty radio. The audience listened carefully as the Doors ran through portions of "Celebration of the Lizard." Ray Manzarek: "The Fillmore East had a light pit [in front of the stage] and I knew something was gonna happen. And [Jim] was just really stoned, and sure enough . . . I used to play with my head down, so I didn't see a lot of the things he did. At one point he's supposed to start singing and he didn't sing and I looked up—and he was gone. And then, sure enough: a hand, another hand, and he comes crawling out of the light pit. And he was fine."

For the second show, Jim was nowhere onstage during a long intro to "Music." Then, as the band vamped into his part, he executed a flying leap over the drum kit and landed in front of the mike, screaming on cue. It was a killer move, and the whole audience had an orgasm right there. A bit later he arched his back and let out an agonized shriek, as if he was being electrocuted. People in the audience screamed. Jim smiled and carried on. The screening of *The Unknown Soldier* clip that night inspired some in the audience to heed the flyers passed out on the street by the Youth International Party before the show, announcing the "First Yip-In" at Grand Central Terminal at midnight. The Yippies wanted to take over the station to protest the war, and some of the Doors' customers were attacked with the Yippies when the New York cops met them in force and beat them bloody.

On Saturday night, Jim again called for quiet and attention as he screened *The Unknown Soldier* for the audience. The news from the Vietnam battlefields had been particularly grim that month, and the Saturday-night Fillmore audience, more in a mood to party, greeted the film with gritty applause. The last song of the set was "Light My Fire." Stoned and bored during the instrumentals, Jim grabbed a bunch of daffodils that had been thrown onstage and began to annoy first the soloing Krieger, then Densmore. Jim tickled John's face with the flowers as the drummer was trying to play his ass off. Finally Densmore smacked Jim's hand with a stick, and the mischief stopped. Jim tied the flower to the ride cymbal, where it hung like a dead canary.

The late show that night was pure arson. "Five to One." "Horse Latitudes" in full fury. Cacophonous "Lizard" extracts. A lovely, liquid "Moonlight Drive." A fast, burning "Light My Fire." They played "The End" as an encore. After the long second set had been ecstatically received and the sated crowd began to leave the theater, Bill Graham announced that if anyone wanted to stay, the Doors would play an encore. The crowd rushed back in and the Doors came out, Jim with a paper cup of New York State champagne in hand, and jammed ("Money," etc.) for another hour. Ray made a fool of himself with a talking blues about how every hippie was really a straight. Off-mike, Jim told the kids closest to him that Ray was talking shit. Then Jim launched into passages from "Celebration," "Texas Radio," and even "Orange County Suite." The show ended at a quarter to four in the morning.

Afterward, Bill Graham took Jim and the band to Ratner's, the old Lower East Side kosher dairy restaurant next door to the theater, for an early breakfast of blintzes and potato pancakes. Albert Goldman, who was profiling Jim for *Vogue,* noted that Jim automatically sat at the head of the table, and decided he must have an authoritarian personality.

T HE REVIEWS FOR THESE SHOWS were predictably ecstatic. "The Doors raise sunken continents in everybody's mind," Goldman wrote. *Crawdaddy* gushed: "We remember things from a million years ago when he sings."

Except for a single gig at the new Strip venue Kaleidoscope on March 29, the Doors spent the next several weeks working on their delayed album. Richard Goldstein was flown in from New York by Elektra to report on the Doors' progress to his readers. Jim picked him up at his hotel, driving a convertible with a chick in the front seat. He took Goldstein to an ashram-type place called the Garden of Self-Realization and dutifully gave him some bitchin' quotes:

"See, there's this theory about the nature of tragedy: that Aristotle [in *Poetics*] didn't mean catharsis for the audience, but a purgation of the emotions for the actors themselves. Dig it: The audience is a just a witness to the event taking place onstage."

"I wonder why they like to believe I'm high all the time. I guess maybe they think someone else can take their trip for them."

"See, singing has all the things I like. Writing and music. There's a lot of acting. And it has this one other thing...a physical element...a sense of the immediate. When I sing, I...create...characters."

What kind of characters?

"Oh...hundreds. Hundreds of 'em."

That night, Goldstein was allowed into Studio B at TTG Sound. The other Doors had just returned from a week-long meditation retreat, where they'd been privileged to spend an hour with Maharishi himself. When Jim finally arrived, he was in his snakeskin jacket and tight-assed leather pants. Goldstein: "We realize instantly that Jim is loaded. Juiced. Stoned—the old way. Booze. No one is surprised.... He deposits a half-empty quart bottle of wine on the control panel and downs the remnant of somebody's beer."

They ran a playback of "Celebration." Jim staggered around the small studio in his high-heeled boots and babbled like a wino: "I'm the square of the Western Hemisphere.... Man...like when somebody'd say something groovy, it'd like blow my fuckin' mind.... Now, I'm learnin'.... You like people, man? Cause I fuckin' hate 'em...fuck 'em...I don't need 'em...All right, I need 'em—to grow the fuckin' potatoes."

Ray took this moment to inform Jim that "The Celebration of the Lizard" didn't work as an album track. It just didn't hang. Goldstein watched Jim deflate into his snakeskin collar. There was a dreadful silence for a while.

Then Rothchild said: "Hey, Jim, bring your notebook to my house tomorrow morning, OK?"

"Yeah," Jim said, downcast. "Sure."

Jim left the room, and returned ten minutes later with a fresh bottle of Courvoisier cognac. He disappeared into the vocal booth and started singing "Five to One." He burped a lot. The others in the studio pretended it wasn't happening. Rothchild cut off the mike. "Jim looked like a silent film of himself." Suddenly Jim burst out of the booth, real drunk, in a total rage. It had just sunk in that "The Celebration of the Lizard" didn't make it. The label didn't want it on the record.

Jim began to blurt. "If I had an ax...man...I'd kill *everybody*... 'cept...um...mah friends."

No one said anything. The stillness was spectral. Then Jim tried to break the tension.

"Uh...I gotta get one of them Mexican wedding shirts."

Robby's girlfriend Lynn asked him what size he was.

"Medium, with a large neck," Jim managed.

"We'll have to get you measured,"

Jim shook his head no. "Uh-uh. I don't like to be measured."

Goldstein couldn't believe this shit. His hero was a lush! Jim crashed with friends or lived in a motel. His "wallet" was his driver's license and a Diner's Club credit card between two pieces of cardboard held together by rubber bands. Jim's girlfriend was fucking someone else. Jim and the other Doors seemed to hate each other. Twenty years later, Richard Goldstein wrote what he had really felt that night:

"The idol has turned into an ordinary alcoholic whose family had learned to tune him out. I'm horrified by his helplessness. Years later, I realized that the other musicians are horrified and helpless in the face of an old friend's self-destruction. Their indifference is actually a desperate attempt to repress their desire to bolt from his sight. But they need him— we all do. The myth of the Lizard King is too important for any of us to face the facts about where it is leading Jim and America. . . ."

THE ATMOSPHERE IN THE STUDIO was indeed tense when Paul Rothchild and three of the Doors decided that "The Celebration of the Lizard" wouldn't be ready in time to make a summer release deadline. Jim was upset, and said he didn't have any other material ready. Rothchild got him to turn over some of his notebooks and started mining them for material, which resulted in several new songs. The Dylan-like "Love Street" was about Pam's old place in Laurel Canyon. "We Could Be So Good Together" had a turnaround copped from Thelonious Monk's "Straight, No Chaser." "Waiting for the Sun" would be left off the album named for it. "My Wild Love," which Bobby Neuwirth suggested be sung a capella, became a chain-gang holler with percussion and snake rattles. "Not to Touch the Earth" was salvaged from "Celebration" as a four-minute, stand-alone album track that included the couplet "I am the lizard king. I can do *anything.*"

"Hello, I Love You" and "Summer's Almost Gone" were revived from the Doors' first demo. Robby Krieger contributed "Wintertime Love" (a waltz whose banal lyrics were gamely crooned by Jim), "Yes, the River Knows" (ditto, but even worse, as Jim is forced to sing about drowning himself in mystic heated wine), and "Spanish Caravan" (psychedelic art-rock with a bridge stolen from Spanish composer Isaac Albéniz's "Partido No. 1").

Three strong tracks, it was hoped, would anchor the new album. "Hello, I Love You" was one of Jim's earliest songs, celebrating the dusky, braless young beauty that Jim and Ray had seen on Venice Beach during the summer of '65. "The Unknown Soldier" would (crucially) end the first side of the LP on a blast of war-weary cheering crowds, shouts of "war is over," and an ominously tolling bell. And the almost satanic "Five to One" would climax the record in a hellish whiff of brimstone, as Jim slithered and roared his unholy screed about leaving his heroin-chipping girlfriend to go out in a car with some sleazy strangers and get fucked up. This was one of rock's most carnally disturbed moments, and definitely Jim Morrison's most aroused performance on record.

Jim was unhappy that "The Celebration of the Lizard" was dropped. In an attempt to placate him, the entire text was published on the gate-fold album sleeve when the record came out that summer. Everyone involved in the Doors' third album described its making as "pulling teeth," or "a nightmare." It was a bad dream from which the Doors never woke. *Waiting for the Sun* almost killed the band.

THE FLIP SIDE OF BREAKTHROUGH

APRIL 1968. Jim Morrison and the Doors went back out on the road with their film crew, trying to finish their cryptodocumentary. For the next few months, Jim would coax and provoke action and reaction at Doors' concerts in an effort to duplicate the spontaneous crowd mayhem the band had witnessed nightly earlier in their career. The Doors' audience had suddenly gotten much younger, the venues they were playing had gotten much bigger, and the dislocation all the band members felt in this lucrative but aesthetically uncool situation would be reflected in the film, and in Jim's efforts to make boring rock shows explode into bloodshed and riot.

Jim loved all this, and bonded with the film crew to the exclusion (and frustration) of the other Doors. Cameraman Paul Ferrara was shooting 16-mm black-and-white film when he had started with the Doors the previous fall, but had switched to color stock by that spring. Large, bearded, biker-looking soundman Babe Hill carried a boom microphone attached to a Nagra reel-to-reel tape recorder. The crew, later joined by film editor (and fellow UCLA alumnus) Frank Lisciandro the following autumn, became Jim's trusted companions and minders outside the Doors—much to the annoyance of the neglected and semidespised Other Three. (Manzarek still refers resentfully to the film crew as "the faux Doors.")

Martin Luther King was shot to death in Memphis on April 4 while supporting striking sanitation workers. Black Americans rioted that night in thirty-nine cities. James Brown went on national TV and pleaded for calm. In West Hollywood, Jim Morrison got loaded while watching the topless dancers at the Phone Booth gyrate to "People Are Strange." Later that night Jim was seen dodging through the traffic on Sunset, yelling "Niggers!" at the top of his lungs, his impulse disorder working itself into a manic state, while his so-called friends tried frantically to quiet him down.

He eventually passed out in the bushes behind the Clear Thoughts Building.

T HE DOORS PLAYED three county fair gigs in California in mid-April (Merced, Santa Rosa, and Riverside) before heading back east. Since Vince Treanor had been promoted to road manager, at least the amplifiers worked on this trip.

The first gig was at the Westbury Music Fair on Long Island on April 19, 1968. (Opening were Spanky and Our Gang, and the 1910 Fruit Gum Company.) Jim was photographed for *Vogue* that afternoon in Richard Avedon's Manhattan studio, and then was filmed riding out to the gig in a Cadillac limo while being interviewed by Albert Goldman. When they got to the gig, some girls were waiting outside the gates. Jim rolled down his window, and a brazen young thing with jaded eyes reached in and put her hand on the considerable bulge of his leather pants, while the camera rolled.)

The concerts were problematic. The first show, at three p.m., was played to many empty seats. The second, evening show had a full house, but by then Jim was loaded on booze and pills. As the band played the intro to "Music's Over," Jim tried to climb onto the stage from the darkened house, and stumbled and fell on his way up the steps. The kids in front gave him some attitude, which he either ignored or responded to with vague threat displays.

As the show progressed, Jim kept taunting the audience, making sexual suggestions to the girlfriends of tough-looking guys, trying to provoke action for the film crew. A fat security guard tried to restrain Jim, and was in turn grabbed and fondled by Jim while he suggested the guy lose weight. Humiliated, the guard ran up the aisle, dropping his police-type hat, which Jim seized as a trophy. Suddenly he let out a piercing scream that froze the blood of everyone in the house. The audience reacted like spectators to a gruesome plane crash. The shocked silence was deafening. Jim was twitching spastically, as if he were having an epileptic fit.

Suddenly the lights came up. The concert was over, but the band was still onstage. People started booing. Jim stood in front of his microphone, looking at people leaving, catcalling to him, or just staring back. In a flash he threw back his head, howled like a coyote, and began to chant and dance like a Navajo shaman consecrating a well. It was an exorcism dance that lasted until a girl dashed out of the audience with a scissors in her hand, intent on a lock of the shaman's curls. Babe Hill stepped in front of her until Jim disappeared into a circle of muscle and was spirited away.

All this gave a Freudian critic like Albert Goldman considerable pause, and his remarks to writer Michael Horowitz about these performances are worth remembering: "It's a little early to be disillusioned, but my hunch is that the Doors are stalling. And they're slipping—as you must in this business when you stall—into the teenybopper circuit. Their audiences are getting much younger, and [the Doors] will become more mechanically repetitive. And it may end up with Morrison sort of peeling off and becoming a movie star.

"The initial vision was one of breakthrough," Goldman continued. "That was the spirit of their first album. That's what got us all excited. That's what raised all the sunken continents in everybody's mind. They evangelically converted everyone. Then comes the moment of truth. You've got the world on your side, but where are you at, baby? What are you going to do about it? You made the girl love you. Now, do you love the girl?

"At that moment, they really begin to get into their problem. The flip side of breakthrough is estrangement. Once you've broken away, it's pretty bleak out there. The rebel cuts himself off. He can't get back in again. It's goddamned Jesus Christ, out there alone in the garden!"

To another friend, Goldman confided that Jim Morrison had absolutely no idea how to behave in a venue bigger than a small theater. "This guy just does *not* know what to do with himself during the parts of the concert when the band is soloing. He's lost, he's wracking his brains, he's making do with goofy, awkward, *extremely* gauche bits of stage business that don't come close to working. You get embarrassed for him. He doesn't know how to entertain a big crowd, and it looks like he doesn't give a damn either."

Like all the other journalists who covered Jim, Albert Goldman was too intimidated and confused by the mixed signals from Jim's personae to publish what he really felt about him. His *Vogue* essay that accompanied Avedon's glam photo (long hair, white Cossack shirt) was just another puff piece about someone who didn't exist, and never had.

L IFE MAGAZINE PUBLISHED Tim Page's photos of the New Haven bust on April 12 ("Wicked Go the Doors") along with its take on the Doors' notorious singer: "Jim Morrison is twenty-four years old, out of UCLA, and he appears—in public and on his records—to be moody, temperamental, enchanted in the mind, and extremely stoned on something."

Life didn't know it, but the Doors were already over. When the Byrds released their new album *Sweetheart of the Rodeo,* in which Gram Parsons introduced southern songs and pedal steel guitars into rock music, it started a trend—country rock—that would take over the whole movement. In Paris and other European cities the students were rioting, building barricades, putting the Doors' erotic politics into practice in the streets. Jim Morrison's moment of godly studness was over, and he alone realized it.

He went on a drunken rampage for about a week. He wrecked his Mustang (again), and then wrecked another rental car when he knocked over a bunch of trees on La Cienega five days later. (He just left the smoking hulks on the street for someone else to clean up.) He poured beer over a GTO's pretty head at the Whisky. She told Jim that wasn't very nice and he said, "I know." The Ohio Express took the stage. Jim was blithering. Suddenly he said to himself, "I'm takin' over. Outta sight." He slapped another young groupie sharply in the face, jumped on the stage, and started to jam with the surprised Ohio Express. The Whisky had to turn off the lights and kill the sound when Jim stuck the microphone down his pants and started to make blow-job-recipient noises. It was the only way they could get Jim off the stage. The bouncers threw Jim out the back door into the alley behind the club. The door slammed harshly behind him. Jim was so drunk he just leaned against the wall for half an hour before he could walk home.

WICKED GO THE DOORS

MAY 1968. The Doors played their first Chicago gig at the Coliseum on May 10, trailed by the film crew. They opened with "Soul Kitchen," interrupted by Jim's insertion of lines from what later became the song "Runnin' Blue." Then he paused "Break On Through" to insert his "There You Sit" poem before charging back into the song like a marauding lion. Then he winked at the film guys and tried to get something going.

He gestured the crowd toward the stage, and seemed mesmerized as the crew filmed the cops trying to control the surging crowd. He was trying out audience dynamics, getting ten thousand kids to be pin-drop silent during "Crystal Ship," then whipping them up to frenzy on hardcore numbers "Back Door Man" and "Five to One." When he shouted, "Wake up!" and recited the stanza from "Lizard," there was an electricity in the silent air. They finished with "Light My Fire" and encored with "The Unknown Soldier"—a performance that communicated all the howling anguish of the song and again caused screams in the crowd when Jim fell to the stage like he'd been assassinated.

He lay there for a long time, and girls up front started to cry. Was he dead? But then he was erect again, and a few minutes later, the Doors left the stage to a roaring ovation. The crowd rushed the stage, trying to get close to the vanished aura of the great band, but somehow the police line held.

The next night, Saturday, the James Cotton Blues Band opened for the Doors at Cobo Arena in Detroit. Earth Opera opened in Toronto, where Jim's microphone (and the film crew's lights) failed to work properly.

Paul Rothchild met with the Doors that week, while they were working on early versions of "Orange County Suite" and "Who Scared You?" and trying to finish their record. Densmore had asked Rothchild what he thought they should do about Jim, who was coming to the studio looking unshaven and dissolute, his long hair dirty and stringy, his eyes horribly bloodshot, his clothes slept in for three days. The mood in the studio was sullen, the usual vibe when the Doors got together around then. Rothchild decided to try to talk it over with the whole band present.

"Jim," Paul began, "we don't get the feeling you want to work on this record anymore. I gotta ask you, man—what are you doing? You're not into it. You don't look like yourself anymore. Can you tell us, like, what's happening with you?"

Densmore: "Jim brushed back his greasy hair and stroked his stubble. He didn't respond verbally, and the usual quiet tension in the room intensified." Jim walked out to the lobby alone, Densmore threw up his hands, and the two others just shook their heads.

The next evening Jim astounded them all by appearing totally cleaned up, shaven, with fresh clothes and a drastic haircut he'd done himself by grabbing his locks in a ponytail and chopping them off with slashes of the scissors. The result looked so absurd that they had to take Jim to Jay Sebring's salon to have the damage fixed before the weekend's big show in San Jose.

Immediately all the groupies began calling each other, coast to coast: "What? He *did? All* of it? *How* short?"

T HE DEAD. The Airplane. The Animals. Country Joe. Big Brother. The Youngbloods. Taj Mahal. The Electric Flag. All these bands supported the headlining Doors at the Northern California Folk-Rock Festival held at Santa Clara County Fairgrounds in San Jose on Sunday May 19, 1968. The Doors went on in the late afternoon in full daylight.

Jim played in his new hairdo, snakeskin trousers, white Mexican shirt, and two strands of blue love beads, and turned in a blistering performance that was only tepidly received by an audience that had already sat through ten bands. Jim spied grizzled rock photog Jim Marshall at the edge of the stage, walked over, and said, "Hey, Marshall, want a shot?" and posed with a lit cigarette stuck in his face.

The next Friday night, May 24, the Doors played a famous show at a minor league baseball field in Tucson. Annoyed by thousands of flashbulbs, Jim scolded the teen girls up front and asked for a cigarette. Suddenly the stage was pelted with a hundred lit Marlboros. Then the power went dead. Silence. Darkness. When the lights came back on, Jim urged the crowd forward, pointing out individuals in the audience he wanted onstage with him. He performed his dangerous microphone-as-lariat act during "When the Music's Over," almost braining Ray. As the young kids broke through the barriers and swirled in front of the stage, the security staff massed around the band so the show could continue, and Jim finished the show singing "Light My Fire" with two Tucson police officers pressed tightly on either side of him.

Next night, May 25, Salt Lake City. The audience was tepid, the house only half sold. Jim tried to get the kids going with crude insults, but it didn't work.

"Are you all dead out there?" he asked. "What did you come here for anyway?" The Doors played four songs, left the stage in disgust, and never returned to Utah.

In June 1968 the Doors' third album was finished, sequenced, and mixed. The first single, "Hello, I Love You," was chosen, according to Jac Holzman, by his son, Adam, who liked the bouncy, bubblegum spirit of the song. Jim was upset that the album sounded bland and filled-out with Robby's less-than-magic songs. Jim knew what the problem was, as he explained to Jerry Hopkins.

"A lot of the songs in the beginning, me or Robby would come in with a basic idea, words and melody. But then the whole arrangement, and the generation of the piece, would happen night after night, day after day, in rehearsals or in clubs. When we became a concert group, a record group, and when we contracted to provide so many albums per year, so many singles every six months, that natural, spontaneous, generative process wasn't given a chance to happen. We actually had to create songs in the studio. [Now] Robby or I just come in with the song and the arrangement already completed in our minds, instead of working it out slowly.

"Do I think my work has suffered? Yeah. I do. If we did nothing but record, it would probably be all right. But we do other things, too, so there's not the time to let things happen as they should."

Jim was resigned that his long-form pieces didn't make the cut. "The Celebration of the Lizard" hadn't worked, Jim told Hopkins, because "I kind of constructed that out of pieces of things that I had. It wasn't really a natural development. It doesn't work because it wasn't created spontaneously. It was pieced together on different occasions rather than having any generative core from which it grew. I still think there's hope for it."

On June 5, Robert Kennedy, the brother of the late president, won the California presidential primary by campaigning as a peace candidate. Lyndon Johnson had opted not to run again, fearful that the divided nation would reject him and his ruinous Vietnam policy. Kennedy thanked his supporters that night at the Ambassador Hotel and was assassinated as he made his way out the back door. It was a murderous year. A few days later, Andy Warhol was almost killed by the disgruntled Valerie Solanis (who had appeared in *I, A Man*) when she shot him three times. Warhol survived, but was never the same again.

AROUND THEN Jim gave a freewheeling interview to John Carpenter, music editor of the *Los Angeles Free Press*. Carpenter liked a drink as much as Jim, and the interview started with Bloody Marys over a late breakfast at the Continental Hyatt House on Sunset, where Jim was staying. Later they walked down to Santa Monica Boulevard in the blinding summer light.

"I really dig L.A. in the summer," Jim said. They ended up, hours later, at Jim's fave topless bar, the Phone Booth. Babe Hill from the film crew joined the conversation as a full-figured girl took off her blouse and began dancing to the Four Tops singing Tim Hardin's "If I Were a Carpenter."

BABE: "Can you imagine the babies that chick could have?"

JIM: "It's bad for their tits when they dance topless. Ask any topless dancer. If they lose them, it's like losing your head. This one, she doesn't work too hard. Just sort of stands there. Bless this house and all that are in it.... [A new dancer comes on.] This one is too satirical. She doesn't take anything seriously. I get the feeling that if you spent a lot of time in a place like this, you'd corrupt your soul. Corrode it completely. But let's hold off on that.... It's weird, you know? People in here, after the initial glimpse, just start going on their own trips; talking, eating, drinking. Do you know what it is? I bet that was the appeal of the neighborhood brothel—the atmosphere, a place for conversation.... I must say, this one, *she* is my favorite. She's out of sight. Ooooo. Ummm. But I think it's a mistake to have their breasts exposed. An error in theatrics. They should be wearing a thin negligee, so there'd be mystery.... I like chicks in Levi's. My taste is like, whoever approaches me, I think it's groovy."

The conversation turned to writing. Jim had switched to Black Russians.

JIM: "The mentality of the writer is like the psychology of the voyeur. Journalists never seem to speak of themselves like other people do. They absorb like a sponge and never speak about their own psyche.... Like, I bet there's more philosophy in some sixteen-year-old chick's mind than you ever dreamed of in your whole cigarette. Some of those letters to those fan magazines are really lonely, deep, and open. I don't read many, but some of them really knock me out. Really open, sincere."

When Tim Hardin showed up at the bar, Jim formally introduced him to each of the girls. Then Jim, really loaded, jumped up and started dancing with the girls, bellowing along with the music. Babe went over and quietly said, "Jim, let's go now." The waitress brought the check ($39.75), which Jim paid with bills fished out of his leather pants. They walked across the street to Barney's and kept drinking.

By prior arrangement, John Carpenter gave the transcript of the taped interview to Pamela Courson, who edited out more than a hundred drunken paragraphs before the interview was published. Jim also penciled in some things he wanted to be quoted saying in the margins of the pages.

T HAT MONTH, June 1968, the Doors played desultory shows around California. Bobby Neuwirth's three-month contract was over, so Jim was back on his own. He reportedly had a fleeting relationship with a well-known male prostitute who worked along the Strip. This hustler then tried to extort money by threatening to expose Jim's secret sexual habits. Jim's lawyer, Max Fink, arranged a meeting between the hustler and an intermediary, who was actually a private detective and leg breaker. The hustler was left bleeding and missing teeth in an alley behind a motel near the Los Angeles Airport, and the blackmail attempt stopped.

June 15: Sacramento Memorial Auditorium. Commanding total silence in the packed hall, Jim let the tension build while he hung on the mike with his eyes closed. Suddenly he let out a volcanic burp that startled the audience and earned a round of applause. The highlight was "When the Music's Over," during which (in the "ear to the ground" section) Jim collapsed and started to twist and writhe on the stage, as if he were having a seizure. It took a while before he got back up and intoned, "*We want the world,* and we want it . . . . NOWWWWWWWW!!!!!!!!"

Late in June, the Doors sucked in Santa Barbara, then played two mediocre shows in San Diego. They were working up to headlining the famous Hollywood Bowl on July 5, a big deal (sponsored by local AM radio giant KHJ) that would be filmed by an augmented movie crew and recorded for a possible live album. Everyone was worried and under extreme stress.

Jim's mental state appeared to be very unstable. He had broken up with Pamela Courson after a tremendous fight at her flat. As the neighbors listened in, she screamed that he had to leave the band before he drank himself to death. Jim told her that if she didn't lay off the heroin she would end up a junkie and a whore. She told him to get his shit out of her apartment, and then threw his books out the window.

Jim was seeing a nice-looking writer named Anne Moore. He'd met her a couple of times, and then one night, at an Elektra press party at the

Whisky, he took her hand and said, "Hi, Anne. You're going home with me tonight, aren't you?" Later they walked a couple of blocks to her apartment because Jim had forgotten where he'd left his car. Jim and Anne Moore were on and off again for the next two years. He would come over for a meal after he fought with Pamela and she'd thrown him out again.

He was living at the Alta Cienega Motel in alcoholic semisqualor. Tim Hardin was shooting up brown Chinese heroin in Jim's bathroom. Jim had a key to the Doors' office, and sometimes he just crashed out on the couch downstairs. Topanga Canyon regulars got used to seeing Jim in his dark blue Mustang, parked near the post office halfway up the canyon, just hanging out, and staring at the mountains as evening fell.

Pamela Courson, meanwhile, left for Morocco with her sometime boyfriend Jean de Breteuil to buy clothes to stock her boutique. *"She has robes and she has junkies, lazy diamond-studded flunkies"* in the new song "Love Street" referred to the count and his cadre of gay blades who hung around Pamela. (Jim changed the junkies to monkeys in the final version.) Later in the month, Pamela publicly took up with hot young actor Christopher Jones, star of the low-budget hippie exploitation film *Wild in the Streets,* about a rock star (patterned vaguely on Jim) becoming president of the United States. The handsome, studly Jones was hanging out at Pam's sparsely furnished pad, eating her sodden lasagna, sitting in Jim's reading chair, going down on his woman. (The small apartment had a large photo of Jim, superimposed over an image of a crystal ship, hanging on the living room wall. Pamela's freezer was still full of beef hearts because, he claimed she told him, that's what Jim liked to eat.)

Pam also had a scene with Paul Ferrara. "Jim went off on some damned tour," Ferrara said, "and I [i.e., the film crew] was left home. I think Pam knew that Jim was with someone else that night. That's the thing that wore her down to a frazzle—that she couldn't control him when he left the house. So she was just very lonely and kind of down, and she figured, well, he's sleeping with [Anne Moore], so I'll do something too. Like she was getting back at him. So she asked me over to dinner. We smoked some pot and she just got real close and cuddly and one thing led to another. It's not something I'm real proud of, but it happened."

A few days later, Jim said to Ferrara, "I heard you were with Pamela."

"Oh, God. I guess so. Yeah." End of conversation.

Jim didn't hold this against Ferrara, and even gave him five thousand dollars later in the year to complete a film project. Pamela's other amours didn't seem to bother Jim, but his sublimated rage came out in other ways—shitty performances, self-negating behavior, and generally abusing himself and almost everyone who depended on him.

DEAD AT THE HOLLYWOOD BOWL

I N EARLY JULY 1968, the Rolling Stones had just finished recording *Beggar's Banquet,* their brilliant new comeback album, in London. Mick Jagger was extremely interested in Jim Morrison because of the adulatory publicity he'd been following in the London music press, and because the Stones' booking agent, Tito Burns, reported huge advance interest in the European tour he was arranging for the Doors later in the year. The Stones hadn't toured America since 1966, and the whole concert business had changed. Everything was bigger and more professionalized. Big American bands like Jimi Hendrix and the Doors had outgrown the electric ballrooms and were performing in the large arenas that the Stones also had to play in order to make any money.

Mick Jagger had no idea how to mount a rock show in an American arena. Tito Burns suggested he fly to Los Angeles and see how the Doors handled performing before ten thousand people at the Hollywood Bowl on July 5. So when he finished mixing the *Banquet* tracks on July 3, 1968, Jagger flew into LAX with his girlfriend Marianne Faithfull and Jimmy Miller, the Stones' producer. Two days later, Mick showed up at the Doors' office, and asked where Jim Morrison was.

January Jansen picked up the ringing pay phone near Room 32 of the Alta Cienega Motel across the street. Jim was lying on the bed, looking at the television with the sound off. Tim Hardin was injecting smack in the bathroom.

Jansen: "The office called. They were in a panic. 'Jagger's here! He's coming across the street!' I said, 'Jim ... uh, Mick Jagger's across the street. He's coming over.' Jim said, 'That's all right.'

"There was a knock on the door, very faint. And Jim nodded and I opened the door. And [Jagger] said, 'Hullo, I'm Mick.' And I said, 'You sure as fuck *are*.' It was like, *wow!* You could feel the energy. And Mick came on in.' "

If Mick, who lived in an elegant house in London's Chester Square, showed any qualms about Jim's frugal motel digs, he hid it well. "Mick made himself comfortable," Jansen recalled. "No, he didn't look around and say, what's with this poverty hole? It was convenient, right across from the office."

The two rock stars had never met before. Jagger was five months older than Jim, and had been a star three years longer. Jim stood up and shook Mick's hand, then retired to the bed, resting for the evening's Hollywood Bowl show.

Mick asked Jim if he meditated before a show.

Jim looked at Mick as if he were insane. "Meditate? No, man. We leave that up to John and Robby."

Mick wanted to talk about stagecraft, and said he wanted to learn how to work a big crowd. He told Jim the Stones hadn't played anywhere in fifteen months and were really rusty. Jim asked Mick about Brian Jones. Mick rolled his eyes and said Brian was having a hard time. He'd lost his woman to Keith a year earlier. Mick said he thought Brian was in Morocco, taping the music of a tribe up in the mountains, a group of musicians who were also magicians. Brion Gysin, a friend of William Burroughs, had told Brian about them.

"You know William?" Mick asked.

Jim shook his head no.

Jansen later told Frank Lisciandro: "They talked about dancing onstage. Mick said he was embarrassed about his dancing. He said the one thing he couldn't do was dance. And he and Jim [commiserated] that it was increasingly difficult to feel comfortable and to feel smooth dancing onstage. The larger the audiences got, the larger the working area was, and the less you could relate to it. Everything had to be more exaggerated. Jim told Mick, 'If you fall, man, you *really* gotta fall.'

"They laughed together at how everything was overblown. They had grown up with movie stars and cowboy heroes and everything, and then all of a sudden they were center stage. They were both kind of boyishly bashful about it, and yet in full command. And it was very evident that they had mutual respect for each other's talent."

There have been claims that Mick gave Jim some LSD-25, which Jagger had gotten from an L.A. friend the day before, and that Jim popped the tabs right after Mick left the motel. When Tim Hardin finally came out of the bathroom, they told him he'd missed Mick Jagger. The zoned-out singer protested that they had to be bullshitting him.

AFTER JAGGER LEFT, Jim called Pamela to tell her about the visit and asked her to pick him up and drive him to the show. She had sent him a beautiful midnight-blue vest, intricately embroidered with gold thread, which she had brought back from the souks of Marrakech. She told him to forget it, because she had company. She told him that he should quit the Doors and be a poet. She'd been telling him this for months now. Pam hated the Doors, thought the whole thing was way beneath his talents, and anyway it was killing him. Jim didn't argue with her, just reminded her that the Doors were paying the bills for her rent, the boutique, and everything else. Pam told Jim that she would be at the concert, and that Christopher Jones was coming along.

THE HOLLYWOOD BOWL was built in Cahuenga Pass in 1922 as a spectacular amphitheater seating eighteen thousand people, dramatically situated in the hills above the city. It was an ideal evening venue for the Los Angeles Philharmonic and the opera companies it was designed for, but was far more problematic when it came to amplified rock shows. The Doors' crew arrived two days early to set up the gear, fifty-four amps lined up across thirty yards of the stage, loud enough to be heard a mile away. New Doors crew member Harrison Ford was an aspiring actor; his chores included some carpentry and (according to unsubstantiated Hollywood lore) finding herbs for the band. He also handled one of the cameras during the concert's four-camera shoot.

The show was completely sold out and hotly anticipated in Los Angeles. KHJ radio jocks noted that the crowd was even nuttier than the one the Monkees had drawn a few months earlier. Steppenwolf opened the hot July evening with their new hits "Born to Be Wild" and "Magic Carpet Ride." The Chambers Brothers roused the teenagers with their long-form psychedelic jam "Time Has Come Today." Mick Jagger, who had gone to dinner with the Doors before the show, sat backstage and watched carefully how things went.

The Doors went onstage around nine o'clock amid a seething mob scene and turned in a subdued performance that disappointed everyone there that night. The firebrand god of rock was absent. The erotic politician, the electric shaman, the Lizard King—none of these personae showed up. Instead Jim shocked everyone and *sang*, crooning his songs in leather trousers and his Moroccan vest, from a fixed spot on the stage, moving very little. He wore a silver cross around his neck, which no one had ever seen him do, and chain-smoked cigarettes, which was also unlike him. Only when he had to scream did he bend at the mike and let go, and occasionally Jim would allow himself to fall into one of his cool, crouching Hopi dances.

The other musicians looked at each other in puzzlement as Jim worked through the hits, and then into songs from the just-released *Waiting for the Sun*: "Five to One," "Hello, I Love You, "Spanish Caravan," and "The Unknown Soldier." After every song, hordes of teens yelled at him to do "Light My Fire." He slipped two sections of "Celebration" into "Horse Latitudes," and three of his new poems ("Accident," "Grasshopper," and "Ensenada") into "The End." Throughout Jim maintained a vacant stare, smiling a little, not bothering to make contact with the audience.

There were several factors involved in this tepid show. Mick Jagger, Marianne Faithfull, and Jimmy Miller were sitting in the front row, so Jim was under Jagger's merciless regard. Pamela and her boyfriend were cuddled up a few rows behind them. The hot movie lights made the Doors' usually dark stage white hot. Jim was obviously uncomfortable with the gigantism of the Bowl, and with the immaturity of the restless kids who laughed at the band, threw things, booed the new songs, and ran around during the show. If, as Pam told Jones, Jim was playing high on LSD, he managed quite well, turning in a musically faultless performance that still bored everyone silly. The kids were expecting raw rock theater bordering on human sacrifice, and got a live TV show instead. John Densmore was furious when Robby told him that Jim had dropped a few tabs of LSD before going on.

Mick and Marianne skipped the party afterward. Jimmy Miller later said that on the drive back to their hotel, Mick Jagger complained the

Doors were boring. The Hollywood Bowl concert had been a financial success but a major downer. The Doors suffered what writer Ellen Sander (now Jac Holzman's girlfriend) called "a dramatic loss of local prestige" as the suburban high school kids badmouthed the band. Mick Jagger had learned how *not* to put on a big rock concert.

Pamela and Christopher Jones went backstage after the show. Jones waited outside while Pam went into the dressing room. Then she stuck her head out the door and motioned Jones inside. When he came in, Jim grabbed Pam and sat her in his lap so that her legs were spread apart. "He just sat there grinning at me," Jones told writer Patricia Butler, "with Pam on his lap, and she was looking at me kind of nervous. But Jim knew about us at that point, and he was trying to get one up on me. But I just stood there and smirked at him, you know? Who was he kidding?"

THE LORDS

JULY 1968. The Doors went back on the road with their film crew. In Dallas on July 9 Jim performed the almost complete "Texas Radio and the Big Beat," a new kind of poem/song inspired by the imperative preaching that Jim heard on late-night Bible Belt radio. He also taunted the cops guarding the stage, mocking them, trying to get them to over-react for the film crew.

In Houston the next night he performed spontaneous verse compositions in the middle of "Back Door Man" using the routines "Can the wind have it all?" and "We tried so hard; maybe we tried too hard." Poetic interjections in "When the Music's Over" included "Winter Photography" and "Count the Dead and Wait Till Morning," material culled from his recent notebooks. Delving into R & B to alleviate his boredom with the much-requested "Crystal Ship" and "Light My Fire," Jim launched the band into "Little Red Rooster" and "Who Do You Love?" Working the police again, Jim tried to get the kids to rush the stage. The cops responded by lining the stage, blocking the band from the crowd's view. Jim yelled out, "If you all aren't gonna come up here, I guess I'll have to try to get through 'em.... This is your last chance!" The cops pulled up even tighter, surrounding the band, and the show was over.

WAITING FOR THE SUN, a mixture of old songs, hastily written filler, and cutting-edge brilliance, turned out to be the big album of the summer of 1968, as the urban ghettos continued to burn and the cops rioted at the Democratic convention in Chicago. (The hot-pink sleeve featured band photos by Paul Ferrara and Guy Webster.) Radio stations that had balked at sexy "Love Me Two Times" and radical "Unknown Soldier" jumped on "Hello, I Love You," the perfect confluence of sonic psychedelia and bubblegum pop. "Hello" was the number-one single in America by the end of July, and the album was number one by the end of August and stayed there for six weeks. Then the blind Latino singer José Feliciano had a huge pop hit with a jazz version of "Light My Fire," which also went to number one.

The Doors were still the biggest band in America. No other group could touch them.

Charged by these solid numbers, Jim stayed on the rampage that summer. In Seattle and Vancouver, Jim whipped the band into a stinging fever and had the audience surging past the cops and onto the stage at the end of the shows, encircling Jim in wild dancing and rapture. "An orgy of experience is the only way to describe the result," opined the *Vancouver Sun.*

These raucous shows were only a prelude to the riots the Doors were about to provoke back east the following month.

THE CONVENTIONAL WISDOM about Jim Morrison is that he stopped caring about the Doors after *Waiting for the Sun* and stopped writing songs, preferring to drink all day and blab his talent away in the bars along Santa Monica Boulevard. But the truth is much more complex. It's true he was often getting drunk with Tom Baker at the Phone Booth or Barney's Beanery, or disappearing with Babe Hill down California Highway 60 and holing up in Palm Springs for days on end. But he was also writing and working on his poetry.

On July 24, 1968, he completed and dated a handwritten manuscript of two sets of poems. These were *The Lords,* subtitled "Notes on Vision," which contained imagery on film and media that Jim had been compiling for at least three years. The second set, *The New Creatures*, compiled more recent poetic interpretations of his adventures and persona as a rock star, charting the psychic territory of national legend and celebrity that no poet since Lord Byron had been able to investigate firsthand. Sometimes stabbingly acute, sometimes banal and derivative, these poems hung together as the inner workings of a rebel and outlaw self-exiled to a spiritual landscape of exaltation and despair. Especially interesting was his notion of the Lords as the hyperreal controllers of human culture and behavior, the invisible high lamas who intercede on humanity's behalf with destiny and the gods.

Jim was determined to become a published poet. He had the poems typed by Kathy Lisciandro, the band's secretary. Michael McClure suggested to Jim that he publish them privately, in a limited edition.

A ROUND THIS TIME, late in July, Jim also tried to quit the Doors. He'd been trying to get back with Pam, but she was insisting he had to leave the band if he wanted to be with her. He knew this was crazy, but he was also physically and mentally worn out. In a notebook, he wrote that he was starting to feel his spirit slipping away, and it scared him. Friends noticed he wasn't laughing so much anymore.

One day he walked into the office, sat quietly on the couch, and looked at Ray Manzarek for a moment before he spoke.

"Ray, I want to quit."

Manzarek had a vision of his world crumbling. Finally, stifling a panic attack, he managed to ask, "Why?"

"I just can't take it anymore."

Ray said he didn't get it. He thought things were cool. The secretary went and got Jim a cold beer. Ray noticed Jim looked tired. Dead tired.

"I'm telling you, Ray. I can't take it."

Manzarek tried to placate Jim. The Doors only played on the weekends, then they went home. Did Jim think they were working too hard?

"No, man."

Ray asked if it was just the studio. Was making the records too rough?

Jim dropped his head. He drained the beer.

He said, "I don't think I can take it anymore."

"But why? What's wrong?"

Jim looked at Ray. "I think I'm having a nervous breakdown."

The office got very quiet.

"Oh, man. No you're not. You're drinking too much. It's starting to get to you."

"No, Ray, I'm telling you that I'm having a nervous breakdown, and I want to quit."

This went on for a while. Manzarek cajoled Jim, told him he loved him, begged him to give the Doors another six months. He promised Jim that if he still felt the same way, they'd break up the band. Kathy Lisciandro suggested Jim go home and sleep for a few days. The office would leave him alone. He could forget about the band. Jim said again that he was having a nervous breakdown, but his friends didn't take him seriously, and were too frightened to comprehend what he was saying.

As he walked out the door, totally alone, Jim mumbled, "I don't feel so good."

This episode was immediately rationalized by the bewildered, fearful Doors and their employees as a typical Morrison ploy to get attention. Nobody around Jim realized that he was indeed suffering a nervous breakdown, one from which he probably never recovered, as his untreated, stress-related condition evolved into numbing self-medication and behavior that could be described as intermittent psychosis.

ONE NIGHT A TOP FORTY band was playing at the Whisky, and Jim went to see them. Pamela Miller and some of her GTO pals were there and tried to make conversation with him, but he was stewed and kept repeating the same phrases over and over. "Get it *on*." "Suck mah momma." "Right on." Later he slid into a booth already occupied by Eric Burdon, former lead singer of the Animals, and his girlfriend, a dancer at the Body Shop across the street. Jim was feeling good. He ordered a beer, and when the girl asked him something about one of his songs, Jim poured the beer over her head.

Shocked silence. Nothing happened. She could only laugh. When she went to clean up, Burdon, a tough guy from brawling Newcastle in northern England, tried a gentle approach. "I said, 'Now listen, Jim, that's not on. You're moving among human beings here. This isn't stage acting.' And he became quite upset at what he'd done, like he'd come out of a trance, and he was very apologetic."

In a flash Jim jumped onstage with the band, and being young kids from the Midwest, they were in awe. *Jim Morrison is onstage with us!* But instead of singing with them, he hogged the microphone and started reciting his "Graveyard Poem," written earlier in the year. The band left the stage, and Jim began berating the crowd about their hippie docility.

"You think you're fucking *revolutionaries? No fucking way,* man. You're all a bunch of *niggers!*" He went on like this as the customers gaped at him. "That's right. Niggers!"

The head bouncer, a black ex-cop, grabbed Jim by the shirt, dragged him off the stage, and threw him out of the club. Someone had called the police, and they were waiting for him. A cop grabbed Jim, but Jim pulled away and his shirt came off. Jim ran into the traffic on Sunset, vaulting over the hoods of the cars, and bolted for freedom, still shouting that they were all a bunch of niggers.

The cops didn't even bother to chase him.

Around this time Elektra threw a party to celebrate the opening of its magnificent new studio and office complex. Jim showed up with his cronies, completely stewed. After a couple more drinks he started muttering that he had paid for all this—the Persian carpets, the oak flooring, the up-to-the-minute electronics—with all the Doors records they sold. Next he was on top of the office manager's desk, trying to stomp her IBM Selectric typewriter to death with his boots. "Get him the fuck outta here!" the execs yelled, and Jim was hustled onto the sidewalk and into a car, still shouting that he had paid for all this shit. (He wasn't wrong.)

Sometime later, the Elektra staff came to work one morning to find a body lying in the bushes in front of the building, sprawled out in a weird position. Someone wanted to call an ambulance, but Suzanne Helms, the office manager, told him to put down the phone. "That's just Jim. He passed out again. Don't touch him. Don't even talk to him."

Later in the morning Jim woke up, brushed the dirt and leaves off his leathers, and walked down to Duke's for breakfast.

INNOCENT BYSTANDER

WHEN THE DOORS WENT back east with their film crew in early August 1968, Jim Morrison was primed. Although half drunk, he played a riveting, focused show with his eyes closed in Bridgeport, Connecticut, on August 1, barely moving at all as a looming summer thunderstorm echoed over the Long Island Sound. The concert had a surreal vibe as Jim bore down, enunciating lyrics and poems with hyperbolic clarity. The audience sat transfixed, and left quietly after the encores "Little Red Rooster" and "The Unknown Soldier."

The next night, August 2, the film crew finally got its riot.

It was a steamy Friday night in New York City. The Doors were headlining the Singer Bowl, in Flushing Meadows, Queens. There was tension backstage. The opening act, the rip-roaring English band the Who, perhaps the hottest group in the world that summer, were angry they weren't headlining, and demanded the Doors' gear not be onstage as they played their incendiary live show that ended in explosions and splintered guitars. During the Who's set, the Singer Bowl's revolving stage malfunctioned, leaving a large part of the audience unable to see the performance and extremely annoyed.

Jim rode to the show in a limo with Jac Holzman and Ellen Sander, who later wrote: "Morrison and 'the boys' had grown apart. He was too crazy, too unreliable, too intellectual, too conceited, but mostly he was too insecure. They shunned him socially, and he retaliated by terrorizing them with the threat that he would quit. He was lonely, as all writers must be, and he often drank himself blind and created a scene. He was also a rather pleasant guy when he wasn't acting out."

On the ride to the gig, Jim flipped through the *Village Voice* and mumbled about how bored he was in New York. The driver got lost. "Fucking anarchy," Jim said. He started singing "Eleanor Rigby." Sander told him he was weird, and Jim said, "I tries." In a traffic jam near the Singer Bowl, Jim opened the limo's window and let a mob of excited kids grope him.

"Will some of you chicks escort me backstage?" he asked. "I might get mobbed or something."

The backstage area was cramped and sterile. Checking the film crew was with him, Jim stepped out into the crowd and was surrounded by kids who seemed afraid to get too close. He signed a few autographs and then disappeared backstage.

Pandemonium ensued when the Doors finally appeared after an hour's delay, ushered through the fifteen-thousand-strong crowd by a newly hired phalanx of black Philadelphia private detectives in stingy-brim hats. Off-duty uniformed police repelled an initial assault on the stage, then formed into a defensive perimeter. Jim had to push his way through the line of tough New York street cops in order to face the crowd.

"Cool down," he told them. "We're going to be here a long time."

He preached to them, screamed, moaned, collapsed, and pussy-footed along the rim of the stage. The kids in front tried to grab at him, and the twenty cops onstage had to pry them away. Jim intercut familiar songs with long stretches of "Celebration" and other snatches of surreal, ad-libbed poetry that mystified the restive Long Island teenagers. When the cops got rough with the kids up front, wooden seats flew onto the stage. Jim picked them up and threw them back into the convulsive crowd. The film crew kept shooting and tried to duck the flying debris.

The last song of the night was "The End." The kids who couldn't see were frustrated, upset, and very loud. Many tried to speak to Jim on-stage. Others kept shouting "Sit down" at overwrought kids standing on chairs to see better.

"*Shhhh,*" Jim whispered. "Hey, everyone! This is serious now. Every-one—get quiet, man. You're gonna ruin this thing. *Shhhhh.*"

He kept interrupting the familiar flow of the recorded version with poetic interjections—"Fall down now, strange gods are coming"—and other improvisations. At one point he shrieked, as if in a nightmare: "Don't come here! Don't come in!" When he began the Oedipal verses, the audience was way ahead of him, yelling "And he walked on down the hall" before Jim spoke the line himself. When Jim got to the climactic "Mother?"—hundreds of young girls screamed in terror. As the band crashed into the finale, Jim collapsed onstage like he'd been shot, and the stadium exploded. Robby Krieger finished the set in an electric storm of reverb and feedback.

Jim wasn't finished yet. As the show was ending, he went to the edge of the stage and made a negative connection with a young Hispanic couple he'd been eyeing down front. He looked at this big Puerto Rican guy and said, "Who's that Mexican slut you're with tonight?"

The guy picked up his seat and heaved it at Jim. The whole stage area erupted as dozens of chairs came flying through the hot, humid air. Jim kept dancing and laughing hysterically. The cops tried to get him off the stage, but he lay down and they couldn't move him. Finally the Afro-American bodyguards hustled the band toward the dressing room. The cops fought with the kids, and a miniriot ensued with a dozen arrests and several injuries, all reported in the papers the next day.

The Doors' road crew had to defend the amplifiers from being torn apart. After the crowd was cleared out, the Singer Bowl looked like it had been bombed.

Pete Townshend, the Who's flamboyant, intellectual lead guitarist, watched this wild drama from the side of the stage. He saw Jim watching impassively as his bodyguards roughed up kids who just wanted to get near him. He thought he had seen it all by then, but he was amazed by Jim Morrison's calculated escalation of the crowd's mood from adulation to rapture to chaos and violence. He wrote the song "Sally Simpson" soon afterward, in a backhand tribute to Jim.

Backstage, as the film crew's camera rolled, Jim comforted a teenage girl who'd been hit in the head by a flying chair. She was bleeding from a scalp wound and trying to stop crying as Jim put his arm around her.

"It's a democracy," Jim said soothingly, looking into the camera with a crooked smirk. "Somebody hit her with a chair. There's no way to tell who did it." Tenderly, Jim wiped blood from her face. "It's already coagulating," he cooed. "She was just an innocent bystander."

When a groupie-looking chick sashayed by in a red dress, Jim grabbed her and stuck his hand up her dress for the benefit of the camera, smiling broadly. Later he asked, "Did you think it looked phony, me talking to her like that?"

O N SATURDAY, AUGUST 3, 1968, "Hello, I Love You" was the top single in the country, blaring mindlessly from every car radio in America. The Doors played the Cleveland Public Auditorium that night, with Jim again working the crowd for the film crew. He arrived at the hall shit-faced, and let the band play "Break On Through" for five minutes without him. When Jim finally appeared, he was clutching a quart of Jack Daniel's in his right hand and giving the sold-out, nine-thousand-seat hall the finger with his left. He began shouting and lurching around, singing incoherently as Krieger tried to drown him out with extraloud shards of feedback and echo. This got Jim mad.

"I can't hear myself! I'm gonna give you a good time, but I want it real soft." He turned to the band. "If I can't hear myself, I'm gonna get a gun and kill some people here." During a long, horrid version of "Five to One" he started talking with the kids up front, drawing laughter, derision, and applause. Then he yelled, "Listen! Listen! I want you to feel it. I'm not kidding! I want you to feel it!"

He missed all his vocal cues during "When the Music's Over," and Krieger kept trying to mask his petulant antics with washes of electronic noise. Jim came back to the microphone. "Softer, baby, softer. Gotta feel it inside. Take it deeeep inside.... Hey, listen. I want to give you a history of *me*. All right! All right! I have a few things to say, if you don't mind . . . I don't know where I am or how I got here, but I did." He began to recite his poems "Vast Radiant Beach" and "The Royal Sperm." He asked for a Marlboro and dozens of cigarettes landed at his feet. The band lit into "Soul Kitchen," but Jim was getting tired and wandered away from the microphone. He seemed to be vomiting at the side of the stage, which drew a loud burst of applause. By the time the band lit into "Light My Fire," Jim's mind had left the building. He kept shouting, "Come on," during Ray's solo. As Robby began his, Jim was yelling as loud as he could:

"YOU KNOW I CAN'T TAKE IT! YOU KNOW THAT! I CAN'T TAKE IT ANYMORE! COME ON! YEAH! COME ON!"

Suddenly Jim dived into the crowd with his live microphone, and it looked like a football scrimmage. Fights started as he was passed over the heads of the audience, chanting the Yippie yell: "DO IT! DO IT!" By the time he made it back to the stage, Jim's voice was gone and the band finished "Light My Fire" and ran off.

The kids kept chanting Jim's name, but there was no encore. They started throwing chairs, wrecking the concession stands, and tearing heavy wooden doors to pieces in a wanton ritual of destruction.

SUNKEN CONTINENTS

* * *

T HE FINAL SHOW of that wild weekend was played at the Philadelphia Arena at Forty-sixth and Market on Sunday night, August 4,
and it was magnificent. Strolling onto the sweaty hockey arena's stage
amid wild cheering and applause at ten-thirty, Jim appeared sober and in
command; he even asked the audience to stop bothering the relatively
young cops who were guarding the stage. As "Back Door Man" bled into
"Five to One," Jim bummed a beer and a cigarette from the audience. He
stood back and watched as Robby played a brazen, distorted solo that
soon turned into a flamenco guitar clinic on "Spanish Caravan."

"What do you want to hear?" Jim asked before the last section of the
show. Hundreds began shouting requests. "One at a time," Jim tried. "I
can't hear you." So he recited "Texas Radio" with its preaching cadences
and images of Negroes in the forest and other exotica. Then "Hello, I
Love You" got a quick reading, followed by "Wake Up!" and "Light My
Fire," during which Jim yelled and twitched and danced around the
mike like a man on fire. The crowd surged forward, and the cops formed
a defensive perimeter, as the Doors finished the song and ran off.

The Doors took the rest of August 1968 off. Jim was obviously
brain-fried, and anyway *Waiting for the Sun* was selling on its own. Unexpectedly, this cobbled-together mélange of pop tunes and art songs
would be the number-one album in America by early September.

THE DOORS IN EUROPE

A FEW MONTHS LATER Jim spoke with Jerry Hopkins about his efforts to document a Doors riot on film:

"It's just a lot fun! [Jim laughed.] It actually looks more exciting [on
film] than it really is. Film compresses everything. Any time you put a
form on reality, it's going to look more intense. Truthfully, a lot of times,
it was *very* exciting, a lot of fun. I enjoy it, or I wouldn't do it.

"It's never gotten out of control, actually. It's pretty playful. We have
fun, the kids have fun, the cops have fun. It's kind of a weird triangle. . . .
Sometimes I'll extend myself and work people up a little bit. Each time,

it's different. There are varying degrees of fever in the auditorium waiting for you. So you go out onstage and you're met with this rush of energy potential. You never know what it's going to be. So I try to test the bounds of reality."

Hopkins asked Jim what he did to test the bounds.

"You just push a situation as far as it will go. You have to look at it logically. If there were no cops there, would anyone try to get onstage? Because what are they going to do when they get there? When they [manage to] get onstage, they're very peaceful. They're not going to do anything. The only incentive to charge the stage is because there's a barrier. If there was no barrier, there'd be no incentive. . . . It's interesting to me, though, because the kids get a chance to test the cops. You see the cops today, walking around with their guns and uniforms, and the cop is setting himself up as the toughest man on the block, and everyone's curious about exactly what would happen if you challenged him. What's he going to do? I think it's a good thing, because it gives the kids a chance to test authority."

J IM MORRISON AND PAMELA COURSON got back together, after a fashion, that summer. He bought her a Jaguar XKE sports car. He instructed the Doors' accountant to reinstate her charge accounts and she went on a massive shopping binge. They stayed in her darkened apartment and listened to *Axis: Bold as Love* and Dr. John's voodoo-rock album *Gris-Gris*. Soon stories about this fun couple were circulating like poisoned blood. She hated his drinking and carousing with his crew. He didn't like her using heroin and nodding off. Pamela slugged Jim at a restaurant. She stabbed him with a fork at home. One night he held a knife to her throat and she called the police. The young cops who responded recognized Jim and all but asked for his autograph while Pamela demanded that they arrest him. The cops ignored her and told Jim to try to behave. As they were leaving, he mischievously showed them a thick wad of unpaid traffic tickets that Pamela had collected. They called the station house and immediately arrested Pamela for ignoring several court summonses. Jim bailed her out a few hours later, and they went back to their folie à deux, upstairs on Norton Avenue.

On television, they watched the Chicago police riot at the Democratic convention that nominated Vice President Hubert Humphrey as their candidate for president. The cops beat anyone they found on the street—kids, protesters, delegates, newsmen. It was a national disgrace.

The Doors were excited because their first European tour was scheduled for September. (The Jefferson Airplane and Canned Heat would appear with them at many of the venues.) They even rehearsed a few times in their workshop, determined to take no prisoners in England, Germany, Holland, Sweden, and Denmark. All the shows had sold out in minutes. Jim asked Robert Gover to come along and write about the tour, hopefully for *Esquire,* which Jim admired for its essays by Norman Mailer. (Gover passed on the opportunity.) Jim reedited and polished his poem "Texas Radio & the Big Beat (The WASP)," for publication in the European tour program.

January Jansen made Jim a new leather suit, with wide red lapels, and a studly leather belt with huge silver conchos. The British music press—*Melody Maker, New Musical Express*—was frothing in anticipation. There were so many requests for interviews that Elektra's London office scheduled a press conference instead. Granada Television, England's most important independent TV production company, wanted to film a documentary of the London shows. The Beatles and the Stones had requested tickets. Jim shaved the beard he'd grown over the summer and had his hair done. He wanted to look his best for what became the Lizard King's final bow.

L ATE IN AUGUST they flew east to play the final dates with their film crew. They performed a carefully organized, almost operatic "Celebration of the Lizard" in Columbia, Maryland, on Friday, August 30. The next night in Asbury Park, New Jersey, Jim walked out and stood silently at the microphone for several minutes as the tension grew spellbinding. At an invisible signal, Densmore kicked into "Break On Through," and the Doors put on a stupendous rock show that no one there that night ever forgot.

Jim missed the band's flight to Albany the next day. He had given up running through airports. If the plane left without him, it was someone else's problem. Bill Siddons had to charter a small plane to get Jim and the film crew to Saratoga Springs for that night's show. Since this was the last concert to be filmed, Jim did his best to be entertaining. Waylaid after the sound check by a pipe-smoking, middle-aged evangelical preacher in a Roman collar, who told Jim that the energy of a rock concert reminded him of religious experience, Jim responded that what the Doors were really about was a form of secular religion. Later, in the dressing room at the Saratoga Performing Arts Center, Jim sat at a grand piano, played some Debussy-like chords, and improvised an ode to Friedrich Nietzsche that included a seriocomic re-creation of Nietzsche's mental breakdown in Turin amid random piano cacophony. "Fifteen years in an asylum, he cried and cried, and laughed and laughed..."

The other Doors and their women, bemused, applauded politely when Jim was done. Then they went out and played a superb show that finished with an impassioned "The End." The band refused to do an encore, but came back onstage to take a bow after a long, thunderous ovation. Suddenly Jim flew into the front rows, and it took a dozen cops to get him back onstage and into the wings. The audience stood on their seats and chanted his name for half an hour before reluctantly filing out. At the Schenectady Airport an hour later, he insisted on sitting in with the Siegal-Schwall Blues Band, who were gigging in the airport lounge.

T HE DOORS WERE IN NEW YORK for a few days before flying to London on September 5. Jim called Pamela and asked her to be with him. She parked her Jaguar XKE at a one-hour meter at LAX and flew to JFK. The cops towed the car the following day and found a pound of high-test marijuana in the trunk. Pam was arrested when she tried to claim the car a few days later, but Max Fink somehow got her off.

T HE DOORS' 1968 EUROPEAN TOUR was a considerable triumph. It had to be, because the European kids were waiting for them. The London music paper *Melody Maker* was beating the drums: "Look out, England! Jim Morrison is coming to get you.... Like Jagger and the Stones, Jim Morrison comes on like a fifties-style rock idol in skintight leather trousers, but is actually a poet of some stature.... His audiences know he isn't kidding."

The Doors responded to this adulation. Almost every show and broadcast was very good, confirming their European reputation as America's coolest band. The brief tour was a testament to what Jim Morrison could still do—*if* he really wanted to. As it turned out, these shows also marked the end of the Doors, as originally conceived. Soon, at Jim's insistence, they would mutate into another kind of group altogether.

They flew to London via Air India on September 2, 1968. The Granada TV crew met them at Heathrow Airport and filmed them as they emerged from customs. On September 5 the Doors performed "Hello, I Love You" on the BBC's *Top of the Pops* TV broadcast. The next day, Friday, September 6, the Doors played the first of their two legendary nights at the Roundhouse, an old, acoustically challenged former railway barn in Chalk Farm.

The early show went off well, but the late show was a killer. Originally scheduled to begin at ten-thirty, it was delayed by the Airplane's (stunning) two-and-a-half-hour set and didn't start until after one in the morning. Many of England's pop aristocrats were there: Paul McCartney, George Harrison, Mick Jagger, Keith Richards, Cream, Traffic, and movie stars Terence Stamp and Julie Christie. As the Granada crew filmed every song, Jim performed with a contained passion and an animal grace that surprised even the other Doors and their crew.

They began with a deadly "Five to One" and tore through seventeen songs. "The Unknown Soldier" was rapturously received by the long-haired young crowd, since the English were generally against the American presence in Vietnam. Jim cut "Crawlin' King Snake" into "Back Door Man," then took the band through an abridged but dramatic "Celebration of the Lizard" that brought down the house. After "Hello, I Love You," they went into "Moonlight Drive," during which Jim recited "Horse Latitudes." After a howling ovation, the Doors came back and jammed on "Money" until the gray London September dawn suddenly broke through the Roundhouse's glass skylights, an epiphany for everyone present.

After a few hours rest, the Doors held an afternoon press conference at London's Institute for Contemporary Art, where Jim thoughtfully fielded questions and deflected political criticism by saying that songs like "The Unknown Soldier" spoke for themselves. Densmore: "Jim dazzled the reporters with his rhetoric. He controlled the conversation with long pauses between sentences while he weighed his answers. You could see the wheels turning as he took the maximum time tolerable before responding."

When a reporter asked about comparisons with Mick Jagger, Jim answered: "I've always thought comparisons were useless and ugly. It's a shortcut to thinking." Another asked about fans coming to him for advice. "I get incredible letters," Jim said, warming to the subject. "But they teach me how to live rather than me teaching them. My fans are intelligent youngsters. *Very* sensitive people."

That night they again played two shows at the Roundhouse. The Airplane, English rock singer Terry Reid, and the Crazy World of Arthur Brown played first. Robby Krieger had gotten over his jet lag and treated the audience to a psychedelic guitar display that burned with fire and originality. The second show again finished at dawn with a half-hour reading of "The End," during which the crowd sat quietly transfixed, as if they were attending a solemn rite.

Jim later said this second Roundhouse show was the Doors' zenith performance. He told *New Musical Express,* "The audience was one of the best we've ever had. In the States, they're there to enjoy themselves as much as they came to hear you. But at the Roundhouse, they were there to listen. It was like going back to the roots. It stimulated us. They took me by surprise, because I expected them to be a little resistant, a little reserved. We'd been cautioned there might be hostility toward an American group. But they were fantastic, is all I can say. It was probably the most informed, receptive audience I've ever seen in my life. I think I enjoyed the Roundhouse more than any other date for years."

P AMELA COURSON JOINED JIM IN LONDON before the Doors left for the continent. He went out to meet her at the airport, and those around the tour noticed they seemed unusually close, loving, and comfortable with each other. She brought along a freshly typed folio of Jim's poems, and he spent hours going over them, penciling in corrections and emendations. Pamela was buying clothes on Carnaby Street and the Kings Road for her new boutique, and she and Jim were seen shopping for antiques and curios on Portobello Road. She rented an apartment on exclusive Eaton Square in Belgravia, and settled in as the Doors barnstormed through Europe, beginning on September 13.

That afternoon the Doors taped a segment outdoors in Frankfurt for ZDF-TV's pop show *4-3-2-1 Hot und Sweet,* miming "Hello, I Love You" and "Light My Fire." The next night, September 14, they played two rowdy shows at Frankfurt's Kongresshalle, with their friends Canned Heat opening. Several thousand American soldiers in the audience cheered lustily for "The Unknown Soldier." The German kids irritated the band by sitting quietly during the show. Jim tried to provoke them by threatening to impale the front rows with his mike stand, but he couldn't get any reaction. They ended the show faster than usual and, according to Densmore, only received polite applause. Jim perked up later when the young promoters gave him a beautiful German girl named Francesca to spend the night with, and they all went out to an Israeli-owned nightclub called Das Kinky.

The Doors flew to Amsterdam the following day. A flight attendant asked Jim for his autograph; he wrote a poem for her on an airsickness bag. *O Stewardess/Observe most carefully/Someday you may pour wine/for the tired man.*

That afternoon the Doors and the Airplane strolled around Amsterdam's old town. Crossing the bridges over the city's canals, they found themselves in a district of quaint, gaily decorated shops and cafés that reminded them of San Francisco. As they were progressing down the street, Dutch kids came up and started giving them blocks of fresh hashish and pills of all varieties and colors. The others discreetly pocketed the dope—Amsterdam was famously tolerant toward recreational drugs—but Jim Morrison swallowed everything that was handed to him, without question. Grace Slick said later that he probably ate an ounce of hash and half a dozen pills that day.

Jim was flying by the time the Airplane opened the show at the venerable Concertgebouw symphony hall at eight o'clock that evening. He seemed bored and manic hanging out with the other Doors in the dressing room, so he hopped onstage with the Airplane during "Plastic Fantastic Lover" and performed a crazed leather dervish dance, getting tangled on the guitarists' electric cords and thoroughly annoying the band. Jim twirled and spun, made himself dizzy, and fell down. Helped backstage, he threw up and passed out.

No one could wake him. His breathing was shallow and he looked green and ghastly. The promoter, afraid that Jim was dying on him, called an ambulance and Jim was carried out cold on a stretcher and transported to a hospital. The doctors examined him and said he had to sleep it off overnight. So the Doors went on without their singer. The audience was told Jim was ill and was offered a refund, but everyone stayed to hear Ray Manzarek sing Jim's parts, and the three Doors played two complete shows without him. Contemporary reviews in the Dutch press indicate that the band pulled this off with flying colors.

Jim woke up the next morning, feeling good and rested, and asked what had happened. John Densmore proudly told Jim that the Doors had survived without him.

SEPTEMBER 17, 1968. The Doors and the British blues band Savoy Brown played the Falkoner Theatret in Copenhagen, Denmark. Recovered from his Dutch collapse, Jim performed a taut, aggressive show that reportedly unsettled the Danish kids, who were unused to psychodrama in their rock concerts. They seemed mystified by "Texas Radio," which Jim was performing as an introduction to "Hello, I Love You." When the kids started a rhythmic clapping between songs, Jim silenced them with, "Aww, stop that!"

The Doors started arguing onstage over what to play next. Jim wanted "Little Red Rooster" but Ray and John didn't want to do blues songs. Jim was petulant but went along when Ray started "Soul Kitchen" instead. "When the Music's Over" was given a perfect performance, with Ray quoting jazz vibraphonist Milt Jackson's "Bag's Groove" during his solo. The Doors also premiered two new songs, "Wild Child" and a fragment of "Touch Me." Robby was playing the Beatles' "Eleanor Rigby" melody during his solo on "Light My Fire." Jim insisted the lights be killed for "The End," which the Doors started with a jarring, science-fiction intro and carried through with a commitment and studied intensity they would display only rarely later on.

At ten the next morning, bleary from lack of sleep, Jim (on a stool) and the Doors taped six songs for Danish television, including "Texas Radio" and a complete performance version of "The Unknown Soldier." Later that day, Grace Slick knocked on Jim's hotel door. She'd been watching him carefully during the tour, but had yet to make contact. If she said something to him, Jim responded with averted eyes and a gnomic non sequitur. "I was fascinated by the way he seemed to go from one side of his brain to the other, ignoring all the synapses in between," she later observed. "And beautiful? He looked like a rabid Johnny Depp, perfectly formed and possessed by abstraction." Grace made several charcoal sketches of Jim, her pretext for knocking on his door being that she wanted to show them to him.

Jim answered the door and smiled at Grace. "Hey—what's up?" She walked in the room and saw a bowl of strawberries on the coffee table. Jim started squeezing the fruit between his fingers, offering the dribble to Grace. They started painting the bedspread with the juice. Then Jim got up, opened the top drawer of the bureau, and closed it again. Then they took their clothes off. Not too much was said. "He was a well-built boy, his cock was slightly larger than average, and he was young enough to maintain that engorged silent connection. At the same time, he was surprisingly gentle. I'd expected a sort of frantic horizontal ritual. Jim mystified me with that otherworldly expression, and his hips never lost the insistent rolling motion that was driving the dance.

"I have no idea how long I was there, but I knew I should leave before I got caught—we both had other relationships—and I felt like an intruder. I dressed as fast as I could. Jim didn't seem to notice, appearing unconscious on the bed, naked, his eyes closed. Without moving a muscle, he said to me, 'Why wouldn't you come back?'"

"Only if I'm asked," Grace said.

But Jim never asked.

The Doors' European tour ended on Friday, September 20, in Stockholm, Sweden. The Airplane, Terry Reid, and Savoy Brown opened. The Doors' first show featured the rarely performed "Love Street," plus "Wake Up!" and "The Hill Dwellers" from "Celebration." The second set featured "The Ballad of Mack the Knife" as a prelude to "Alabama Song." Both shows were taped for later broadcast on Sweden's main pop station, Radiohuset.

Many Doors fans feel these final Scandinavian concerts were the last true Doors shows, with a bardic singer in full command of his powers, a potent icon of desire, an agent of change in the original, leather-clad package, still looking like a romantic lord and basically playing it straight. Soon Jim Morrison would force changes that made sure the Doors would never be the same again.

A POET'S TOUR

THE DOORS FLEW back to London on their way home. Jim settled into placid domesticity with Pamela in an expensive furnished flat overlooking the private gardens of Eaton Square. They invited Ray and Dorothy Manzarek to breakfast, and Ray was pleased to see Jim at ease for once, cooking bacon and eggs for them, squeezing juice, and making tea. He wrote later that it was the most adult thing he'd ever seen Jim and Pam do. "They seemed quite at home and quite happy. It was the calmest and happiest I'd seen Jim since his 'nervous breakdown.'"

On September 23, probably at the invitation of George Harrison, Jim visited the Beatles at EMI's Abbey Road studio, where they were recording *The White Album*. Some Beatles experts claim that Jim can be heard singing backing vocals on archival outtakes of "Happiness Is a Warm Gun," but his name does not appear on the seemingly meticulous studio production logs for that date.

On October 4, Jim and Pamela watched the independent ITV Network's broadcast of Granada's documentary, *The Doors Are Open*. This was a ten-song digest from the last Roundhouse show, interwoven with material from the London press conference and an interview with Jim. The producers also spliced in footage from antiwar demonstrations and from Vietnam, using the Doors' performance as a template for reporting political dissent and generational revolt. Jim said later that he didn't think much of the film, but that the British filmmakers had made the best of what they had to work with.

Jim walked for miles throughout London. Notebook notations mark the names of places he visited: Cheyne Walk in Chelsea, the Poets' Corner in Westminster Abbey, the bookstores in Charing Cross Road, Mayfair, Spitalfields, the bright lights of Leicester Square. He stopped to listen to a young violinist in a rag hat playing in front of the Royal Court

Theater in Sloane Square. Jim and Pam ate roast beef and Yorkshire pudding at Simpson's, and went to the movies: *Rosemary's Baby, The Trip, Blow-Up, Weekend.*

I N MID-OCTOBER Jim took a black cab to Heathrow to meet Michael McClure, his new literary mentor and collaborator. McClure, nine years older than Jim, was the youngest of the Beat poets (and possibly the least talented), but he was Hollywood handsome and totally hip. He lived with his wife and kids in San Francisco, rode motorcycles, and had just ghostwritten the memoirs of the Hell's Angels leader Freewheelin' Frank Reynolds. Pamela Courson's sister, Judy, was dating McClure's agent, Michael Hamilburg, who brought the rock star and the poet together again. Jim and McClure had met in New York earlier in the year to discuss the possibility of Jim starring in a film adaptation of McClure's play *The Beard,* which was about to open in London. The American movie producer Elliott Kastner had expressed interest in this project, and McClure had set up a meeting in Kastner's London office.

Jim and McClure first spent several days talking and visiting locations associated with great English poets. With British poet Christopher Logue, they paid homage at the site of William Blake's house, now occupied by a hospital. McClure showed Jim a poem he had written on the flight over about Percy Shelley, and Jim immediately wrote a spontaneous poem in reply.

"I liked Jim," McClure later told interviewer Frank Lisciandro. "I liked his intelligence. I liked his style. I liked the way he moved. He was a pretty well-integrated human being, both physically and mentally adept, the whole individual working in one direction. You could sense the poet there."

McClure was staying with Jim and Pamela in Belgravia, and one night Pamela deliberately left a sheaf of Jim's poems out on a desk for McClure to inspect. McClure read them through, and was very impressed. In the morning Jim was irritated at Pamela for this, and told McClure that the poems were private, and not for publication.

McClure: "He was afraid the poetry would be adulated because he was a rock star and that it wouldn't be taken seriously by the people he wanted to take it seriously. And it was for that reason I suggested he first do a private publication of those poems.... When I saw them, I was moved. A wonderful first book. I didn't see *The Lords*. I saw *The New Creatures*... which is a book of imagistic poetry with hints of seventeenth-century Elizabethan drama, [and] tastes of classical mythology. It's a kind of romantic personal viewpoint, in a nineteenth-century Shelleyan/Keatsian sense. *Snakeskin jacket/Indian eyes/Brilliant hair*... His poems are almost narratives rather than being transcendental visions. Some of them could be Roman poems, except for their very Englishness—goddess hunters, bows and arrows, people with green hair walking by the side of the sea. It's a little bit like science fiction. A little bit like some Roman poet writing in Latin had been reading nineteenth-century poetry.

"And I said, 'Jim, this is real fine. You should publish it,' but he was concerned. And I said, 'Publish a private edition.' 'What would I do with it?' he asked. And I said, 'Give it to people, and see what responses you get, and then decide what you want to do about commercial publication.'"

Jim said he would think about it. Meanwhile, Jim read the manuscript of *The Adept*, McClure's just completed novel about a cocaine dealer, and loved it.

McClure: "It's a mystical novel, an adventure novel about an anarchist sixties idealist coke dealer, who is also a motorcycle rider—sort of a sociopathic idealist back in the sixties when there were such people. The characters are based on people I knew. People believed in drugs, sold only certain drugs, more harmless types of drugs. Coke was thought to be a diversion, a rarity, not a social plague. People were making fortunes and using the money to do things like back plays. I had a play at the Straight Theater in San Francisco [financed] by someone much like this person in *The Adept*.

"The [original] idea was to talk to Kastner about a film version of *The Beard* starring Jim, but after some serious talk we decided there was no way in 1968 that the play could be done without censoring it for the film media. So we decided against talking to Kastner about the project. Jim loved *The Beard* and wanted to play Billy the Kid, but when he read *The Adept* he was sold, and wanted to do that instead."

Kastner received Jim and McClure in his office in Soho, London's movie quarter. Jim was growing a beard and putting on weight. McClure was scruffy. Both were immensely hung over. Kastner asked about *The Beard.* "Jim said that we'd changed our minds," McClure recalled, "that we didn't want to do *The Beard,* but a new project based on *The Adept.* Jim explained the novel in elegant detail to Kastner. He told the story with a great sense of drama, great detail, and full recall of what happens in it."

But Kastner passed on the project. It was too close in subject matter to Dennis Hopper's coke-dealer movie *Easy Rider,* then in production and already the talk of the Hollywood industry. Also, movie people were interested in Jim as he had looked in 1967, not the bearded, bleary, biker-looking poet of late 1968. But Jim was adamant that *The Adept* would be a perfect movie vehicle for him, and assured McClure he would find backing for the project back in Los Angeles.

J IM AND PAMELA flew back to Los Angeles together on October 20. The mountains and hills east of the city were on fire as the hot, dry Santa Ana winds fanned the flames. The atmosphere was stifling.

The Doors should have been ready to start making their fourth album but the band's affairs were in disarray. They were upset that the thirty thousand dollars they had spent on their documentary seemed to be down the drain. As edited by Frank Lisciandro, *Feast of Friends* came in at under forty-five minutes, an awkward length for anything but an hour-long television show with commercials, and the grainy, shaky, anarchic footage was obviously too raw and experimental to be broadcast on American TV as it then existed. While *Feast* brilliantly captured the chaos and frenzy of the 1968 Doors concerts, it was judged an expensive waste of celluloid by everyone who saw it except Jim, who screened it on his return from London.

"The first time I saw the film I was taken aback," Jim told Jerry Hopkins a few months later, "because, being onstage and one of the central characters of the film, I had only seen things from my point of view. Then, to see a series of events that I thought I had some control over, to see it as it actually was . . . I suddenly realized, in a way, that I was just a puppet of a lot of forces I only vaguely understood."

What forces do you mean?

"Well, I guess I mean there was a lot more . . . a lot of the activity going on around me that I thought I understood . . . well, seeing the film I realized I was only aware of a tiny section of reality, just one lonely chink in the wall. There was a whole stadium out there. It was kind of shocking."

The other Doors were also shocked because their money was gone. They wanted to abandon the project, but Ferrara and Lisciandro begged for another chance to edit the film and convinced Jim to let them try. He rented an office for them in the Clear Thoughts Building at 947 North La Cienega, across from Elektra, and turned it into an editing suite for the film crew and general clubhouse, at his own expense.

NOT LONG AFTER they came back from Europe, Jim began having problems urinating. Max Fink sent him to an old friend, Dr. Arnold Derwin, a gynecologist who practiced on Wilshire Boulevard and treated celebrities discreetly, after normal office hours. Derwin diagnosed an unspecific urethritis—a venereal disease—possibly acquired from the German girl Jim had been with in Frankfurt. Pamela went nuts when Jim told her he had a case of clap, and accused him of getting it from homosexual encounters. A few days later, she flew back to London with Christopher Jones, who was about to costar with Anthony Hopkins in *The Looking Glass War*. They moved into the London Hilton together, while Jim took up with Anne Moore in Los Angeles and went into the studio with the Doors.

Jim Morrison was dried up. He didn't have any new material for the Doors, and didn't seem to give a shit, so *The Soft Parade* would be mostly Robby Krieger's record. Paul Rothchild was in his most anal-aggressive phase, taking hours of studio time to obsess with engineer Bruce Botnick over microphone placement and sound levels, all of which made Jim insane with boredom. Rothchild was also insisting the Doors had to stay current and follow the Beatles, the Byrds, and Blood, Sweat and Tears with rock music's newest trend—horn sections—and even with string orchestrations on some tracks. Jim just wanted to play bar-band R & B at that point, and hated the direction rock music was going.

Robby's new song "Touch Me" grew out of a fight with his girlfriend, Lynn, who had taunted Krieger with "Come on, come on—*hit* me! I'm not afraid of you." Jim Morrison suggested "Touch Me" instead. At the early sessions for the new album, Rothchild brought in Curtis Amy, thirty-nine, a black jazz musician who had played with Dizzy Gillespie and recorded for World Pacific, to put an energized tenor sax solo onto the ride-out of "Touch Me." (Manzarek: "We told him, 'Play it like Coltrane.'") Another early track was the stupendous "Wild Child," with Jim's lyrics grafted onto Robby's melody.

A film crew captured the vocal sessions for "Wild Child" in Elektra's paisley-walled studio. Jim was singing in the isolated vocal booth, smoking cigarettes and wearing a pinstriped Van Heusen dress shirt. Robby was fingering the song's complex riff on the neck of his horned red Gibson SG, and griping about the end of the vocal, in which Jim stepped out of character and intoned, "Remember when we were in Africa?"

"That's the stupidest ending I ever heard," Krieger commented.

Jim, stoned, just laughed at him. "What's 'stupid' about it?"

Krieger: "It doesn't have anything to do with the rest of the song." Robby was argumentative and annoying, but as the band's secret weapon, he alone could confront Jim on matters of artistic worth.

Jim: "Ahh, don't worry about it."

Around this time, the legendary Italian director Michelangelo Antonioni was in Los Angeles, preparing his first American feature film, *Zabriskie Point,* an atmospheric hippies-in-the-desert saga with a cast of attractive young unknowns and a typically opaque plot. Antonioni was interested in rock music—he had famously featured the Jeff Beck/Jimmy Page dual-guitar Yardbirds in *Blow-Up*—and had been referred to the Doors by none other than Mick Jagger. According to Antonioni, he met with Jim Morrison at Elektra studios, and had asked for a song for his movie that would capture something of the disturbed grandeur of southern California in 1968.

Jim and the Doors responded with the harsh cubist composition "L'America," which Antonioni summarily rejected for his pretty but useless film, released late in 1970.

THE DEVILISH SANTA ANA winds kept blowing all that autumn, roaring down the canyons at eighty miles an hour, pushing smog and negativity back into the Los Angeles Basin from the east. The peaks of the San Gabriel Mountains, east of Los Angeles, were aflame with wind-driven wildfires. "I see your hair is burning," Jim wrote in a notebook. "Hills are filled with fire. If they say I never loved you, you know they are a liar."

Without Pamela Courson's taming influence, Jim Morrison went ape. He was drinking to blackout almost every night. His cronies had to take him to his motel and pour him into bed. He was banned from the Troubadour for screaming maniacally during other musicians' sets, and for slapping a waitress who had asked for an autograph. He was walking around West Hollywood, picking up skinny, boyish-looking girls, taking them back to his motel, and trying to sodomize them. (Often, he couldn't get it up.) He was driving the Blue Lady, his rebuilt Mustang, around town and up the Pacific Coast Highway, often blind-drunk.

"Jim and I used to argue about his excesses," Paul Ferrara told writer Patricia Butler, "and he would [say] ... 'It doesn't matter.' And I would say, 'Yes, it does, you're going to fucking kill yourself.' ... One night, Jim was driving—he had a Shelby Mustang—and I think Babe [Hill] was in the front seat, and I was in the back with Frank [Lisciandro]. From the Whisky a Go Go, if you head east on Sunset you come to Halloway Drive that dips down toward La Cienega. There's like six or seven stoplights. Jim floored the car and went screaming through every light for six or seven blocks, regardless of color. He literally pushed it to the floor and that was it. Man! We must've been going a hundred miles an hour. That car was *fast*."

Jim would bring bottles of whiskey to the Doors' recording sessions. When he went to the bathroom, John Densmore or Vince Treanor tried to empty out most of the booze in hopes that Jim could get through the evening's work.

LET HIM CRY

JIM MORRISON AND THE DOORS went back on the road in the first half of November, touring Midwestern cities on the weekends. Six linebacker-sized black bodyguards from Philadelphia's Sullivan Detective Agency protected the band from their fans and the local cops. The Doors badly needed cash, and "Touch Me" was about to be released as the next Doors single. But the tour was hastily organized, promotion was inadequate, and many of the shows didn't sell out. (Jim Morrison hated playing to empty seats.)

In Milwaukee on November 1, the band came back for an encore after a good, workmanlike show. "OK, OK, OK, baby," Jim yelled to a raving crowd. "This one's gonna bring the house down." Robby tore into the "Gloria" chords and the Doors attacked the song with pure abandon. Two nights later in Chicago, where their last appearance had been raucous, Jim led the band through a mesmeric, almost sinister performance. They played Robby's new song, "Tell All the People" and an almost complete "Celebration of the Lizard." The encore was "Light My Fire" in a breezy, radiolike version that sent everyone home happy.

Richard Nixon was elected president of the United States on Tuesday, November 5, an event that would have consequences for Jim Morrison. The following Thursday, the Doors played the Arizona State Fair and Jim let fly with multiple curses and crotch grabs, inviting the crowd to leave their seats as if he was trying to provoke the uniformed highway patrol cops guarding the stage. Between "Tell All the People" and "When the Music's Over," Jim Morrison walked to the edge of the stage and in a bitter tone announced:

"Well, we have a new president... [booing, catcalls]... That's right... He hasn't made any mistakes... *yet!*... But if he does, *we're gonna get him*... [applause, shouts, general concurrence]... That's right! Right on! Right on! Right on! WE'RE NOT GONNA STAND FOR FOUR MORE YEARS OF THIS BULLSHIT!"

There was loud and prolonged cheering. Several hundreds kids rushed the stage and were pushed back by the increasingly aggravated cops. The balconies started to empty onto the floor. Firecrackers and sparklers were tossed onstage, and were put out with a fire extinguisher. Someone cut the backline power and the house lights were brought up. Ten thousand kids voiced their anger and the power went back on.

The cops moved in closer, and the band finished with a savage "The Unknown Soldier" as hundreds of clothes were thrown onstage. Jim, laughing, threw back as many as he could before disappearing behind the curtains. Outside the hall afterward, there were a dozen arrests for disorderly contact, and ten kids were taken to the hospital with minor injuries.

But this was more than another typical, anarchic Doors concert. Jim Morrison's FBI file contains a report about this show, although it is heavily blacked out with censored deletions. The FBI's unidentified informant, citing eyewitnesses and newspaper clippings, alleges that Jim Morrison made unspecific threats against President-elect Nixon in Phoenix that night.

Jim's Morrison's chaotic performance in Arizona—filthy lingo, inflammatory politics, dirty moves—had also angered the locals who had co-produced the show with Rich Linnel, and who may have lost money. Word began to filter out—through booking agencies, concert industry newsletters, and insurance company tip-sheets—that the Doors were bad news—riling the authorities, using obscenities as part of their show, drinking onstage, playing to empty seats. This was the kiss of death for a touring band.

Some of the Doors' next gigs in the Midwest were downsized from classy venues to hockey rinks. This, coupled with a ferocious turn in the weather and the vagaries of Jim Morrison's love life, put him into a foul state of mind. Jim was irritable and destroyed his mike stand in Madison, Wisconsin, on Friday, November 8. (An encore of "Celebration" left the college-age crowd stuck to their seats in wonder, according to press accounts, staring at the vacant stage after Jim had walked off.)

The next night in St. Louis an early blizzard had kept most people home. The Doors were supposed to play at prestigious Kiel Auditorium, but were quickly downgraded to the grungier St. Louis Arena. Jim was pissed. Appearing onstage to a sparse crowd, with a bottle of whisky in his right hand, Jim denounced what he repeatedly called "this old fuckin' barn" and proceeded to give the audience a drunken show that visibly disgusted the band. Jim either glared at or ignored the vocal, excited audience. He played most of the show with his eyes closed and the microphone pressed close to his face. He seemed unable to finish many of the songs. His white poet's shirt came loose, his beard was thick with new bristles, and he pawed the stage with his boot in one of his off-kilter shaman hops that seemed almost comical.

The kids up front noticed the atmosphere was tense onstage. Robby seemed upset, played with his back to the audience, stared at his amps, sadly shaking his head at Jim's shit-faced yawps. Densmore looked furious. The kids up front would catch Jim's cold, flat stare and have to look away. Ray was soloing with his head down, playing his ass off on "Light My Fire," sending the message that whatever crap Jim might be pulling, you were just getting what you paid for.

Jim kept getting worse, slurring lyrics, embarrassing the Missouri teenagers up front by rubbing himself to obvious erection with the microphone stand. A big, biker-looking guy in the front row with his daughters bellowed at Jim to cut it out, and he did. Then Jim left the mike stand, sat down on the edge of the stage while Ray was soloing, and put his head in his hands.

A seventeen-year-old girl, Poe Sparrow, was about ten rows back, on the aisle. She later recalled:

"A sudden irresistible force was pulling me toward Jimmy. He sat, shoulders slumped, elbows on his knees, holding his head. My fingers gripped my camera nervously as I stopped three feet in front of him. Perspiration dripped from his hair and trickled across his leather pants. Slowly, he raised his head. . . . I was *aghast*. I was looking into the face of an utterly exhausted, bewildered man/child. I wanted to cradle his weary head, to soothe. . . . The moment his eyes focused on mine is frozen in eternity—soft and vulnerable, etching pain straight through to my cortex.

"Then he changed, undergoing a transmutation so swift it sent me reeling backward. He smiled, mouthing words I couldn't hear, lost in the wall of sound. But it didn't matter, because Jimmy was gone, and in his place was the Lizard King. I remember a wave of shock, of backing up fast, unable to avert my eyes. The rest of the concert is a complete and total blank. I have no memory of returning home."

Sunday night in Minneapolis was the last show of the tour. A cute, extremely excited teenage girl rushed over at the airport and asked Jim for an autograph. Jim had been sleeping off a drunk on the plane, and slurred, "You'd eat your own shit, wouldn't you?" Densmore wanted to kill him, but the chick's boyfriend told Jim, "That's OK, man. Whatever you gotta do to get through."

The band vamped on "Soul Kitchen" for five minutes before Jim emerged to roaring acclaim and checked out the audience. "OK, OK, man—let me get a good look at you." The front rows were full of blond kids smiling at him, so Jim put on a good show. During "When the Music's Over," he started laughing insanely and doing comedy bits, getting laughter and applause. Jim almost always talked to the audiences as his equals, rarely talking down to them. He'd ask them simple questions, and listen to the responses.

There was a long delay after this, and the kids got restless, but eventually some issue was settled and local hero (and Elektra artist) Tony Glover came out with his harmonica and stayed with the Doors for the rest of the show. Glover had interviewed the band that afternoon for *Circus* magazine. He and Jim did several harp-poem jams together on "Back Door Man" and "Love Me Two Times," which turned into Elvis Presley's "Mystery Train," a motif that the band would later adapt for jam sections during shows.

T HE EVENTS SURROUNDING Jim Morrison during the next three weeks, in November 1968, are both unclear and still in dispute. What is certain is that this crucial period changed the lives of everyone involved with him.

The Doors continued working on their new album at Elektra Sound Studios. "The Soft Parade," Jim's episodic rock opera, which had been left off the last album, was resurrected and improved. Jim complained about singing the lamely provocative lyrics of "Tell All the People." Robby refused to change them, so Jim insisted that from then on all Doors songs should have individual publishing credits—a huge rift in the solidarity of the band. George Harrison visited the *Soft Parade* sessions, observed Paul Rothchild's compulsive knob-turning, and made a few wry comments about it being as tedious as the Beatles' sessions had become.

Then Jim disappeared. One day he just didn't show up, and his cronies either didn't know where he was, or wouldn't say that Jim had flown to London to get Pamela Courson back. She was in bad shape, having broken up with Christopher Jones. She had put her trust in Jones, and thought her life with Jim was behind her. Jones then wrote an innocuous letter to his ex-wife, the mother of his daughter, and left it for his agent to mail. But Pamela intercepted the letter, read it, and took it as a betrayal. She was shattered. She was buying heroin from Jean de Breteuil's connections, the same dealers supplying Keith Richards's habit. When she ran out of money and was alone and frightened, she called Jim. The tone of her voice scared him. He got to London as fast as he could.

At first Jim couldn't find Pamela, and had to ask that effete junkie, the Comte de Breteuil, whom he hated, where she might be. When Jim tracked her down, Pamela said she wasn't coming back—unless he quit the Doors. Jim argued with her in the Bag O'Nails, the popular, exclusive nightclub. They fought. He got drunk, started crying, called her names. She threw her drink in his face at midnight—a few people applauded— and stormed out. An hour later, she knocked on the door of a mews house that Jones had moved into, near Cadogan Square.

"Where's Jim?" Jones asked, knowing he was in London trying to reconcile with Pamela. She told him.

"So you just left him sitting there, crying? Why don't you go get him?"

"I don't think so," Pamela said, coming in for the night. "Let him cry. He likes it."

THE GODDESS OF JUSTICE

J IM MORRISON AND PAMELA COURSON flew back to Los Angeles during the last week of November 1968. That was it for the Doors.

Bill Siddons told Jim about the Buick commercial first. Jim had come into the Doors' office to read his mail. The staff was surprised to see him, but no one could ask where he'd been. Jim had a full beard again, and didn't look well, also being jet-lagged and maybe drunk. Bill took Jim into his office and told him the good news—that the Doors had sold "Light My Fire" to General Motors for a Buick advertising campaign. When the ad agency needed a quick answer and they couldn't find him, the other three had approved, posthaste. Max Fink had signed off on the deal, having Jim's power of attorney.

Jim listened quietly, with growing anger, as Bill outlined the deal that would bring the Doors sixty thousand badly needed dollars for the rights to use Robby Krieger's song to promote Buick's new muscle car, the 1970 Gran Sports GS455, on radio and TV. It was going to be *Come on, Buick, light my fire!* on the airwaves from coast to coast. Jim Morrison sat there in shock. He couldn't believe it. They told him it was Jac Holzman's fault. (Elektra would get twenty grand as its share.) Soon the band

and its management met in emergency session. Jim's remarks were quoted (thirty years later) by Ray Manzarek:

"You *can't* have signed without me. . . . *Why,* man? We do everything together. Why'd you do this without me? . . . *So what?* Couldn't you have waited for me? . . . FUCK YOU GUYS!"

Total silence. Jim had never screamed at them like that. He was blind with rage and looked distraught. He got up and stomped around. "Fuck this, you guys. I thought we were supposed to be *brothers.*"

Ray tried, "We are, man. Nothing has changed."

Jim looked at him sharply. "Everything has changed. *Everything...* because I can't trust you anymore. . . . You guys made a pact with the devil."

Ray cursed at Jim.

"I *know* you, Ray," Jim said. "You're only in it for the money." There was a moment of silence. Robby told Jim there was nothing anyone could do. It was a done deal.

"Oh, yeah? We'll fuckin' see about that." Jim was raving now, started talking about smashing up Buicks, onstage, with a sledgehammer. Everyone was in total shock. Bill Siddons: "He felt betrayed. His partners had betrayed him. They had sold out to corporate America without asking him. He just didn't get it." Jim got on the phone to Abe Somer, the band's lawyer. "Threaten 'em with a lawsuit. Tell them anything, but stop the fucking contract."

But it was too late. The commercials were filmed and broadcast in a limited way, mostly in the South and Midwest.

Bill Siddons: "That was *it*—the end of the dream. That was the end of Jim's relationships with the other members of the band. From then on, it was strictly business. That was the day Jim said, 'I don't have partners anymore. I have associates.'"

The other Doors went into shock. Other rock bands worked every night, made serious money on the road. The Doors could only work three nights on the weekends—the maximum that Jim Morrison could handle. Robby Krieger: "After doing a show, we [the other Doors] were spent. We'd go to our rooms and crash. But Jim was just getting going: partying, hanging out—on through the next day. Then another show the next night, and Jim just kept going. That's why we never did long tours.

Jim would get 'tired.'" The Doors thought selling Robby's song to Buick was a good way to offset this handicap. Hell, they had other songs too. There was real money there. They were dead wrong. Jim Morrison refused to sell out.

Bill Siddons: "I knew Jim had a lot of serious problems. I didn't know what they were. I just knew he would put more alcohol into his body than anybody.... I thought he was trying to commit suicide, because the quantities didn't make any sense to me. He operated in Jim Land, and nobody operated there but Jim."

J IM WAS SO ALIENATED AND PISSED OFF THAT, for a while, it was questionable whether he would show up to tape the Doors' two-song appearance on CBS's red-hot *The Smothers Brothers Show* on December 4, 1968. But they needn't have worried, because Jim Morrison had the same cash flow problems as everyone else. There was a new record to promote, and Jim arrived on time at CBS's Burbank studios in full leathers, no beard, and great hair. This would prove to be the last appearance of the Lizard King, who, as it turned out, was never seen alive again.

Robby Krieger showed up with a wicked-looking black eye, gotten in a barroom brawl over a pool table. Jim had mouthed off, and avoided being trashed by rednecks only because Babe Hill had blocked the door with his body after Jim bolted. So the drunken morons smashed Robby in the face instead.

Tom and Dick Smothers had a comedy act that mocked the pretenses of the early sixties folk revival. Their eighteen-month old television show was radical for the times, with anti-Nixon jokes before the new president had even taken office, irreverent, double-entendre satire, and cutting-edge musical guests. So the Doors went whole hog for this show, performing "Wild Child" and "Touch Me," appearing (on the latter) with tuxedo-clad horn and string musicians from the Smothers' band.

Elektra had provided an instrumental mix of the songs, over which Jim Morrison was required to sing live—a tough assignment requiring ultraprofessional, split-second precision. He almost nailed it. Performing with his golden microphone, emoting into the cold red eye of the TV camera, "Wild Child" was perfect. But Jim (horribly) missed his vocal cue on the second verse of "Touch Me." Since the show was taped, there was talk of a retake, but Curtis Amy had mimed the song's jazzy ride-out so well that the director told them to forget it. The Smothers were happy with the flawed, real-life version of the Doors they had captured. Indeed, the CBS broadcast later that month (December 15) had unusually high ratings. Jim looked like a gray-eyed Achilles in his leathers and long hair. He never looked that good again.

It was also the Doors' last appearance on commercial television in America. Inevitably, the Smothers' show would be canceled six months later, in the spring of 1969, after protest diva Joan Baez dedicated a song to her husband, David Harris, who was going to prison for refusing to fight in Vietnam.

O N DECEMBER 8, 1968, Jim Morrison was twenty-five years old. The office had a little party for him, with a cake and candles. Afterward Jim walked down the stairs with Bill Siddons's pretty blond girlfriend, Cherie. "He said to me, 'Well, I made it to twenty-five. Do you think I'll make it to thirty?' And we both knew he wouldn't make it to thirty."

A few days later, Jim brought the Doors' teenage office boy, Danny Sugerman, home to Pamela's flat for supper. Sugerman was a twitchy high school kid from a troubled family who hung around the Doors' office. Bill Siddons tried to get rid of him, but then Jim hired him to help answer his voluminous fan mail. They walked over to Pam's place, where she greeted the boy with the same steely glare and open contempt she displayed to anyone connected with the band. Danny noticed Jim's books stacked in milk crates against the walls, floor to ceiling. After shouting at Jim for bringing some kid home for dinner, Pamela served a delicious lasagna, drank a glass of wine, and then nodded off in a heroin stupor, her head almost in her plate at one point.

"Quick, *take off*," Jim whispered, grabbing his jacket. Pam came to and started screaming again as they ran down the steps.

"Jim—where the fuck are you going? Answer me, Jim! God damn you! Jim!"

"Run," Jim advised, "before she starts throwing stuff. That chick has an arm like you wouldn't believe."

Sugerman says they went to the Whisky, and Jim got him in without an ID. They sat at the bar and Jim ordered four straight double vodkas and a glass of milk for the kid. Primal black rocker Bo Diddley started playing around ten o'clock; as soon as his jungle telegram started throbbing out of the speakers, Jim vaulted over the railing, crashed onto the dance floor, and pressed up against the stage, whooping and hollering. He grabbed one of the mikes, and started bellowing along with Bo. They exchanged words, and then suddenly Jim was raging at the kids around him, calling them niggers, telling them they were pieces of shit. They were kicked out of the Whisky. Jim spent the rest of the evening watching the topless girls dance at the Phone Booth, and the night on the office couch.

THE YEAR 1968 had been a bad trip for everyone, around the world. The Doors' final show of Bloody '68 took place at the Los Angeles Forum in Inglewood on December 14. The big arena, home of the mighty Los Angeles Lakers basketball team, was sold out. "Touch Me" was already on the radio in heavy rotation, and climbing the charts.

Jim was candid about his misgivings in a preconcert interview: "I don't know what's gonna happen," he said when asked about the band's future. "I guess we'll continue like this for a while. Then, to get our vitality back, maybe we'll have to get out of this whole business. Maybe we'll all go to an island by ourselves and start creating something again."

There were several opening acts. A traditional Chinese musician (hired by Ray) was booed off the stage while thrumming his primitive lute. Sweetwater, a country rock band, fared a little better. Lurid, volatile rockabilly demon Jerry Lee Lewis played "Great Balls of Fire" and "Whole Lotta Shakin' Going On" and got booed for his efforts by the teenage audience.

"Ah hope y'all get *heart attacks*," Lewis told the kids, and walked out in a huff.

The Doors' performance was rudely received by the kids because the band was showcasing new songs backed by a horn section and a string quintet. "Tell All the People" opened the show and hardly anyone clapped. Other new songs and "Spanish Caravan" drew yawns and shouts for "Light My Fire," which continued through "Touch Me" and

"Wild Child." When they band finally condescended to play "Light My Fire" the audience came to life, flaring their lighters in a massive tribute to the band. The Doors played the song for their lives, and a tumultuous ovation thanked them when it was over.

Then there was a long pause. Jim sat down with his legs dangling off the stage, and started asking the kids up front, in a tone bitter with mockery, what they *really* wanted. Most of them said they wanted to hear "Light My Fire" again.

To the astonishment of the audience, Jim suddenly asked, *"Is everybody in? The ceremony is about to begin."* He then finished the Forum concert with an alternate version of the complete "Celebration of the Lizard." Jim shrugged off protests and catcalls and recited in a swaying fervor, changing lyrics and adding new imagery. After twenty-five minutes, as he intoned the final "Palace of Exile" section, Densmore, Krieger, and then Manzarek left the stage. Jim finished the long poem—*"Tomorrow we enter the land of my birth / I want to be ready"*—and then walked off to near silence.

There was no ovation, and no encore. Eighteen thousand kids watched the empty stage as the house lights came up, and then filed out in a whisper of mystification.

After the show, when the giant parking lot was cleared, Jim went out in the dark and played kick-the-can with Pamela and a special guest, his younger brother, Andy Morrison.

P AMELA COURSON'S BOUTIQUE, Themis, named for the Roman goddess of justice, was open by Christmas 1968. No one quite believed the money Jim had poured into the shop, with its décor of precious woods, fine silks, Moroccan hangings, and walls covered with peacock feathers. Stepping into Themis out of the blinding California sunlight, a customer's eyes had to adjust to a grottolike darkness lit by scented candles. The shop was on the ground floor of the Clear Thoughts Building, where Jim and the crew had their clubhouse, but they weren't allowed in the shop. Themis was deliberately expensive and fashion-forward, way ahead of its time. Pamela's sister Judy ran the business, while Pam and the Count de Breteuil took off on buying trips to Milan, Paris, and Marrakech.

Jim was proud of Pamela's enterprise and energy. "Jim was always giving her stuff," Paul Ferrara recalled. "Money, clothes, cars, dogs, anything she wanted. He pampered the hell out of her. She'd want something, and he'd call Max [Fink] and say, 'Give her whatever she wants.' Money meant nothing to Jim. It was immaterial to him if he spent a dollar on her or a hundred thousand dollars, as long as she was happy."

When Pamela said she wanted a place in the country where she could get away from it all, Jim paid for a secluded cabin, behind an old tavern, up in tranquil Topanga Canyon.

He wouldn't marry her, though. "Everyone knew Jim had Pam where he wanted her," a friend of hers said later. "And besides, he didn't trust her for a minute. He just loved her. That's all." The Doors' accountant later estimated that Jim spent a quarter million preinflation dollars on the boutique, which became a hip fashion spot in late-sixties L.A. (Miles Davis was an occasional customer in 1969/70), but never made any money. Pamela took perverse pleasure in overcharging the other Doors' wives when they shopped there.

Jim and Pamela tried to stick together. He lived with her when he could. In private and in public they kept to themselves. If they went to dinner in a group, they spoke only to each other. John Densmore and girlfriend Julia gave a Christmas party that year. Jim and Pamela went, and just sat quietly on the steps together, like a quiet, reserved suburban couple. Everyone thought that was really sweet.

BOOK THREE

JAMES DOUGLAS MORRISON

CHAPTER SEVEN

LORD OF MISRULE

The secret enemy, whose sleepless eye
Stands sentinel, accuser, judge, and spy,
The foe, the fool, the jealous, and the vain,
The envious who but breathe in others' pain,
Behold the host! delighting to deprave
Who track the steps of Glory to the grave,
Watch every fault that daring Genius owes
Half to the ardor which its birth bestows,
Distort the truth, accumulate the lie,
And pile the pyramid of Calumny....

—LORD BYRON

ROCK IS DEAD

THE EARLY DAYS OF 1969 saw a seismic change in the rock music movement when Led Zeppelin landed in Los Angeles and stormed the Whisky a Go Go in a frenzy of Jimmy Page's atomic riffs and the hysterical caterwauling of Robert Plant. Led Zepp's explosive arrival immediately consigned the Doors and their ilk to old-farthood as far as the Strip's teenaged customers were concerned. (Gram Parsons's hot new country rock group, the Flying Burrito Brothers, did the same thing to the Byrds and Buffalo Springfield.) There's no hard evidence that Jim Morrison saw Led Zeppelin perform this early, but he did frequent the Whisky, and he surely heard about Zeppelin's antics from his various girlfriends. A surviving notebook from this era contains the titles of two blues songs—"Killing Floor" and "How Many More Times"—that Zeppelin performed in excelsis on their first American tour. Several people claim that Jim Morrison was disturbed by Plant's hypersexual posturing, and remember him saying that this riff-banging, power-mad English band represented the death of rock as he knew it.

During January 1969, the Doors were working in Elektra's studio, very slowly, while Paul Rothchild compulsively layered horns and strings onto their songs. Jim had totally lost interest, and the others were useless. This was the album on which Paul Rothchild virtually *became* the Doors, churning out "product" for the label.

Jim was reworking his screenplay about a murderous nomad crossing the southwestern desert. Initially titled *The Hitchhiker—An American Pastoral,* the script's atmospheric desert imagery and cast of mythic American hobos and lowlifes seems to have been modeled on the surreal world of Michael McClure's *The Beard.* The scenario included a homicidal hitcher, Billy Cooke, murdering whoever picked him up: a homosexual, a sheriff, a pilot who had served in Vietnam and his family, plus a cute car-hop. The *Hitchhiker* screenplay referenced Picasso, the Rolling Stones, the dead body of Che Guevara, and other late-sixties icons. After his capture and execution, Billy joins a trio of mythic hobo archetypes— Doc, Blue Lady, Clown Boy—in a surreal desert eternity. The script was never finished and survives in only fragmentary form, but it would serve as the template for the short movie Jim financed later that year, when he finally had some time on his hands. Viewed with the advantage of hindsight, *The Hitchhiker* uncannily recapitulated the dangerously adrift psychic climate in Los Angeles in 1969 that spawned the so-called Manson Family's berserk murder spree later that summer.

Jim was also writing in a death-haunted notebook titled "Dry Water," whose several poems reflected the personality crisis he was experiencing. ("Dry" poetry, in Jim's language, referred to verses read aloud, without musical accompaniment.) "Dry Water" fairly boiled with dark imagery: hangmen, tombstones, *The velvet fur of religion / The polish of knife and coin.* . . .

Friends noticed that Jim was morose and more depressed than usual. He was becoming weirder with girlfriends like Pam Zarubica and Gayle Enochs, abusing them verbally, and callously breaking their hearts. One of his tricks was to call up a girl and invite her over to Room 32 at his motel, where she would find him already in bed with someone else.

S OME NIGHTS JIM WOULD SKIP the Doors' boring recording sessions and hang out at the Whisky. One night he went to the club with Elektra exec David Anderle, who watched in horror as multiple drinks triggered an enzyme rush that transformed Jim from a bearded, reticent poet into a psychotic werewolf who needed to be physically ejected from the crowded club. It was the last time Anderle went out with Jim.

At this point, the only person who could calm Jim down when he did his changeling number (besides Pamela) was Eric Burdon. Jim respected Burdon, a British Invasion legend in his own right. Speaking of Burdon to a British reporter later that year, Jim was forthright: "I like anyone who'll get drunk with me, for the right reasons, in the right way."

Burdon lived in a rented house in Beverly Hills, drank as much as Jim, and was almost as miserable. The difference was that Burdon could handle it. Or could until Jim showed up at his house one night with an entourage of feral hippies who moved into the house's big vestibule and held an orgy and wouldn't leave for three days straight. Annoyed, and no fool, Burdon resolved the situation one midnight by firing a handgun into the hall's vulgar golden chandelier. Jim's entourage cleared out within seconds.

T HE DOORS' ONLY SHOW that month was a twenty-thousand-seat sellout at Madison Square Garden in New York City on Friday, January 24, 1969. It was the Doors' biggest payday ever. Jim arrived a few days early with his UCLA friend Alain Ronay, and moved into the Plaza Hotel.

One evening Elektra invited some rock journalists to Jim's suite, including Patricia Kennely, the young editor of *Jazz & Pop* magazine. (Kennely was impressed that Jim stood up to greet her when she walked into the room.) She and the other writers were less impressed when Jim got drunk, lost his cool, and humiliated writer Ellen Sander, who had once called Jim "a Mickey Mouse de Sade" in print. Jim had never forgotten it.

Jim and Ronay spent evenings in the Village, drinking incognito at the Lions Head, the Cedar Tavern, and McSorley's. On the night before the concert, Jim drunkenly interrupted Tiny Tim's act at Max's Kansas City by pretending to give him head. At four o'clock in the morning, Jim called Robby Krieger's room and intoned, "This is God calling. I have decided to kick you out of the universe."

The great rhythm and soul group the Staple Singers opened the show at Madison Square Garden. The Doors (with three horns, a string section and Harvey Brooks on bass) ran through a set heavy with new songs ("Soft Parade," "Tell All the People," "Wild Child") and golden oldies: "Light My Fire," "Back Door Man," "Five to One." The show was lit by the Doors' new lighting director, Chip Monck, and untold thousands of cheap camera flashes, bathing the huge arena in a strange, stroboscopic light. Jim Morrison—bearded, fleshy, alert—made up for the shortcomings of the venue with an intimate, passionate performance that surprised everyone familiar with his burgeoning reputation as a hopeless drunk. At the show's midpoint he took off his expensive leather jacket and flung it to the kids, who ripped it to shreds like a sacrificial goat.

Between songs he involved the audience in a joke. Pointing to the left half of the arena, Jim solemnly intoned, "You . . . are . . . *Life*." Pointing to the other half, he announced, "And you are . . . *Death!*" After a pregnant pause, Jim delivered the punch line. "I straddle the fence . . . and my balls hurt!"

This was Jim Morrison's idea of humor in early 1969.

The concert finished with "When the Music's Over" and its scarifying plea for redemption and salvation. Jim, singing in a yellow halo while the band was bathed in blue, inserted the fantasy/memory poem called "Stop the Car" that described jumping out of a moving vehicle. It always ended with an agonized wail—"*I can't live . . . through each slow century . . . of her moving!*"—before the band resumed the song they were performing.

Despite their impeccable L.A. provenance, the Doors had been a quasi–New York band since their Ondine shows three years earlier, and Jim Morrison pulled out the stops that night, cementing the Doors' media rep as one of the great rock bands in the world. Later that night, Jim shivered pitifully in an uptown Chinese restaurant because he'd thrown his coat away. His teeth chattered as he drank a dozen beers.

ONCE HE WAS BACK IN L.A., Jim wanted out of the band again. His old lady hated the Doors and was really bugging him. Jim couldn't quit the band outright, his attorney explained, because he was contractually obligated to produce three more albums; and anyway he needed cash flow to finance the old lady, the booze, and, increasingly, cocaine, plus the expensive weekends in Palm Springs for his moveable feast of friends. But Jim Morrison was determined to separate himself as much as possible from the other Doors. At Jim's insistence, individual song credits would be assigned from then on, so that Jim couldn't be accused of writing lame lyrics like Robby's "Wishful Sinful" or "Tell All the

People." This also involved separating Jim's potentially lucrative music publishing business from the other musicians. The fact that this goal was so assiduously pursued shows that the Doors' original 1965 pact—equal veto power and equal revenue shares—was all but dead.

Jim also signed a will on February 12, 1969, in his attorney's Beverly Hills office. He had a considerable estate by this time, with rumored investments in California ranch land and oil wells. Prepared by Max Fink and witnessed by Paul Ferrara, the document declared that Jim was a resident of Los Angeles County, was unmarried, and had no children. Jim's entire estate was willed to Pam—"Pamela S. Courson of Los Angeles County." In the event that Pamela failed to survive three months after Jim's death, the estate was to be split between Jim's brother, Andrew Morrison, and sister, Anne R. Morrison. Pamela Courson and Max Fink were appointed as co-executors of the one-page last will and testament of James D. Morrison.

T HE OTHER DOORS and their management were, as usual, semi-oblivious to Jim's obvious distaste and discontent, let alone his mental status. The band's office was working feverishly on the next Doors tour, their biggest and most ambitious ever, which would begin in Miami on March 1, 1969, and run through seventeen cities over two months. Vince Treanor built a massive new state-of-the-art sound system that could be trucked from gig to gig, freeing the Doors from depending on primitive arena PA systems.

The Doors were the first rock band big enough to pioneer "arena rock," where a single act could sell ten to twenty thousand seats in any given city on any given date. While lesser, younger bands—Fleetwood Mac, the Allman Brothers, Santana—were still playing the electric ballrooms, the Doors and Jimi Hendrix were starting to sell out huge halls where their split of the ticket revenue amounted to real money if their management had the muscle to actually separate the cash from the (usually crooked) local promoters. It would be the Doors' first "real" tour, testing whether Jim Morrison could work more than just on the weekends. To capitalize on the tour, in February 1969 Elektra rushed out Robby's "Wishful Sinful" as the second single from the Doors' unreleased next album. ("Touch Me" had eventually reached the Top Ten late in 1968.)

Jim Morrison, when he showed up at his personal desk in the Doors' upstairs office to look at his mail and make phone calls, watched these feverish preparations for the Doors' big tour with detached interest. If he knew what was going to happen next, he didn't let on. After the tour's first gig in Miami, Florida, on March 1, the band was planning to take a few days off and vacation in the Caribbean. Jim, Robby, and John all reserved houses on the north coast of Jamaica, where they planned to chill with their old ladies before a long concert tour of the Northeast and Midwest.

On Tuesday, February 25, 1969, the Doors were recording at Sunset Sound. Jim laid down two stentorian versions of "When I Was Back in Seminary School," his scary southern gospel radio riff, plus a blues titled "Build Me a Woman"—also known as "The Devil Is a Woman," lifted from Robert Johnson's "Me and the Devil." A new bootleg record of the unreleased Robert Johnson recordings had just appeared, and Jim immediately reworked "Love in Vain," which the Rolling Stones would soon appropriate. He also cut a sing-song fragment called "Whiskey, Mystics, and Men," with accompaniment by the band.

That evening, the Doors and their entourage went out to supper together at a local Mexican joint, the Blue Boar, where they stuffed themselves in a private dining room and drank beer and tequila for a couple of hours. Well lubed, they returned to the studio and started jamming. Jim sang Elvis's "Love Me Tender" and, as the band played free-form R & B, started improvising about the death of rock and roll. He kept repeating, "Rock is dead," and *"Listen, listen, I don't wanna hear no more talk about revolution,"* as if trying to damn the rock movement as something that was definitively over. *"I'm not talking about no* revolution," Jim sang. *"I'm not talking about no* demonstration. *I'm talking about . . . the death of rock and roll. . . .* The death is rock, is the death of *me. . . .* And rock is dead, . . . We're dead! All right. Yeah. . . . Rock is dead!"

This was then interspersed with a memory riff. The singer was now a child, overhearing his mother complain about him to his father. "Mama didn't like the way I did my thing. Papa says, 'You gotta *hit* him, baby.' . . . And I'm feeling real bad, *real bad, real bad."*

The "Rock Is Dead" jam—forty-five minutes of primal bar-band R & B— was Jim Morrison's disgusted, explicit farewell to the rock movement that had launched him into immortality. It summed up the depressive, changing climate of the youth movement of 1969, when the Haight-Ashbury had become a slum of panhandlers, burnouts, and runaways. Led Zeppelin was hammering its way to the top. Ken Kesey had denounced LSD. The Nixon presidency escalated the war in Vietnam and had started persecuting its critics. The Doors had lost the avant-garde, and were now hated by the same writers who had fawned on them the year before. Jim Morrison's original audience—college students and bohemians who responded to the long silences and mannered gestures of rock theater—had been replaced by dopey high school kids, pressed together like goats, giggling at "The End" and catcalling to Jim, "Hey, you wanna fuck me?" It was all too much. For Jim, rock was truly dead.

Jim later explained: "We needed another song for this album. We were wracking our brains trying to think—what song? We started out throwing up these old songs in the studio. Blues trips. Rock classics. Finally we just started playing, and went through the whole history of rock music—blues, rock and roll, Latin jazz, surf music, the whole thing. I called it 'Rock Is Dead.' I doubt if anyone will ever hear it."

The "Rock Is Dead" jam session remained officially unreleased for almost thirty years, but was notoriously bootlegged and became familiar to fans of the Doors. Tapes of this session also featured an early Doors version of Elvis's "Mystery Train." This would soon become a Doors concert staple when the band was prodded by Jim Morrison into more conservative, and personally manageable, artistic terrain.

MASS HALLUCINATION IN MIAMI

THE LAST WEEK OF FEBRUARY 1969 found Jim Morrison in San Francisco, where he attended some of the Living Theater's epochal shows with Michael McClure. If Jim Morrison was looking for some transcendent way to move his band and his public persona out of dreary, repetitive rockdom and into a more artistically valid next level, he surely felt that the dangerously avant-garde Living Theater offered a portal into the future.

If Freidrich Nietzsche killed Jim Morrison, then the Living Theater most definitely killed the Doors. In February 1969, the Living Theater was living out its destiny as outlaw heroes on the jagged edge of that countercultural happening known as Guerrilla Theater. These nomad actors were the living embodiment of the notion that dramatic catharsis was about the actors, not the audience. Founded in New York in 1952 by Julian Beck and Judith Malina as an off-Broadway acting company, the Living Theater had presented beatnik plays (most notably Jack Gelber's 1959 heroin drama *The Connection*) with mixed success before being hounded out of America by the tax authorities in 1963. The troupe evolved into a stateless tribal band, moving across Europe and putting on their confrontational, anarchic plays wherever they landed—until the cops got wise and urged them to move on. By the time the actors reached California in 1969, the troupe was legendary for nudity, obscenity, anarchy, antiauthoritarianism, and violence. Their three-hour productions of *Frankenstein, Antigone,* and *Paradise Now* challenged every given in western civ—borders, morals, laws, behavior, received wisdom—in a loud, argumentative presentation that deployed seminaked actors moving among the audience, chanting, "I can't travel without a passport," and "I can't smoke marijuana," in a flat, provocative monotone that conjured either indignation or ennui. Michael McClure called the troupe "eagle angels of the anarchist spirit." They often camped out, en masse, with Keith Richards and Anita Pallenberg in London and Italy.

Jim Morrison loved the Living Theater. These were actors and artists living a vagabond life, one step ahead of the narco squad and the sex police, moving from country to country and spreading the demented chaos of total artistic freedom. The troupe was emblematic of the sixties spirit of reclaiming and embracing the senses. If Jim Morrison thought rock was dead, he might have thought the Living Theater was reason for living. When he learned the company was headed to Los Angeles, he had the Doors office buy six tickets for all four nights that "Le Living" was playing at USC's Bovard Auditorium. Jim Morrison attended every performance.

Jim was staying in San Francisco with Michael McClure and his family. Babe Hill was in a nearby motel. Jim was in a good frame of mind, singing to McClure's children at the breakfast table. The two poets, Morrison and McClure, had a heavily bonded companionship going. This may have been the era where Jim wrote the lines that later appeared in "The Soft Parade" about loving your neighbor until his wife gets home.

Jim and McClure (both "raging drunk" according to McClure) attended the Living Theater's *Paradise Now* at San Francisco's Civic Auditorium. As they walked in, the company was already down to jockstraps and panties, blabbing about repression and social control, with chaotic abandon in the air. Big Rufus, the Living's only black actor, was standing by the door. Jim looked at him and immediately started yelling "NIGGER" as loud as he could. McClure was shocked that Jim's racism was so open and violent-sounding. So McClure yelled "NIGGER" at Rufus, too, which actually diffused the scene because McClure and Rufus were friends. Jim was really nuts, wild-eyed and frothing, and kept yelling "NIGGER." So McClure started riffing on it, trying to control it, yelling "JULIAN BECK IS A NIGGER! JUDITH MALINA IS A NIGGER!" Meanwhile the audience was getting upset and shouting protests. Some fainthearted customers scurried out. Eventually the troupe pushed Jim and McClure onto the stage, where they partook in theater games and exercises with audience members. Jim was portly, bearded, unrecognized. He got completely into it; at one point he took off the exquisite Moroccan leather jacket he was wearing and flung it into the audience, as if he were at one of his concerts. Jim was having the time of his life, participating in the hippest theater in the Western world, which must have been a dream come true for the onetime Florida State theater arts student.

Michael McClure: "The next day, I was sick and hungover and cleansed and fearful and trembling. [It was] frightening and cleansing, but it had started out violently. Jim had gone into the area where one's yelling was connected with violence, and it had to be carried out and exorcised."

Michael McClure may have been exhausted, but Jim Morrison was just getting started. He went to all four nights of the Living Theater's Los Angeles run. He whooped it up and got involved in the shows, but in a more careful and subdued way than in San Francisco. Again, his bushy beard and long hair enabled him to appear incognito, looking like an intelligent biker on 'shrooms instead of the rock icon he had left behind forever.

NOW IT WAS LATE FEBRUARY 1969, and the Doors were going back on tour. The plan was for Jim Morrison and Pamela Courson to fly to Miami together. After the Doors' first gig in Jim's home state, the loving couple would fly to Jamaica, where Jim had rented a house for a winter vacation. Everyone knew they grew the best herb in the world in Jamaica, where no one had ever even heard of the Doors.

But on the last day of February, as they were packing their bags, Jim and Pam got into a horrendous fight. Some think Pamela told Jim she was pregnant, by someone else, possibly Christopher Jones, and that Jim flipped out. Others say the argument related to Jim's homosexual contacts and involved Pamela's threats to reveal them. Whether or not either of these scenarios is accurate, Jim Morrison was disturbed and upset, in extremis. In the limo on the way to the airport, the fight escalated into near violence, and Jim told Pam that she had to go home. She wasn't coming along. Jim would go to Miami, and on to Jamaica, by himself. Jim Morrison was furious now, and someone—some band—was going to pay dearly.

A FEW WEEKS EARLIER, the students at the University of Miami had been polled to find out their favorite rock group, which would be invited to play at the school just prior to spring break. The students chose the Doors, and the band had been invited to play at Convention Hall in Miami Beach. But the band's management accepted instead a better offer of twenty-five thousand dollars from local Miami promoters, who had more experience putting on rock shows.

The Doors' problems in Miami started days before the band left Los Angeles. The local promoters—who ran Thee Image, Miami's electric ballroom—weren't burdened by any great reputation for probity. Other California bands told Bill Siddons that they had been ripped off by Thee Image, with oversold halls and underreported gross ticket sales.

On Saturday, March 1, 1969, the Doors and their gear flew to Miami without Jim, who missed the flight. Bill Siddons waited at LAX until Jim showed up and sent Pamela home. Siddons: "We found a flight that went through New Orleans, where we had a couple of drinks at the airport bar. By the time we got to Miami, I noticed that Jim's facial muscles had slackened, the only way I could tell how drunk he was. So I knew he was real drunk on the way to the gig."

The Miami promoters had met the earlier plane and loaded the

Doors' brand-new tour equipment into their truck. When Siddons arrived, hours later, with a stone-drunk Jim, the Doors' booking agent informed Siddons that the promoters had removed the seats from the so-called "Dinner Key Auditorium" (in reality an old seaplane hangar reeking of filth and damp), and had oversold the hall by thousands of tickets. When Siddons, backed up by his black detectives, threatened that the Doors wouldn't play, the promoter and his brother, a karate black-belt supervising a thuggish crew, countered that the Doors wouldn't see their expensive new equipment again unless they appeared, as contracted, that night. Siddons told an interviewer later that the brother threatened him if the band didn't play.

No one said a word as Jim staggered into the dressing room. Jim was heavily bearded, and wore a full black ensemble with a silver cross around his neck and a black leather broad-brimmed hat banded with a silver skull-and-crossbones pulled down over his blazing eyes. He looked about as dread as it was possible for a rock star to look in 1969. Jim Morrison was *home,* back in Florida for the first time in years. He was about as drunk as one could be and still put on a rough semblance of a rock show.

Jim checked out the audience before he went on: uncounted thousands of kids, mostly teenagers, crammed against a flimsy stage at one end of an evil-smelling old barn. Jim was (unwisely) briefed on the contentious, extortionate vibes of the show, the dodgy promoters, the threats. The band's agent said it was the worst venue he'd ever seen. Vince Treanor warned the band that the stage was poorly built and could collapse. By showtime, Jim was mad as hell and totally liquored up. He proceeded to destroy his career in his family's home state.

The worst, and one of the most important, rock concerts in history started late. John Densmore noticed immediately that the stage was shaking. Promoter Ken Collier, flashing the V-fingered peace sign, introduced the band by asking the audience to keep its cool. A tape made by an audience member captured a series of off-key harmonica notes played by Jim as the band tuned up onstage. Thousands of Kodak Instamatics flashed like lightning bolts. Kids were shouting stuff at Jim, and he responded:

"Yeah! OK! Right on. *Right on.* Looky here! . . . I ain't talking 'bout no revolu*tion.* And I ain't talking 'bout no demonstra*tion.* I'm talking about having a good time!" He told the crowd they all should come to L.A. that summer and rub their toes in the sand. Then he pumped it up. "Are you ready? Are you ready? Are you ready? Are you ready? Are you ready? Are you ready? Are you ready? Are you ready?"

The Doors started pounding out "Back Door Man."

Robby Krieger: "Jim started rapping 'Rock Is Dead' instead of singing. He was pissed off. People were expecting a freak show instead of rock and roll, when they came to see the Doors, and he hated this. He was venting his anger on this audience."

Jim: "FUCK! *LOUDER!* COME ON, BAND, GET IT *LOUDER!* YEAH, BABY! *LOUDER!*"

They got through the first two verses and into Robby's solo. Someone threw a plastic bag of orange Day-Glo paint, which burst on the stage, spattering Jim and Robby.

Jim: "Yeah. Hey. All right. Suck on me baby, suck it . . . mmm. . . . You gotta get it . . . way down low. Softer, sweetheart. *Soft, soft, soft, soft, soft.* Sock it to me. Come on, softer. Mmmmm." He started soliciting from the audience. "Hey, listen. I'm lonely. I need some love. Come on. *Come on.* Ain't nobody gonna love my ass?"

As Jim invited the audience onto the stage to give him love, the band shifted into "Five to One." Jim managed two verses and then Robby played his spiky guitar solo. Jim, enraged, started in on the customers.

"You're all a bunch of fuckin' *idiots.* You're a bunch of *slaves,* man. How long you think it's gonna last? How long you gonna let it last? How long you gonna let them push you around? How long? . . . Maybe you love getting your face stuck in shit. *COME ON.*"

Jim paused as John Densmore pounded on, and the audience noise rose to howls of protest and alarm.

"Maybe you love gettin' pushed around. You love it, doncha? You love it! You're all a buncha *slaves.* Buncha *slaves!*" He jumped back into the song—*"Your ballroom days are over"*—and then: "Hey, I'm not talkin' 'bout no revolution, no demonstration. I'm talkin' about gettin' out in the streets. I'm talkin' about having some fun. I'm talkin' about dancing. I'm talking about loving your neighbor—*until it hurts!* I'm talking about love. I'm talking about love. I'm talking about love. Love. Love. Love. Love. Love. Love. Love. Grab your . . . fuckin' friend and love him. Come on. Yeah!"

The audience at this point had turned into a churning, tidal mass of flesh. The band started "Touch Me," but Jim wasn't in the mood. He took off his leather coat and threw it into the crowd. He traded hats with a cop, and then threw both of them into the crowd. The band kept trying to play "Touch Me."

"Hey, wait a minute. Wait a minute. Hey, wait a minute. This is all fucked up. You blew it. Too fast. Wait a minute. I'm not gonna go on." The band kept playing but Jim was adamant. "Now, wait a minute. I'm not gonna take this shit. I'm copping out, man. Bullshit!"

Ray stopped playing, then started again, and stopped when Jim wouldn't sing. The band started up "Love Me Two Times," which Jim performed in a dead monotone. He got down on his knees and pretended to give Robby's guitar a blow job during a fiery Krieger solo. They went into "When the Music's Over" and Jim sang as if he were underwater, slurring his lyrics to incomprehensibility. Then he started to rap about the Living Theater:

"Hey—listen. I used to think this whole thing was a big fuckin' joke. I used to think it was something to laugh about. And then, the last couple of nights, I met some people who were doing something. They're doing something, and I want to get on that trip. I want to change the world. *Yeah! Change it. Come on!* The first thing we're gonna do is take over the schools! [Audience applause] Then we're gonna ..."

Jim paused to halt a fight in front of the stage, and went into a new vocal riff, "Away in India," as the band vamped on a blues progression. For the next five minutes Jim spoke with the kids up front. He asked for a cigarette and dozens were thrown onstage.

He told the crowd he was from Florida.

"You know, I was born right here in this state. You know that? [Applause] ... Yeah, I was born right here in Melbourne, Florida, in 1943." He went on in this vein, insisting he wasn't talking 'bout no revolution, no demonstration. He grabbed at his crotch, teasing the crowd. Someone yelled, "Take it off." Hecklers began to curse as Jim chanted more anarchic exhortations, and eventually concluded "When the Music's Over." Then he screamed, "WAKE UP!" and recited the "Lizard" stanza, which led into "Light My Fire."

During the solos, Jim's friend Lewis Beech Marvin, the Topanga supermarket premium heir, handed Jim a live lamb. Marvin was planning to follow the Doors' tour with the lamb, which he regarded as a symbol of the vegan pacifism he espoused.

Jim held the lamb to his chest. Five thousand flashbulbs went off. Later he remembered being surprised that the lamb was so placid and unafraid. He could even feel its heart beating. "I'd fuck her," he told the audience, "but she's *too young.*" Everyone laughed. (A photo of Jim and the lamb later appeared on the band's live album.)

As the band finished "Light My Fire," Jim began grabbing at his crotch and exhorting the crowd to come up on the stage. "All right! All right! I want to see some action out there." He yelled this five times. "I wanna see you people come on up here and have some fun! Come on now, let's get on up here! No limits! No laws! Come on. Come on! Let's do it." People jumped on the stage. Someone poured champagne over Jim's head.

Then Jim decided to perform a striptease. Off mike, he asked if the kids wanted to see his cock, and began unbuckling his belt. Everyone could see he was wearing boxer shorts, which interested the band because Jim hardly ever wore underwear. "VINCE! VINCE!" Ray Manzarek yelled over to Vince Treanor—*"Don't let him do it!"*—and Treanor ran onstage and stuck his thumbs in the waistband of Jim's leather pants so he couldn't pull them down. Jim started doing a crotch peekaboo routine with his shirt. Thousands of flashbulbs recorded the scene.

Promoter Ken Collier ran on the stage and told Jim, "Someone's going to get hurt." Jim brushed him off and yelled, "We're not leaving until everyone gets their *rocks off!*" Jim grabbed his crotch—Collier said he reached into his pants and fondled himself—and seemed about to take off his pants when Collier's brother tried to take the microphone away. Jim pushed him off the stage. One of the local karate guys then grabbed Jim and flipped him over his back into the crowd, which caught him. Landing on his feet, Jim led the audience in a wild pagan snake dance around the cavernous room. (Siddons: "The audience looked like a giant whirlpool with Jim at the center.") Then the stage itself began to tilt and collapse. John and Robby stopped playing and ran for the dressing room. When John jumped off the sinking stage, he landed on the lightboard, which crashed apart in a sparking fury.

Ray [in a radio interview twenty-five years later]: "It was Dionysius calling forth the snakes. The stage was collapsing. I played the riot—

screaming, crunching chords. Part of me was saying, 'We're in serious trouble here.' ... But I knew Jim never did it [exposed himself]. What happened in Miami was a mass hallucination."

After the shirt had been ripped from his back, Jim extricated himself from the bacchanal, followed by local photographer Jeff Simon, who snapped a picture of a bleary, barechested Jim on the balcony a few moments later, surveying with dazed satisfaction the aftermath of the chaotic scene he had orchestrated.

The Miami concert, and the Doors as originally conceived, were over.

FBI FILE

NOT MUCH WAS SAID in the dressing room after the Miami show. It was, after all, just another royally screwed-up Doors gig. The band even laughed off the show with the off-duty Miami cops who were providing security backstage. Jim had sobered up and spoke about the Living Theater and wanting to change the band's direction. When the hall was emptied, discarded clothes, underwear, and shoes were swept into the middle of the floor in a huge pile measuring five feet high. The Doors' road crew rounded up their amps and prepared to truck them to the band's next gig in Jacksonville, Florida, on March 9. On March 2, the band left Miami for their Caribbean vacations. Robby and John (with their girlfriends) and Jim flew to Montego Bay in Jamaica. They were picked up and delivered to their vacation rentals: Robby and John to a house near Ocho Rios, Jim to a villa owned by a retired British major up in the hills above the town.

Jim hated Jamaica immediately, and began scribbling freaked-out observations in his notebooks. He was never really comfortable around black people, and Jamaica in 1969 looked like a West African country, with people darker than he had ever seen before. He was estranged from Pamela, and disoriented as he rattled around a colonial manse with only the silent Jamaican servants for company. The telephone crackled uselessly when he picked up the receiver. The butler rolled a spliff for Jim that was the size of a corncob. After a few draws, Jim was almost paralyzed with fear and paranoia.

In his Jamaica notebook he wrote, "I *must* leave this island, struggling to be born from blackness." He spent a couple of days by the "sick turquoise" swimming pool, watching the huge turkey vultures making passes over his tanning body, as if he were carrion. Homesick, scared, and alone, he evidently worked on a new poem, "An American Prayer," a long, emotional elegy to his country in all its wonder and disease. "America, I am hook'd to your cold white neon bosom.... I am drawn back home/your son in exile/in the land of Awakening.... Give us an hour for magic."

Finally Jim panicked and fled the major's house. He turned up late at night, drunk, at John and Robby's rental and started hanging out, much to John's dismay, because Jim immediately saw that their girlfriends were bored to death. He recruited the girls, Julia and Lynne, to go out drinking with him in the bars of the tourist hotels.

THERE WAS TROUBLE in Miami now. Larry Mahoney was a young reporter for the *Miami Herald* who had been a student at FSU at the same time as Jim, and may have known him there. Two days after the Miami show, Mahoney began writing inflammatory articles about the Doors' appearance, one of which suggested that Jim Morrison had exposed himself at the Dinner Key Auditorium. In "Rock Group Fails to Stir a Riot" on March 3, Mahoney reported that Jim flouted the laws of obscenity, indecent exposure, and incitement to riot. "Many of the nearly twelve thousand youths said they found the bearded singer's exhibition disgusting, Included in the audience were hundreds of unescorted junior and senior high school girls.... Morrison appeared to masturbate in full view of the audience, screamed obscenities, and exposed himself. He also got violent, slugged several Thee Image officials, and threw one of them off the stage before he himself was hurled into the crowd."

Vince Treanor saw this article before he left Miami and called Bill Siddons in alarm. They both knew that Jim hadn't unveiled his considerable manhood. Neither had taken their eyes off him during the performance.

Larry Mahoney then began leading a press campaign against the Doors, describing the band's concert in the *Miami Herald* as an "orgasmic" rite of depravity. He called Miami's acting police chief and asked reporter-type questions. He called the Dade County district attorney. Did they know a rock star had exposed himself in Coconut Grove? The cops tried to defend themselves, saying they had been too busy dealing with 2,500 ticketless fans outside the hall to arrest the star of the show.

The FBI dossier concerning Jim Morrison contains a report on the show. The name of the informant is blacked out. Drawing on Mahoney's reporting, the informant declared that Jim exposed himself. "[Informant] advised that he is conducting an investigation and warrants will be obtained for Morrison's arrest on misdemeanor charges. The matter will be discussed with the Florida State Attorney's office to determine if Morrison can be charged with a felony." On March 5 Mahoney reported that the Miami police had issued an arrest warrant for Jim, charging indecent exposure and disorderly conduct by profanity. This article hedged its bets about the exposure. "The self-styled 'King of the Orgasmic Rock' reportedly simulated masturbation and unzipped his pants during the blue-language performance." An assistant state attorney was said to have taken a statement from one of his office boys that Jim had displayed his penis, and that the state of Florida was considering pressing charges.

It was all rubbish. There were several professional photographers covering the concert that night, and thousands of flash cameras. The only image that comes close to indecent exposure is one where Jim has one hand in his pants and another reaching for his crotch.

But Jim Morrison was in big trouble, much bigger than anyone realized. Officials at both the FBI and in the vindictive Nixon White House still believed that Jim had made threats against the famously paranoid Nixon. The FBI's notorious COINTELPRO operation was currently neutralizing, sometimes violently, the government's critics and perceived enemies. They were already harassing John Lennon, who had made outraged statements against Nixon's policies. The thuggish prosecution and subsequent police threats against Jim Morrison jibe with what details can be gleaned from his censored FBI file to indicate that no less than the evil, blackmailing director of the FBI, J. Edgar Hoover, may have had a hand in the persecution of Jim Morrison.

M EANWHILE, the Doors' lucrative tour was suddenly canceled. The Concert Halls Management Association (CHMA) put out the word that the Doors were poison. Their insurance company canceled their policies. Big money dates in Jacksonville, Pittsburgh, Philadelphia, Providence, Toronto, Detroit, Cleveland, Cincinnati, Boston, Buffalo, Dallas, Houston, and other towns were immediately spiked. Suddenly, almost mysteriously, the Doors dropped off the radio, as if they'd been banned from airplay. Bill Siddons reached the group in the Caribbean, told them the tour was off, and suggested they return to L.A. instead. Jim was warned that he could be arrested if he landed in Florida, so he caught a flight to New York instead on March 8.

President Nixon sent a letter of support to a "Rally for Decency," held at the Orange Bowl in Miami on March 23, 1969, to protest the Doors' behavior. Miami's Catholic archdiocese took part, as did local paragons of decency like Jackie Gleason, the obese, alcoholic TV comic, and Anita Bryant, a former Miss America who would later lose her corporate spokesperson jobs for homophobic remarks. Kate Smith sang "God Bless America" at this farce, which only half filled the huge football stadium. It was a dark night for Nixon's so-called Silent Majority.

EVERYONE AROUND THE DOORS was completely freaked out about the canceled tour and the enormous loss of revenue—except Jim Morrison. He seemed relieved. The whole thing had been on his shoulders and now he was free. He came home to L.A. and met with his lawyers about what to do. He kept growing his beard, put on some weight, and dressed down. Pamela Courson supposedly told friends that Jim had admitted to her that he had flashed his meat in Miami. She asked him why he had done it, and Jim said, "Honey, I just wanted to see what it looked like in the spotlight." This is probably apocryphal, but Elmer Valentine, who owned the Whisky, also claimed that Jim told him he thought he might have fished it out.

With time on his hands, Jim immersed himself in other interests. He published the poem "Dry Water" in the *Los Angeles Image,* a counterculture magazine. Sometime in March (the tapes are undated), Jim gathered his notebooks and taped more than an hour's worth of poems, lyrics, and fragments in either Elektra's studio or at Sunset Sound. The engineer was John Haeny, who had been Elektra's chief engineer since the beginning of the year. This recording session yielded forty spoken-word

Morrison poems, some of which ("Bird of Prey," "Under Waterfall," "Orange County") were sung by Jim a capella, as if musical accompaniment could be recorded later. Among the pieces were "Indians Scattered on Dawn's Highway," sections of "An American Prayer," two versions of "Texas Radio," "Stoned Immaculate," and "Motel, Money, Murder, Madness." There were also several fragments that were later united into the posthumous poem "Far Arden." (Arden was the family name of William Shakespeare's mother, and the "Forest of Arden" is the setting for *As You Like It*.) Jim spoke, chanted, and sang in a bell-clear baritone, reading from his notebooks in carefully thought-out cadences, as if he had rehearsed material he had repeatedly polished and refined. Some have speculated that these tapes were meant to be released in some form if Jim went to jail for the Miami concert. Portions of these poems were eventually adapted and used by the Doors to carry on Jim's image long after he had died. Poets and critics who have heard these visionary taped experiments agree that Jim Morrison was creating a new American poetry that worked on a very high level, one that didn't necessarily transpose successfully to the printed page.

THE FILM CREW ALSO "FINISHED" *Feast of Friends* that month. Though never released as a feature film, the rough-hewn, semisurreal *Feast of Friends* perfectly captured the frenzy of the Doors' moment in 1968, and it was immediately and energetically entered (by Frank Lisciandro) in several important American film festivals throughout 1969. (Segments have been excerpted in many of the Doors' commercial videos since 1985.)

Jim, in part to keep his film crew together, segued immediately into his next cinematic project, the experimental demo movie *HWY,* based in part on Jim's *Hitchhiker* screenplay. Jim had Max Fink incorporate a new film company, HWY Productions, in late March 1969, which employed Jim's faithful entourage of Ferrara, Hill, and Lisciandro.

During Easter week, this team took Jim's Mustang and another car and began filming sequences of Jim hitching, driving, buying gasoline, and walking along the desolate highways around Palm Springs and in the high California desert near the Mojave. This was Jim Morrison acting the role of the Killer on the Road, the homicidal nomad of the vivid fantasies he'd imagined while hitchhiking in Florida as a teenager. Wearing a scraggly beard and a brown fleece jacket, Jim looked creepily dissolute and menacing. He played matador with the cars that passed him by as he tried to thumb a ride. This grainy, jumpy footage would be assembled into a scenario that implied that Jim's character had murdered the owner of the Mustang and was headed into town, bent on further mayhem.

After the desert escapade, there were Godard-like sequences of a car entering urban Los Angeles from the desolation of the desert. West Hollywood was shown by night from a rooftop, with the Phone Booth's neon sign flashing red. Then Jim was filmed at his only real home, the Alta Cienega Motel. From the pay phone, he called Michael McClure in San Francisco. McClure wasn't aware that film and sound were rolling, or that Jim wasn't speaking in earnest.

Jim: "Hi. How you doin? I just got back into town.... L.A.... I was out in the desert for a while.... Yeah, in the middle of it.... Hey, listen, man, I really got a problem. When I was out on the desert, you know ... I don't know how to tell you ... but, uh, I killed somebody.... Just, um, this guy gave me a ride, and ... he started giving me trouble, and I just couldn't take it, you know? And I wasted him.... Yeah."

Years later, Frank Lisciandro asked Michael McClure about this phone call.

McClure: "When Jim said something like that, it wasn't something I would totally believe—though it's not something that would be totally impossible. [I think] he wanted to connect outside the film world and the rock and roll world.... I think if he had killed somebody he would have wanted to talk to me. I was nine or ten years older. I think I told him, 'Take it easy. Figure out where you're at. Keep your equipoise.' I think he was really in a state ... [I didn't know] that the call wasn't a prank.... But Jim wasn't a violent person."

RAY MANZAREK claims the Doors confronted Jim about his drinking at a band meeting at Robby's parents' house in the Pacific Palisades, where the Doors had worked on some of the *Soft Parade* songs. In his memoir, Ray said they all told him he was drinking too much and that it looked like he was killing himself. According to

Manzarek, Jim acknowledged his problem, saying simply and sadly, "I know I drink too much, Ray. I'm trying to quit."

That was enough for the Doors. Jim knew it was what they wanted to hear. So he didn't quit. He just kept boozing with Babe Hill at the Palms.

M AX FINK, Jim Morrison's Beverly Hills attorney, was contacted by the Federal Bureau of Investigation late in March concerning criminal charges against Jim relating to the Doors' Miami concert. The FBI got a federal judge to issue a warrant for Jim, citing interstate flight to avoid prosecution. This was absurd, since Jim had left Florida before any charges had been filed, and Florida only declared him a fugitive of justice (in a warrant signed by Governor Claude R. Kirk Jr.) on April 18. Fink was getting the distinct impression that somebody in the FBI wanted Jim Morrison put away in prison. The situation was extremely serious, and potentially very dangerous for Jim.

On or about Friday, April 4, 1969, Jim Morrison and Max Fink arrived at the FBI's downtown Los Angeles office, where Jim was arrested. By prior arrangement, a U.S. magistrate immediately released James Douglas Morrison—an active-service admiral's son and major, heavy-duty American rock star—on $5,000 bail.

PURE EXPRESSION OF JOY

I T WAS A DEADLY QUIET SPRING in West Hollywood. The atmosphere was humid and claustrophobic. The Doors' April 1969 concerts were canceled. They were blacklisted by CHMA, the concert hall managers' trade association. No one would book them. They couldn't get a job. Jim was hiding out, sometimes with a teenage girlfriend, at the Landmark Motel on Fountain Avenue.

Jim had an advance copy of Neil Young's solo album *Everybody Knows This Is Nowhere,* and played it repeatedly. (He told a friend that he thought "Cinnamon Girl" had been written about Pamela Courson.) He was buying cocaine. He was reportedly seen (many times) on such an errand at Steven Stills's house in Laurel Canyon. He was reading Norman Mailer's satiric protest novel *Why Are We in Vietnam?* He fought with Pamela, and spent unbelievable amounts of money keeping Themis afloat. He watched the news, none of it good. He drove his dark blue Mustang up to Topanga and just sat in the car, near the post office, drinking beer, watching the light change over the mountains, and listening to the radio. Marvin Gaye's "I Heard It Through the Grapevine" was big. He drank with his crew and, glazed over, watched the swaying tits of the strippers at the Phone Booth. He caught an advance screening of Dennis Hopper's coke movie, *Easy Rider,* and wrote in a notebook that he found it moving (although this entry is ambiguous).

One afternoon he picked up an eighteen-year-old girl named Lana Elliott on Santa Monica Boulevard. She drove him to her family's tract house out in the valley, where Jim played Wiffle ball with her younger brothers, and sat around the dinette chatting with her mom. Snapshots of this visit show Jim heavily bearded and looking trim, well kept, and relaxed.

A ROUND THIS TIME "The Soft Parade" reached fruition in the recording studio. "Parade" was Jim's major statement of the era, a testament to his mixed emotions of exaltation and futility. It was also the Doors' last epic, a seven-part suite assembled by Paul Rothchild from many disparate source tapes. It began with "When I was back there, in seminary school"—Jim's howling impression of a Bible-belting radio preacher. "Can you give me sanctuary?" was a heartfelt and poignant acoustic plea for "soft asylum," which evolved into "Peppermint Miniskirts," an uptempo jingle with a pointedly ambiguous imperative—"Make love with your neighbor, till his wife gets home." Then the Doors started rocking, hard, and Jim got into it—"This is the best part of the trip . . . pretty good, eh?" They shifted into their Latin tinge, and Jim sang a beautiful, extremely moving declaration of his existential despair:

> All our lives we sweat and save
> Building for a shallow grave

The piece then built as the Doors rocked out and Jim screamed lyrics of blinding, cut-up imagery that recalled "Horse Latitudes," *The Soft Ma-*

chine of William Burroughs, and the poetic exhortations of the American Beat fathers. As assembled by Paul Rothchild from a multiplicity of takes, "The Soft Parade" became an elegy to the Sunset Strip ambience of the tragic sixties, and a highly emotional summation of almost everything Jim Morrison and the Doors had been through for the past four years.

O N APRIL 27, 1969, the Doors flew to New York, where over the next two days they taped an edition of the public television arts program *Critique,* produced by Channel 13 and broadcast over the PBS network the following month. The seven songs they taped constituted the band's first performance in two months. Jim was almost incognito in a heavy beard, dark shades, black jeans, a T-shirt, and a noticeable paunch. He also looked dead eyed and maybe drunk, and crooned "Tell All the People" and "Wishful Sinful" like Dino on Quaaludes. Riffing during "Build Me a Woman," he rhymed *motherfucker* with *Sunday trucker,* probably to aggravate the obscenity charges against him in Florida. The Doors played well on "Alabama Song" and "Back Door Man," but Jim Morrison only seemed to come to life when they swung into "The Soft Parade" and its evocation of American lives devoid of meaning. Jim screamed and postured in a work of astounding video art that became one of his most potent performances captured on film.

The band returned the next day, April 29, to tape the interview section of the show, moderated by their local champion Richard Goldstein, who had been instrumental in inviting the disgraced band to perform. Sitting in front of their instruments, Jim hid behind his long hair and dark shades, like he didn't want to be there. Ray and John did most of the talking. Jim only spoke when prompted by Ray. Asked what he wanted to do next, Jim's hesitant answer spoke volumes about his aspirations:

"I'd like to do a song, or a piece of music, that's just a pure expression of . . . ah . . . *joy.* Pure—like a celebration of *existence,* y'know? Like the coming of spring, or the sun rising—something like that. Just pure, unbounded joy. I don't think we've really done that yet. The feeling that I get from most of it [the Doors' music] is kind of a heavy, sort of *gloomy* feeling, y'know? Like someone . . . not quite at home, not quite relaxed: *aware* of a lot of things, but not quite sure about anything. I'd like to do one where there's a feeling of being totally at home."

Later, Jim said he "admired poets who can get up and recite. Music gives me security that can make it easier to express myself, rather than reading it 'dry.' I'd like to work like that."

Jim also spoke cogently about the origins of rock and roll as a blending of black music and blues with folk music brought over from Europe, what he called "the West Virginia, high-lonesome sound." Asked about the future, with intriguing prescience Jim in 1969 predicted the techno music that emerged twenty-five years later: "I can envision one person with a lot of machines—tapes, electronic setups—singing and speaking, and using a lot of machines."

"**A**N AMERICAN PRAYER," Jim's new long-form poem, received its public debut on May 1, 1969, when Jim read it at Sacramento State College at a poetry reading headlined by Michael McClure. (Two nights later, Jim appeared at the Whisky in L.A., with Eric Burdon and a blues band, for three songs.) He kept refining the new poem, and read it again at the end of May, at a benefit for Norman Mailer's quixotic campaign for mayor of New York City. This took place at Cinematheque 16, a small screening room in Hollywood, along with readings by Michael McClure, Michael Ford, Tom Baker, and Mary Woronov. Jim, nervous and ill at ease, read from "An American Prayer" before midnight screenings of *Feast of Friends* and Warhol's *I, A Man*. Robby Krieger also appeared and he and Jim improvised a couple of blues songs, plus Elvis's "I Will Never Be Untrue."

There were rumors that Jim would campaign for Mailer in New York, but this never happened. "I was interested in the actual mechanics of political organization," Jim told *Rolling Stone* a few weeks later, "and also I think he would have been a good mayor. Mailer has come into an increasingly rich and complex moral stand, and I think he has a lot of imagination. . . . He's an anarchist, he's a communist, he's a capitalist. He's a husband, a father, a lover, a conservative, a politician, a hero, a writer, an intellect. He's hit more bases than anyone I can think of who's running. . . . And I like his idea of turning [New York] into a city-state, because New York is a special place. It should have some sort of political independence. I'm sure they need all the help they can get, but I don't know if I'd even have been any use in the campaign."

* * *

O NE OF JIM'S ACTIVITIES that spring was to supervise the private publication of his film journals, written while he was at UCLA, and a collection of short pieces and poems from his notebooks. On this he had help from Michael McClure, who showed him some of the private publications of the Topanga artist/writer Wallace Berman. The material was typed by the Doors' secretaries, and taken to Western Publishing, a Los Angeles printer. Jim read and corrected the proofs himself at his desk in the Doors' office. *The Lords* was issued as a sheaf of loose pages contained in a folder embossed with the title *The Lords/Notes on Film.* *The New Creatures* poems were bound between manila hardboard covers with the title stamped in gold on the cover. Both editions of a hundred copies were credited to James Douglas Morrison. When they arrived from the printer, they were stacked in a corner by Jim's desk, and were given away to friends and fans of the Doors. (Copies of these rare first editions, especially ones signed by Jim, fetch thousands of dollars today when they appear on the market.)

Michael McClure gave some copies to his agent, who sent them to an editor at Simon & Schuster in New York, who immediately acquired rights to the books and arranged to publish them in 1970. Jim Morrison was as thrilled as he could be, considering that he seemed to be in a chronic state of depression. It was the beginning, he wrote in a notebook, of his "real" career.

PLEASED TO BE ALIVE AT THIS TIME

J UNE 1969. Jim Morrison sat with *Rolling Stone's* Jerry Hopkins for a crucial interview that portrayed him as a changed man when it was published the following month. The paper's cover portrayed a bearded, brooding, denim-clad poet rather than a fetishistic bastard angel. The text gave the impression that "Jim Morrison"—lurid, stoned, erotic politician— had been replaced by "James Douglas Morrison," a thoughtful veteran poet with something to say. Of all his interviews, this one (published July 26, 1969) came closest to portraying what was actually on Jim's mind. It also repositioned the Doors' lead singer as a rational artist in the wake of the disaster in Miami.

Jim was initially reluctant to talk to *Rolling Stone*. He thought the paper's coverage of Miami and its aftermath had made him look like a fool or a clown. But his record label and the Doors' publicist talked him into it. The paper's editors sweetened the deal by agreeing to publish some of Jim's new poems. Hopkins's interview took place over several sessions at the band's office; the nearby bar the Palms; and at the Phone Booth, where Jim drank rounds of boilermakers (shots of whiskey and chaser glasses of beer) while half-naked, tit-jiggling young girls gyrated to "Hello, I Love You" and "Love Me Two Times."

Jim told Hopkins that America needed something like a national Mardi Gras, a great bacchanal, when a Lord of Misrule would govern the land for a day. As he had during his recent TV appearance, Jim wanted to talk about the future of music, and predicted several coming trends: world music, punk, and techno. "Obviously there'll be a new synthesis... like Indian music, African music, Eastern music, electronic music.... Some brilliant kid will come along and be popular. I can see a lone artist with a lot of tapes and electronics, like an extension of the Moog synthesizer, a keyboard with the complexity and richness of a whole orchestra. There's somebody out there, working in a basement, just inventing a whole new musical form. We'll hear about it in a few years." (Cue techno, twenty-five years later.)

Jim told Hopkins about the "Rock Is Dead" session in February. "The initial flash is over. The thing they call 'rock,' which used to be called rock and roll—it got decadent. And then, there was the rock revival sparked by the English. That went very far. It was articulate. Then it became self-conscious and incestuous, which I think is the death of any movement.... The energy is gone. There is no longer a *belief*.... I think the kids that are coming along next aren't going to have much in common with what we feel. They're going to create their own, unique sound.... So maybe after the Vietnam War is over—it'll probably take a couple of years—it's hard to say—but maybe the deaths will end, and there will be a need for a new life force to express and assert itself." (Cue punk rock, which came alive the year after the Americans were driven out of South Vietnam in 1975.)

Asked to name musicians he had liked as a kid, Jim was both reticent and expansive. "It's like the way I feel about writers. I can't single any-one out. Really. I think we're an incredible gifted country in popular mu-sic, incredibly rich. Think of the people who came out of America in the last ten to twenty years. You know, down the road, it's going to be inter-esting to look back on blues and rock. It happened so fast. From a his-torical vantage point, it'll look like the troubadour period in France. I'm sure it will look incredibly romantic."

Hopkins must have looked bemused, but Jim was serious about his pride in his generation. "Well, *look* at us," Jim said, pursuing his point. "We're *incredible,* man. I guess I mean people who ride motorcycles and have fast cars and interesting clothes, who are—*saying things,* expressing themselves, honestly. *Young* people. So, yeah, it seems romantic to me. *I'm pleased to be alive at this time.* It's incredible. I think we're going to look *very good* to future people, because so many changes are taking place, and we're really handling it with a flair."

Hopkins asked what songs Jim liked.

"I'll tell you the truth. I don't listen to that stuff [rock music] much. I like singing blues—those free, long blues trips where's there's no specific beginning or end. It just gets into a groove, and I can just keep making up things. Everybody's soloing. I like that kind of song, rather than just a 'song.' You know—just starting on a blues trip, and seeing where it takes us."

Jim felt differently about the allure of poetry: "It's so eternal. As long as there are people, they can remember words and combinations of words. Nothing else can survive a holocaust but poetry and songs. So long as there are human beings, songs and poetry can continue."

Jim had an expansive view of religion, and one consistent with both his rituals and his demons. For Morrison, religion could be anything: women, drink, drugs, philosophy, literature. It all fit the bill. "Religion is what you think about and work at most," he said. But while his actions over the years sometimes suggested otherwise, his own view of religion centered on what he called "the game of art and literature." He said, "My heroes were artists and writers." The cross he wore in Miami was "al-most an accident really. I was raised in a Christian culture, and the cross is one of its symbols, that's all."

Hopkins asked Jim about his parents. Why had he claimed they were dead?

"I just didn't want to involve them. . . . I guess I said my parents were dead as some kind of joke. I have a brother, too, but I haven't seen him in about a year. I don't see any of them. This is the most I've said about this."

At the end of the sessions, when prompted for any further topics he'd like to cover, the interviewer noted Jim's reputation as a "heavy juicer," and he replied, "On a very basic level, I love drinking [liquids]. But I can't see drinking milk, or water, or Coca-Cola. You have to have wine or beer to complete a meal . . . [Long pause] . . . Getting drunk, you're in complete control—up to a point. It's your choice, every time you take a sip. You have a lot of small choices. It's like the difference between suicide and slow capitulation."

When asked to explain, Jim said: "I don't know, man. Jeezus! Let's go next door and get a drink."

The last page of the published interview was taken up with four long stanzas of an early version of "An American Prayer."

> *Do you know we are being led to*
> *slaughters by placid admirals*
> *& that slow fat generals are getting*
> *obscene on young blood*
> *---*
> *(When the true king's murderers*
> *are allowed to roam free*
> *a 1000 magicians arise*
> *in the land)*

This was the first time that any rock star had published a work of poetry in a national publication. At the end of 170 lines of often-rhyming verse, the poems were credited: "© 1969 James Douglas Morrison."

THE ADEPT

JUNE 1969. While the other Doors were struggling with cash-flow issues, Jim Morrison was living on a movie advance.

"I'm working on a screenplay with Michael McClure," Jim told Jerry Hopkins. "It's called *The Adept* and its based on one of Michael's unpublished novels. He types, and we sit there with the novel out, and just invent. It's a contemporary American story that reminds me of *The Treasure of the Sierra Madre*. Three guys in search of a psychic treasure. A guy named Nicholas who lives in New York. A friend of his, Rourke, who's a revolutionary turned neocapitalist [cocaine dealer], and they both have long hair.... They fly to Mexico and meet up with a black guy named Derner. They venture out in the desert and meet a half-breed border guard to make a score. I'm not gonna reveal the whole plot. We're looking for a producer now."

This screenplay was part of a sclerotic Hollywood's quest for new talent. In 1969 the parking-lot company Kinney National bought Warner Bros./Seven Arts. Kinney boss Steve Ross hired Ted Ashley, who had been the Doors' booking agent, to run the studio. Jim showed Ashley the *HWY* footage, but Ashley passed on Jim's project. Jim then mentioned McClure's coke-dealer manuscript in a meeting with MGM executives, and since it sounded a little like *Easy Rider,* Jim and McClure were given a cash advance to write a screenplay under the supervision of producer Bill Belasco. (Agent Todd Schiffman claimed that this was part of a three-picture deal he struck with MGM on Jim's behalf.) Jim and McClure spent two thousand dollars to score an ounce of pharmaceutical cocaine, half of which they kept in an MGM executive's office safe so they wouldn't be tempted to snort it up all at once.

McClure moved into the Alta Cienega Motel. Belasco paid for a two-room office on the top floor of the office building at 9000 Sunset Boulevard, a couple blocks down from the Whisky. Jim and McClure made a no-booze-during-the-day deal that was good until six o'clock. They came in with copies of the novel at ten o'clock every morning. McClure says that Jim was never late.

McClure recalled: "Since Jim had been at UCLA film school, he said we should do an outline [treatment] before we did the script, but I didn't think we had to. We started working directly from the novel. But Jim was right: we should have done the treatment.... [After a while] we realized that we were just sitting there rapping it to each other, so we hired a secretary and began dictating it. We did this all day for three or four weeks."

They were ingesting so much cocaine that Jim's depressive mood improved noticeably. Bill Siddons confirmed that Jim once snorted a full ounce of cocaine in eight days, a stupendous intake.

"Not while we were working on *The Adept*," McClure said later, "but either before or after, Jim was doing massive amounts of coke. I don't mean he was doing it like a cokehead, but Jim would score some grams and share them, and then he'd snort the rest of them in a few minutes or a few hours. It was a large amount of coke.... But this was typical. I just took it as Jim's hedonistic gluttony. Jim was a glutton for experience. One of the things I admired about Jim was the intensity with which he sought out pleasure—for the experience."

Jim was up at Pamela's a lot, according to McClure, who went home to the family in San Francisco on weekends. After a few weeks, they had about two hundred pages of action and dialogue. To make the payday, Jim cut the huge script by himself, in one coke-fueled night, to a typed, ninety-page screenplay, and gave it to Belasco. Nothing happened. Dennis Hopper's *Easy Rider* came out in August 1969 and was a huge success, depressing the market for coke-dealer movies. And anyway Jim Morrison now looked like a cross between R. Crumb's guru "Mr. Natural," and Allen Ginsberg—hairy, funky, and uncool.

McClure: "Despite Jim's mental acuteness while we were working, he had a depression setting in regarding his physical self. It was dawning on Jim [during the summer of 1969] that he wasn't going to get himself back in shape.... I think he was feeling some despair about himself. But despair for Jim was like hangovers. He didn't acknowledge them."

They ran out of movie studio blow. The project died. McClure was watching Jim deteriorate and wouldn't pursue it any further. He was even relieved when the producer paid it off. A year later, MGM head James Aubrey, who had once predicted Jim would be a major movie star, declined to pick up the studio's option to renew Jim's contract. *The Adept* was published as a novel, to good reviews, two years later. The opening sentences ring a certain bell:

> Listen, my dear reader, my fine punk asshole, my lovely hypocrite, and you shall hear what it is to be a healthy full-grown male animal with hair down to the ass and a fine set of muscles. No, not down to my ass but down past my shoulders. A rich brown curling hair.... I can take that hair and pull on it—tugging like a chick—and assume a mask of petulance. Without that assumed gesture, I look like a handsome Irish or Jewish mystic. I

appear rather feminine and beautiful. It is doubtful I look more than twenty-five years old."

(Jim Morrison's screenplay of *The Adept* is in the Michael McClure archive at Simon Fraser University in Canada.)

RAMOS GIN FIZZ

IN THE SPRING OF 1969, the Doors finally finished cutting *The Soft Parade*, their first album using eight-track technology, horns, and strings. The record had taken a year to make and cost a fortune to produce. And nobody liked it. Paul Rothchild had micromanaged the music into the ground and driven the musicians nuts. Jim was bored to death. One night, Rothchild asked him for another vocal take of "Easy Ride." As the tape was running, Jim started complaining. ". . . But before I begin, I must say that the collective archive is getting me *down*. And you know what I mean. So, if there are any desert islands available, *please* turn me on to them."

The Doors also owed Elektra a live concert album, but their concerts had lately been so erratic and screwed up that Paul Rothchild told the band he couldn't cut and splice tapes from different performances to make a coherent album. The Doors decided to try to record a live album at the Aquarius Theater in July, in front of an audience of friends and fans. They would also use the sessions to try new material and rejigger themselves into the existential bar band that Jim was insisting on.

Jim was hanging out with Michael McClure while they worked on their screenplay, and he and McClure were seen together at predominantly gay parties in Hollywood. Todd Schifman, who booked the Doors, saw them together and assumed they were a couple. If Jim wanted to break into the higher circles of American poetry, whose alpha males were mostly homosexual, it didn't hurt to have a certain kind of private reputation.

"Jim Morrison was *way* into being gay," Schifman told Miss Pamela—years later, when it was safe.

"Jim and I were playboys," McClure told Frank Lisciandro. "And we did what we did."

Jim was also seen at local theater productions. He went to see a stage version of Norman Mailer's *The Deer Park*. He attended plays put on by the Company Theater repertory group, but walked out of *Children of the Kingdom,* about a rock star, when the protagonist seemed to resemble him. He gave money to the L.A. Art Squad, guerrilla muralists. He went to the movies a lot: *Midnight Cowboy, True Grit, The Wild Bunch, Butch Cassidy and the Sundance Kid.*

He helped Pamela Courson move into a rented house in the Hollywood Hills that he paid for. She had put her wedding ring back on and was calling herself Pamela Morrison again. She complained all the time and was adamant that Jim leave the Doors. She related to Jim's colleagues and cronies with total contempt and steely, silent glares. She liked her stylish clothes, the Porsche 911 Jim had bought her, marijuana, red wine, cocaine, and heroin. She had her usual other guys, on the side. On the arm of Jean de Breteuil, she partied with the French consular crowd, in those days a fast and wealthy set of swinging aristo-diplomats transplanted to L.A. Hashish arrived in the diplomatic bag, and other stuff as well. They all drove flashy convertibles. The men were suave and beautifully dressed, as opposed to Jim, who looked like Allen Ginsberg with better hair. There are photos of Pamela at these consular affairs (one was published in *Paris Match)*, which sometimes devolved into orgiastic after-parties in private homes.

It was well known in the Doors' milieu that Pamela Courson had Jim Morrison by the balls, and that he mostly didn't measure up to her expectations. One afternoon, Jim woke up in her house to find Pamela gone. The dog was gone too. He staggered to the bathroom. SOME SEX SYMBOL, she had lipsticked on the bathroom mirror. CAN'T EVEN GET IT UP!

"She was really frustrated because she actually wanted to make a home for him," a photographer friend of Jim's recalled. "Jim preferred motels. He chose motels for their neon signs. He would just disappear. He was a like a Zen monk. No possessions. Had a credit card and a frayed driver's license in his pockets—nothing else."

Jim lost many of his notebooks in greasy spoons and bars. The Doors' staff would find him asleep in his clothes on the office couch in the morning. He was recklessly generous, buying people things, giving money away. He would visit Venice Beach and buy out the pamphlets of the street poets and the trinkets of artisans that appealed to him. When his old lady wrecked her Porsche, he bought her another one. The whole thing was wild, saw-toothed, stone free.

THE DOORS WENT BACK to work on a weekend in mid-June. They played two theater shows in Chicago on June 14. The first Doors show in almost four months went off so well that Jim was jubilant during the second, which started after midnight. Heavily bearded with a bushel of brown hair, his paunch covered by an untucked Mexican shirt, looking like Che Guevara with a band, Jim kept jumping in the smoky air and running around the stage with unusual energy as the band burned through new songs like "Ship of Fools" and warhorses "Back Door Man" and "Light My Fire." They also played the brand-new, still evolving, totally thrilling "Roadhouse Blues" for perhaps the first time in public. Jim kept doing jokes and little routines that had the audience laughing and applauding the unexpected good vibes.

The next night in Minneapolis he was a little more subdued. Kids were yelling at him, goading him about Miami. "Take it off," they heckled. "Show it to us." "Jerk off." It seemed that Jim was upset, but he just shrugged it off. "Nah—you ain't gonna get that one again."

Tony Glover appeared and they jammed on "Gloria" and the Doors' new "Maggie M'Gill" for a while. The band took a break and asked for requests. The kids yelled out song names for a long ten minutes, before the Doors perplexed them with a full-bore "Celebration of the Lizard." The audience gaped in dumbfounded silence as Jim screamed out, "There's been a slaughter here," and the band comped expertly behind Jim's post-Beat recitations and songs. The encore was "Light My Fire" and earned them a standing, affectionate ovation.

The promoter put out a statement the next day to the effect that the Doors were prompt and professional, had offended no one, and that they had put on a good show.

A FEW DAYS LATER Jim and Frank Lisciandro flew to Atlanta. Lisciandro had entered *Feast of Friends* into competition at the Atlanta International Film Festival, where, to the Doors' general astonishment, it won a prize. During the flight Jim told a petrified Lisciandro, who was afraid of flying, they he wouldn't mind going in an air crash. He just didn't want to die in bed or OD. They sat through *Feast of Friends* as it was screened, and Lisciandro noticed that during the fourteen-minute Hollywood Bowl version of "The End" that finished the film, no one moved a muscle. That night they attended a party at a communal house in a student neighborhood. Jim paid for the beer, helped make snacks, and chatted amiably with the young southern kids who politely pressed in on him. The next night, Saturday, June 21, they attended the awards ceremony and dinner at the Regency Hyatt House Hotel. Jim got through it completely drunk. For once he managed to behave, though, politely chatting with the Atlanta society types at his table.

Lady: "And where are you from, sir?"

Jim [shades, leather pants, suede jacket]: "From the top, ma'am. [He pointed upward and smiled.] "From the top."

Jim spoke briefly with documentarian Murray Lerner from New York, whose Newport Folk Festival film had also won an award. Jim ordered six bottles of decent French wine for the table, and guzzled it from his water glass, which he had emptied into his soup bowl. "I never eat soup," he told the woman on his right.

After three glasses, Jim was incoherent. He relieved himself into one of the empty wine bottles and put it back on the table. When it was time to accept the gold medal for *Feast of Friends,* he staggered, zigzagging to the stage, took the award from the local beauty queen who presented it to him, and gave her his room key in return.

The next morning Lisciandro found him in the hotel bar, looking almost healthy, drinking his usual hangover cure, a Ramos Gin Fizz. He had three. Then he insisted they drive to New Orleans. They drove on the back roads, two longhairs from L.A., stopping in country stores for cold Cokes. Unlike the paranoid scenario of *Easy Rider,* where southern rednecks murdered the flamboyant hippies, they were treated with politeness by everyone they met. (People in the Deep South had seen a lot stranger things than hippies.)

In a French Quarter bar called the Roach, Jim asked the band, who sounded like Canned Heat, if he could sing. No pictures of Jim in a beard had yet appeared. The band said sure. Jim called for "Crawlin' King Snake" and stood silently at the mike for half a minute, concentrating, tapping his foot while the band vamped on the song's Detroit boogie. At the right moment, Jim Morrison began to sing and the place just froze. The band recognized Jim's voice immediately. People started murmuring. Then he improvised on "Little Red Rooster," an electrifying, intensely personal performance for the thirty people in the joint. He did another blues, and, ignoring pleas for more, went back to his table. The guitarist announced it had been an honor to work with Mr. Jim Morrison.

The next day, strolling around the Quarter, they came upon Rudolf Nureyev, the Russian ballet star, who was sightseeing by himself. Lisciandro introduced Jim to Nureyev, trying to explain who Jim was.

"You have big beard, like old Russian," Nureyev told Jim. "Is good way to hide, no? I cannot grow such beard. You never see ballet dancer with beard."

They flew back to L.A. late the next night. Jim went off to crash at Pamela's quiet house up in the hills above Hollywood.

THE OLD BLUES MAN

I N LATE JUNE 1969, the Doors flew to Mexico City. As usually happened with their honest, decent, totally amateurish management, the band got fucked. They had originally agreed to appear May 31 at the largest bullring in the world, the Plaza Monumental. This fell through at the last minute when the repressive Mexican government found out who the Doors were. Eight months earlier, in October 1968, student protesters had been machine-gunned in the main public square by the Mexican army, and hundreds had died. The authorities now feared riots if a big American band incited a huge crowd of teenagers, and decreed the Doors would not appear in the bullring.

Instead the Doors were booked into an upscale supper club, El Forum, where Rat Pack acts like Sammy Davis Jr. usually appeared. They played four shows (for five grand each) to packed houses of rich Mexican kids in coats and ties and their dolled-up dates. This was annoying, but Jim greeted the audiences in Spanish and introduced the band as Ramon, Juan, and Roberto. Jim wore a loose floral shirt and worked the crowds: emoting, gesturing, drawing passionate ovations, especially for

"The End." The band was astonished when the orderly kids roared out the climactic lyrics with Jim in a volcanic dual catharsis of band and audience. The Mexican promoter later told Jim that the Oedipal section of "The End" was highly respected for its daring lyrics. In Mexico, he explained, everyone wanted to kill their fathers and fuck their mothers.

D URING THE FOUR DAYS the band was in town, a pretty girl discreetly attached herself to Jim at the club and stayed close. (Twenty years later, she was the much-respected, charity-supporting wife of one of the highest officials in the Mexican government.) John Densmore's old lady had an abortion. During the daytime, Jim and the band went sightseeing, climbing the sacrificial steps of nearby Aztec pyramids (with Jim in full beard, leather pants, clunky Frye boots), and visiting the Museo de Antropologia. The Doors got rave reviews in the Mexican press, and these 1969 concerts are still recalled as a defining moment by the Mexican elite of a certain age.

But elsewhere things were still dark for the Doors. Good money gigs in Hawaii and Seattle were canceled. Rumors circulated in the band's agency that local FBI offices were warning promoters off the Doors. Letters concerning the "filth" the Doors were peddling continued to find their way to J. Edgar Hoover and were filed in the Doors' dossier. Then, on July 3, in England, Brian Jones died (mysteriously, at twenty-seven) in his swimming pool, and it really shook Jim up. The founder of the Rolling Stones had been an idol to Jim, but stardom had meant more to Brian Jones than music did, and he had suffered a long public decline for two years. He'd been fired from the Stones, had gone to alcoholic fat and pill-addled sloth. He'd been repeatedly arrested for drug possession by crooked cops in London. He'd lost his treasured girlfriend, who left him for his best friend, Keith Richards. Rumors that Brian had been murdered began in London, and reached L.A. almost immediately. Brian Jones's death began a series of weird rock star extinctions that would only end in a Paris bathtub two years later, to the day, after Jones's still-unexplained death.

Brian Jones's trajectory from heroic rock star to pathetic ghost must have given Jim Morrison pause, because in the days after Brian's death was announced, Jim asked Elektra exec Steve Harris what would happen to the Doors if he, Jim, suddenly died. In a burst of energy, Jim feverishly composed what some think was his best poem, "Ode to L.A. While Thinking of Brian Jones, Deceased." It's also his saddest poem. The title is redolent of the elegiac odes of Shelley, Keats, and Lord Byron, but the style owes more to the Beat strophes of Kenneth Patchen. They capture Brian's "porky satyr's leer," and evoke the rock star's early, cathode-ray aura: "You were the bleached / Sun / for TV afternoon." Brian Jones had gone off to "meat heaven" with the cannibals and jews: "I hope you went out / smiling / Like a child / into the cool remnant / of a dream."

Michael McClure saw it clearly, transparently. Brian Jones, in his tragic decay, had become Jim Morrison's metaphor for himself.

T HE NEW AQUARIUS THEATER on Sunset had recently been the Hullabaloo, and many other previous incarnations, but in the summer of 1969 it housed the Los Angeles company of *Hair,* the smash-hit "American Tribal Love Rock Musical." Needing a place to record tracks for the Doors' live album, Elektra hired the Aquarius on a Monday night, when the theater was normally dark. The Doors played two shows on July 21. Ticket holders were given printed copies of Jim's new Brian Jones elegy as they entered the theater, marking these concerts as Jim's tribute to the founder of the rock movement.

The Doors had just played a blistering R & B sound check, to an empty house. As the audience filed in, they found "Mr. Natural" seated on a stool at center stage, wearing Army/Navy workman's clothes. Some thought he was one of the roadies, because Jim Morrison looked like a hip railway employee. Illumined in a mystifying blue spotlight, Jim was relaxed and comfy, wearing blue-tinted, wire-rimmed shades, and ready to work. The rock star bullshit was passé. This was a dignified way for Jim to carry on, the Greek god pose having outlived its usefulness.

At eight o'clock Jim drawled, "Well, we've wanted to record a live album in our hometown—so we're gonna do it—tonight!"

Densmore began the tom-tom throb of "Back Door Man" and the Doors commenced their next incarnation as a postpsychedelic roadhouse band. The first show ran through the hits and premiered new jams like "Mystery Train," fading into Jim's "Away in India" jam-aria, and concluded with a skewed reworking of Robert Johnson's "Crossroads."

This cool triad of blues songs was utilized by Jim through the rest of his career. They also tried out Curtis Mayfield's "People Get Ready" and a complete "Celebration of the Lizard." Jim sang the whole show sitting on his stool, almost motionless, bearing down with concentrated ferocity. There was cool extemporaneous poetizing as Jim recast "Light My Fire" with angry new verbal riffs: "Dead cat in a top hat / suckin' on a young man's blood."

The second show was even longer, and looser. "The evening is *ours*," Jim announced. "We can stay here as long as we want." In addition to re-shaping the Doors, Jim was repositioning himself. During "Back Door Man" (in both shows) he sang, "I'm an old blues man." It was a persona he played for the next year, as if picking up the bluesman role that had been fumbled by Brian Jones. Somebody had to carry that flame. But "the old blues man" was an identity that would be as impossible for Jim Morrison to sustain as it had been for Brian Jones, deceased.

The second Aquarius set debuted new songs: "Make Me Real," "Universal Mind," "Blue Sunday." Jim interrupted "Gloria" with his poem "Coda Queen." The band performed Robby's "Peace Frog" without Jim. The Aquarius management had stipulated that Jim not touch the ropes the *Hair* actors used to launch themselves over the audience. But, during the second show, the archrebel couldn't contain himself, and swung off the balcony like Tarzan at the beginning of a truncated but fiery "Lizard" rite, a crazed and fevered performance of this ultimate sixties epic.

The Doors played more than twenty songs. Then they screened *Feast of Friends*. The audience left, spellbound, at three in the morning. But Elektra was unsatisfied by the Aquarius shows. The Doors sounded clunky to them. Jim sounded like he was blurting out some of the lyrics. Paul Rothchild was worried they hadn't gotten it. Execs thought the Doors sounded listless. While the band's gear was still set up, they played another private session at the theater the next afternoon to record more for the "live" album. They redid "Peace Frog," "Blue Sunday," "Maggie M'Gill," "Build Me a Woman." They jammed the blues a lot, and Jim ad-libbed some paranoid lines that became known as "The Assassination."

So died the Lizard King. Hail the Old Blues Man. The subsequent press reviews recognized that the Doors had left the pop star crap behind them and had opted for something mature and serious:

Cash Box: "... the best and most powerful performances ever witnessed locally."

Los Angeles Herald-Examiner: "... assertive ... demanding ... brilliant."

Los Angeles Free Press: "There was Jim Morrison, more the rabbinical student than the sex god, and looking more comfortable in the new guise.... How can Morrison be accused of singing less well just because the hostility and the sensuality has given way to something richer textured, fuller, more aggressively grim? They have approached Art, no matter how much they have offended, amused, or even thrilled the rock critics. The standards by which their art must be measured are older and deeper." (The Doors loved this review and soon afterward hired its author, Harvey Perr, to do PR for them.)

So the Doors now had their template for the future, as a white R&B band with some psychedelic hit records. Most people thought they were finished, but in this guise the Doors would produce the two albums that yielded their most enduring songs, and Jim's most timeless imagery of the American night—the roadhouse, the queen of the highway, the peace frog, the rider on the storm.

IN SAN FRANCISCO ON JULY 25, Bill Graham presented the Doors in the Cow Palace along with Elektra bluesmen Elvin Bishop and Lonnie Mack. The fourteen thousand seats sold out in an hour. The next night the Doors headlined at the University of Oregon, supported by a new band, Alice Cooper, that took the old Doors theatrics to an even lower level. The day after that, they flew to Washington to play the Seattle Pop Festival with every major act of the day: Led Zeppelin, the Burritos, Vanilla Fudge, Ten Years After, Santana, the Flock, Charles Lloyd, the Byrds, the Youngbloods, Spirit, Bo Diddley, Chuck Berry, and many more.

Jim arrived by helicopter, drunk. This was noticed by the "road mangler," Gram Parsons's famous road manager Phil Kaufman, who bundled Jim into the back of a rented Cadillac to keep the equally inebriated and cocaine-suffused head Burrito company. Kaufman had to throw Jim out of the Cadillac a few hours later, when it was time for the Doors to go on. Standing by the side of the stage was Robert Plant, a twenty-one-year-old Englishman who was lead singer of Led Zeppelin.

Ten months earlier, Robert had been too poor to afford to see the Doors in London. He loved all the California bands, but he really had it for the Doors. Now his band was the hottest in the world. Led Zeppelin had captured the Whisky and Sunset Strip earlier in the year, had conquered America with constant and virtuosic touring, and now their second album, *LZ II,* was the number-one record in the world on the strength of monster licks like "Whole Lotta Love." Led Zeppelin would go on to dominate the 1970s as the rock movement's biggest act during its greatest years.

Robert got a bad dose of the Doors. Jim treated the kids in the audience with contempt after they seemed bored with "When the Music's Over." They cursed and laughed at him in return. He didn't even look like "Jim Morrison." Some thought Jim was the guy in Canned Heat. The kids up front could see that Jim was using the microphone stand to arouse himself. He tried rapping to them during "Light My Fire" and someone threw a cup of beer at him. Jim gave him the finger. Someone else cursed him and Jim let fly: "Hey, hey, hey—you bigmouth bastard, say that again. *Get it all out—*all your little hatreds, everything that's boiling inside you. Go ahead—LET ME HAVE IT!"

"Fuck you," a dozen kids yelled.

"That's the word I wanted to hear," Jim sneered. "That's the very little word." Then he blurted his life story to twenty-two thousand strangers: "I read in the paper that some headshrinker . . . said people like me who perform onstage are *crazy.*"

Applause. Jim raised his voice: "I read that they didn't get enough love, when they were kids." Then he started shouting: "I DIDN'T GET ENOUGH LOVE."

After performing "The End," Jim arranged himself in a cruciform position, alone onstage under a bloodred spotlight. The other musicians had split, the applause had died down, but Jim held the pose for an agonizing three minutes while the roadies cleared the stage for the next act. Finally the red spot faded, and Jim walked off the stage and into the waiting helicopter.

The next act was Led Zeppelin, six hours away from infamously drubbing groupies with dead sharks at their seaside hotel. They played for almost three hours and put on a spellbinding display of the best that rock could be. When Zeppelin returned to London, Robert described the Doors to the music paper *Melody Maker:* "It seemed like [Jim] was—screwed up. . . . He hung on the side of the stage and nearly toppled into the audience. . . . He was just miles over everyone's head. It seemed he realized the Doors were on the way down. He went onstage with that opinion and started immediately saying things that nobody could get into."

THERE'S BEEN A SLAUGHTER HERE

AUGUST 1969. Jim Morrison was moving around L.A., sleeping in motels, or sometimes at Pamela's house. He kept a room at the Chateau Marmont, where Tim Hardin could be found nodding off. He wasn't washing much, and sometimes smelled bad. He attended two screenings of Agnès Varda's new film, *Lions Love,* in which he had appeared as an extra late in 1968. (Varda, an intense, persuasive woman, insisted that Jim come to France and observe the French style of making quality films, on the run.)

Jim was writing the next Doors album, and trying to avoid promoting the new one, the less-than-magic *The Soft Parade.* Other than the title track and the great singles "Touch Me" and "Wild Child," the album sounded trite and plastic. Jim's "Shaman's Blues" and Robby's "Runnin' Blue" were immediately forgettable. Except for "Touch Me," Rothchild's horns and string sections sounded dumb. (Jim had ordered the string tracks pulled from the songs he had written.) Even the dark-blue album jacket was boring, unthinkable for a Doors record. The rock critics dumped on the album with unprecedented contempt. The Doors, they wrote, had let everyone down. The whole thing was a bummer.

Jim spent time driving around L.A. and into the high Mojave desert with his friends. He would disappear for days into his secret lives. There were rumors he had a teenage girlfriend in California's Central Valley. Seemingly death-haunted, he sometimes parked his car and drank beer outside 1403 North Laurel Avenue in Hollywood, the building in which F. Scott Fitzgerald died of a heart attack in 1940.

On August 9, the hippie Svengali Charles Manson, frustrated by music industry rejection of his songs and other showbiz snubs, dispatched his witchy young whores into town, where they butchered movie star Sharon Tate in her Beverly Hills house (which belonged to record producer Terry Melcher), along with Jim Morrison's former hair stylist, Jay Sebring, and four other houseguests. The next day they murdered a middle-aged couple named LaBianca, chosen at random, a few miles away. The arrests of Manson and his girlfriends would only occur later in the year, so Hollywood was locked down, in a state of shock and panic. Steve Stills and David Crosby armed themselves. "They're killing anyone with property," Crosby shouted over the phone to a reporter. Heavy-duty paranoia descended upon the land.

About a month later, for reasons that remain unclear, Jim Morrison was questioned by police detectives investigating the Tate-LaBianca murders. There was a rumor going around town that Jim had talked about the murders—before they happened. Jim may also have been tied to the case through Sebring, or through connections in Topanga, where the Manson family had lived, or through acquaintance with one or more of Charlie's girls, who were pimped by Manson and were known to offer the back-door services that Jim enjoyed. Over the years, several of these (still-imprisoned) women have claimed that they knew Jim Morrison, but similar claims about other contemporary celebrities are considered highly suspect, and remain unproven.

T HE DOORS either were not invited or refused to perform at the Woodstock Music and Art Fair, held in an alfalfa pasture in upstate New York over three days in the middle of August 1969. This was the biggest jam of the sixties, in which a half-million kids famously gathered for three days of peace and love. It was an even bigger reprise of the Monterey Pop Festival, which the Doors hadn't been invited to. Jac Holzman, Bill Graham, and Bill Siddons all begged and pleaded with the band, but were told that Jim had sworn he would never play outdoors again. (The Band, widely considered as the Anti-Doors, were the Woodstock headliners of record.) Jim was relieved. He spent that weekend with some friends in the desert, hiking through the fifteen miles of palm oases and rocky gorges in the hidden Indian canyons near Palm Springs.

On Monday, August 18, Jim and Babe Hill drove down to San Diego for an arts festival on a college campus. *Feast of Friends* was screened, and Michael McClure and other major poets were reading their work. Late the following night, Jim and the poets were sitting outside, under a tree. Everyone was drunk. Robert Creeley peeled off his clothes and rolled down the hill. Richard Brautigan was sitting quietly, listing slightly to port. Babe Hill said something to Jim, who reached over and smashed a beer bottle on Babe's head. Everyone gaped, slack jawed. Babe hadn't even flinched. Michael McClure tried to diffuse the tension: "Hey, Jim, that was a rotten thing to do to Babe."

McClure: "Jim said, 'Oh, yeah?' He picked another bottle and broke it over his own head. Immediate self-retribution. It was touching and crazy."

SEPTEMBER 1969. The Santa Ana winds were starting up again, blowing the desert back toward the ocean in a spiraling vortex of gritty negativity. Jim was looking, and feeling, downhearted. An undated notebook contains versions of some of his most troubled poems of this era. But his correspondence with his editor at Simon & Schuster regarding his intention to publish *The Lords and The New Creatures* in 1970, neatly typed by the girls in the office, indicate that Jim Morrison was still able to navigate in the real world when something interested him.

Halfway through the month, the Doors went back out on the road. They headlined a rock and roll revival show in Toronto on September 13, having been added to the old-old-school bill of Berry/Diddley/Jerry Lee/Little Richard when tickets failed to sell. At the last minute, John Lennon, bored with the floundering Beatles and fired by respect for the primal rockers (especially Chuck Berry), showed up with Eric Clapton and the Plastic Ono Band, making this rare Beatle appearance into a media event.

The show had been going on for hours when the Doors flew in and were escorted to Varsity Stadium by a hundred color-wearing Vagabonds, a biker gang. The band was less than thrilled to hear they would follow John Lennon and Eric Clapton, but managed to play really well. The chugging new "Roadhouse Blues" was a big hit with the bikers (and still is), and "Wake Up" startled the exhausted crowd to attention. (In the aftermath of the still-unsolved Tate-LaBianca murders in Los Angeles, people began to pay closer attention when Jim yelled, "There's been a slaughter here!" as part of "Celebration.")

Introducing the last song, "The End," Jim paused and delivered a brief encomium to "the illustrious musical geniuses" the show was meant to honor. "The Doors seemed rather down," the *Toronto Globe and Mail* reported the next day. "Their songs are full of morbid images, and their vibes were depressed and dramatic. But Morrison's greatness as a performer is still evident in his bursts of movement and his exciting climax at the end."

They played Montreal the following night. A short tour of England had to be canceled when Jim's legal problems in Florida prevented the office from confirming the dates. If Jim had meant to kill off the Doors, it was working.

The next weekend, they played Philadelphia and Pittsburgh. The shows only took off when Jim began reciting, "When I was back there in seminary school" to open "The Soft Parade." Jim was crooning, chanting, whispering, screaming, as he took the audiences through the song, bearing down on his bleak verses on the fragility of life. In Pittsburgh, the kids got so excited by "Light My Fire" that the cops stopped the show. Bill Siddons came onstage and said that the band would do another song if everyone got back into their seats. Order restored, the Doors came back and threw down a fiery "Soul Kitchen," and then disappeared behind a curtain and into their waiting limousines.

T HE ROLLING STONES came to Los Angeles in October and entered the Doors' orbit, tangentially. Things looked good for the Stones. Their new single, "Honky Tonk Woman," was on the radio every ten minutes. Cash-strapped Mick Jagger was trying to relaunch the Stones, with new material, as an arena rock band in the mold of the Doors. He and Keith Richards were even trying to rip off the Doors' rock-theatric sound for their new Stones album, *Let It Bleed,* which they were mixing at Sunset Sound with Doors engineer Bruce Botnick. Jagger was adamant that a new production called "Midnight Rambler" had to have the same doomy soundscape as "When the Music's Over." (The female role in "Rambler" was sung by Merry Clayton, a studio vocalist who was the wife of Curtis Amy, who had played sax on "Touch Me.") Jim ran into Mick a couple of times at Stephen Stills's house in Laurel

Canyon when Jim showed up to score cocaine. Mick invited Jim to see the Stones' first show in Phoenix on November 11.

Jim was in San Francisco at the end of the month. He wasn't feeling well. Jack Kerouac had just drunk himself to death in Florida, and Jim avidly read *Rolling Stone*'s accounts of his funeral in Lowell, Massachusetts. Jim and Michael McClure went bar-hopping, and Jim—incognito in heavy beard and blue windbreaker—would ask whatever band was playing to let him sing a couple of songs, just for the hell of it. The sheer adrenaline of belting bar-band blues made Jim feel more like himself after a couple of drinks. On October 31, *Feast of Friends* was screened at the San Francisco Film Festival, alongside *One Plus One,* Jean-Luc Godard's semidocumentary about the Stones. Jim and Frank Lisciandro were shocked when the audience responded to the amateurish, jumpy-looking, totally authentic *Feast* with loud booing and catcalls. Jim split fast and disappeared.

On Sunday, November 9, Jim and attorney Max Fink flew to Miami, where they were met by local lawyers representing Jim. (The Living Theater had just performed *Paradise Now* in Miami, without official harassment.) By prior arrangement, Jim was arrested at the Dade County Public Safety office late that night in order to avoid a media circus, and was released on five thousand dollars' bail ten minutes later. But those ten minutes were crucial. Jim immediately told his lawyer that he had been threatened by the cops who took his mug shots and fingerprints. When Jim got back to L.A. and resumed working in the studio, he told Ray Manzarek that he was in real trouble. "Hey, pretty boy," one cop had taunted. "Wait'll we get you in Raiford [prison], boy. We'll see about that long hair."

Ray later said, "Jim was scared. We all were."

ROADHOUSE BLUES

NOVEMBER 1969. The Doors started work on *Hard Rock Café,* the working title of the next Doors album, which had to be all killer, no filler, if the band was going to continue. It was also the last original

LORD OF MISRULE

351

album owed to Elektra under the original Doors' contract, whose requirements would be satisfied by a live album and a greatest hits anthology to be released in 1970. Elektra and Atlantic Records were being absorbed into Kinney National's Warner Bros. Entertainment conglomerate, WEA, and Jim was telling friends he didn't want to record for a large corporation.

To the surprise of everyone who knew what was going on, Jim Morrison stepped up and saved the Doors' career with "HWY 9," which was the original title of "Roadhouse Blues," the blustery bikers' anthem that the Doors began recording that month at Sunset Sound. He was telling people that he was taking control of the Doors, and, true to his word, he proceeded to write ninety percent of the next Doors album.

"Hey, gentlemens, gentlemens," he cajoled the band, as the tape was rolling. "Now, the subject of this song is something you've all seen at one time or another. It's an old roadhouse. We're down in the South . . . or in the Midwest . . . or maybe on the way to Bakersfield, and we're driving a '57 Chevy to that old roadhouse. Can you dig it? You know? It's about one-thirty, and we're not driving too fast, but we're not driving too slow either. We got a six-pack of beer in the car, a few joints, and we're listening to the radio, and driving to . . . the old roadhouse. Dig it? [Sings:] *Welll, I wanna tell you something I know . . . Money beats soul every time. Come on!*"

Crucially present in the studio for "Roadhouse Blues" and "Maggie M'Gill" was rockabilly guitar star Lonnie Mack, on bass guitar. Ray Manzarek's left hand had never been an adequate bottom for the Doors, and Lonnie Mack, an authentic veteran of roadhouse R & B, now gave the Doors a kick they had never known before. (Jim can be heard shouting, "Do it, Lonnie, *do it*," as Mack rocks the track hard.) "Roadhouse Blues" as sung by Jim late in 1969 was so convincing and studly that it can be seen as the fulfillment of the "pure expression of joy" that Jim had talked about on PBS earlier in the year. Dripping with bar-band bravado, the song had all the Doors' late-period trademarks: boozy shouting, the ashen lady, a harmonica part (played by John Sebastian), a drunken-sounding last verse, and in-your-face existential angst: *"The future's uncertain,"* Jim sang, *"and the end is always near."*

"Roadhouse Blues" was a fast ride up Topanga Canyon Boulevard on a bright midnight with Jim Morrison. The canyon road was narrow and winding. You had to keep your eyes on the road and your hands upon the wheel. "Roadhouse Blues" was a new kind of Doors masterpiece. The label knew right away it had the makings of a classic. Paul Rothchild had blown it with *The Soft Parade.* Maybe the new direction imposed on the Doors by Jim Morrison might bear some fruit—and some hit records—after all. Equally promising was Jim's "Maggie M'Gill," which they had been playing live for almost a year. "Maggie" was Jim's shaman rock piece, a tom-tom war dance. The Old Blues Man emerges as the "illegitimate son of a rock and roll star / Mom met Dad in the back of a rock and roll car."

At the time "Maggie M'Gill" was recorded, there were three paternity suits against Jim Morrison being defended by Max Fink's office. All were still pending when Jim died, and so were unresolved. Over the years, at least one semicredible son has emerged, claiming to have been born of one of Jim's girlfriends in 1969.

EVERYONE THOUGHT that Tom Baker was an asshole. The hip, good-looking young actor was one of Jim's fave barflies, someone who could give Jim some intelligent backtalk, someone who could hold it over Jim that he'd been with Pamela Courson first. He also could provoke Jim into doing stupid shit, wrecking the car, hurting himself, drinking to blackout. He once goaded a shit-faced Jim into trashing Elektra's offices during a company party. Tom Baker had a certain ironic, Hollywood kind of cool, and he was extremely funny, but he was a useless human being and really bad news.

So Jim took Tom along to attend the opening of the Rolling Stones' 1969 tour in Phoenix on November 11, 1969. The Stones had not played for a paying audience for more than two years and were scared shitless. Brian Jones was gone, replaced by a young kid named Mick Taylor, who played the electric guitar like an Andalusian troubadour. The sixties were over, man. It was a whole new era. Jim was excited. He'd never seen the Stones, except on television. Jim had to be there, up front in Phoenix, like Jagger had been at the Hollywood Bowl. He grabbed a handful of tickets from Bill Siddons at the Doors' office—"Hey, maybe we'll meet some chicks"—and took off with Baker.

They got really drunk at the airport. Giggling, they staggered to their seats. After lift off, Tom Baker began hassling the stewardesses, ragging them for being slow with the drinks up there in first class. Jim just sat there, looking vaguely like a buffalo hunter, just chortling and getting even more juiced. Tom started throwing peanuts at the stews—one of them was really cute—and touching them as they passed by. Halfway to Phoenix, the captain came back and told them to cut it out and said no more drinks. But Tom Baker was such an idiot that five minutes later he groped one of the girls, who got really mad. The captain came back again, and then another time when Baker wouldn't stop. Jim was in hysterics. What an asshole! When the plane touched down, the cops had other plans for Mr. Morrison and Mr. Baker than escorting them to the local arena to see the Stones. They booked Jim and Tom for interfering with a flight crew, a federal offense, and jailed them overnight. In the morning they were arrested by U.S. marshals and charged with felony counts of assault, intimidation, and threatening a flight attendant. Max Fink flew in and got them released on $2,500 bail each. Baker was broke, so Jim paid his bail so that Tom could go home too. They were back in Phoenix on November 24, 1969, to plead not guilty to air piracy charges worth, the judge advised them, twenty years in prison. Their trial was set for February 1970.

JIM WAS ON and off with Pamela. He probably wanted to be more on with her than he was. He paid for her epic shopping binges on Rodeo Drive in Beverly Hills, with Pam muttering, "He owes this to me," to her pals as she plowed her way through YSL Rive Gauche. She was famous (and hated) around town for her luscious French suede boots, expensive Italian shawls, and for the Stellazine antipsychotic medication in her pocketbook. Jim was hemorrhaging money into Themis to keep it going, financing Pam's buying trips and stock purchases. Still a great beauty at twenty-three, she often looked ghostly and malnourished, she said, because Jim preferred her body to be skinny and boyish. Many assumed she was using heroin, especially after she nodded off at a party given by Ahmet Ertegun, the suave Turkish president of Atlantic Records, who was rumored to be courting the Doors once the Elektra deal was over. After Pam was revived, Jim went berserk—jumping on the leather sofa, reciting poetry, and reportedly trying to damage Ertegun's ugly paintings—and had to be "helped" to the limo in which Pamela had already slipped into unconsciousness.

The Doors had been trying to get Jim to shave and clean up for months, but nothing worked until a publicist landed a photo shoot with the short-lived New York entertainment magazine *Show,* which had a regular feature about some celebrity's favorite shop. Themis would be billed as Jim Morrison's exclusive hippie haberdasher. When photographer Raeanne Rubinstein arrived from New York, she was greeted at Themis's door by Jim Morrison, clean shaven and freshly styled, wearing an absurdly modish Nehru jacket. Throughout the day-long shoot, Jim was helpful and considerate, posing with "Pamela Roselily" (as she would be identified in the captions) and her gay-looking flunkies, and by himself, holding huge rock crystals and wearing ugly tie-dyed clothing he otherwise wouldn't have been caught dead in.

Rubinstein was intrigued. "They were a type of couple that I was not unfamiliar with in those days," she told writer Patricia Butler. "They seemed to have a kind of sweetness and gentleness about them. A kind of ethereal quality, like they weren't quite there. They were great in that romantic, dreamy way that people tended to be then if they were among the lucky ones, which Pam and Jim really were."

But it was all an illusion. The rags Themis sold were made cheaply and soon came apart at the seams. The lucky couple's grace and serenity depended on champagne, smack, and pills. Jim was very down around the time of his twenty-sixth birthday on December 8, 1969. He got so drunk on cognac at his birthday party at Bill Siddons's house that he started to urinate on the carpet until Bill held a glass to catch the stream, since Jim couldn't get up from the couch. A notebook that can be roughly correlated with late 1969 contains several drafts of his bleakest poem, "I Am Troubled." Jim again totaled the Blue Lady, his Mustang, then called Max Fink and reported it stolen. The Rolling Stones' tour ended in shame and recrimination after the December 6 disaster at Altamont Speedway, in which the Hell's Angels providing security for the band indulged in human sacrifice in front of the stage during the Stones' performance. Charles Manson and his gang had been arrested, but the vibes were still insane.

According to Max Fink, Jim showed up at his house at two-thirty on a cold December morning to confess that a male hustler was leaving graphic, blackmailing phone messages that threatened to go public with details of Jim's midnight ramblings in the gay L.A. underworld. Max handled this new problem quietly, as he had before.

Max Fink later claimed that Jim Morrison gave him a new set of golf clubs that Christmas, along with a scrawled note thanking Max for being "the only father I've ever known."

CHAPTER EIGHT

THE SOUL
OF A CLOWN

Love cannot save you from your fate.

—JIM MORRISON, 1970

IS EVERYBODY IN?

BY JANUARY 1970, an American had walked on the moon. Another half a million Americans were in South Vietnam, where thirty thousand young Americans had already died. Jim Morrison kept writing, almost compulsively, long poems and song lyrics about his obsession with the country of his birth: *The American Night;* "An American Prayer": *"American boy, American girl / Most beautiful people, in the world."*

James Douglas Morrison, American poet, went back to press, privately publishing the final version of the antimilitarist poem "An American Prayer" in an edition of one hundred copies, bound in manila cardboard and stamped in gold. The printed poems were duly stacked in the Doors' office near Jim's desk, and over the next year were mailed out, often inscribed and signed, to fans who wrote letters to him. Jim was also working on a long piece called "Anatomy of Rock," a surreal, misogynistic meditation on a psychotic high school featuring images of crashed school buses and raped cheerleaders. He was also reworking the more coherent "Dry Water" poems, which would be published later in the year in the rock magazine *Circus.*

Jim seemed in good spirits in those days. It seemed to his anxious dependents that he might have gotten over the hump, and it gave them false hope. True, he was a shadow of his former self. Jim was pudgy and often drunk, but at least he had survived. He was softer now, more quiet, less dangerous. He was writing poetry, filling notebooks, working on songs all the time. The Doors hired professional bodyguard Tony Funches to look after Jim after the six-foot-six black giant had successfully minded Mick Jagger through the Rolling Stones' American tour and the debacle at Altamont. Tony Funches worked often with Jim that year, and, along with Babe Hill, at least ensured that the Doors' lead singer wasn't murdered in a tavern brawl like Christopher Marlowe.

Jim had shaved and cleaned up for Pamela's photo shoot. Grabbing this rare opportunity for a beardless album cover, the Doors quickly scheduled a photo session in the brief span before Jim's heavy beard grew in again. Henry Diltz, a musician as well as a photographer, shot the band in various locales in Venice Beach, using both stills and video in the hazy, pale winter light as the band walked along the beach, under the pier, and up to a wall where graffiti was scrawled: "POT." Jim was casual, quiet, and cooperative. Later Diltz drove the band in his VW bus to L.A.'s downtown skid row, where he photographed them at the Hard Rock Café, a wino saloon on Fifth Street, which had been there since the Depression of the 1930s. They spent an hour buying boilermakers for the old regulars and getting them to talk.

"[Jim] didn't talk much himself," Diltz recalled later. "He'd just sit there and nod and have that little smile on his face, like he was drinking stuff in, observing life and people." After a while, Jim wanted to check out a few other decrepit, last-legs bars before they ended the shoot at the Morrison Hotel at 1246 South Hope Street, a $2.50-per-night flophouse that Ray had found nearby. (The manager didn't want the Doors to be photographed in the hotel lobby. When he was called away briefly, the band rushed inside and Diltz shot them through the plate glass window.) There was no mistaking the down-and-out ambience these photographic images evoked. The Doors would be telling their fans that they had hit bottom. The Morrison Hotel was a fleabag for the lost human dregs of the city at the edge of the desert. It could only go up from there, and—for a while—it did.

Jim Morrison was actually living in the quite comfortable Continental Hyatt House, the notorious rock hotel on Sunset Boulevard. When Led Zeppelin stayed there, the local groupies called it the Riot House, but most of the time it was quiet and anonymous. Jim seemed in higher spirits than usual, occasionally terrifying the management by doing his human fly routine on his eleventh-floor balcony. He also took more interest in the mixing of the crucial new Doors album.

THE *MORRISON HOTEL* songs document the Doors returning to the rootsy R & B they had all grown up on. Their manager, Bill Siddons, later claimed that it was the album that killed the band, but, for Doors fans, the best tracks were a welcome blast of gritty early-seventies social realism following the hedonistic styles of the sixties. In *Jazz & Pop,* Jim called it "an album about America." He also spoke of the band as the new Doors.

The six songs on the album's first side formed a suite titled "Hard Rock Café." "Roadhouse Blues" was the America of the truck driver, the biker, the man of the highway, forever on the road. His only refuge is the netherworld behind the saloons, where people like to go down slow. Rockabilly guitar and bluesy harmonica supported Jim Morrison's astounding, impassioned performance in a song that reached an almost unbearable emotional intensity until Jim released the energy with his bacchanalian "Let it *roll,* baby, roll."

But this was Jim's only masterpiece on the new album. "Waiting for the Sun" was an outdated psychedelic ballad that had been left off the album named for it. "You Make Me Real" was a hopped-up boogie. "Peace Frog" was a funky and very cool Robby Krieger riff that needed lyrics, which Paul Rothchild found in one of Jim's current notebooks, under the heading "Abortion Stories." "Blood in the streets in the town of New Haven." Other name-checked locales included Venice, Chicago, and "fantastic L.A." The dying Indians on dawn's highway made a spectral appearance in the bridge of one of the greatest of all Doors songs. Then there was Jim's insincere crooner/parody song, "Blue Sunday," and "Ship of Fools," a contemptuous, jazz-rock ecology song mocking the hubris and pretense of the moon landing.

ONE NIGHT, during the *Morrison Hotel* sessions, Jim arrived late at the studio with some guests he'd met during a film industry event he'd attended with Agnès Varda and Jacques Demy. The men were in evening dress, the women in gowns. Jim had invited the group to watch the band record. One was Laurence Harvey, the English movie star. No one paid much attention, and Paul Rothchild kept rolling one of his compulsively calibrated joints. Then someone recognized Jim's other guest as Tom Reddin, and slowly it dawned on everyone that he was the L.A. chief of police. Rothchild freaked—he had already done prison time for pot—and discreetly packed up his attaché case as Jim stifled his glee at his producer's extreme discomfort.

T HE ALBUM'S SECOND SIDE was titled "Morrison Hotel." "Land Ho!" was a Robby Krieger sea chanty that Jim gamely acted out. "The Spy" was Jim's sleepy mystery blues, featuring a honky-tonk piano, creepy paranoia, and thoughts of deepest, secret fears. (The title was again borrowed from a novel, Anaïs Nin's *A Spy in the House of Love*.) Robby Krieger wrote the pretty melody to "Queen of the Highway," and Jim wrote the lovely, elegiac lyrics of California reverie— "Take us to Madre." Ray Manzarek used the au courant Fender Rhodes electric piano (prominent in Miles Davis's current band) to jazzy effect on the extremely touching "Queen" (*"Naked his children / Out in the meadow"*), one of the greatest late-period Doors songs. "Indian Summer" was an evening raga loosely based on the flamenco sections of "The End." The album ended with the Lonnie Mack–driven bass-line thump of "Maggie M'Gill," in which Jim Morrison bloviated with a drunk-sounding bluster that resounded with downward-spiraling alpha-male bravado, like it had been recorded in a roadhouse on the highway to hell.

T HE DOORS REHEARSED in their downstairs "workshop" that month. The band planned to tour as much as they could, and now worked out a more rambling, jamming style that dispensed with every outmoded convention of rock theater and evolved into a loose R & B and rock show roughly modeled on the presentation style of jam bands like the Allman Brothers and the Dead. While they dutifully reprised their jukebox singles and staples like "Back Door Man" and "Five to One" during their 1970 shows, the Doors also developed long concert sequences such as their "People Get Ready" jam, which began with Curtis Mayfield's soul classic, segued into Elvis's "Mystery Train," and then blended into "Away in India," a vocal/band improvisation based on their old "Latin BS #2" riff from their earliest days at the Whisky. Other songs were often interpolated: "Crossroads," Robert Johnson's spooky blues newly updated by Cream on their live album *Wheels of Fire;* Chuck Berry's "Carol," which the Stones had played on every show of their '69 tour; Barrett Strong's "Money"; "Who Do You Love"; "Heartbreak Hotel"; "Little Red Rooster"; bar band perennial "Louie Louie," and "Universal Mind" ("I've been doin' time / In the universal mind"), which Jim based on a central image in Rimbaud's *Illuminations.* At Jim Morrison's insistence, the Doors' 1970 concerts were less about tragic catharsis and more about havin' a real good time, and letting it roll, baby, roll—all night long.

T HE ROADHOUSE BLUES tour began on January 17, 1970. The Doors played four shows over two nights in the Felt Forum, the four thousand-seat theater under Madison Square Garden in New York City. (Lonny Mack's trio opened.) They began the first show with a blazing "Roadhouse Blues" and then Jimbo stepped up to the mike in his preacher mode:

JIM: "All right. All right. [Cheering] Hey, listen—listen—listen, man. I don't know how many of you believe in astrology . . ."

Front row girl: "You're a Sagittarius!"

JIM: "Yeah, that's right, baby, that's right. I am a Sagittarius—the most *philosophical* of all the signs."

Front row girl: "I love you. So am I!"

JIM: "But anyway, I don't believe in it."

Front row girl: "I don't either!"

JIM: "I think it's all a bunch of bullshit, myself." [Loud cheering] "But I'll tell you this, man. *I tell you this.* I don't know what's gonna happen, man . . . BUT I WANT TO HAVE MY KICKS BEFORE THE WHOLE SHITHOUSE GOES UP IN FLAMES. [loud cheering] ALL RIGHT! ALL RIGHT!" [Ovation in packed theater]

The Doors were on the money that night. They played new songs in the first show like "Peace Frog" and "Blue Sunday" and "Ship of Fools."

The young audience, now Zeppelin's children, hadn't heard these yet and didn't dig Jim crooning "Blue Sunday." They yelled for "Light My Fire" and went crazy when it was finally played. The encore was a killer "Soul Kitchen." Something annoyed Jim backstage between shows, but no one knew what it was because Jim had arrived separately from the band, with his own crew, and they kept everyone out of his dressing room. When he walked onstage for the second show he grumbled, "Well, everything is fucked up—as usual."

This show was a Doors R & B clinic: "Crawlin' King Snake," "Build Me a Woman," "Back Door Man." They played nothing from *The Soft Parade*, although they tried to fire up "Wild Child" twice before giving up. (*Parade* was their worst-selling album and apparently a source of embarrassment, but it had already won a gold record, the Doors' fourth in a row—a record for an American band.) Jim made sarcastic comments about New York, holding up a skinny joint thrown onstage and saying it was a typical New York number. After some boys got onstage and had to be dragged away from Jim, he said, "Typical New York. The only people to rush the stage are guys."

They finished with a spine-tingling version of "The End" that began with Ray tinkling bells and Jim shouting, "Bring out your dead," in a whiskey-soaked voice, like a corpse collector working the Black Death. By now the song's tale of a spiritual journey that ends in patricide and incest could be taken as a joke. When the killer awoke before dawn, the kids up front squealed, *"He put his boots on!"* It was hard to play off this, so Jim used his ironical voice until he came to the door. Robby played his Andalusian goat song. "Hey you old fool—I wanna kill you.... Woman? I wanna...FUCK YOU, MAMA, ALL NIGHT LONG." The band paused in a tone-drop, then exploded into white noise behind Jim's gruesome howls and a writhing drop to the stage, seemingly in terrible agony.

The New York shows were being recorded, so the next night, Sunday, January 18, the Doors warmed up with "Roadhouse Blues" and funky, blistering "Peace Frog" and then cut loose with rarities like "Moonlight Drive" and the entire "Celebration of the Lizard." Jim got the rowdy audience to become totally silent. ("Shhhh. All right now. Shhhh. Have some respect. Show some respect. Shhhh.") His crowd control techniques always worked well. When it was as quiet as a church, Jim launched into *"When I was back there in seminary school,"* and the kids broke into loud, spontaneous applause that even drowned out Jim's crazed radio preacher act. Tapes of this late show reveal that after singing, *"I tell you we must die,"* during "Alabama Song," Jim said, "Hope not," just off-mike.

For a final jam on "Gloria," Jim simply told the audience, "Please welcome a very talented guy." This was John Sebastian, a local hero from his hit-song days with the Lovin' Spoonful. He had played on *Morrison Hotel,* and Paul Rothchild was producing his new solo album. Sebastian was about to play some nights at the Bitter End on Bleecker Street, and a few days later Jim went to catch one of his late shows. Those who recognized Jim standing in the back of the club, in a wool shirt and Frye boots, were shocked at his glazed eyes, dead expression, and bloated affect. The *Village Voice,* which had so championed the Doors, now lowered the boom: "[Morrison] has become a shadow of himself, with his face grown chubby, his body showing flab, his once shoulder-length hair receding into his forehead."

That week Jim got drunk and passed out at Max's, totally jive and uncool. Paul Morrissey said he just seemed overwhelmed. One of his New York lady friends told Jim that he was the subject of widely circulating rumors in the gay demimonde, rumors well known among the Warhol people (like Dotson Rader, who published them), that Jim Morrison liked to have sex with men. Jim just laughed it off and told the woman that he wasn't gay.

THE LIZARD QUEEN

ON THE COLD MONDAY NIGHT after the New York shows, Elektra gave a lavish party for the Doors in the penthouse of the New York Hilton. The band's contract with the label was up, and other companies were clearly interested in signing them. Elektra wanted to keep the Doors, and the party was a way for Jac Holzman to let the band know it was valued. It was a media-heavy crowd. Andy Warhol was expected, and some of his people crashed. Jim had Pamela on his arm. She was in full L.A. regalia: beautiful appliquéd shirt, Persian slippers, and an embroidered Moroccan waistcoat. As usual, she was the most beautiful woman in the room, but Jim was the center of attention, as people came up to kiss him or just touch his shoulder. He stayed sober and was gracious. They were among the last to leave the party, and as they slid out the door, Pamela whispered to Holzman, "Well, Jac, in case we're on Atlantic next year, thanks for a *swell* party."

Jim had put her up to it. "I almost died," Holzman later recalled.

At this affair Jim resumed contact with Patricia Kennely, the editor of the music monthly *Jazz & Pop*. He had met her at the Plaza Hotel two years earlier. Kennely was twenty-four, pretty, very smart, with the requisite red hair. After Jim's death, Patricia Kennely began making some astounding claims. While it is clear she and Jim Morrison had some kind of relationship in 1970 (they were photographed together at the magazine's office, and *Jazz & Pop* would publish Jim's new poem "Anatomy of Rock" in its September 1970 issue), the true extent of what Kennely has described as a passionate romance ending in an occult blood wedding has yet to be confirmed by reliable, independent sources.

Whereas his sex partners in Los Angeles have described him in this period as impotent and sometimes brutal, Kennely has claimed that he was a gentleman stud capable of multiple erections and marathon love sessions in her bed. She told Jerry Hopkins, after Jim died, that he once tore her diaphragm out of her vagina because it annoyed him.

She describes Jim as being mostly sober. In West Hollywood, Jim could be seen lurching across the street to Monaco Liquors at noon, but when he was with her in New York, she claimed, they only used cocaine and a little pot. In L.A., Jim was generally seen to be morose, taciturn, and laconic. With Kennely in Manhattan, he was the soul of witty repartee, classically allusive dialogue, and poetic aperçus—on demand.

She says that she became Jim's wife in a candlelit marriage ceremony conducted by priestesses of Wicca, the ancient goddess religion. This rite involved blood transfer, swords, incantations, and magic circles. She published a photograph of a document, a Wiccan wedding bann, attesting to this ceremony on June 24, 1970, complete with a signature that looks like Jim Morrison's. (The names of the other priestesses are blacked out in published copies, supposedly to protect their privacy.) She says that Jim fainted during the wedding and crashed to the floor. When he revived, they carried on, and she says that Jim later fucked her seven times in two hours within the magic circle of the rite.

According to her, she became pregnant by Jim. She pursued him but he tried to avoid her, aside from a secret meeting in Miami during his trial. She says that Jim promised to be at her side during an abortion in New York, and that he failed to keep his promise. She claims Jim wrote many letters to her, later indicating in one of these that he would leave Pamela Courson to be with her.

Patricia Kennely later changed the spelling of her name to Kennealy, and retold and elongated her story in her 1993 memoir *Strange Days*, which described in uncanny detail an alternative Jim Morrison that no one else who knew him was able to recognize. Her tone throughout the book is angry, venomous, secretive, and defensive. But she hedged about some of her bizarre claims by writing that she might have hallucinated the whole thing. She also wrote that she was high on marijuana, cocaine, and tranquilizers during the period in question. After she left music journalism, she wrote mythic romance fantasies for a living.

Not everyone believes Patricia Kennealy's claims. She hasn't yet produced any of the letters she says Jim wrote to her. Former Elektra employees who knew and worked with both Jim and Kennealy can only vouch for her being at certain places at certain times, and for her claiming she was pregnant by him. Over the years, Patricia Kennealy cleverly inserted herself into Jim Morrison's saga via the media, first in *No One Here Gets Out Alive*, and then in Oliver Stone's 1991 movie *The Doors*. Kennealy even appeared in the movie as one of the priestesses at her alleged witch wedding to Jim. (She later further changed her name to Patricia Kennealy-Morrison.)

Girlfriend pregnancy and abortions were an everyday thing with Jim, whose lawyer now had multiple paternity suits to deal with. But an occult wedding was something else. Whether this, or indeed any of Kennealy's claims regarding Jim Morrison, can ever be reliably corroborated will determine if her vivid stories will survive as history, or just as a romantic subfable of the legend.

Morrison Hotel was released early in February 1970 and revived the Doors' career by selling half a million units in just two days—the group's fifth gold album. Lonnie Mack and Ray Neapolitan were credited on bass. John Sebastian was identified as "G. Puglese," reportedly because the saccharine songsmith was embarrassed to be associated with the Doors. The Doors played Winterland Arena for Bill Graham on February 5 and 6, their last shows in San Francisco. Jim came on full-steam, and Robby's guitar was so loud that people felt like their ears were bleeding. The next night they sold out the Long Beach Arena, with the Flying Burrito Brothers and blues hero Albert King opening. When the Doors came out, Jim was breathing fire. He blasted into "Roadhouse Blues" and launched into an eighteen-song show punctuated by poetry, comedy, and his tuneless harmonica bleats. At the end of the "Soul Kitchen" encore, the audience was filing out when Jim appeared onstage with a live mike. "OK, listen, listen. Does anyone *have* to go home early tonight? . . . You'd like to listen to some more, right?" The kids ran back to their seats and the Doors played for another hour, finishing one of their longest concerts well after one o'clock. The hall was reportedly swarming with plainclothes police and vice squad detectives, but the Doors had been warned, and Jim didn't say *fuck* all night. All four Doors hung out at a press party after the show. "Better than ever," commented the *L.A. Free Press.*

The next weekend the Doors again played well during two shows at the Allen Theater in Cleveland. Less than two months after Hell's Angels had killed an armed man in front of the Rolling Stones at Altamont, there was some consternation when the local chapter of the motorcycle gang lined up in front of the stage in full colors. But they just wanted to groove and boogie like everyone else. These stocky, bearded bikers identified with Jim, who looked a little like them, dressed like them, said straight out that he represented lost ideals of freedom, and sang about roadhouses, highway queens, and the spiritual lure of the American road. "Roadhouse Blues" was the beginning of the strong affinity between bikers and the Doors that continues today.

Two nights later, the Doors played the Chicago Theater, with the Staple Singers opening. The first show went well, but Jim was drunk for the second and turned it into a stark display of his poetic skills that left the audience confused and disappointed.

A BEAUTIFUL HUMAN BEING

JIM MORRISON and Tom Baker had to show up in Phoenix on March 26, 1970, to be tried in a federal court under the recently enacted skyjacking laws. No one could believe how stupid this was. It was, in the vernacular of the day, "the pits." Tom Baker had been clean shaven when he'd harassed the stewardesses as they'd flown to see the Stones five months earlier. Now Baker had a beard, and Jim Morrison was newly shaven, at Max Fink's misguided insistence. (Fink had also dressed Jim in a white shirt, rep tie, navy-blue blazer, and gray flannel trousers for the trial.) Confused by the prosecution's questions, the stewardess who had filed the complaint pointed at beardless Jim as her tormentor. The judge duly found Jim Morrison guilty of assault, even though Jim had done nothing. Tom Baker was acquitted, compounding the farce.

Sentencing was delayed while Max Fink frantically tried to convince the judge that it was a case of mistaken identity. Baker could have stood up for Jim, who was paying the lawyers, but of course he didn't. The word soon got around that Baker was the biggest asshole in L.A., and he stopped getting work as an actor. Soon after this, Jim got into a barroom brawl with Baker that ended up at the Doors' office. Jim called the cops, who responded and tossed Baker out. Baker couldn't believe that Jim had phoned the police, and the two rarely saw each other again.

Around this time, Jim learned that Felix Venable had died, probably from alcohol poisoning.

FOR TEN YEARS, Jim Morrison had styled himself a poet. This ambition was realized in April 1970 when the venerable New York publisher Simon & Schuster issued *The Lords and The New Creatures*. This slim volume contained the complete texts of Jim's privately printed volumes, and was dedicated to "Pamela Susan Courson." The book's lurid purple dust jacket featured Warhol-type multiple images of Jim as Dionysius, while the jacket flap depicted a heavily bearded, long-haired American poet. The author's credit read: "Jim Morrison was born in

Melbourne, Florida, in 1943. Mr. Morrison is a graduate of UCLA, where he studied cinema in the Theater Arts Department. His ambition is to be a film director."

Michael McClure remembered that when Jim saw the first copies of his book, tears coursed down his cheeks. "This is the first time in my life," Jim told McClure, "that I haven't been completely fucked."

And yet, Jim *was* completely fucked. Apart from a brief notice in *Rolling Stone,* Jim Morrison's first published poems got little press attention and were ignored by the "serious" poetry community. There was absolutely no recognition of a new American poetic voice at work. Jim had even told McClure what would happen: that no one would take him seriously as a poet. "He was right," McClure later recalled. "He did *not* get the reaction he should have gotten. Everyone was cautious, because [Jim] was a rock star."

I N APRIL 1970, the Doors went back out on the road in three-day weekend bursts. "We could tell his energy was giving out," Ray said later in a radio interview. "He was really depleting his energy with alcohol." But they all needed cash—Densmore had bought a house, and Themis was bleeding Jim dry. Some of the shows were ragged, a few were desperate. "The first night would be OK," Ray said. "The second night he was drinking during the show. By Sunday night he was mostly hanging on the mike," trying to stay upright.

On April 10, the Doors played two shows at the Boston Arena, a dreary hockey rink off Massachusetts Avenue. Both Boston shows were recorded for the live album. Jim seemed subdued and wobbly during the first set, and only came to life in the "People Get Ready" jam. He found an energy source for the second set, which didn't start until after midnight, with a two a.m. curfew in force. He stormed the stage in a fury, twisting and gyrating like a demon during a hellacious "Break On Through." As "Alabama Song" oompah-ed along, Jim climbed up the stack of amps and then lost his footing, crashing to the stage and finishing the song flat on his back. Recovering, he sang Gershwin's "Summertime," "Fever," "St. James Infirmary," and recited his sadly prophetic "Graveyard Poem." Another poem was called "Adolf Hitler" and started:

"Adolf Hitler is still alive / I slept with her last night." He gave a new song, "Been Down So Long," its premiere performance.

Before he could launch the finale, the arena's management cut the power. *"Cocksuckers,"* Jim muttered into the mike. Manzarek ran over and put his hand over Jim's mouth before he could start really cursing, but it was too late. The Doors were being watched; they would be blackballed nationally if Jim got arrested again onstage. As it happened, the manager of the Salt Palace in Salt Lake City, where the Doors were scheduled to play the following night, was checking up on the band in Boston and heard the obscenity. The Utah gig was immediately canceled.

Two nights later, they played in Denver—and played well, with Jim pacing the stage, getting himself hard with the mike stand, and crashing to the floor in an extended epileptic spasm. Next weekend: Honolulu Convention Center, April 18. Someone brought "da kine" backstage, "Maui Wowie," the most potent marijuana known to man. The Doors played for two hours in an inspired ganja trance. Jim stopped "Road-house Blues" because he didn't like the lighting. He started singing *"Love hides in the strangest places,"* a riff that he kept performing that year. After the jam "People Get Ready/Mystery Train/Away in India/Cross-roads/People Get Ready," Jim launched into "Baby, Please Don't Go." The encore of this stoned soul picnic was "The End," interrupted for a poetry reading: "Stop the Car/Ensenada/Coda Queen." The audience cheered for ten minutes after the band left the stage, but there was no encore.

Two days later in Phoenix, Jim was acquitted of assault charges when the Continental Airlines stewardess testified that she had made a mistake in identifying him as the man who had harassed her.

THE STAPLE SINGERS opened for the Doors at the Philadelphia Spectrum on May 1, 1970. Lead singer Mavis Staples was the equal of (or better than) the titular Queen of Soul, Aretha Franklin, and it was to the Doors' credit that the Staples supported them in so many concerts. Elektra was rolling tape again, as the Doors always seemed to play well in Philadelphia, one of America's great music towns. On the afternoon of the show, at Jim's request, he was interviewed in his hotel room by critic Michael Cuscuna for the jazz magazine *Downbeat*. Jim wasn't an avid jazz fan, but he told Cuscuna that he read every issue of *Downbeat* because it was about music, rather than personalities.

"The Doors brought many innovations to rock," Cuscuna wrote in his preface to the interview. "It was the first successful synthesis of jazz and rock.... The Doors were the first to introduce the theater song into the current popular music.... The group's second album, *Strange Days,* was one of the first concept albums in the underground, and certainly the most subtle.... The third disk, *Waiting for the Sun,* sounded as if the now-successful Doors were trying to imitate themselves. *The Soft Parade* was an overproduced and overarranged collection of obvious songs. The spirit of the Doors had all but disappeared."

Cuscuna wasn't shy about confronting Jim with his analysis. Jim was used to being interviewed by fawning sycophants and paid-for rock critics. He had to think about his replies. "Jim speaks slowly and quietly," Cuscuna continued, "with little evident emotion, collecting his thoughts before he talks. No ego. No pretentions."

Jim: "Really? Disappeared? Umm. I like all four albums...equally. But I'm really proud of our second record because...it tells a story. It's a whole effort. Someday it will get the recognition it deserves. You know? I don't think many people were aware of what we were doing."

Jim patiently explained that the first two records were worked out in clubs, six nights a week. The next two albums, he said, were studio productions and suffered accordingly. Jim did say he was proud of one late achievement. "One thing about the fourth album that I'm very proud of is that 'Touch Me,' which was also a single, was the first rock hit to have a jazz solo on it, by Curtis Amy on tenor saxophone." But Jim Morrison was clearly dissatisfied with what he was doing. Cuscuna described Jim's rap as a lamentation, and quoted his ambivalent remarks:

"Working in clubs, we had a lot of fun. And could play a lot of songs. A lot of things were going on. Now, we play concert after concert. And we have to play the things the audience wants to hear. Then we record and go out into the concert halls again. And the people, man, are very demanding, and we don't get to do a lot of new or different things. I really want to develop my singing. You know? I love the blues, like Joe Turner or Freddie King. I want to get into that...St. James Infirmary... *feeling.*"

Jim Morrison had intuited that *Downbeat* would "get it." Michael Cuscuna wrote: "In Jim Morrison, I found to my surprise a beautiful human being who, not unlike [bassist/composer] Charles Mingus, has been a victim of sensational publicity and harassment by silly journalists. Jim Morrison seems trapped in the routine of success, with a public image to live up to, while his best musical and cinematic ambitions remain stifled and/or untapped."

BORN UNDER A BAD SIGN

THE SEMISURREAL ROADHOUSE BLUES tour continued on Friday, May 8, 1970, as the Doors played a lot of R & B at Cobo Arena in Detroit. Jim was lively and precise, sang like he was trying to move the stars in the sky, and was the object of a flimsy rain of panties and bras, which he periodically gathered during the show and piled on one of the amplifiers. "Roadhouse Blues" was now a huge sing-along on the joyous "Let it roll" chorus. John Sebastian played guitar on blues numbers "King Bee" and "Rock Me." A hard-core "Break On Through" was incredible. "Five to One" stopped the show.

Jim, to moronic heckler: "Hey, man. Yeah, *you*. Have you taken a good *shit* lately?" That shut him up.

"When the Music's Over" was a shattering meltdown, with "Lizard" bits, scary voices, horror effects, and incredible energy. "PERSIAN NIGHT!" Jim cried at the climax, and the crowd became tumescent with catharsis and began shouting back at Jim in an orgasm of rock communion. After a long show, Jim refused to budge, even though the band's contract stipulated the music had to be over at midnight. "Don't let them push us around," Jim growled, and the kids stayed put as he began "The End" at eleven-thirty. The song took almost an hour as Jim inserted recent poems ("Vast Radiant Beach," "Come, They Crooned, the Ancient Ones") before he walked on down the hall. The Doors had sold out the huge room, but so angered its managers by playing late that Bill Siddons was told they would never work at Detroit's major rock venue again.

After shows in Columbus and Baltimore, Jim went to New York to appear at a benefit poetry reading at the Village Gate for Timothy Leary, who was being railroaded to jail after being arrested with a few joints. Jim was present for part of the evening, listening to Allen Ginsberg recite, but he said he was too nervous to read his own work. The following night, Jim was in the light booth at the Fillmore East when the Jefferson Airplane took the stage. As they were playing, Ginsberg came in and introduced himself to Jim. Now that Jim wore a full beard, there was a slight resemblance between the two poets, something that would have been unthinkable two years earlier. Between songs, a heckler started bothering Grace Slick, and when he began blurting incoherently, Grace tartly observed, "Yeah, they told me that Jim Morrison was here tonight."

Jim, embarrassed in front of Ginsberg, murmured, "Thanks a lot, Grace."

MAY 1970. Four students attending a protest rally at Kent State University in Ohio were shot and killed by National Guard troops. Neil Young's brave song about this, "Ohio," jammed the radio within a couple of weeks. Jim was away from his usual haunts for much of the month. He was seen at a screening of Jean-Luc Godard's *Two or Three Things I Know About Her* at the Thalia Cinema in Manhattan. He was seen in Palm Springs, in Topanga, and in San Francisco, where Jim and Babe drank in North Beach bars with Michael McClure. Wearing his heaviest beard yet, Jim was unrecognizable when he asked to do a couple of songs with the bar bands. But it didn't take long for the customers to figure out who was singing, once they heard his voice. The Miami obscenity trial was going forward, despite massive efforts to get the indictments quashed. The trial was now scheduled for the late summer, putting the Doors' second European tour in jeopardy. Jim began to do trial preparation with Max Fink. This is when, according to the lawyer, Jim described being sexually abused as a teenager, and confirmed a later relationship with an older man while in junior college in Florida—probably the owner of the coffeehouse where Jim first got onstage. (In his unpublished memoir, Fink claimed that this man had tried unsuccessfully to contact Jim after the Doors' success.) Fink said that Jim insisted to him that he was not a "fag," and claimed that Jim had told him that his behavior in Miami was "a good way to pay homage to my parents."

People who knew him well say that Jim was generous with money and now had almost no possessions of his own. He drove leased cars from Cahuenga Auto, a nearby dealership. Around this time, Jim paid for the publication of the *Mt. Alverno Review,* a poetry anthology edited by his friend Michael Ford to help master poet Kenneth Patchen—a favorite of Jim's—with medical expenses. Charles Bukowski contributed a poem, as did Jim. His began, "We reap bloody crops on war fields."

Jim's essential conservatism came out in a thoughtful interview he gave to CBC radio later that month:

"I keep an enlightened pessimism about things, so I don't get disappointed when things don't turn out like I wanted. No, I don't want a revolution. A revolution is really just a switch from one faction to another. And I think a revolution in this country would be a disaster. Democratic ideals are still worthwhile. We just need to change a few leaders, change a few laws.

"Most people feel completely void and helpless about controlling their own destiny. It's sad. I think people should be more involved, rather than designating all their power to a few individuals. One of the tragedies of our time is that decisions are made for you, in which you have no input at all."

Jim said he was saddened so many people accepted the status quo.

"I lament that so many people are living a quiet, ordinary, well-mannered life when so many ... *injustices* are going on. I think that's sad. It's almost as if people are programmed by some higher form of life, from birth to the grave, to live a well-ordered, programmed existence. It's tragic, man. It is. Let's be aware of life in all its complexity."

Jim's solution was to live an artistic life.

"I'm hung up on the art game. You know? My great joy is to give form to reality. Music is a great release, a great enjoyment to me. Eventually I'd like to write something of great importance. That's my ambition—to write something worthwhile."

Unlike his devotion to creativity, he was reluctant to discuss sexuality—though he had clear views on the direction society was headed. "I can't talk much about sex. I'm stuck in the repressed generation of five or ten years ago. Sex will always be a mystery to me. ... The repression of sexual energy has always been the tool of a totalitarian system. ...

Let's face it—we got to the moon first on the basis of a lot of repressed sexual energy.

"I think each generation supercedes the last in intelligence and awareness, and I think there's been a giant step recently [with younger kids]. There's an incredible awareness of events that far surpasses the people I grew up with. I may be twenty-six, but I'm over the hill as far as they're concerned. I like to be pessimistic, but they're far better equipped to handle what's coming than my generation."

Jim's views about future progress were quite prescient.

"The new heroes might be political activists, computer scientists—people who have an understanding of how society works. I don't really know about the future. The future will have to take care of itself. We can make little stabs at it, but it'll just happen, I guess."

JIM WAS IN BAD SHAPE when the Roadhouse Blues Tour continued at the Seattle Center Coliseum on June 5. Master blues guitarist Albert King and his quartet opened for the Doors there and in several other cities, and there are backstage photos of Morrison (bearded, in a blue T-shirt and a pair of black jeans he wore onstage for the next few months) lighting the six-foot-four-inch King's big cigar. There was bad blood between Jim and the five thousand Seattle kids (in a fifteen-thousand-seat arena) from the beginning; strange vibes left over from Jim's theater-of-cruelty performance at the Seattle Pop Festival a year earlier. Jim recited "Love Hides" and "Adolf Hitler" during "Back Door Man." Drinking beer onstage, he ruined "When the Music's Over" with aggravating amplifier feedback. He tried talking to the restless kids, thanking them for their patience: "It takes a while for us to warm up." He insulted Seattle: "It reminds you of a late thirties version of twenty years into the future. You know what I mean?"

The "Mystery Train" jam then collapsed, shamefully. Jim grabbed at his crotch. There were long, boring pauses between songs. The concert was a total rip-off, and the hall cut the power at twelve-thirty. As Jim was led offstage, he was heard muttering, over and over: "It's gonna be all right. All right." John Densmore was so upset he refused to get into the helicopter with Jim. The Doors were called "an anachronism" in the *Post-Intelligencer* the next day.

The next show was Saturday in Vancouver, and Jim hit his stride. He watched Albert King play a stellar version of "Born Under a Bad Sign," and then King joined the Doors onstage, playing his scarlet Gibson Flying V on some of the chugging R & B songs. Speaking in a bell-clear voice that resounded with conviction, Jim interpolated the long poetic passages "Across the Sea" and "There You Sit" between sections of "The End."

O N JUNE 10, 1970, a Dade County judge denied Max Fink's legal motions to stop Jim Morrison's obscenity trial, now set for the end of August. Jim began doing more interviews, letting himself be photographed as a hirsute street poet with a beer belly. He shuffled around West Hollywood on foot, in engineers' overalls. (Robby called him "Engineer Bill.") Jim was quieter now, more given to contemplation than provocation. He could sometimes be seen reading on a bench along Santa Monica Boulevard. Other times his behavior was really outré. He would vomit on people without warning. He pissed on walls in public. He was bruised from jumping out of moving cars at high speed, a new kick. He had alcoholic tremors on some mornings. He was trying to keep hold of the notebooks he was working on, rather than lose them as usual, and mentioned to friends (and an interviewer) that he wanted to write about his obscenity trial. The lyrics to "Riders on the Storm" and "L.A. Woman," in all their harrowing, downhearted beauty, come from this desolate period of almost suicidal alcohol poisoning.

"I don't think [Jim] purposely wanted to change his image from rock star to drunken bum," Robby Krieger said later. "It just happened that way, when he started drinking too much, and he'd get sloppy and fat. I don't think he wanted to be that way at all. I remember he tried out for a couple of movie parts, a Steve McQueen movie, and stuff. I could see that he was real embarrassed at the way he looked. . . . He cut his own hair and beard, and it looked terrible. . . . He came back from the audition and he was pretty embarrassed. [Michael Douglas would eventually get the part.] So I don't think he purposely tried to look that way, like some people would say."

Somebody decided they had to get Jim out of town. Pamela was supposedly in France, but she was actually hanging out in Morocco with Count de Breteuil and Paul and Talitha Getty at the Gettys' villa in

Tangier. So Jim flew to New York. He had walking pneumonia and was coughing his lungs out. He was reportedly seen by Michel Auder, the husband of Warholite actress Viva, in the rooms of a heroin dealer at the Chelsea Hotel. Patricia Kennealy claimed she married Jim in a voodoo rite on June 24.

On June 26 Jim flew to Paris with Doors' publicist Leon Barnard, supposedly to do advance work on the band's European tour scheduled for September. They checked into the Hôtel George V. Jim immediately took a liking to the bistro across the street, Bar Alexandre, and especially to an artfully curved city bench in front of the bar, where he spent the jet-lagged, early morning hours gazing up into the bright midnight of the summer solstice in northern France. It was Jim Morrison's first taste of Paris, and he loved the ancient city's magical ambience immediately. The Doors had never played in France, and no one knew him there.

Jim's friend Agnès Varda was back in Paris. She and her husband, Jacques Demy, had moved to California after the success of *The Umbrellas of Cherbourg,* and Varda had tried to get Jim to star in one of her films—without success. Varda and Demy had enjoyed their house in the Hollywood hills, with a pool and a Cadillac convertible, but the more radical Varda had deplored the shallow materialism and the callousness she found in their California reverie. But she and Jim had bonded, and they talked for hours about film. One of the reasons he had come to France was to visit the set of Demy's new movie, *Peau d'Âne.*

Varda, forty-two years old, with black bangs, was crisp, passionate, and authoritative. She lived in a big Left Bank apartment dominated by an Alexander Calder mobile. She invited Jim to her daughter's birthday party soon after he arrived. He came with presents, got loaded on cognac, and crashed onto the table when he blacked out. The kids thought he was kidding and laughed. He woke up soon afterward, and carried on as if nothing had occurred.

A few days later, they took the train down to the country, where Demy was shooting his film at the majestic Chambourg château in the Loire valley. Varda briefed Jim (according to notations in a surviving notebook) on the weird scenes in French cinema since a coalition of students and workers had come close to toppling the government in 1968. *Cahiers du Cinéma* was now Marxist. Jean-Luc Godard was now a Maoist. The New Wave was finished. Henri Langlois, founder of the Cinémathèque in Paris, had been fired by culture minister André Malraux, but then was rehired after a street riot that had begun the whole process. Jim told Agnès (sarcastically) that nothing like this could ever have happened in L.A.

It was visiting day. Agnès Varda always shot Super-8 footage on her husband's sets, and her film from that afternoon includes ninety seconds of Jim Morrison, heavily bearded and with long hair blown by the wind, sitting on the lawn in conversation with cinema goddess Catherine Deneuve and New Wave hero François Truffaut. They had an idyllic lunch at a big table under some trees, and Jim drank it all in with the heroes of the New Wave, along with the three bottles of wine he emptied. (The English title of Demy's film is *The Magic Donkey*.)

In search of the elusive Pamela Courson, Jim and Leon Barnard then flew to Tangier, checking in at the luxurious El Minzah Hotel, scoring some hash at Achmed's rug bazaar across the street, where the Rolling Stones got their dope when in town. Pamela and the count weren't there, having fled to the de Breteuil villa in Marrakech. Jim and Leon hung out in white-hot Tangier for a couple of days, drinking at the famous Parade Bar, where the expat community held court. (Several years later, a girl from Long Island claimed that she was the mother of a son fathered by Jim during a one-night stand during this brief time in Tangier.)

It isn't known how long Jim spent abroad, but he was back in Paris in early July, looking funky and unwashed. He was having problems with his credit cards, which had been refused by the Hôtel George V. So he spent several nights at a cheap youth hostel on the rue Saint Jacques, in the Latin Quarter, registering as James Morrison. He attended a screening of Godard's new film at the Cinémathèque, and appears in a snapshot taken afterward in front of the building, standing just behind Godard himself (although the two never were introduced). He spent the long summer nights wandering the quays of the Seine, drinking wine with the *clochards* who slept under the bridges. A British music paper published a report that Jim was seen at a Pink Floyd rave in London's Hyde Park on July 18.

He was definitely back in Los Angeles by the end of July, and starting to drink heavily again after finding Pamela Courson living with Jean de Breteuil (who was now in the country illegally, and pushing heroin to his celebrity friends). Jim's pneumonia came back, and he visited the doctor, a rare occurrence. He mostly stayed at his motel and at the more comfortable Riot House on Sunset, where he annoyed the management by hanging off his eleventh-floor balcony by his hands, which impressed the English bands that also stayed there, but scared the hell out of the Rotarians from Cedar Rapids and the Young Methodists from Mountain Grove.

IMPRESSIONS OF MY HANGING

BY AUGUST 1970, *Absolutely Live,* the Doors' two-LP "live" album, was climbing the charts, on its way to being the band's sixth gold record. There was nothing "live" about it. The tracks had been assembled (with more than two thousand separate tape splices) by Paul Rothchild and Bruce Botnick from at least six different shows in 1969 and 1970. In interviews, Jim couldn't quite get excited about the record: "It's a fairly true document of what the band sounds like on a fairly good night.... There were a few cuts that we did for the first time onstage that have flaws in them but... in a live thing, it's just that one shot."

He may have looked like a dissolute biker, but Jim Morrison was still a great bullshitter.

Paul Rothchild told Jerry Hopkins: "[*Absolutely Live*] shouldn't have been released. It was difficult to convey the Doors live, on tape.... The Doors were not great live performers, musically. They were exciting, theatrically and kinetically, but as musicians they didn't make it. There was too much inconsistency, too much bad music. Robby would be horrendously out of tune with Ray. John would miss cues. There was bad mike usage, and you couldn't hear Jim at all."

ON AUGUST 5, Jim was more down than usual. His woman was using heroin, in cryptojunkie mode, and was fucked up a lot. The next day he had to fly to Miami to stand trial, a huge waste of money and energy. He tried to be philosophical about it to Howard Smith of the *Village Voice*: "I might even buy a suit, try to make a good impression.... Suit and tie... Kind of a, um, *conservative* dark blue suit. Not one of those paisley ties, but more of a . . . Yeah. I'll get a suit, and take some tranquilizers, and just try to have a good time. Maybe I'll keep a diary of the whole thing and publish it in *Esquire*—my impressions of my hanging."

That night he got seriously loaded at the Palms. Falling-down drunk. Jim left the bar with someone he'd been drinking with, who dumped him on the front step of a West Hollywood bungalow when Jim could no longer walk. In the morning, the lady of the house thought she had either Charlie Manson or a dead body blocking her doorway. The cops arrested Jim for public intoxication and let him go. It was his eleventh, and last, arrest. Someone got him cleaned up and on a plane to Miami later that day.

ON AUGUST 6, Jim and his entourage—Max Fink, Babe Hill, Tony Funches—flew to Miami and checked into the Carillon Resort Hotel in Miami Beach. They were joined by Mike Gershman, a publicist whose Los Angeles firm also represented the Rolling Stones. The other Doors, who expected to testify at Jim's trial, arrived a few days later. The proceedings were supposed to begin on Monday, August 10, but were postponed for two days. The judge was Murray Goodman, a Republican appointee who was up for reelection that fall. Goodman was a political hack, widely regarded in Miami legal circles as either crooked or an idiot, who was later tried (and acquitted) on bribery charges. (Max Fink later claimed the judge told him in private that the case could be resolved for fifty thousand dollars. Fink says he declined the offer.)

Jim wasn't helped by the fact that the judge hated Jim's local attorney, Robert Josefsberg. Or that sixty-two-year-old Max Fink referred to Miami as "one of the most immoral cities in the United States" during a press conference. The county's prosecutor was a relatively hip young assistant state attorney, Terrance McWilliams, who sucked up to Jim—asking for signed copies of his records—while doing his best to send him to prison. The judge made it clear early on that he wasn't going to postpone the trial so that the Doors could play shows, so the band reluctantly canceled their European tour, scheduled for early September 1970. The whole scene in the Metro Dade Justice Building had the stink of corruption to it. It was obvious to Miami's veteran legal observers that Jim

Morrison was being railroaded to prison under the watchful eye of the paranoid Nixon administration. Somebody was out to break the Doors financially and physically, and it quickly became apparent that no one in the media was going to stand up for Jim Morrison in his hour of need.

The six-person jury was sworn in on August 14, 1970. That night Jim and his crew went to see John Fogarty's hard-rocking band, Creedence Clearwater Revival, play in Miami Beach. Then they went to the Hump, a hotel club, to see Canned Heat play. Bob Hite called Jim up to the stage, where he did "Back Door Man" and other blues tunes for almost an hour.

They had to push past a crush of TV crews, radio reporters, and fans on Monday, August 17. (The nationally famous thief Murph the Surf was being tried on a robbery charge in the adjacent courtroom.) Jim sat at the defense table, taking notes, as the testimony began. After opening statements, during which Max Fink claimed the charges against Jim were baseless and motivated by unsavory local politics, two witnesses, Betty Racine and Colleen Clary, testified that Jim Morrison had exposed himself—for ten seconds, according to ponytailed drugstore cashier Miss Clary. Another prosecution witness, the one who had signed the original complaint, turned out to be an employee in the prosecutor's office.

Max Fink picked their stories apart during cross examination, and asked the court to be allowed to present "community standards" evidence, exposing the jury to the public nudity in the *Woodstock* movie and the Miami production of *Hair*. The following day, photographer Jeff Simon, who was five feet away from Jim during the entire concert, testified that he didn't see Jim whip it out. More than a hundred of Simon's photos were introduced as evidence. On August 20, Judge Goodman ruled that "community standards" were irrelevant to this case. With the jury excused, Fink excoriated the judge's ruling, drawing applause from spectators. But the ruling stood.

T HE DOORS PLAYED two California shows that weekend. Friday night in Bakersfield the kids were packed in front of the stage like penned animals and the Doors played for three hours. Jim bore down, concentrating furiously, performing "Celebration" with careful enunciation, requesting cigarettes from the audience, and consuming maybe a gallon of beer. The next night in San Diego, he introduced the show by yelling, "This whole thing started with rock and roll, and now it's out of control!" Again, the Doors played a great show, which no one could have known would be the last of its kind, the end of an era that had begun five years earlier in the hopeful sunshine of a summer's day on Venice Beach.

Judge Goodman's kangaroo court reconvened on Tuesday, August 25. A female police officer testified that the cops had been afraid to arrest Jim because they thought it would provoke a riot. Max Fink pointed out that the arrest could have been made after the show, but that nothing had happened. Fink insisted that "a media-fueled hysteria" had eventually forced police to file charges against an innocent artist. Two days later, the prosecution played the jury the tape of the show, which sounded coarse, seditious, and chaotic, but offered no proof that Jim had displayed his regenerative organ.

Judge Goodman then adjourned for the weekend so the Doors could perform at the Isle of Wight Festival, off the south coast of England, one of the last great outdoor events of the decade. Jim Morrison, already depleted and exhausted, flew from Miami to London on Friday, August 28, and was then shuttled to the festival site on Saturday the 29, arriving in time to perform the Doors' evening set before one of the largest audiences ever assembled in Europe.

A year earlier, Bob Dylan and The Band had headlined the Isle of Wight, and the vibes were good. The Beatles had come to see them, along with the Stones. In 1970, the Doors and Jimi Hendrix were on top of the bill, along with the Who, Sly and the Family Stone, Miles Davis, Chicago, Free, James Taylor, Joan Baez, Leonard Cohen, and many more. But things had gone awry at East Afton Farm from the start. Two hundred thousand paying customers were penned in by high fences and police dogs, while an equal number besieged the site, testing the defenses, demanded to be let in for free. During Joni Mitchell's set, as she was trying to perform the soulful songs from her now-legendary *Blue* album, turmoil broke out when gate-crashers stormed the perimeter. One of the protesters ran onstage, grabbed the microphone, and yelled, "This festival is a hippie concentration camp!" Joni Mitchell burst into tears. But she finished her Saturday afternoon set, and was followed by Tiny Tim and Miles Davis's *Bitches Brew* band. The English band Ten Years

After—stars of Woodstock—played next. The Doors were then told they could go on, but they were all so exhausted and jet-lagged that they deferred to the British power trio Emerson, Lake and Palmer.

Jim Morrison hadn't slept in forty-eight hours and was pretty much drunk. He wore a clean white shirt under a dark-blue embroidered Mexican jacket, and was heavily bearded. Backstage, he was approached by Murray Lerner, who was filming a documentary on the festival. Lerner, who had met Jim at the Atlanta Film Festival the previous year, asked him if he could film the Doors. "Sure," Jim replied. "You can film, but you're not gonna get an image" because the stage was so dark. Lerner proceeded to shoot the entire Doors set (in very low light), which began at two o'clock on the morning of August 30 with "Back Door Man," worked its way by rote through the first two albums, and finished with miscellaneous poetic interpolations during "The End." (Some estimates put the audience that night at six hundred thousand, one of the largest ever recorded.) The Doors played for more than an hour, with "Ship of Fools" the only recent music presented. Jim chain-smoked cigarettes and hung on the microphone stand, barely moving at all. A careful review of Murray Lerner's footage reveals that Jim performed the *entire* concert with his eyes tightly shut, on automatic pilot, as he expertly sleep-walked through the Doors performance at the Isle of Wight. "It was one of the worst shows that I remember," Robby told *Mojo* magazine thirty years later. "Jim was so bummed about his trial, and he was just going through the motions. If you *listen* to it, it sounds pretty good, but if you watch [Lerner's footage], Jim's like, *stone faced.* He never moves from the mike." (The Doors were then followed by an explosive marathon from the Who, at the top of their game, and Sly Stone, who was still churning out stupendous funk as the sun came up over the weary festival.)

Jim crashed at a local inn. The next night, he appeared backstage and was giving a laconic interview to several journalists, who were startled to hear Jim Morrison say that he thought the Doors performance the night before was probably his last. Asked if that meant he was leaving the Doors, Jim replied, "The future's uncertain. I'm just not gonna make any plans right now." Jim was speaking on tape about his filmic ambitions to reporter John Tobler when he spied Murray Lerner's lights following the Jimi Hendrix Experience onstage. "Hey *look*," Jim said with sudden enthusiasm, "there's a *real* movie going on."

Jim Morrison watched from the wings as Hendrix, resplendent in a flame-colored suit, played his "blue wild angel music" in one of his greatest (and last) concerts ever, dedicating the new song "Machine Gun" to "all the cats fighting in Vietnam." At the end of a volcanic reprise of "Voodoo Chile," Hendrix gestured to the huge crowd and sang out, *"If I don't see you no more in this world, I'll see you in the next world—don't be late!"*

Hendrix was dead within three weeks.

APATHY FOR THE DEVIL

JIM MORRISON WAS BACK in Miami for the resumption of the legal proceedings against him on September 2, 1970. The Isle of Wight show was to have been the start of a lucrative European tour that would have taken the band to Germany, Italy, Switzerland, and Paris. All the dates had been canceled because of Jim's trial commitments. The atmosphere in off-season Miami was subdued, even morose. The scene at the trial was totally weird. At one point, a big fat woman cornered Jim in the hallway. She was squealing—"Jimmy! Jimmy!"—and hugging him. An embarrassed Jim later told his lawyer that she had been the beautiful high school girl with whom he had lost his virginity eight years earlier.

The prosecution rested on September 2. Max Fink had sixty rebuttal witnesses. The judge ruled that he could present only seventeen. The next day the judge declared an eleven-day recess, infuriating the band, which had canceled its tour. The trial was costing a fortune in both money and morale. Jim wanted to return to L.A. because Pamela sounded so stoned on the telephone, slurring her words or laughing uncontrollably, but the lawyers talked him out of it.

Patricia Kennely also arrived in Miami, claiming that Jim had married her and that she was pregnant. Babe asked Jim about all this. "I don't know *what* I did," Jim told him. "I was drunk. Maybe I did, but there was no emotional involvement with her."

The tension at the Carillon Hotel was diabolical, so Jim and his crew—Babe Hill, Frank Lisciandro, and Max Fink—retreated to the Bahamas for a few days of fishing, snorkeling, and drinking rum. Back in

Miami, they went to an Elvis Presley concert, an almost papal rite at the huge Convention Center, strobe-lit by Instamatic flashes, during which Elvis strutted and posed in a succession of iconic tableaux. Jim was impressed by Elvis's great band, which included guitarist James Burton, drummer Ronnie Tutt, and bassist Jerry Scheff.

The local press was particularly craven about Jim's legal ordeal in their town. *The Miami News* reported: "Attired in a tan suede jacket with sheepskin lining, Morrison looked like a ranch hand in search of a barber. An unidentified friend was far more flamboyantly attired in tapestry coat and rust-colored bell-bottoms." The papers sent young reporters to cover the trial, and they would approach Jim in the hallways almost on bended knee, according to Mike Gershman, as if Jim were taboo, or not quite real. Their questions were shallow and useless, the TV coverage was dumb, and no one bothered to notice that a major political fix was in. Then again, a lot of people in Miami thought Jim Morrison was getting what he deserved—and maybe even what he wanted.

A few months later, Jim told *Rolling Stone*'s Ben Fong-Torres: "You know, I thought there was a possibility of it becoming a major, groundbreaking kind of case, but it didn't turn out that way. It actually received very little national attention. And in a way, I was kind of relieved, because as the case wore on, there were no great ideals at stake."

A HIGH SCHOOL STUDENT, Steve Rosenberg, attended the trial almost every day. When the crowds died out as the case dragged on, Jim noticed him in the halls and answered Steve's respectful questions about what poetry he liked (Rimbaud), and what music he was listening to (Pink Floyd). During a recess, Jim asked if there was a Burger King around, and Steve drove him to the nearest one in his mother's '63 Chrysler Newport. Jim liked the car. "Cool air-conditioning," he commented. "Really blows a lot of air." He had two Whoppers and a thick shake. "He was fat, bearded, a little spacey," Rosenberg recalled. "I had to draw him out. Then I just drove him back to the courthouse."

A few days later, Rosenberg found Jim and Babe Hill in the bar of the Carillon. Then they went up to Jim's suite. Babe disappeared and returned with two young girls. Steve guessed they were both around seventeen. They all smoked some pot and drank Scotch whiskey. Jim and the two girls went into the bedroom. One girl soon came out, half-undressed, and motioned for Babe to come in too. The door closed behind them. Steve stopped attending the trial.

COURT RECONVENED ON SEPTEMBER 14. The legal procedures and defense witnesses were so boring that Jim stopped taking notes. Jim testified two days later, the other Doors the day after that. The judge was being a prick, and the press ignored the trial. The Doors' own publicist filed stories for *Rock* magazine, which came out weeks later. Jim's mood sank to a new low on September 19 when word of Jimi Hendrix's death in London got out. (Jim and Babe were both tripping on acid when they heard Hendrix had died.) The official version was that Hendrix had swallowed a handful of Quaaludes and had choked to death when he vomited while in a coma. But it was well known in the music business that Hendrix was leaving his manager, and so was worth more dead than alive to certain people.

After the moves to dismiss (denied), the closing arguments, and Judge Goodman's highly unorthodox directive to find the defendant guilty, the jury returned with its verdicts on September 20, 1970. Jim Morrison was found guilty on misdemeanor counts of indecent exposure and "open profanity." He was acquitted of public drunkenness, and of the felony charge of lewd and lascivious behavior.

None of this made any sense. The whole trial had been a farce. (Goodman had already commented in open court, while the jury was deliberating, that there was no real evidence that Jim had exposed himself.) Sentencing was postponed until October. Jim's bail was raised to fifty thousand dollars, and he now faced an almost certain prison sentence that could get the judge reelected as a Nixonian law-and-order enforcer.

This new bail order came down on a Sunday evening, so that it would be hard for Jim to make his bond and he could be jailed overnight. But Max Fink had been prepared for this. He had several certified bank checks in various amounts at the ready, so the cops couldn't get Jim behind bars.

The lawyers told Jim not to worry. They would win on appeal. Jim talked to the press after the verdict. "This won't affect my style," he told the *Miami Herald*. "I maintain I didn't do anything wrong." He went on to say, with a straight face, that he wanted to do a tour in Australia, playing parish halls instead of big auditoriums.

Max now told Jim to get out of Florida—immediately. But Jim was in no hurry to get back to Los Angeles. Pamela had fallen apart and was in the hospital, being treated for malnutrition and dehydration related to chronic heroin use. (Pam was said by her friends to have been suicidally depressed in Jim's absence.) Jim now elected to drive back to California, with Babe Hill for company, and they took their sweet time. Jim wanted to see his old haunts, so they stopped in Clearwater, where Jim had been in junior college. Both got thrown in jail for a few hours when Jim started a fight in a bar. Let loose, they drove on to Tallahassee, where an unusually nostalgic Jim stopped at the motel where he had lived as an FSU student.

Then they drove straight to New Orleans, where they tarried for a few days and got, in Babe Hill's words, "as drunk as a couple of walruses." Touring the city, Jim bought a postcard at St. Louis Cathedral and mailed it to the Doors' office. "Don't worry," he wrote: "The end is near,—Ha Ha." The card depicted the sacrifice of the Lamb of God. Jim visited Congo Square, site of the old slave market and the place where African rhythms were first heard in America. One night he got up and jammed the blues with one of the bar bands in the French Quarter, thanking them politely when he'd sung his fill. (These musicians later mutated into Kansas, a successful touring band of the early 1970s.)

In Tennessee, Jim and Babe got busted at a speed trap. They had to follow the cop to the county courthouse, where the judge let them go for a hundred dollars in cash.

I N OCTOBER 1970, Jim Morrison drove into a Los Angeles scoured dry by the easterly Santa Ana Winds. "I see your hair is burning," he wrote. "Hills are filled with fire. If they say I never loved you, you know they are a liar." In fact, he loved Pamela Courson so much that he went into a deeply morbid tailspin when he learned that she had run off to France with Jean de Breteuil after the count had sold Janis Joplin the heroin that had killed her at the Landmark Motel on October 4, 1970. The evidence for this is circumstantial, but compelling. One of the GTOs was in Joplin's motel room that evening, and saw de Breteuil, who was known to be dealing star-quality Chinese heroin. Janis Joplin was found by her manager the next day, with her arm still tied off and six dollars in her dead hand, supposedly the change the dealer gave her for the dope. She had been recording a solo album with Paul Rothchild that would later be titled after the nickname her friends called her: *Pearl.*

Jean de Breteuil freaked when he heard Janis was dead. An illegal alien, he faced life in prison if the cops connected him with the singer's death. He went to Pamela Courson, told her he had to get out of the country immediately, and begged her to come with him. She left Jim a long note, which he found when he went to see about their dog. Jim read the note twice and then burned it over the stove. That night, Jim and the crew were commiserating over Janis Joplin's death at Barney's Beanery, where she had sometimes liked to hang out.

"You're drinking with number three," Jim murmured. "That's right. Number three."

THE CONTINENTAL RIOT HOUSE evicted Jim after the police responded to reports of a man hanging from an upper floor balcony by his hands. The cops smelled pot when they entered Jim's suite, and busted Babe Hill for possession. So Jim moved to the semisleazy Chateau Marmont Hotel, taking a bungalow near the pool. Tim Hardin was shooting dope in the bathroom, leaving red streaks of blood in the sink. Jim started trolling the city for women, calling up old flames, trying to get laid. Some girls only slept with Jim because they felt sorry for him. Some claimed that Jim was impotent, or brutal toward them. He paid for one abortion, then another. He was spending real money on cocaine, which ameliorated the effects of his toxic alcohol intake. He suffered from chronic nosebleeds. He was smoking three packs of Marlboros a day, and sometimes coughed up blood.

But Jim Morrison was also writing some of his most beautiful lyrics. The Doors would soon enter the studio to record the album they had agreed to make for Jac Holzman, in return for which Holzman upgraded their royalty rate from seven to ten percent, and (in a gesture of unprecedented generosity that cost him millions over the years) returned Elektra's share of the Doors' publishing rights to the band.

In addition, Jim had filled several recent notebooks with new poetry and images. Much of this new work was extremely troubled and disconsolate. The many references to impotence, cancer, and his penis in these poems, along with contemporary rumors that swirled around Jim and Pamela, have led to speculation that Jim had been diagnosed with penile or testicular cancer, or a debilitating venereal disease such as syphilis. While no proof of this has ever surfaced, and Jim's extant medical records remain sealed, it is hard to explain away poems like "Lament for the Death of My Cock" and other similar elegies.

Around this time, Jim decided to record another solo poetry session. If the work sounded good, he told his friends, he could release a spoken word album. He spoke with movie composer Lalo Schifrin about providing orchestral settings for some of these poems. He even had the album jacket in mind when he replied to a letter from a college art student, T. E. Breitenbach, who had sent Jim samples of his work—clearly showing that Jim was actively and creatively engaged in the preproduction of the album.

The letter was typed, probably by Jim's secretary, Kathy Lisciandro, dated October 9, 1970. In it he asked Breitenbach to do a triptych, the left panel depicting "a radiant moonlit beach and an endless stream of naked young couples running silently along the water's edge," where "a tiny infant grins at the universe, and around his crib stand several ancient, old people." In the center panel would be "a modern city or metropolis of the future at noon, insane with activity," and the right panel "a view through a car windshield at night on a long straight desert highway." These vivid scenes of death and rebirth were reflective of the new beginning Jim himself was seeking. Jim closed the letter by assuring Breitenbach that if he could create "something related to these themes" in the next five months, Jim would use it.

Included with Jim's letter were signed first editions of *The New Creatures* and *An American Prayer*. In this letter, Jim seems to have two recent poems in mind, "Vast Radiant Beach" and "Come, They Crooned, the Ancient Ones." T. E. Breitenbach finished the triptych a few months later, in 1971, but was informed by Kathy that James Morrison had moved to France for a while.

* * *

IT WASN'T ALL GLOOM and doom for Jim in late 1970. His pals say Jim never stopped being funny, and liked to kid around. He sang R & B songs all night with a pickup band at John Densmore's hippie wedding. Jim was a football fan, and had season tickets for Los Angeles Rams games at the Coliseum. One of his notebooks contains a game score and the notation "RG & F4," which probably denoted Rams quarterback Roman Gabriel and the famous defensive line that included Deacon Jones and Roosevelt Grier, known as the Fearsome Foursome. Sometimes Jim put on sneakers and a headband, and played touch football in Redondo Beach with his friends, who say he could still run if he wanted to, but that Jim got winded long before anyone else. He was twenty-six years old, but could have passed for forty. Around this time, in response to an unfavorable review, he dictated a note to writer Dave Marsh at the Detroit rock magazine *Creem,* which concluded: "I am not mad. I am interested in freedom. Good luck, Jim Morrison."

On October 14, 1970, Jim taped an interview with the rock magazine *Circus.* Since the phones in the darkened office kept ringing, Jim took writer Sally Stevenson to the little garden in back that featured a small pool, with four big goldfish sucking at the surface for attention. The recent shocking deaths of Jimi and Janis came up quickly.

Jim: "I think the great creative burst of energy that happened three or four years ago was hard to sustain for sensitive artists. You know? I guess they might be dissatisfied with anything except 'the heights.' When reality stops fulfilling their inner visions, they get depressed. But that's . . . not my theory of why people die. Sometimes, it could be an accident. Sometimes, it could be suicide. Sometimes, it could be . . . murder. There are a lot of ways people die. I don't know."

Asked how he thought he would die, Jim answered, "I hope at about age a hundred and twenty with a sense of humor and a nice comfortable bed. I wouldn't want anybody around. I'd just want to drift quietly. But— I'm still holding out, because I think science has a chance in our lifetimes to conquer death."

Jim said he was facing eight months in jail, and was worried about it. He called the Miami trial "more a political than a sexual scandal." He continued: "I think I was just fed up with the image that was created around me, which I sometimes consciously, most of the time unconsciously, cooperated with. It just got too much for me to stomach, so I just put an end to it in one glorious evening....I told the audience they were fucking idiots to be members of an audience. That's how I felt at the time."

Asked to speak candidly about himself, Jim replied: "I think of myself as an intelligent, sensitive human being with the soul of a clown—which always forces me to blow it at the most important moments."

Any regrets? "I'm not denying that I've had a good time these last few years. I've met some interesting people in a short space of time that I probably would not have run into in twenty years of living. I can't say I regret it. If I had to do it over, I think I would have gone for the quiet, undemonstrative artist, plodding away in his own garden."

MR. MOJO RISIN'

IN OCTOBER 1970, with Pamela Courson in Paris, Jim Morrison began a passionate affair with a friend's sexy wife. Eva Gardonyi was a young Hungarian woman with a much-talked-about wild streak. She was a little older than Jim, and had gone to law school in Budapest before arriving in Los Angeles as the bride of refugee filmmaker Frank Gardonyi, whom Jim had met while filming *HWY*. Slender, sultry, hyperflirtatious, Eva had charmed Jim (and everyone else) with her worldly, Central European manner. (Even Pamela Courson liked her.) Jim Morrison had his eye on Eva to the extent that he showed up at her house on the same day her husband walked out on their marriage.

Eva recalled in an interview with Frank Lisciandro: "So Frank left at five in the afternoon. At eleven o'clock, somebody's knocking on the door, and there's Jimmy, and he's got two suitcases. The taxi was pulling away. It was funny—with *suitcases*—because he never traveled with anything."

Jim had two bottles of champagne and a jar full of cocaine.

Eva: "It must have taken him a lot of drinking...to get the nerve that he would do it! As soon as I opened the door, he put his foot in

there—like he wasn't sure that I'm going to let him in—and he kept pushing me back, saying 'I love you, I love you,' and he didn't stop doing that
until he got me into bed. He left the suitcases in the living room and
ended up in my bedroom, and it was *very* bold. I was surprised. I was
flattered. I was stoned. . . . He said for a long time before, he had a crush
on me, which I didn't know."

Jim liked Frank Gardonyi, and Eva said he felt guilty about carrying
on with his friend's wife, so only a few people knew Jim was living at her
house while recording *L.A. Woman.* He spent the afternoons at the
band's makeshift studio, and came back to Eva's late at night. "He enjoyed playing house," she said later. "He just so many times said it was
nice to be home and have dinner and just lock the door." They would
stay up all night and go to bed together as the sun rose over the hills.
They went to the movies when Jim had free time, or drove out to Zuma
Beach on the Pacific Coast Highway. He carried a notebook and was always stopping what he was doing to pull it out and start writing, mostly
poetry. Eva says he was having difficulty sleeping because of his drinking, and often worked in his notebooks when he couldn't fall asleep.
"We took a long acid trip together," she recalled, "but he wrote pro-
fusely, all night long." He was in a fever of creativity. When he came
back from the recording sessions, he played the old Doors albums and
sang along with them. He also sang the *L.A. Woman* songs to her—
"Love Her Madly," "Hyacinth House"—and wanted to know what she
thought.

She said that Jim complained to her about the Doors. "You know, by
that time he wasn't on good terms with any of them. He was deeply disappointed with all of them." She also said that he always spoke of
Pamela with total affection. "She was quick, Pamela. She had the clarity
of a child, with very good intuitions, and an innocence that Jimmy loved
in her a great deal. She was easy to burst into laughter, and look at life
in the sweet child manner. He said, 'She was a child when we met, and I
feel responsible for her because she never grew up.' She had believed in
him, and he appreciated that. I know that they had been starving together. And he forgave her a lot of things. Even though at times she was
impossible to be with, he would say, 'She's a sweet child.' Somehow he
just needed to take care of her. Somehow they always gravitated back to
each other after every little escapade."

Eva told Jerry Hopkins: "We really got it on. Neither of us was expecting it. He loved life and so did I. The only bad thing was, there was too much cocaine, which blew our minds. . . . He thought I was crazier than he was, and he wanted to see how far I'd go. One evening he came home and he had all this coke and champagne. He learned that I freak out real bad. Sometimes, I like to have . . . being from Transylvania . . . I told him I liked to drink blood. And he said, 'Well why don't we drink some blood?'" Eva found some rusty razor blades and started cutting her hands as Jim watched in passive horror. "Suddenly we had blood all over the place," she said, "and we freaked out and danced in the moonshine. And after that we got very scared [about] where it could go, because the mornings after these freakouts are really sad. Waking up, and all these pools of blood . . ."

Years later, Eva was sure of at least one thing. "People say Jimmy was self-destructive, and [they] talk about all he might have been, but he loved living. He had great plans for his life. When I drove badly, he would hang on and say, 'Oh Eva! Don't kill me! You know I love living!'"

THE DOORS NOW HAD a one-album deal with Elektra, but the sessions had begun inauspiciously. Paul Rothchild, who had produced the band's six gold records, arrived at the early rehearsals and hated the music he heard. He was fed up anyway, and brokenhearted from having to finish Janis Joplin's album by himself. At Sunset Sound, he listened to the Doors noodle away on the jazzy bits of "Riders on the Storm" and thought the new music wasn't happening. He didn't like "Love Her Madly" either. They played "L.A. Woman" for him as a slow blues. Jim seemed distracted, and wasn't singing well. Paul Rothchild walked into the control room and told engineer Bruce Botnick that he wasn't going to do the record.

Back in the studio, Rothchild told the band that he thought their new music—four or five songs—was boring. He said he was very sorry, but he didn't feel up to making another record with them. The fifth Door was quitting. "We were bummed," Robby said later, "because he'd done all the others ones, and . . . he didn't like the music. He said, 'It sounds like cocktail music,' about 'Riders on the Storm.' We were going, 'Oh shit—what do we do now?' We'd never been in that position before."

But Jim Morrison seemed pleased by Rothchild's decision. Some claim that Jim didn't want to work with Rothchild anymore, and had often complained that Rothchild's slow, meticulous methods had robbed the Doors of spontaneity and made the band sound uptight. Krieger has pointed out that Rothchild's sessions were so drawn out that a bored-stiff Jim Morrison would often be too liquored up to sing. Whether or not Jim Morrison "got rid of" Paul Rothchild is still an open question.

The band quickly decided to produce an album themselves, with Botnick as coproducer and engineer. Then the Doors decided to record in their own building. Elektra didn't want them wrecking their studios, and Sunset Sound was expensive. The Doors could save a fortune by transforming their offices into a cheap recording studio. Two years earlier, Elektra had installed a mixing console in an old northern California farmhouse to try to record a "Big Pink" country-rock knock-off by some musicians led by teenaged Jackson Browne. This soundboard, later used by the Doors to record at the Aquarius Theater, was now installed upstairs at 8512 Santa Monica Boulevard, while the mikes, monitors, keyboards, and pinball machines were set up downstairs.

To toughen up their sound, the Doors added two musicians. Bassist Jerry Scheff had toured and recorded with Elvis Presley, and Mark Benno was the hot rhythm guitar player in Leon Russell's band. On uptempo songs like "L.A. Woman" and "Love Her Madly," the Doors now recorded as a hard-rocking sextet.

This was the group that cobbled together one of the greatest records the rock movement produced, in only a couple of months, beginning only a few weeks after Jim had been sentenced to jail time. The brilliant "L.A. Woman" began life as a slow blues assembled by Jim and Robby about the strippers at the Phone Booth ("never saw a woman so alone"). But "L.A. Woman" exploded in the studio, according to Manzarek, when the bass and rhythm guitars kicked the Doors in the ass. "We smoked a joint and just *locked in.* God, did we capture it!" There was a minor problem adding a bass part to "Riders," but when Scheff began to figure it out, Manzarek says it was just "spooky. That song became itself in the recording studio. Those two songs were born there." Bruce Botnick suggested that Jim overdub his vocal with another, completely whispered vocal track. This would give "Riders" its ghostly, otherworldly mystique.

Jim solved the lack of an isolated vocal booth by recording, mostly live, in the tiled bathroom. He actually spent a lot of time in the bathroom, because Babe Hill was constantly crossing the boulevard to Monaco Liquors for fresh cases of the Mexican beer Jim liked: Tecate, Bohemia, and Dos Equis. Bill Siddons later said that the thirty-six beers Jim drank in one day during the *L.A. Woman* sessions might have been his all-time record.

Krieger remembers Jim coughing a lot while making the album. He had never recovered entirely from a late spring case of pneumonia.

I N A SENSE, Paul Rothchild might have been right about what he heard in the late-1970 Doors. A lot of the music was formulaic, white R & B. "The Changeling" hit a good R & B groove as Jim grunted out his new imperative: "See me change," etc. "Been Down So Long" was a blustery blues inspired by the title of the late Richard Farina's novel *Been Down So Long It Looks Like Up to Me.* "Crawling King Snake" was *Hooker 'n Heat* without much of the latter. Another blues, "Cars Hiss by My Window," was a lonely motel lament that contained the chilling, prophetic line: *"A cold girl will kill you in a darkened room."* In one of the great Doors moments, Jim drunkenly *sang* a Little Walter harmonica wail at the end of the song, an uncanny vocal approximation of the harp solo Jim Morrison had always wanted to be able to play.

Robby Krieger's "Love Her Madly" was an uptempo pop song (sung with conviction by Jim) that Elektra chose as the first single. "Hyacinth House" was a sad folk-rock ballad crooned by Jim, a plaintive wish for romantic rebirth. *"I need a brand new friend that doesn't bother me."* Robby has said that the song refers to his parents' house, where it was first worked out. Others have pointed out that Oscar Wilde and his circle used *hyacinth* to refer to the rent boys they buggered, and that Jim was reading a lot of Wilde in this period.

"L'America" was left over from having been rejected by Michelangelo Antonioni for *Zabriskie Point.* Its rattlesnake maracas and gothic organ conjured America as a carny-type horror show, but the track was both experimental and unresolved. Even less successful was "Orange County Suite," Jim's failed attempt to forge another album-ending epic like "The End." (Ray: "[It was] Jim on piano chords. This was for Pamela, his Orange County sweetheart.") But the music was dolorous, and the maudlin lyrics described a resigned acceptance of a dead-end romance. The band again rejected "Orange County Suite" as a total bummer.

If there's greatness in the last Doors album, it lies in a triad of longer songs. "The Wasp (Texas Radio and the Big Beat)" dated to 1968, but was recut for *L.A. Woman.* This was Jim beaming authoritarian cadences and superlurid beatnik imagery—*"the negroes of the forest"; "stoned, immaculate"*—out to pagan America.

"Riders on the Storm" was Jim Morrison's ultimate existential statement. It echoed a popular song from Jim's childhood, Vaughn Monroe's 1949 hit record "Riders in the Sky." Acknowledging humanity's fragility, and essential solitude, amid a soundscape of thunder and rain, the song was also an explicit warning not to pick up Jim's psychotic alter ego: the demonic hitcher, the killer on the road—or *"sweet family will die."* "Riders" was also an explicit, extremely poignant plea for tender, womanly love. Nothing Jim Morrison, or any other auteur of the rock movement, ever wrote was as melancholy, true, and compelling as "Riders on the Storm."

"L.A. Woman" was the album's title track and centerpiece. It was a driving song, reporting what Jim Morrison experienced as he wheeled around Los Angeles, the deserts, and the beaches. Freeways, demonic wildfires, the city of night: all flashed by as an electric piano and rhythm guitar powered the band. A bolero described a topless bar. *"Motel, money, murder, madness / Let's change the mood from glad to sadness."* Mr. Mojo Risin' (an uncanny anagram of "Jim Morrison") made his priapic appearance, solemnly invoked as the final incarnation of "The Changeling." Jim blurted out drunken, ironic love calls as the song built into its ecstatic climax, and he finished his last masterpiece with blubbery, unrepentant shouts of desperate triumph.

WHEN THE MUSIC'S OVER

JIM MORRISON TURNED twenty-seven years old on December 8, 1970. Late that afternoon, he took his recent notebooks into the

Village Recorders, a studio in West L.A., and read, sang, and played piano and tambourine for three hours. Present were engineer John Haeny, a beautiful Austrian girl named Florentine Pabst, and Frank and Kathy Lisciandro. Frank's photographs reveal the poet as heavily bearded, with the longest hair of his life, wearing a football jersey bearing the number 66.

Jim began the taping by saying, "OK—let's do a bit and listen to it." Reading from notebooks and typed versions of poems, he began with "In that year we had a great visitation of energy," and kept going through twenty-two distinct poems and songs. He recorded "The American Night" seated at the piano, playing chords. Other poems included "Book of Days," "Ghost Song," "White Blind Light," and "The Holy Shay." As in his first solo poetry session two years earlier, he sang several songs a capella, including "Bird of Prey," "Winter Photography," "Under Waterfall," and "Woman in the Window."

Almost all the poems were dark. They described sex, rape, napalm, bleeding virgins, and impending death. In "Bird of Prey" he kept asking, "Will I die?" His dysfunctional sex organ was a preoccupation: "I sacrifice my cock on the altar of silence."

At some point a bottle of Irish whiskey was opened (Haeny says the Lisciandros brought it, but Frank later denied this), and the session got somewhat looser. They all took a break and walked over to the Lucky U, Jim's old UCLA haunt, for Mexican food and beer. Back in the studio, Jim started improvising blues lyrics, and then asked Florentine and Kathy to read a lengthy new poem in unison, which took a long time to get right. While listening to the playback, Jim suddenly blacked out. He pitched forward, crashed down, and took a couple of mike stands with him. After a few seconds of unconsciousness, Jim woke up laughing. He yelled, "Wait a minute! Wait a minute! Start 'em again. They're great!"

Jim worked for another hour, reciting his poetry in a calm, contained voice with a hint of melancholy and world-weariness. He listened again to the playback of the two girls reading together, and his reaction was captured on tape: "Brilliant. Brilliant. Oh, my God. I can't believe it. This was *incredible.*" One of the last lines he read was "Love cannot save you from your own fate."

* * *

THREE DAYS LATER, on Friday, December 11, the Doors went out for what turned out to be one last weekend of concerts. The Friday night shows were at the State Fair Music Hall in Dallas, Texas. In the first, the Doors played some of their new songs: "Love Her Madly" with no vocal, "The Changeling," "L.A. Woman." Jim seemed tired, and became truculent as he swilled malt liquor from a can. Between shows, there were questions about whether Jim could (or should) go on. He looked haggard, seemed exhausted, and was unusually drunk. But Jim managed to take the stage, although he sang with his back to the audience and hung onto the microphone stand to avoid keeling over. The band hustled the show along, barely pausing between songs. "Riders on the Storm" received its first (and last) public performance. During the finale, "Light My Fire," Jim tried to cavort around the stage, but he collapsed into Robby and both men crashed to the floor and almost fell off the stage. There was no encore.

The next night, December 12, 1970, the Doors were booked into the Warehouse, New Orleans' famed electric ballroom. Jim looked somewhat abstracted as the band began with "Soul Kitchen," but he shouted out the lyric with conviction, and the full house settled in for what they thought would be a great show. Four songs in, Jim started to come apart. He tried to tell some lame jokes, and no one laughed. When the band got going again, he forgot the lyrics. Between songs, he was lurching around as if he was having a seizure, and the big room got quiet as the music-savvy crowd intuited that something was very wrong.

Then, in the middle of "Light My Fire," Jim Morrison died onstage. He stopped singing and stumbled to the drum riser and sat down. He missed his cue at the end of the guitar solo, unable to stand, so the band anxiously went through another instrumental cycle. When it was time for Jim to finish the song, John Densmore disgracefully rammed his boot in the middle of Jim's back and sharply pushed him upright.

Standing again, shaking with anxiety and rage, Jim burst into a tormented fury. He grabbed the mike stand and began smashing it onto the stage floor, again and again, until the wooden planks began to splinter. The kids in front looked on in shock. Then the mike stand broke in two.

Jim only stopped when Vince Treanor walked out from behind the amps and laid a calming hand on his shoulder. Jim put his arm around Vince for support, and stood there, staring, breathing hard, while the Doors finished the song. Then Jim dropped the microphone and staggered off the stage. The show was over.

So were the Doors.

Everyone was deeply shaken by what had happened. Ray Manzarek later said that he had witnessed an occult process, the evaporation of Jim's life force, the dispersal of his chi. The band had been through almost every conceivable permutation of hard rock nightmares, but the abject horror of Jim's collapse in New Orleans now jolted them into a new awareness of reality. The limo ride back to the Pontchartrain Hotel was desolate. Jim tried to make small talk, but the others were silent. When Jim got out of the car, Ray said, "OK. It's finished."

Before they flew back to Los Angeles the following day, the Doors and their handlers agreed to suspend concert performances. Jim Morrison never appeared onstage again.

DECEMBER 1970. Nixon was bombing Cambodia. Despair reigned supreme over the land. Bill Graham decided to close both of his Fillmores, West and East, so the rock movement was almost over. Elektra released *13*, the first Doors compilation album, and it was an immediate bestseller. Somehow the magic of the songs and Jim Morrison's voice continued to hold. The rest of Jim Morrison's year was spent working on *L.A. Woman*.

Bruce Botnick's producing style was laid back compared to Paul Rothchild's, and Jim responded well to the relaxed ambience. He appeared sober to sing his parts, and generally took more responsibility. *"Did a little downer 'bout an hour ago,"* Jim sang on the last verse of the title track. (The published lyric reads, *"Just got into town about an hour ago."*)

Jim was moving between the Chateau Marmont, the Alta Cienega Motel, Eva's house, and Pamela's empty flat on Norton Avenue. Elektra publicist Diane Gardiner, who lived downstairs, says that Jim would sit silently in a dark corner of her apartment and just watch people as they came and went. Mirandi Babitz described him as "flabby and pale and strange-looking." A girl at the Whisky asked Jim for an autograph, and he wrote, "Love, Arthur Rimbaud." He gave intelligent interviews, crammed with insights and good quotes, to journalists who then called him a has-been, and "the bozo prince of pretentious rock."

Pamela Courson returned from France before Christmas, having left Jean de Breteuil in Paris. She was wasted and weighed about ninety pounds. But she regained her strength and kept pressuring Jim to quit the Doors and return to France with her. Her oft-repeated fantasy was that Jim could be a poet, she could be his muse, and they would buy a house and be happy together at last. If he didn't come, she told Jim, she was going back to Paris by herself.

Patricia Kennely claimed that she ruined Pamela's birthday on December 22 by flying to L.A. and confronting Pamela with the news that she had aborted Jim's child. (Kennely says she was staying at Diane Gardiner's downstairs apartment when this took place.) But Pamela was too smart to fall for sniveling recriminations, and simply cut her would-be rival dead with a bored, offhand remark. Unbeknownst to Kennely, there had been *many* aborted children in Pamela Courson's five years with Jim Morrison. Other girls' dead babies were the *least* of Pamela's problems with her man.

Jim preaching in 1969: "When I was back there in seminary school …"

Morrison Hotel photo session, Venice Beach, 1970. (EDMUND TESKE / MICHAEL OCHS ARCHIVE)

Jim and François Truffaut on a Jacques Demy film set at Chambourg in France, spring 1970.
(THALIA ARCHIVE)

During his obscenity trial in Miami, Jim posed in the lounge of his hotel with unidenti-fied guests and his two bodyguards, Tony Funches, seated at left, and Babe Hill, seated right. (THALIA ARCHIVE)

Top: Jim performing, eyes wide shut, summer 1970. (CARL SAMARTINO / MICHAEL OCHS ARCHIVE) *Bottom:* an exhausted Jim Morrison at the Doors' workshop during the *L.A. Woman* sessions in early 1971. (EDMUND TESKE / MICHAEL OCHS ARCHIVE)

Shortly after his arrival in Paris in March 1971, Jim was photographed with a Polaroid camera as he stood by the bedroom window of the apartment where he died. (THALIA ARCHIVE)

Jim shaved off his beard while in Morocco a few weeks later in the spring of 1971. (THALIA ARCHIVE)

Jim at the Bar Alexandre in Paris, April 1971.
(HERVÉ MULLER)

French journalist Hervé Muller and Jim in Paris the same month.
(HERVÉ MULLER)

Pamela and Jim with Hervé Muller in Paris, June 1971.
(GILLES YÉPRÉMIAN)

Jim Morrison and Pamela Courson in Paris, June 1971.
(HERVÉ MULLER)

One of the last known images taken of Jim, June 1971.
(GILLES YÉPRÉMIAN)

For twenty years after Jim died, in July 1971, his Paris grave was an international pilgrimage site, covered in graffiti and backpackers' offerings. (ARCHIVE OF ROCK)

Today, Jim's grave is one of the most visited tourist sites in Paris, after the Eiffel Tower and the Louvre. The Greek inscription can be translated as "True to his own spirit." (PHILIP DALECKY)

CHAPTER NINE

LAST TANGO
IN PARIS

The world on you depends
Our life will never end
Riders on the storm...

AFTERNOON OF A ROCK STAR

JIM MORRISON HABITUALLY watched the news on television. In January 1971, he heard fascist-looking Spiro Agnew, the vice president of the United States, mount a vitriolic attack on rock musicians for spreading "drug culture among the youth of America." (Agnew would continue these antirock tirades until he was disgraced and forced from office in a payoff/corruption scandal in 1973.) Jim was fascinated by the Manson trial, which ended late that month with life sentences for totally insane Charlie and the three idiot girls who butchered Sharon Tate. It was also gradually dawning on the music business that the Beatles had broken up in late December 1970, after almost ten years as a band. George Harrison's Hindu gospel anthem "My Sweet Lord" was dominant on the radio.

The Doors, now in their sixth year, finished recording *L.A. Woman* in their workshop studio during a final two-week spurt in the middle of January 1971. At their studio/office, the windows were boarded shut and the walls covered with heavy mover's quilts. One day Jim was late to the sessions, and remorsefully gave the other five musicians and Bruce Botnick a dollar each in reparations. The Doors would begin mixing the eight-track tapes almost immediately, at Poppy Sound in West Hollywood.

The band, especially Jim, was adamant that the Doors were on hiatus and not playing gigs. An English tour was canceled, and the Doors' agency was told not to book the band anywhere. While the issue was never openly discussed, everyone was worried that Jim was quitting the Doors after the album was done. The Elektra contract had now expired. Pamela Courson, the Doors concluded, had won her long battle to get Jim out of the band. Engineer John Haeny recalled: "Once Jim had quit, he never mentioned to me that he had any intention of rejoining. His focus was on his poetry. After our initial recordings of his poetry, he realized he needed to organize his thoughts. That's what he went to Paris for. It was important to him that the world perceive him as a poet. That's why he signed a contract with Elektra to make a poetry album—with no participation from the Doors."

AROUND THEN, Jim was killing time one bright winter afternoon with his friends at the Garden District Café on La Cienega. Joni Mitchell was talking quietly with her manager at a nearby table. Jim was doing an interview with writer Dan Knapp, of the *Los Angeles Times,* who noted Jim's long brown hair, already beginning to show gray streaks at twenty-seven, and his heavy beard. "Excessive eating had run him to fat, but that only seemed to accentuate his good nature, his quiet, intelligent conversation. . . . Only three or four too rapidly finished screwdrivers too quickly washed down with bottles of beer hinted at the demons that were said to drive him."

Jim couldn't say he was leaving the Doors. This would hurt sales when the record came out. But he pretty much said it anyway when asked about the Doors. "The next album . . . um . . . may just be the other guys, you know? Doing their thing—um . . . instrumentally. Heavy blues stuff." As the afternoon wore on, Jim and his entourage headed up to the office, where "the other guys" were listening to mix-downs of the new songs. Bored, Jim stopped for five minutes to pet a stray dog he seemed to be familiar with on Santa Monica Boulevard. The group headed down the street to the Palms, where they played pool and drank more beer. At the nearby Little Club, Jim switched back to screwdrivers. At closing time, his head was almost down on the bar.

A waitress now joined the party, which headed by car to the Chateau, where Jim was staying in one of the two-story bungalows close to the hotel's pool. Babe Hill went off to find some grass. Laughing, Jim said, "He gets his hands on any cocaine, that's the last we'll see of him for a few days." The waitress was pressed up against Jim, and her blouse was half open. Once everyone was inside, Jim cracked open a quart bottle of Smirnoff vodka, and drank most of it himself. Babe returned with an ounce of pot and they smoked most of that as well. Tony Funches showed up in a T-shirt with COCAINE spelled out like the Coca-Cola logo.

At four in the morning, they watched an old movie on TV with the sound turned off. Mexican music from a border station blared from a radio. The waitress looked over at Jim, and went up to the bedroom. At dawn, Jim climbed up on the roof and tried to swing down into his bedroom window from the rain gutter. But the gutter broke and Jim fell two floors. He bounced off the roof of the shed behind the building, and landed hard on his back on the concrete sidewalk.

At first, he couldn't breathe. Then he couldn't get up. His friends ran out to help him. Jim told them not to call an ambulance. The waitress split. Funches helped him into bed. Jim slept through the next day, then woke up with chest pains and coughed up some blood. Jim wondered if he might have punctured a lung. His leg hurt badly. They took Jim to the doctor, who examined him, found nothing was broken, and apparently just gave him some painkillers for badly bruised ribs and told him to take it easy. Jim Morrison walked with a slight limp for the next few weeks.

Jim was apathetic, according to Densmore, about the mix-down of the Doors' new album. In Jim's mind, he was already gone. He did attend a singles meeting with Jac Holzman when the record was close to completion in February. *Morrison Hotel* had sold well and been a good comeback for the band, but it had no singles or radio action. "Riders on the Storm" was the obvious choice, but it was too long for AM radio. Holzman proposed Krieger's "Love Her Madly" as the first single from *L.A. Woman.* Jim Morrison nodded in assent. Later he and Holzman had a drink together. Jim told the famously reserved label boss, somewhat tauntingly, that he ought to hang out more, let go a little, walk along the edge of life. Holzman only answered, "Yeah, Jim—but I think it's important not to *bleed.*"

In an interview with the *L.A. Free Press,* Jim said he was proud that he and the Doors had never sold out. It was a band that remained rebels to the end, and if Jim was leaving, at least his integrity was intact. As if he were speaking for Brian Jones, Jimi Hendrix, and Janis Joplin, as well as for himself, Jim said: "For me, it was never really an 'act,' those so-called performances. It was a life-and-death thing, an attempt to communicate, to involve many people in a private world of thought."

THE LAST INTERVIEW

THE EARLY MONTHS of 1971 were hard times for Jim Morrison. Pamela, dumped by her count, was hurt and angry. Jim was drinking and fucking up. He crashed another car. He insulted Danny Sugerman's sister with comments about her breasts. He reeled drunkenly into Themis, knocked over some clothes racks, and was beaten about the head with a heavy purse by an outraged customer while Pamela screamed bloody murder at him. Jim tried to tape an antiamphetamine radio spot at the Doors' office, but couldn't bring himself to say "Speed kills." He tried to ad-lib, but he was tipsy, and kept coming out with jokey lines like "Stay away from speed, man. Take downers instead." Paul Rothchild saw him at the Elektra office and said that Jim looked like a haunted man.

February 3, 1971. Jim was watching the third lunar landing at Atlantic Records chief Ahmet Ertegun's hotel bungalow with a bunch of Ahmet's upscale friends. As Alan Shepard and Edgar Mitchell bounced around the moon (images that would be used as the original MTV logo a decade later), Jim was guzzling Scotch and looking sullen, but he carefully took in Ertegun's gossip about the Rolling Stones, now signed to his label. The Stones were leaving England, Ertegun said, one step ahead of the taxman. The whole band was moving to France; they were looking for houses on the Riviera, where they would record their next album in exile. There were some astringent comments made about the easy availability of heroin the closer one got to Marseilles. Jean de Breteuil's name came up, because he was supposedly living at Keith Richards's house in London.

When Ertegun told an off-color anecdote involving midgets in India, Jim suddenly got up, steadied himself, and shouted, "You think you're gonna *win*, don't you? Well, you ain't gonna win. Us *artists* are gonna win, not you capitalist pigs." There was dead silence, and Jim walked out. People shrugged. Who cared what that asshole thought?

Jim returned later and apologized to Ertegun.

B EN FONG-TORRES was an editor at *Rolling Stone* magazine, then based in San Francisco. When working in Los Angeles, Ben usually stayed with Elektra publicist Diane Gardiner, who lived downstairs from Pamela Courson. One day in February, Fong-Torres was hanging out when Jim Morrison came in, looking for Pamela. America's greatest rock star was virtually unrecognizable—fat, hairy, limping. Fong-Torres immediately asked for an interview and turned on his cheap Sony cassette recorder. Jim told a couple of dirty jokes and then agreed to talk on the record. A new country rock band's annoying album played in the background. Pamela Courson showed up a few minutes later and sat in on the recorded interview.

It would be Jim's last.

Jim was candid about the end of the Doors. "We're kind of . . . off playing concerts. We're making our last album. That's right. We're at a crossroads of our career. The Doors are already an anachronism for the younger people, you know? Each generation wants new names, new symbols, new cycles."

Fong-Torres mentioned Grand Funk Railroad, in 1971 the biggest American rock band. Jim changed the subject to the new singer-songwriters like Joni Mitchell and James Taylor who he was more interested in. "There's a certain moment when you're right in time with your audience—and then you *both* grow out of it. You just have to realize it. It's not that you've outgrown the audience. It's that you *and* the audience are too old for it. You have to go on to something else, and let the younger people do it now."

Asked what that meant, Jim replied, "I'd like to write and direct a film of my own. It's all in my head." The conversation turned to *HWY,* which had played in several film festivals in 1970, and been booed in San Francisco as an incoherent ego trip. Pamela Courson giggled and coughed. In her little-girlish voice, she ventured, "It didn't have enough action."

The interview paused while Jim ordered food and beer on the telephone. "Do you take credit cards?" he asked. "What's the address here?"

Fong-Torres asked Jim about getting fat. "He's *not* fat," Pamela laughingly protested. "I *like* him the way he is!"

"I drink a lot of beer," Jim said. "It's the only thing I drink when I'm recording. It gives me energy and keeps me going all night. Getting heavier, for me, is just part of the natural aging process—filling out, you know?" Some people came in, and Jim politely explained he couldn't get up because he had a bad leg. When the food arrived a few minutes later, the tape recorded a dog barking at the delivery boy. "Sage!" Pam yelled. "Be quiet!"

Fong-Torres wanted to know about Miami. Jim was philosophical about his legal troubles. "It was a case of me trying to reduce the whole thing to a certain level of absurdity," Jim said. "And it worked too well. If I didn't have almost unlimited [financial] ability to defend myself, I'd be in jail right now for three years." Jim said that the trial had some positive effects. He had gotten out of L.A. for the first time in years, and in Nassau he had learned to scuba dive, describing it as "a floating intrauterine experience."

Speaking of the Doors, Jim recalled: "We came along at a weird time. The English groups, you know, had already done it. (Pamela: "Yes. That's right.") We came at the tail end of a rock revival from England. I think it was the success of these English groups that gave hope to a lot of musicians over here. We said, 'Sheeeyit! We can do the same thing, man.'"

The conversation turned to the changes in the rock scene. People weren't dancing at clubs in San Francisco anymore. Many were wiped out on pills. Pam began making the case that rock music was on a downhill trajectory.

Jim concluded: "What the people want right now is a band that's just totally casting aside the past, and all the [music] business associations. They have to say, 'We're doing this for a *reason*. It's *not* 'cause we want to make a lot of bread off you people.' They [rock fans] want to feel that the group is part of their community, rather than something laid on from somewhere else."

A RETIRED HOLLYWOOD LAWYER who played golf with Max Fink said (in 2002) that he believed Fink might have received a warning concerning Jim Morrison about a month before Jim left for Paris, which would have been in early February 1971. According to this attorney, who spoke on condition of anonymity, Fink was given a tip by an associate of Mickey Rudin, the prominent Beverly Hills attorney whose clients included Frank Sinatra, and who had ties to the Nixon administration. This retired lawyer was given to understand that Fink was quietly told that his famous client would be neutralized in prison—murdered or incapacitated—and should be gotten out of the country before his legal appeals were exhausted and his passport confiscated. France, which has no extradition treaty with the United States for so-called sex crimes, was suggested as a logical place for Jim to take refuge. No direct or documentary evidence for this warning exists, only the unverifiable word of a respected former associate of both Rudin and Fink. Whatever the accuracy of this account, within one month Jim Morrison was in Paris, living incognito as a lodger in an apartment house, under the assumed names of James Douglas and/or Douglas James.

O N FEBRUARY, 9, 1971, the first tremor of a massive earthquake hit at six o'clock in the morning. Pamela was in bed, and Jim had passed out in his reading chair. The ground began to shake with increasing violence. Suddenly Jim awoke to people screaming. The walls of the apartment building quivered. Jim and Pamela ran outside into Norton Avenue and watched the hills above Hollywood shake up and down. The sky was a sickly yellow, pierced by lightning bolts. An acrid smell of ozone and organic decay filled the air. The earthquake registered 6.5 on the Richter scale, and the aftershocks lasted for hours. For the next few days, they watched constant TV images of chaos and devastation. Sixty-five people had died. At one point Pamela looked at Jim and said, "We've got to get out of here—now."

Pamela left for Paris on February 14. She and Jim first drove to Orange County to see her parents. Jim took her to the airport, put her on a plane, and promised he would join her in a few weeks. The next day she checked into the Hôtel George V, hooked up with the Count de Breteuil again, and set about looking for a place for Jim to live.

After Pamela left, Jim carried on as before, spending many of his nights in her empty apartment, whose furniture, except for her bed and his reading chair, was now covered in sheets. The winter in L.A. had turned cold, and people were traumatized in the wake of the earthquake. Craving female company, he combed through his notebooks, calling old girlfriends and women who'd given him their phone numbers on napkins, matchbooks, ticket stubs. "He was the biggest mercy fuck in Hollywood," one woman said. "Everyone felt so sorry for him."

Early in March, Jim told the Doors he was leaving town. At the Doors office, he told his erstwhile comrades that he had to take a break, that he needed time off. Asked if he was sure he wanted to leave before *L.A. Woman* was finished, Jim said the album was almost finished, that it sounded good, and he trusted them to do a good job. There was a long pause, and no eye contact.

Ray asked Jim how long he would be gone. "I don't know," Jim answered. "Maybe a year."

Ray later wrote: "We all said, 'Where are you going?' Jim said, 'Paris.'" And then Jim quietly said good-bye and walked out of the mixing session without any ceremony. The Doors were totally shocked. Ray Manzarek, in his memoir, wrote that they were "dumbfounded." None of them had a clue what was happening with Jim.

"MY FEELING," Frank Lisciandro said later, "and the feeling of those who knew him closely, was that [Jim] was leaving for good, for as long as he could get away from L.A. He was through with that part of his career and his life."

In his last days in Los Angeles, Jim was more sober, more human. He seemed relieved that a difficult phase of his life was now over. He was still limping slightly from his fall. He cleaned out his desk at the Doors office, and was especially nice to the staff, as if he wanted to leave on good terms. The HWY Productions office in the Clear Thoughts Building was closed. The Elektra contract had been fulfilled. He made the financial arrangements with the band's accountant necessary to see him through a long exile. He went to several film screenings: The Stones' *Gimme Shelter,* Donald Cammel's *Performance,* and George Lucas's *THX 1138* (with a score by Lalo Schifrin).

One winter afternoon he was hanging out at Bill Siddons's house in Long Beach, chatting with Siddons's attractive blond wife, Cheri, who was pregnant with her first child. Jim teased her about not being asked to be the baby's godfather, and was assured that he could do the honors with her next child. This seemed to please him.

I N MARCH 1971, Janis Joplin's poignant "Me and Bobby McGee" was huge on the radio in L.A., and Jim was saying his good-byes. On March 3, he showed up at a party at Elektra's expanded offices and refurbished studio. Jac Holzman told Jim he was surprised to see him. Jim joked that he wanted to see what he'd paid for. Holzman took a few people, including Jim, over to the Blue Boar for supper later. Jim sat next to his friend, composer Fred Myrow, who asked Jim when he was coming back to Los Angeles. Jim replied that he wasn't coming back.

Holzman: "There was a poignancy to that evening. Jim, who was usually quiet in groups, was unusually so that night: half there, half somewhere else. I could feel the finality hanging in the air. As we left the restaurant, we all said our good-byes to him. We had enjoyed a lifetime together, in the blazing arc of rock and roll. Jim and I hugged each other, and then he turned, somewhat awkwardly, and walked away. I watched and wondered if I would ever see him again."

Another night, Jim and Babe Hill visited Pamela's sister Judy, who was still running Themis. They talked about magic over dinner, and later Jim began calling numbers from her address book at random, asking whoever answered if they believed in magic. Most hung up on him, but one of Judy's neighbors responded enthusiastically that, yes, he believed in magic. Jim then emptied his pockets—four twenty-dollar bills—and slipped the money under the man's door. He called the neighbor back and said, "Magic has just left you a gift," and hung up.

A few days later, Pam Miller—"Miss Pamela" of the GTOs—was walking down La Cienega on her way to audition for a TV commercial. Jim Morrison, driving a convertible full of his buddies, spotted her and executed a deft U-turn in the middle of afternoon traffic. "He wanted to say good-bye to me," Miss Pamela recalled. "And he was just so *sweet*, so full of life. I hadn't seen him in a long time, and I thought, *Wow—something good is happening for Jim.* Because the truth was that Jim Morrison was a down-and-out figure before he left for France. Everybody thought he was, like, pathetic. We were all used to seeing him in a really bad way.

He was quite a debauched, drunken sot before he moved away, and he'd become almost a sad fixture in Hollywood. It was obvious that the reason he went away was to start afresh, and I could see it was already happening. He had his big beard, but he was slimming down, and looked really good and vibrant; and he was actually smiling. I said, 'Jim! You look great! How are you?'

"He just said, 'I wanted to say good-bye. I'm going to France.'"

JIM DIDN'T PACK MUCH. He took prints of his two films, *Feast of Friends* and *HWY;* as many notebooks as he could find; the typed manuscripts of his unpublished poetry; the two quarter-inch tape reels of his solo poetry readings; his Super-8 movie camera; a few copies of his poetry books; his personal photo file (including color transparencies of himself, a recent publicity photo of Joan Baez, pictures from the Miami trial, and selected Elektra eight-by-ten-inch promotional glossies of himself); and a few precious books and clothes. He left his library and some files in Pam's apartment, and told the Doors' accountant to pay the rent while they were gone. Judy Courson took the dog.

Jim kept postponing his departure. He helped a girlfriend through an abortion after she had refused his request to have the child. He played touch football with friends. The weekend before he left, Jim and Babe Hill took a cabin cruiser the Doors had bought, a few grams of cocaine, and a couple of girls out to Catalina Island for a weekend of alcoholic fun. After a rough crossing, they got a hotel room overlooking Avalon Bay and enjoyed an enormous, beery breakfast at the local hash house, Big Mike's.

During his last days in L.A., Jim saw Tom Baker for the first time in almost a year. He kept Babe Hill by his side constantly. They went to see a closed-circuit broadcast of the Ali-Frazier fight from New York on March 8. They got into their own fight with some greasers over the pool table at the Palms. They walked along Venice Beach, and went to the Santa Monica Pier for lunch. That night Pamela called from France and told Jim she'd found a cool place for them to live. The next morning Jim announced to his friends that he was definitely leaving that night for Paris. He didn't see the other Doors again. Ray said later they were surprised to hear that Jim had actually gone.

Babe brought Jim to the airport. Waiting for the Air France flight, they settled into a cocktail lounge, with well-wishers Frank and Kathy Lisciandro, and Alain Ronay, and began ordering drinks. The conversation was animated. Jim talked about a dream of buying an old church in the south of France and turning it into a place to live and write. By the time the third round was consumed, Jim had missed his flight. Babe had to bring him back the next evening and put him on the plane. In those days before computer networks, no one noticed that Jim Morrison was skipping the country illegally, against his bail restrictions, with a six-month jail term (and warnings of violence) hanging over him. France was already a safe haven for hundreds of young Americans avoiding the Vietnam-era draft, as well as for a few legendary rock stars escaping punitive taxation and puritanical prosecutions for alleged indecency. (A public indecency conviction in America was insufficient to warrant extradition by the French government.) Pamela had been right about one thing. For the first legendary rock star to quit and walk away from it all, Paris was the logical place to begin a new career in poetry and film.

Jim Morrison arrived at Orly Airport early on the morning of June 12, 1971. He took a taxi to the Hôtel George V, and was shown to Pamela's room. No one answered the knock. When Jim was let in by the porter, the room was empty and cold, as if no one had been living there for some time. Jim went across the street to the Bar Alexandre, ordered a double whiskey, and waited for Pamela to return.

CITY OF LIGHT

S HE WAS KNOWN among a certain louche element of the Parisian *jeunesse dorée* as "Pamela Morrison," wife of the famous American rock star. With her cool California beauty, fashion-forward wardrobe, long straight hair, paid-up credit cards, and ready laugh, Pamela was now a familiar figure in upscale Saint Germain hangouts like Café de Flore, Les Deux Magots, and Brasserie Lipp as a companion of the young, well-connected Count Jean de Breteuil. Her acquaintances included young models and actors, a few diplomats, and café habitués such as *les minets* (gay fashion kids) and *les michetons* (handsome young men, impeccably dressed and groomed, who hung around le Drugstore and were employed as gigolos by fashionable but lonely women of the quarter). Through Jean, Pamela had become friends with the gamine model and starlet Elizabeth Larivière, known professionally as "Zozo." Zozo lived in a large apartment on the Right Bank, and when Pam learned Zozo had a job coming up in the south, she arranged for Jim to rent the flat while Zozo was away that spring.

Sometime in the middle of March 1971, Jim moved into the second-largest bedroom of a fourth-floor apartment in a handsome nineteenth-century Beaux Arts building at 17, rue Beautrellis in the Fourth Arrondisement. The large, slightly shabby flat was furnished with the typically overstuffed antiques of the bourgeoisie. There were elegant marble fireplaces, parquet floors, plaster reliefs on the walls, and the ceiling of the salon was painted with a blue sky and puffy clouds. The leaky bathroom, smelling of old-fashioned French plumbing, had a bidet, a toilet, and a narrow tiled wall tub that was equipped with a handheld shower. (Zozo had padlocked her bedroom while she was away.) Jim's room faced the morning sun, and he moved a leather-covered writing table by the big window. As the day progressed, he would move the table to the other side of the flat, so he could sit in the sun as it warmed the courtyard in the rear of the building. A concert pianist lived across the courtyard, and the sound of her daily exercises seemed to please Jim. On the apartment's lobby mailbox, he taped a handwritten label for the postman: "James Douglas."

Judging from entries in surviving notebooks, Jim began to explore Paris immediately. He visited his friend Agnès Varda at her apartment at 84, rue Daguerre. Jim played with her daughter, Rosalie, a bit. Mostly he just sat with Agnès and a few friends in her garden. Varda later told German journalist Rainer Moddermann: "[Jim] didn't say a superfluous word. He didn't like gossip. We used to meet relatively often, but I cannot say we ever talked much. We respected him. His greatest wish when he came to Paris was to remain here, incognito, as someone who just wanted to write his poems." Jim also told Varda that he had both his films with him, and that he wanted to set up some screenings for them in Paris. Varda told Jim this might take some time in the present (anti-American) political climate, but that she would see what she could do. Pamela later told Jim that she didn't like Varda. Jim replied that if anything ever went wrong, Varda would be the only person in Paris that Pamela could completely trust.

A T FIRST Jim made notes on his wanderings through the Marais, the old quarter in which he lived. During the Renaissance it had been the most elegant part of Paris, but had since become a funky and bohemian neighborhood dotted by stupendous landmarks of its past grandeur. Jim was drawn to the busy cafés around the place de la Bastille. He and Pamela toured Les Halles, the teeming (and now vanished) food and produce markets. There was a large Jewish population along the rue des Rosiers, cool shops on the rue des Franc-Bourgeois, and many vibrant dive bars catering to gay men and lesbians in the medieval streets off the rue Saint-Antoine.

A Parisian friend of Pamela's, Victor Lamy, who sometimes walked with Jim, recalls that he would emerge from his building in the early afternoon and walk to the boulevard to buy the International *Herald Tribune*. Then he liked to walk back up rue Beautrellis, past the repertory Théâtre Espace Marais (where Beaumarchais's *Le Mariage de Figaro* was playing), and continue past the large and cheerful elementary school, l'École Massillon, until he reached the Seine. His favorite route took Jim across the Pont Marie and along the Île Saint-Louis, the exclusive island in the middle of the river. Spring had arrived early in Paris that year, and on sunny days Jim would often sit at one of the outside tables of the brasserie at the head of rue Saint-Louis-en-l'île and drink a beer or two, either Stella Artois or Kronenburg. Refreshed, Jim pressed on across the footbridge to the Île de la Cité, where he sometimes paused to light a candle in one of the quiet chapels of Notre-Dame Cathedral.

Victor Lamy remembers that Jim was very attentive to the street musicians. There was music everywhere in Paris: American kids strumming guitars in the place Saint-Michel, European kids bowing violins, English and Irish buskers, gypsies playing accordions in the metro. "Jim usually emptied his pockets for these scruffy musicians," Lamy said. "He stopped to listen to almost every one he saw, and he gave each one a few francs, or a large roll of bills if that was all he had with him. Another thing was that he wasn't recognized. He had this freedom, a different thing for him. He wore a suede jacket, a nice dress shirt, corduroy trousers. He looked like any twenty-seven-year-old American postgraduate student at the Sorbonne."

Jim then crossed to the Left Bank. Sometimes he kept walking along the river, browsing in the bookstalls; other times he wandered through the Sorbonne, the University of Paris, and paused amid the many bookshops. Paris was still in the grip of the revolutionary events of 1968, and Jim often stopped to watch (with total fascination) student demonstrations turn into miniriots in the streets. (The government was paving over much of the Latin Quarter because the demonstrators of '68 had ripped up the city's classic old cobblestones and thrown them at the riot police. In 1971 Jim Morrison saw the last of the old Paris streets before they were lost forever.) Sometimes Jim stopped for a drink at Pamela's hangout, the Café de Flore, erstwhile haunt of existentialist heroes Sartre and de Beauvoir, and sometimes at the Deux Magots, where Hemingway and Scott Fitzgerald contemplated the façade of Saint Germain-des-Prés, the oldest church in Paris. Jim always had a spiral notebook or a bound journal with him, and often seemed lost in their pages. (Several times that spring, Jim was recognized and photographed—once smoking a cigar—by young American tourists.) Jim then usually recrossed the Seine on the Pont des Arts, caught the #1 metro at the Louvre, got out at the Saint Paul station and walked home along the rue Saint-Antoine, sometimes stopping for a bottle of whiskey, a bag of fresh strawberries, or a ten-cent fresh baguette.

When the weather was fine and he didn't feel like walking, Jim often hung out in the exquisite place des Vosges, two blocks from his room. This seventeenth-century square of red-brick mansions was usually full of children and their nursemaids, and Jim liked to sit for hours and write, or just watch the children playing in the sandboxes. It was one of the most historic places in France: the site of medieval jousts, royal palaces, and Renaissance military parades. Victor Hugo's house was in one corner of the square at No. 6; No. 8 had been the home of Théophile Gautier, who had written *The Poem of Hashish*. When Jim woke up (or came to), he often had coffee and croissants on the terrace of Ma Bourgogne, the Alsatian restaurant on the northwest corner of the square. He told many of the people he met that spring, including Philip Dalecky, that the place des Vosges was his favorite spot in Paris.

P HILIP DALECKY WAS ZOZO'S BOYFRIEND. He was tall, sympathetic, about twenty. He spoke good English, played guitar, and was recovering from a near-fatal motorcycle crash. Jim took a liking to him immediately. When Zozo was in Paris, Philip and Jim hung out together at No.17. "He was very, very quiet, and so you wanted to be quiet around him," Philip says. "You almost had the feeling like he was recovering from something, trying to get his strength again. His mannerisms, his way of walking, were very slow—almost effeminate in a way. I didn't really know who he was, so it was very relaxed between us. We went out a few times with the girls to restaurants in the quarter, or to a bar in the Marais or Les Halles. Jim and Pamela did not speak French, and both were shy in public, so they sort of stuck close together. But there was always a good feeling between us, and I really liked him a lot."

One day Philip and Zozo came by the apartment to drop off her luxurious fur coat in the closet of her locked bedroom. They found the atmosphere very tense, as if Jim and Pam had been arguing. Zozo and Pam spoke for a few moments while Philip sat with Jim.

On the way downstairs, Zozo whispered, "Pamela just came in from a fuck with a *micheton*." Philip asked how she knew. "She told me—girl to girl."

O NE AFTERNOON in early April Jim was drinking on the terrace of l'Astroquet, a bistro on the boulevard Saint Germain. He heard some American voices at the next table and started a conversation. Jim said he had language difficulties in Paris, and the isolation of this was beginning to get to him. It was nice to hear some familiar voices. The Americans turned out to be members of Clinic, an American band trying to get a break in Europe. The leader, Phil Trainer, finally asked if he was Jim Morrison. Jim nodded yes. They said they hadn't known Jim was in Paris. "Nobody knows," Jim said. Out came the guitars, and they jammed on blues songs for an hour or so. Jim was chain-smoking Marlboros and was coughing and spitting constantly. They all ended up drinking wine and whiskey at the apartment of someone Pamela knew.

Jim smoked heavily, kept coughing, and got so loaded they had to put him in a taxi. It took five minutes for Jim to remember the address.

Jim had cut down on alcohol when he first arrived in France, but after a month he started again, and the heavy, compulsive smoking began to take its toll. When Jim coughed up blood in April, Pamela took him to see a doctor at the American Hospital in Neuilly. A physical exam and a lung X-ray turned up nothing obvious, and Jim was told to get some rest in a warm climate, if possible.

Jim and Pamela thought of the Côte d'Azur, where the Rolling Stones had just established themselves in their tax-related exile. But Jim wanted to see Spain and more of Morocco, so they left Paris in a rented car on April 10 and headed south into the lush and wet European spring.

THE LAND OF THE MOORS

JIM MORRISON DROVE their rented Peugeot sedan at a relaxed pace southward toward Lyon, and then headed for Spain. They picked up a few girl hitchhikers as they drove through southwest France, stopping for a night in Toulouse. The gray weather turned to sunshine after they crossed the Pyrenees and progressed through Catalonia. They both used the Super-8 movie camera, and a sequence shot in Madrid's Prado museum shows Jim staring impassively at Hieronymus Bosch's immense "The Garden of Earthly Delights," which Jim had written about in college, with hundreds of damned figures seething in various degrees of torment. Jim sat in front of the painting for an hour, completely transfixed. They then drove on to Andalusia, a pilgrimage Jim had wanted to make for years. In Grenada, they visited the Alhambra, the great Moorish palace whose gardens, architecture, and vistas were one of the wonders of the world. Jim was so taken with the poetry of the site that he insisted on visiting for several days in a row. Pamela shot film of him sitting by the great fountain guarded by stone lions. Jim stood up, a beatific smile on his features, and walked toward the camera with his arms stretched wide, until only one Morrison eye filled the last frame of the sequence.

They abandoned their car when they learned their insurance was no good once they crossed the Strait of Gibraltar. In Tangier they stayed both at the Hotel Minzeh and at the palatial home of Paul and Talitha Getty. Paul was the eldest son of the founder of Getty Oil. Talitha was a lovely Dutch actress. She was a good friend of Jean de Breteuil, and one of his clients as well, sharing her husband's taste for heroin. (Talitha Getty would die of a heroin overdose in Rome later that year.) While shopping in the European section of the old port town, Jim bought a copy of Paul Bowles's novel *The Sheltering Sky* at the Librarie des Colonnes on the Avenue Pasteur.

Jim and Pamela flew on to Marrakech, the ancient, red-walled desert caravan terminus, where the Comtesse de Breteuil, Jean's mother and the grande dame of expatriate society, lived in splendor at the Villa Taylor, one of the great estates in the old palm oasis outside the tumult of the old city. Jean was then living in Keith Richards's London house, but Madame de Breteuil had already met Pamela, and warmly received her and her "husband." They were given the top floor bedroom of the villa's tower, with surrounding views of the snowcapped peaks of the Atlas Mountains. The countess told them that Winston Churchill had often stayed there when he came to Marrakech to paint after the war.

One of the servants functioned as their guide, and they spent days exploring the souks of the ancient medina. Jim loved the warren of sandy streets, dark alleys, and mud walls. The women were veiled, and the men wore djellabas with pointed hoods that gave them privacy. The sounds and smells were those of Africa, Jim noted in a journal (that he left behind). In the evenings they often ate in the savory, open-air restaurants of the Djemaa el Fna, the "Square of the Dead." This was where the old salt caravans had stopped after crossing the Sahara, and it now served as a bus terminal and market. After dinner, they watched teams of acrobats and various bands of traditional musicians who competed for coins. Jim listened intently to the professional storytellers, who drew huge crowds of country folk with their shouted tales of magicians and djinns. Surviving Super-8 footage shows Jim and Pamela in a horse-drawn carriage in the evening, being driven out to the Menara oasis as the sun set over the mountains.

Jim wanted to swim in the hot desert air, so they moved to the Hôtel Marrakech, which had a pool. One afternoon Pamela came down to the pool, wearing a new white silk djellaba she had bought in the souk. She saw a cool-looking guy whom she thought she knew, talking to a couple of girls. Drawing closer, she saw it was Jim. He had shaved off his beard during the night. His hair was brushed back. He looked like himself again. Later, she told friends in California that at that shining moment, she immediately fell in love with Jim all over again.

T HEIR TRIP LASTED around three weeks. On May 3, 1971, Jim and Pam flew from Marrakech to Casablanca, and then on to Paris. When they got to their apartment, Zozo and some friends were in temporary residence, so Jim and Pam checked into l'Hôtel, an exclusive small hotel in the rue des Beaux-Arts. L'Hôtel was famous for its discretion, and many celebrities felt comfortable there. It was also famous because Oscar Wilde had died in one of its rooms. (His famous last words: "Either that wallpaper goes, or I do.")

Pamela had a huge problem now, because Count de Breteuil was in London and she wanted heroin. Jim told a friend of Zozo's that he didn't want Pam scoring on the street, and anyway, he supposedly said, "Scoring is a man's job." Around that time, a *Paris-Match* photographer saw a friend sitting with Jim at the Café de Flore and said hello. A few minutes later, the friend came over to his table, explained that Jim Morrison wanted some heroin, and did he know where they could find some?

The upscale, junk-using denizens of Paris usually ended up at the Rock and Roll Circus, very late at night. The Circus was a big discotheque on the rue de Seine, modeled on the American electric ballrooms of the sixties. The walls were decorated with large murals of English rock stars (and Jimi Hendrix) dressed as clowns. The club was famous for Led Zeppelin having jammed there two years earlier, but now had a somewhat sleazy reputation for the drug and sexual commerce in the dark downstairs bathrooms. Yet it was often packed with *le jet-set* and French movie stars, and the new Chinese heroin ("China White") was sold openly in the club's dark corners. One prominent notebook entry of Jim's was published by his literary executors after his death: "The Chinese junkies will get you in the end."

If Jim was getting heroin for Pamela, he was not to be outdone in the self-destruction sweepstakes. He was drinking heavily to match her heroin stupor, and began to act out while they were still living at l'Hôtel. One rainy morning at dawn, he opened the tall window of their second-floor room to let in some air, and then stood up on the iron railing just outside. As Pam looked on, Jim either jumped, or lost his balance and fell out the window. There was a loud thump. Pamela ran to the window and saw Jim sprawled on the roof of a parked car. When she got to the street, he was already wiping the muck off his suede jacket. She tried to get him to come up to bed so she could call a doctor, but Jim said he'd see her later and ran off to look for a drink.

They were at l'Hôtel for a couple of weeks, and then moved back to the rue Beautrellis. Alain Ronay, Jim's old friend from UCLA, arrived in Paris sometime in May and started hanging out. Ronay spoke the language and could get things done. He helped Jim carry firewood up the four flights from the lobby, because Jim thought the building's heat was inadequate and said he was cold unless he sat by the fire. Pamela was stoned and in a trance most of the time. Jim seemed angry and frustrated that she wasn't really living with him, and was quite content with her own independent life and friends. As the days got warmer, Jim walked to the Place des Vosges almost every afternoon, sat in the dark shade of the plane trees near the sandbox, and wrote in his spiral notebooks. One day he opened the *Herald-Tribune* and read the obituary of Warhol's ex-muse Edie Sedgwick, who had died in California of an overdose of barbiturates.

AN AMERICAN IN PARIS

IN MAY 1971, Gilles Yéprémian was an eighteen-year-old rock music fan who occasionally hung out with his friends at the Rock and Roll Circus in hopes of seeing some of his heroes. One late night (May 8, 1971), he was checking out the original French rock star, Johnny Hallyday, as Johnny and his entourage got increasingly rowdy in the club's restaurant. As Johnny got louder and more annoying, the club's tough bouncers started hovering nearby. Suddenly Gilles saw what he describes as "a shadow" leaping over his left shoulder. This turned out to be Jim Morrison, who was electing to leave the crowded club by tramping over the tables and across the laps of the other customers.

Drinks were knocked over in the dark. Candles were upset. People were shouting.

"They had wanted to throw Hallyday out of the Rock and Roll Circus," Gilles recalls, "but they couldn't, because this guy was a national icon. It was much easier to throw Jim out instead, because they had no idea who he was. He looked like an American student passing through Europe in an old green army jacket, blue jeans, and boots."

The bouncers tossed an extremely drunk Jim into the club's outdoor vestibule. Gilles Yéprémian had recognized Jim, and followed them outside. Jim tried to get back in, but a bouncer barred his way and Jim fell down. Jim began bothering other customers as they tried to step over him. Jim then started kicking the glass doors with his boots, and it looked like the bouncers were going to sort him out. Yéprémian had the good sense to intervene.

"I asked him: 'Jim? Are you Jim?' And he looked away and said, 'Yeeeah.' I said, 'OK, OK, let's go. Come with me.' " Gilles got Jim upright, and dragged him to a taxi idling outside on the rue de Seine.

Gilles asked Jim where he wanted to go, but Jim had passed out. The only place Gilles could think to stash a comatose American rock star was the flat of his friend Hervé Muller, a well-known Parisian rock critic who was also France's premier Dylanologist. Gilles gave the driver Hervé's address—#6, place Tristan-Bernard—and the taxi set off. As the sun was about to rise over Paris, Jim woke up while they were crossing the pont de la Concorde over the Seine. "Stop the car," Jim shouted, and jumped out. Gilles paid the driver and asked him to wait. Jim hopped onto the parapet of the bridge, began shouting, and Gilles was afraid he was going to jump into the river. This also attracted the attention of two patrolling Paris cops, who stopped to see what was going on. *"Jim,"* Gilles whispered. *"Take care. Police are coming."*

"Fuck the pigs!" Jim roared. Gilles got Jim back into the taxi, but the driver was hesitant until Jim threw a huge wad of francs into the front seat. The driver became even more nervous, and gave back the money.

When they arrived at Hervé's building, Jim was shouting again. Begging him to be quiet—it was five in the morning—Gilles started helping Jim up the six flights of stairs to Muller's flat. This took forty minutes. Halfway up, as Gilles was prodding him along like a mountain guide,

Jim turned to Gilles and stage-whispered, "Shhhh. Everyone's *asleep,* damn it."

Finally, they knocked at the door. Inside the young writer was asleep with his girlfriend, Yvonne Fuqua, who eventually opened the door a crack. (A Belgian chick, a houseguest, thought the knock was a police bust and was busy throwing her stash out a rear window.) Muller, who wrote for the main French music magazine *Rock et Folk,* was incredulous. Gilles: "I said to Hervé, 'It's me, and I have *Jim Morrison* with me.' Hervé answered, 'Fuck off, Gilles, *it's six in the morning!*'" But he opened the door, and Jim—really gone now—brushed past Hervé until he reached the bedroom. Jim collapsed on Hervé's bed and immediately passed out. They tried moving him, but this proved impossible.

Hervé and Yvonne spent the rest of the morning in sleeping bags in the living room. When Jim finally woke up that afternoon, he washed and got dressed, walked into the main room, and asked Hervé Muller: "Where am I?" Muller explained the situation. Jim shrugged, asked to borrow a hairbrush, and invited Hervé and Yvonne to breakfast at the Bar Alexandre. The food was superb, and Jim was in a good mood, discussing films and poetry and gently improving Hervé's command of California idiom. He talked about Pamela, saying they were just back from Morocco. He ordered a bottle of cognac, drank most of it out of his water glass, and soon got hellacious, bothering respectable people at nearby tables and throwing food. (They normally didn't let hippies into the restaurant, but since Jim was already known for leaving obscenely large cash tips, the bistro's staff left them alone.) Hervé, not one to lose an opportunity, was taking photographs of the whole scene. After two hours, Jim staggered over to his favorite bench in front of the Alexandre and passed out. When they tried to revive him, Jim came to and started yelling: "Where do you want me to go? I don't want you to take me there! *No! No!*" He seemed delirious and tried to stagger away.

With difficulty, they got Jim back to Hervé's apartment. Jim was agitated now, wouldn't leave the stairwell, and was screaming so loudly that the elderly concierge called the police. When the cops arrived, Jim had passed out and all was quiet. He slept until late the next day.

Hervé Muller drove Jim home. Pamela was waiting in the flat, and Hervé wondered if she would be angry that Jim had disappeared for two nights. "Oh," she simply said when Jim had introduced Hervé. "He's been with you, then."

The next day, sensing an international scoop, Hervé tried to conduct a mini-interview with this American rock star who was hiding out in Paris. Jim refused to discuss the Doors, and only would say that he was looking for a venue to show the films he had with him, *HWY* and *Feast of Friends*. Jim mentioned wanting to buy an old church, somewhere in France, to use as a house and a writing studio. He told Hervé that he hadn't seen the Doors in a while, but he thought that, for sure, the band would try to continue on without him. That was all Jim would say about his late career.

I N LATE MAY 1971, Jim moved back into 17, rue Beautrellis. He invited Alain Ronay to use the other bedroom for a few weeks because he was lonely and wanted company. The Doors' office had mailed him an acetate copy of *L.A. Woman,* and Jim listened to it repeatedly. John Densmore claimed that Jim called him from Paris, a few weeks later, to ask how the album was doing and to inquire about the first single, "Love Her Madly." Ray Manzarek said that in fact the anxious drummer had called Jim, because the Doors were getting, and turning down, increasingly lucrative tour offers, since no one yet knew Jim had split. Densmore claimed that Jim told him he would return eventually, and the Doors would tour the *L.A. Woman* songs. (Cynics also point out that John Densmore was probably the last person Jim Morrison would have called from Paris.)

Gilles Yéprémian said that when Jim got the Doors' record, he did muse out loud about rejoining the band. But from the way he said it, Gilles could tell Jim didn't mean it.

Bill Siddons said he talked with Jim on three separate occasions. He said that Jim always seemed in good shape and sounded happy. Siddons told writer Patricia Butler: "We talked to him about coming back, and all we ever got was 'Ahhh, no plans! I'm having a great time. Maybe someday we'll do another record, but—no plans!'"

Jim was also in touch with accountant Bob Greene when his money ran low. He sent touristic postcards ("the women are great & the food is gorgeous") to the office, and wrote letters to Michael McClure and a girlfriend in San Diego. He and Pamela took a day trip to the château de Courson, an old country mansion southwest of Paris famous for its gardens.

Sometime during these days, Jim wrote the two drafts of "As I Look Back," a nostalgic poem that would remain unpublished for twenty years. Ronay later remembered that in Paris Jim often spoke about his parents with affection, telling funny stories about his family. Before he had left Los Angeles, Jim had heard through old navy family channels that his mother was concerned for his health. In Paris, according to Ronay, Jim asked Pamela to call his parents in Washington to assure his mother that reports of his poor health were exaggerated.

O NE DAY JIM AND PAMELA came to lunch at Hervé's flat with Jim's new friends: Hervé and Yvonne, Gilles Yéprémian, and another music journalist, Henri-Jean Hénu. Pamela was mistrustful and didn't speak, preferring to hide behind Jim's shoulder. They opened a bottle of Corsican wine, but Jim hardly touched his. Hervé was surprised Jim didn't get drunk. Instead he thanked Hervé for helping him when he was drunk, and gave Muller a signed copy of his privately printed *An American Prayer*.

Gilles: "Jim was very friendly, but it wasn't possible to discuss the Doors with him. If we mentioned the music, he just turned off completely." Hervé says that Jim did say he felt too old to be a rock star at the age of twenty-seven. Jim mentioned that they were planning to drive to Switzerland, but Yvonne suggested they go to Corsica instead, because the wine they were drinking was so delicious and the weather would be warm. Pamela turned and asked, "Oh, Jim, can we go there?" He laughed and said, "Sure, babe. We'll go next week."

After the meal, they sat down to listen to music. Jim was shown Hervé's vast record collection and asked to choose. Gilles said that for the rest of the afternoon, Jim spun all of Hervé's Buffy Sainte-Marie albums.

On May 18, Jim and Pam flew to Marseilles, on their way to Corsica. At the airport Jim's shoulder bag was stolen. Gone were his wallet, passport, plane tickets, and several notebooks. They flew back to Paris, where Jim got new papers, then on to Corsica, where it rained for ten days and they were bored. Film footage from this trip features Jim and Pam wandering unhappily through a gloomy graveyard under lowering, ominous skies.

One long evening early in June, Jim and Alain Ronay were standing on the top step of the long staircase leading up to Sacré-Coeur, the great white church at the summit of Montmartre in northern Paris. A band of black African musicians was banging away, and Jim stopped to listen awhile. Gazing off to the east, Jim asked Ronay about the large green hill he could see, all the way across the city. Ronay explained that it was Père Lachaise, Paris's great cemetery. It dated from Napoleon's time, and was where honored citizens like Chopin, Balzac, and Edith Piaf were buried. Jim insisted they visit immediately, but their taxi took an hour to fight through heavy traffic, and the gates were shut by the time they arrived.

Jim and Alain returned to the cemetery a few days later. They walked among the impressive monuments of the great artists and the florid nineteenth-century tombs of the stolid bourgeoisie. When Ronay said he found the place a morbid experience, Jim protested that he liked the cemetery's spooky tranquility in the midst of the city, and that he definitely wanted to be buried in Père Lachaise when he died.

NO ONE COULD SAVE THEM

T HROUGHOUT JUNE 1971, Jim Morrison carried a white plastic shopping bag from the Samaritaine department store with him whenever he went out. There were usually one or two spiral notebooks inside, plus a file of Jim's personal photographs, the quarter-inch tape reel of his 1970 birthday poetry reading, a pack of Marlboro cigarettes, a Bic lighter, two or three ballpoint pens, a photocopy of an interview with Jean-Luc Godard ("Film and Revolution" by Kent Carroll) that had been published in *Evergreen Review,* and an article about the Doors ("Morrison Hotel Revisited") torn from *Jazz & Pop.* One of the notebooks was titled "Tape Noon." It was filled with death-haunted poems, prayers, obscenities, a version of "American Night," and phrases about the street riots he saw in Paris. One of the final pages bore a single, seemingly desperate line: *"Last words, last words—out."* Jim Morrison obviously sensed that his time was nearing its end.

Early in the month, Jim and Pamela flew to London for a few days. They had been happy there once, back in 1968, and now perhaps sought to recapture some of the romance of that time. Alain Ronay was already in London, and reserved a room for them at the Cadogan Hotel, near Sloane Square. Pamela immediately disappeared for a while, probably to Cheyne Walk in nearby Chelsea, where Jean de Breteuil was living in Keith Richards's riverside mansion, doling out heroin to former pop star Marianne Faithfull, who had abandoned her career (and boyfriend Mick Jagger) for the life of a full-time addict.

Marianne later wrote in her memoirs: "Jean was a horrible guy, someone who had crawled out from under a stone. I met him at Talitha Getty's house. He was her lover, and somehow I ended up with him. What I liked about him was that he had one yellow eye and one green eye—and a lot of dope. It was all about drugs and sex. He was very French and very social. He was only with me because I'd been with Mick Jagger. In that froggy way, he was obsessed with all that.

"I went back to London with him, to Keith Richards's house. Keith and Anita [Pallenberg] were in the south of France. Jean had shown up there with a lot of that pink smack, so they were happy to see him. It was 'Listen, man, when you're in London, stay in Cheyne Walk.' I lived there with him for a few months."

Jim was more fatalistic about Pamela's habit now. It even seemed to Ronay that Jim preferred Pamela when she was doped up. She was easier to deal with when stoned, and Jim made it clear he didn't care that much anymore. Ronay says that Jim told him: "There's only two choices you can make, man. We've each made our own. I'm on the side of life. She's on the side of death. We can't do anything for her . . . so just don't worry about it. You know what I mean?"

One night in London, as they were riding down the Kings Road in a black cab, Ronay told Jim that Oscar Wilde had been arrested for the crime of sodomy at the Cadogan Hotel, and later had died at l'Hôtel in Paris. "You better watch out that you don't follow too closely in his footsteps," Ronay teased. "You might end up like Oscar."

Jim didn't laugh, and turned away as if he'd been hurt. Ronay felt like an idiot.

Jim also had a terrible spasm of coughing in London. He coughed for more than three hours, bringing up dangerous-looking pink sputum. He passed out (possibly after a snort of heroin) and had trouble breathing for more than an hour. Pamela, herself narcotized, asked the hotel for the name of a doctor, but it isn't known with any certainty whether Jim was examined while he was in London.

Back in Paris a few days later, unable to concentrate on his writing, Jim again went to see a doctor at the American Hospital. Jim was now heavier than on his previous visit because he was drinking and eating more than usual. He told the doctor about the fall from l'Hôtel, and said it had aggravated an old leg injury, which was again very painful. Again, Jim was told to stop smoking, cut down on alcohol, and (according to hospital records) was prescribed an antispasmodic medication to curtail the coughing spells. These pills often left him groggy and unable to write. An entire page of one of Jim's Paris notebooks, which possibly dates from this month, was filled with the tortured, repeated scrawl: *God help me.*

AROUND THIS TIME, Jim hired a young Canadian girl named Robin Wertle as his secretary. She was fluent in French, and tried to get her new boss organized. Robin arranged all his typed poetry into new files, and bought an expensive leather case to house them. She hired a Portuguese woman to clean the flat. She made the dinner reservations and did currency transactions. She and Jim went out and bought an Olivetti typewriter, and Jim began to dictate his business letters to her. He was being offered movie roles of varying degrees of interest, and also answered a couple of fan letters that had found their way to "James Douglas."

Sometimes Pamela's Parisian friends came over to visit and sniff heroin with her. Jim disliked them and would retreat to a far corner of the big apartment with Ronay, who was ten years older and contemptuous of these rich, overdressed young addicts. When Jim objected to the company she kept, Pam threatened to stuff the apartment with "cotton candy," the fluffy pink Chinese heroin that Jean de Breteuil was getting from the so-called French Connection in Marseilles. It was a higher order of dope, much stronger than most of the young heroin users were accustomed to, and subsequently there were unusually large numbers of fatal overdoses in France that year. One day, Jim blithely told Ronay to pay no attention if Pamela threatened to kill herself.

Another of Jim's notebooks was headed *Paris Journal.* It was one long poem filled with remorse and anger—a stunningly bitter epic that evoked carnal desire *("eating pussy til the mind runs clean"),* the Beat poets, heroin *("I hope the Chinese junkies get you"),* and the omnipresent specter of the homicidal hitchhiker. Paris landmarks like "the candle-forests of Notre Dame" were sketched in elegiac washes of color. The pages of these notebooks almost smelled of drugs. One page contained a single sentence: *The poppy rules the world.* On the last page, Jim drew his personal totem—the hitcher waiting, beside an empty highway. (Both the *Tape Noon* and *Paris Journal* notebooks made it back to California with Pamela. Sections of these texts would be published by Jim's executors in 1990.)

O N JUNE 11, Jim went to see a play. Hervé Muller had gotten press tickets for American director Robert Wilson's *Le Regard du Sourd* ("Deafman Glance") at the Théâtre de la Musique. Pamela didn't want to go, so Alain Ronay used her ticket. It was a colorful avant-garde production performed in French, enlivened by Wilson's bold staging that combined elements of architecture and painting. (Wilson later famously collaborated with composer Philip Glass on the opera *Einstein on the Beach.*) But the pacing was very slow, and Jim became bored and thirsty, and wanted to leave after the first act. Ronay persuaded Jim to stay, and later Jim seemed fascinated by the final tableau of naked actors, pretending to be dead, surrounding the assassinated revolutionary Marat, who had been stabbed to death while lying in his bath. After the play they went to a café for drinks. Jim thanked Hervé Muller for the evening. It was the last time Hervé saw Jim Morrison.

THE LAST BRIGHT MIDNIGHT

ONE DAY AROUND JUNE 15, Jim Morrison went out walking. It was high summer in Paris and everything was green, but there was also a brisk northern chill in the air. He crossed over to the île Saint-Louis, then made his way to the quai d'Anjou. He stopped at the house marked No. 17 and sat on the parapet overlooking the river, making a note about Charles Baudelaire, who had once lived in a garret at the top of the house. Then Jim crossed to the Left Bank and made his way to the Odéon, where he bought a paper. Nearby was a cheap, second-floor recording studio that he'd come across on an earlier walk. He went upstairs and hired the studio for an hour so he could listen to his poetry tape, which he was carrying around with him. Lately he had worried that the master tape, still at the Village Recorders in Los Angeles, would be stolen and fall into the hands of bootleggers. The studio engineer played back sections of the tape for Jim, some of them twice. Before he left, Jim said he might want to do some fresh recording, and the owner told Jim he could come back anytime.

Jim walked on to the Café de Flore, where he sometimes found Pamela and her friends. Using the pay phone next to the bar, he phoned Agnès Varda to see if any progress had been made regarding getting *Feast of Friends* and *HWY* screened at the Cinémathèque Française. Varda had no news for Jim, and reminded him that no one in France had heard about these experimental films, now already somewhat dated. Politically (and *everything* was political in 1971 Paris), there was little interest in screening an American rock star's murderous fantasies. The Vietnam War had killed France's always-keen interest in American culture, for the time being.

Jim went out to the Flore's terrace and proceeded to order straight-up whiskeys until he had gotten his alcohol fix. Noticing an annoying racket nearby, he focused on two young American street musicians who were working the cafés for spare change. The guitarist wore a buckskin jacket, and the singer wore a cowboy hat. They were murdering Crosby, Stills, Nash and Young songs, one after the other. Jim, pretty drunk, loved them immediately. After they performed "Marrakech Express" and nobody gave them any money, Jim introduced himself and graciously invited them to have a drink. He told them about the nearby recording studio, and asked if they felt like walking over with him and doing a session. The two guys couldn't believe it.

"Wait, man, hold on. You are shitting us, right? Are you *really* Jim Morrison?" An hour later, they found themselves in the studio. The fifteen-minute tape has survived.

Jim was running real loose. His American accent sounded very stoned and very southern. The studio people were unhappy that he was obviously drunk. They ran a businesslike operation that usually recorded jingles and classical musicians, and told Jim archly that they were very busy and he could have a half hour maximum with the two freaks he had brought along. Jim spent the first five minutes amiably cajoling the two guys, trying to get a sound out of them. The guitar player, a droll hippie troubadour, was only semicompetent, and the mind-blown singer *("I'm cutting a track in Paris with Jim Morrison!")* was hopeless when they handed him a studio guitar. They couldn't even get in tune. Jim mentioned that the bored engineer on the other side of the glass was frowning, and tried to explain: "Um . . . It's because he's not an instrumentalist."

He asked the two hippies what they wanted to do. The guitar player suggested three obscure songs, but Jim had his own plan. He said, "Let's try something. I wrote this one myself"—and launched into an astounding version of "Orange County Suite," the unfinished, unrealized paean to his old lady that had been rejected from at least two Doors albums.

It was a drunken, and mostly ad-libbed, recording. The musicians were incompetent. Yet, listening carefully (to one of the bootleg versions of the tape that have since sold thousands of CDs), one hears the authentic *last* of Jim Morrison, two weeks before he died, as he roars spontaneous verses and imagery about his hardhearted woman, his anguish, and his obsessions, easily deploying a poetic champion's compositional facility for the natural cadence and spontaneous rhyme: *Well, her father has passed over / And her sister is a star / And her mother's smoking diamonds / And she's sleeping in the car.*

But, to the guy in the control booth, the session was a travesty, and when Jim stopped versifying, after nine minutes, the engineer motioned that he wanted to stop the tape. Jim: "OK—but I want to hear it. Can we hear a playback, please?"

Jim gave the two hippies all the money he had on him after he paid for the studio time. The engineer handed him the box of quarter-inch tape. In a shaky scrawl, Jim inked in the name of his ad hoc Left Bank street band: JOMO AND THE SMOOTHIES.

Jim stayed up all night on June 21, the summer solstice. The sky stayed light until almost twelve o'clock, and for hours Jim walked along the quays of the Seine by himself, enjoying his final bright midnight.

O N A WARM SATURDAY evening in late June, Pamela was hanging out at Café de Flore when she ran into her L.A. friend Tere Tereba, an aspiring writer who had helped out in the early days of Themis. Tereba noticed that Pamela was part of "a notorious entourage of Parisian hangers-on" who quickly disappeared to the Flore's upstairs dining room to get away from the noxious tourists on the terrace. Pamela invited Tere to come by rue Beautrellis the next day for tea.

Tere stopped for fresh fruit at one of the abundant open-air shops on the rue Saint-Antoine before going upstairs at 17, rue Beautrellis, which she found "most beautiful and grand." Jim Morrison opened the door to the fourth-floor flat, wearing a buttoned-down shirt, khaki trousers, and desert boots. "He is clean shaven, and, except for the long brown hair framing the soft, childlike face, he could be mistaken for a college senior from Middle America." Tere complemented Jim on the roomy, comfortable apartment. It was a sublet, Jim said. "Can't get anything like this in L.A.," he murmured.

Jim made the tea. He was upbeat, and eager to chat. He loved Paris, he told Tereba. He was writing all the time. He showed her the "Paris Journal" notebook, said it was nearly finished, and almost ready for private publication. When it was time for supper, Tereba suggested they dine at la Coupole, the legendary Montparnesse bistro immortalized (for Americans) by the Lost Generation writers: Ernest Hemingway, Scott Fitzgerald, and Gertrude Stein. In the taxi, Jim said something about how "they threw away the blueprint when they made this city." Tere heard about their trips to Spain, Morocco, and Corsica. Jim mentioned he was going to write something about their time in Marrakech. He said he had felt that while they were in the desert, they had gone back in time.

L A COUPOLE WAS PACKED with Parisians of all stripes. The restaurant's central pillars still bore decorations by Picasso, Modigliani, and Chagall. But the tumult of the diners and the bustle of the waiters reminded Jim of someplace he'd been in another life. "It's really cool here"—Jim smiled—"but I can't help thinking this place reminds me of Ratner's"—the funky dairy restaurant next to the old Fillmore East on New York's Lower East Side.

During the meal, Jim said he was aware that the Doors were rehearsing new material without him. He said he had been offered a costarring role, with actor Robert Mitchum, in a movie version of Mailer's *Why Are We in Vietnam?* but he was turning this down so he could stay in Paris and write. He also mentioned his efforts to get his films shown. And then, to the waiter: "Monsieur—*s'il vous plaît*—some *mousse au chocolat* for the ladies—please?"

They passed through another student demonstration on the ride back to the Marais. The students were singing and chanting slogans. Red-and-blue Viet Cong flags fluttered in the air. The sinister riot cops, in their long black raincoats, formed a defensive line in the street. Jim wanted to watch, but Pamela insisted that the driver proceed. Tere said she was returning to L.A. in a few days. Jim said that he was surprised she wanted to go back. She said he told her: "I won't be back in L.A. until September—at the earliest."

SHE'LL GET OVER IT

T HE LAST NOTEBOOK Jim Morrison worked in is now in a private collection in Paris. He had obviously started the spiral-bound steno pad before he left L.A., since the first entry is *Cahuenga Auto 466-3268.* The first twenty pages of the notebook are full of stanzas and imagery written in Jim's large-lettered handwriting. There are almost no crossouts, as if the notebook represented a confident and finished sequence of poems.

Several pages are variants of older poems, such as "The Ancient

Ones," "Winter Photography," and "The Hitchhiker." Other pages contain only one or two lines, but variations in the writing style indicate they may have been thought over for days. The notebook contains both wonderful new poems and scabrous jottings: *JERK-BAIT SCROTUM, INC* and *Fuck Shit Piss Cunt*. A previously unknown poem, "Impossible Garden," refers to "a beautiful savage like me" and "the most insane whore in Christendom." A new song lyric, "Now You Are in Danger," seems to sum up Jim's Paris idyll: *Let the piper call the tune / March, April, May, June*. The next page contains short lyrics for a blues song: *We're two of a kind / We're two of a kind / You want yours, and I want mine*.

Page 17 contains one line: *She'll get over it*.

The notebook continues in various states of passionate anguish.

Page 18: *What can I say? What can I do? I thought you found my sexual affection stimulating*

Page 19: *UMHM / Glorious sexual cool / I'm finally dead*

Page 20: *In that year we were blessed / By a great visitation of energy*.

This notebook was in Jim's plastic bag, along with two tape boxes, Jim's photo file, and some random papers, when Jim ran into Philip Dalecky in the street. Jim thought he had recorded something interesting in "Orange County Suite," but couldn't listen to the tape reel because he only had a cassette player at home.

Philip Dalecky: "I remember that I was walking along rue de Rivoli when I ran into Jim. We had a drink together in a bar, and he said he needed to make a cassette from a reel-to-reel tape he had in his bag. I said I could help him, and we went over to my place [5, rue Chalgrin] near the place de l'Etoile, about a five-minute walk from the bar. I had a little home studio with a Revox [tape recorder] and a K7 [cassette] deck, so I did the job. We had another drink, then Jim quickly left with the cassette, like he was really excited to listen to it. I went back to the studio and noticed Jim's plastic sack on the floor. I ran to the window, but he was already halfway down the block. I shouted, 'Hey, Jim! You forgot this!' He looked back at me, over his shoulder, and he shouted: 'All right—keep it—see you later—Bye!'"

Philip put the bag in a drawer. The next day he went to Saint Tropez with Zozo, who had a film job. He never saw Jim Morrison again.

* * *

JUNE 28, 1971. Pamela wanted to see some countryside, so with Alain Ronay they made a day trip to the horse races at Chantilly, along the picturesque River Oise north of Paris. The day was gray and cool, and everyone wore sweaters. The changing scenery, which they filmed from the speeding car, looked like real-time Impressionist paintings. They stopped for lunch at the village of Saint-Leu, where Ronay made the last photos of Jim and Pamela as they snuggled over their coffee cups, both sad eyed and exhausted by their competing binges of epic self-destruction. But Jim smiled broadly into Ronay's camera, which followed Jim and Pamela as they shopped in a country flea market for a few minutes.

THE FOLLOWING DAY, Robin Wertle was working with Jim. She was trying to reach someone at the Cinémathèque to discuss Jim's films, which now included a recently received print of Granada TV's agitprop documentary, *The Doors Are Open*. But no one was interested. The Doors had never played in France because the second European tour had been canceled during Jim's trial in Miami. Outside of a few thousand fans of American rock, Jim Morrison was unknown in his palace of exile.

Jim also dictated a letter to the Doors' accountant, Bob Greene, which was typed, undated, by Robin Wertle and mailed on June 28, 1971. In it, Jim was adamant about cutting ties to his former life, saying that "Paris is beautiful in the sun, an exciting town, built for human beings" and asking if it would be possible to "stay here indefinitely." He also asked Greene to send a financial statement and a copy of the Doors' partnership agreement, and informed him that he and Pamela had decided to turn over Themis to Pamela's sister and her husband, so that they could eventually be "completely clear of any involvement." In conclusion he wrote:

> Any luck on the credit cards? We could use them made out to both our names. What's the problem? And if you'd send our

check when you receive this—house bills are catching up. Please send $3,000 [about $25,000 in current money].

> Give our best to all,
> Later,
> Jim.

Nico, Jim's old flame, was also in Paris, staying with friends near the Champs-Elysées, trying to write songs. On that Friday evening, June 29, she was in a taxi that was stopped at a red light near the Opéra, when she saw Jim Morrison walking down the boulevard. Nico was surprised. She'd had no idea Jim was in Paris. She thought Jim looked good, if a little heavy. She was reminded of the furies of their love affair four years earlier. She opened the car window to call to him, but the light turned and the cab shot forward, and the moment was lost.

Alain Ronay moved out of Jim's flat at the end of June because Pamela would be staying at 17, rue Beautrellis for a while. She had been living, off and on, at Jean de Breteuil's Paris flat, but the debauched count had returned from London with Marianne Faithfull in tow, and three was a crowd. Jean and Marianne moved into l'Hôtel, however, and Jean was soon supplying both Marianne and Pamela with Chinese heroin. The count also had a highly desirable test pressing of *Sticky Fingers,* the not-yet-released new Rolling Stones album, which Jim Morrison listened to repeatedly when Pamela borrowed it for a night.

Alain Ronay, who was supposed to return to California in a few days, moved into Agnès Varda's house. (Varda's other houseguest was director Bernardo Bertolucci, with whom she was working on the script of *Last Tango in Paris.*) Ronay unburdened himself to Varda regarding the Morrison/Courson household's dangerous, perhaps fatal, problem with heroin. Varda immediately said that they had to intervene. Identifying Pamela as the source of the problem, she called Jim and arranged for an elite yogic healer to visit 17, rue Beautrellis in an effort to cure Pamela's toxic need for heroin.

Her name was Monique Godard. She was much in demand, and very expensive. She was slim, pretty, stylish, wore a miniskirt, and had a good reputation as a spiritual counselor to some of the most important people in Paris. Ronay had doubts about her supposed powers, but he served as translator in the hope that Monique Godard could somehow save Pamela from herself. At first Pamela wouldn't come out of the bedroom, so Monique spoke with Jim for a while, discussing Nietzsche's views on suicide and other topics related to impending death, which, Godard noticed, seemed to preoccupy Jim. When Pamela finally emerged into the living room, she was floating in a white silk djellaba, repulsively stoned and too far removed from reality to contend with her situation. Monique Godard recoiled from Pamela Courson in instinctive horror, said a concerned farewell to Jim Morrison, thanked Alain Ronay for his help, and fled the apartment.

ACCORDING TO HIGHLY UNRELIABLE ACCOUNTS, something very bad apparently happened to Jim Morrison on one of the last nights in June. Hervé Muller, whose life was later threatened when he conducted his own investigation into Jim's last days, found people in the heroin underworld who swore that Jim had bought some smack from a Chinese dealer called le Chinois, and a local kid, known as Petit Robert, in the basement crapper of the Rock and Roll Circus. They claimed that Jim had snorted a big load in the toilet, passed out, and turned blue. Someone murmured, *"Il est mort."* The people he was with—"two guys"— carried Jim out of the bathroom, through the kitchen the Circus shared with the adjacent Alcazar nightclub, and out the Alcazar's entrance on the rue Mazarine. They bundled Jim into a cab, got him upstairs on the rue Beautrellis, threw him into the bathtub, and split. Somehow, Jim came through it and recovered.

This unverifiable but often-repeated story—that Jim Morrison had OD'd at the Rock and Roll Circus—became part of the local drug lore, and will forever cast doubt on what really happened to Jim two nights later.

THE PASSION OF JIM MORRISON

JULY 1, 1971. Paris was now cool in the mornings, heating up in the afternoon. Jim slept most of the day. He was possibly recovering from his underground adventures on the Rive Gauche. He awoke depressed and in a foul mood. He had tried to work in an old notebook, but nothing came to him. With difficulty he managed to send a telex to Jonathan Dolger, his editor at Simon & Schuster in New York, who had informed Jim that *The Lords and The New Creatures* was being reprinted as a paperback. Jim wanted the old photo of himself on the book's dust jacket replaced by a softer, more recent, less lupine portrait by Edmond Teske.

At about eight o'clock Jim and Pam walked downstairs and began to order their supper at Vin des Pyrenées, the old bistro down the street. Jim was recognized by two German students sitting next to them. Jim wanted to move to another table, but Pamela said the kids were harmless. Bickering, they raised their voices. Jim got up and walked out. Pamela called out that he could go fuck himself. She tossed some hundred-franc notes on the table and stormed out after Jim. The German kids saw them enter No. 17. They had seen Jim in Frankfurt back in '68, and now here he was. They decided to mount a vigil, and it paid off.

Just before midnight, Jim came out. They followed him to another bistro, Le Mazet, on rue Sainte André-des-Arts. Jim sat on the terrace in the warm night air, ordered a *pichet* of red wine and a *croque monsieur,* a top-broiled ham-and-cheese sandwich. Jim stayed for an hour, until he was recognized by a young American Doors fan and induced to pose for a snapshot taken by the waiter.

Alain Ronay noticed immediately that Jim was shaky when he arrived at No. 17 the next afternoon, July 2. The shutters were closed and the flat was dark. A Super-8 film projector was propped on a chair, pointed at a blank wall where a painting had been removed. Jim seemed downhearted and was coughing. Ronay suggested they go for a walk and get something to eat, and then Jim would feel better. As they strolled through the Marais, Jim tried to sound upbeat, but Ronay could tell it was forced. They walked over to the rue des Rosièrs, the center of a district of synagogues and delicatessens. Jim stopped to buy a red cut-glass Star of David pendant on a silver chain for Pamela that had earlier caught his eye in the window of an old jewelry store. Jim was trembling, moving very slowly, and Ronay picked up expressions of anxiety in all of Jim's gestures and remarks while the transaction was completed.

Finally, out on the street, Jim collapsed onto a bench, wracked by hiccuplike spasms in his chest. His breathing was fast and shallow, and he was changing color. Ronay was concerned and wanted to get a taxi to the hospital, but Jim waved him off until the spasms stopped. They decided to eat some lunch at Ma Bourgogne on the place des Vosges, just a few blocks away. Jim ordered a steak and *frites,* and seemed better after two glasses of wine.

Walking on, they visited a shop on the rue Tournelle that stocked rare films in 16-mm versions. Jim wanted to ask about some Fritz Lang titles he was interested in. They also stopped at a cobbler, an Orthodox Jew, who was reworking a pair of new Frye boots that had been shipped from California. Jim had wanted them made a little wider, but they weren't ready yet. Out in the air again, Jim suffered a complete reversal, and was again doubled over by another spasm of hiccups. Saliva poured from his mouth. He immediately turned and headed home. Ronay, appalled and concerned, noticing Jim's agitated emotional state, followed him. There was firewood to be carried upstairs from the courtyard, and Jim grabbed a few splits. He was so winded by the time he reached the fourth floor that he dropped the wood and had to sit on the top step before he could find his key.

Ronay could see that Jim Morrison was frightened. Pamela wasn't around, and Alain was supposed to meet Agnès Varda for an early supper at five-thirty. Jim panicked when Ronay said he had to leave. "Don't go away," Jim begged. Another coughing fit shook his body. He tried to get Ronay to read the cover story in the latest issue of *Newsweek*: "The Heroin Plague: What to Do About It." He said he also wanted Ronay to read the interview with William Burroughs in *Paris Review.* He said he had to send another telex and needed Alain to help with the unfriendly functionaries at the telex office. He seemed desperate not to be left alone.

The telex office was closed when they got there. The workers were on strike. Jim began to hiccup violently in front of one of the cafés in the place de la Bastille. Ronay wanted to duck into the Metro to keep his date with Varda, but Jim asked him again not to go just yet. "Come on, Alain, stay for a short beer with me. Don't leave now, man. Do it for an old friend."

They went into the big tourist café and Ronay asked the waiter to hurry their drinks. A new series of chest spasms rocked Jim, and he closed his eyes, leaned his head back, and tried with all his will to control the hiccups through deep breathing. Ronay immediately had the sensation of looking at a pale, ceramic death mask of Jim Morrison. When Jim finally opened his eyes again, Ronay must have looked alarmed. Jim asked, "What did you just see?"

"Nothing, Jim. Nothing."

Jim called for another round of beers. He asked Ronay to hang out for a while longer, and then join him and Pamela for a movie at nine o'clock. They were going to see *Pursued,* a new Western starring Robert Mitchum. Ronay stood up and said, "Forgive me, but I really have to go." He ran over to the Metro entrance, but turned and looked back to the café. Jim was still sitting there, and he also turned and stared at Ronay for a moment. Ronay, his brain reeling, plunged underground to keep his date with Agnès Varda.

N O ONE STILL ALIVE CAN SAY with complete confidence what took place in the fourth floor, right, apartment at 17, rue Beautrellis on the morning of July 3, 1971. Only two people, Pamela Courson and Jean de Breteuil, were fully party to the tragic death of Jim Morrison, and both died soon after. But it is accurate to say that in the frenzied days immediately following July 3, an improvised, risky, remarkably skillful and cynical cover-up, abetted by determinedly lax procedures by the local authorities, enabled an American rock star's sordid and potentially scandalous heroin overdose, with obvious but messy criminal implications and enormous financial consequences, to be officially decreed a common heart attack by the City of Paris.

Pamela Courson told several versions of her story: one to the police; one to Alain Ronay and Agnès Varda; and others to friends in California over the next three years. Jean de Breteuil blurted out his story in Morocco, where he felt safe, three days after the events. Hervé Muller published findings that indicated Jim had really died in the toilet of the Circus a day or so earlier. Taking all of these sometimes dubious, thinly sourced narratives into account, one can construct a speculative timeline that considers all the variants of the painful, heartbreaking final hours of Jim Morrison's life.

Pamela Courson said they did go to the movie. On a bright and warm summer's night, they walked through the village Saint-Paul, past the crumbling old city wall, down the narrow passage Charlemagne, and found a cab at the Saint-Paul taxi stand. *Pursued* was director Raoul Walsh's attempt to inject a film noir sensibility into the standard Hollywood western format. It was playing, ironically, in an art house near the Pelletier Metro. After the movie, they ate some sweet-and-sour Chinese food at one of the late-night restaurants on the rue Saint-Antoine. Jim washed his food down with several beers. At one o'clock, they called it a night and went back to their flat.

Jim was restless. He was sipping whiskey out of the bottle, possibly in pain from his various injuries and ailments. He sat at his desk with an open notepad, but couldn't focus. Pamela was cutting lines of heroin on a mirror with a credit card. They both began snorting the drug, using rolled-up money. Jim started threading Super-8 films of their travels into the projector. Pamela said they sang together as they watched their dark, jerky, out-of-focus movies of Spain, Morocco, and Corsica on the wall. Jim (according to Pamela in all her narratives) played old Doors records—even "The End"—far into the night. Between reels, they broke for lines of the strong Chinese junk.

If the neighbors can be believed, early that morning Jim Morrison became very upset. Raging, he opened the apartment's door and went into the hall before someone dragged him back in and slammed the door. A year later, the woman who lived directly upstairs told Philip and Zozo that on the night their friend had died, she had been awakened by a disturbance. She had opened her door with the chain on, and had looked out to see "Monsieur Douglas"—naked and screaming on the staircase.

According to Pamela, Jim started coughing again, and had trouble clearing his throat. Pamela eventually told Jim they should go to bed. It was three o'clock on Saturday morning.

Jim asked Pamela for another line, or two, before bed. It was her stuff, bought from Jean, and at home she was the one who doled it out (although she also maintained that Jim had his own stash as well). Jim was still awake when Pamela nodded off in a heroin stupor.

She woke up with a start, maybe an hour later. It was four o'clock and very dark. Jim, lying next to her, was gurgling horribly. It sounded like he was drowning in his own mucus. But she had heard this before, and tried to wake him up. She couldn't rouse him. She slapped his face. Nothing. She hit him hard, again and again, until he began to come to.

An awful scene now ensued. Rousing himself, in obvious pain, Jim staggered to the bathroom. Someone—Pamela couldn't remember who—turned on the water in the tub, and Jim lowered himself in. Pamela went back to bed and passed out again. She awoke, in a cold sweat, to terrible retching sounds. Jim, still in the bath, was now vomiting up chunks of pineapple and vivid clots of blood. Pamela rushed into the kitchen, fetched an orange Le Creuset saucepan, and ran back into the bathroom. Jim vomited some more into the saucepan. When the nausea passed, she flushed the stuff down the toilet. She later said she thought she had to empty and wash out the basin three times. She said that Jim now told her he felt better, and to go back to sleep. Sometime around five o'clock, as the sky was turning light, Pamela Courson, overcome with heroin and fatigue, fell back into bed. As she was drifting off, she thought she heard Jim calling out to her: "Pamela—are you there?"

Perhaps an hour later, Pamela woke up again. Jim hadn't come back to bed. Morning light filtered through the louvers covering the windows. She got up and went to the bathroom. The door was locked from the inside. She shouted at Jim, rattled the heavy door, but there was no response.

At six-thirty on Saturday morning, Pamela called Jean de Breteuil, who was in bed with Marianne Faithfull. Marianne was stoned on Tuinals but remembered when the call came in.

"I got to go, baby," Jean said. "That was Pamela Morrison."

That woke Marianne up. "Jean, listen to me. I've got to meet Jim Morrison."

"Not possible, baby. Not cool right now, OK? *Je t'explique* later. I'm right back."

He was at the flat within half an hour. Pamela, dressed in her white silk djellaba, was out of her mind, and incoherent. The count calmed her down, gently broke a glass pane in the bathroom door, turned the lock, and let himself in.

They found Jim Morrison, dead, still in the bathtub. Blood was still drying under his nose and mouth, as if he had violently hemorrhaged. There were two large and lividly purple bruises on his chest. The bathwater was dark pink, as if Jim bled out until his heart stopped. Pamela later said that he looked relaxed for the first time in months, his head turned slightly to his left, a slight smile on his lips. "He had such a serene expression," Pamela said later. "If it hadn't been for all that blood . . ."

Pamela started slapping Jim, talking to him, freaking out. Then she got halfway into the tub with Jim before the count pulled her away and dragged her out of the bathroom. With cool calculation, amid terror and considerable anguish, Jean told Pamela that he was leaving town. Janis Joplin was one thing. Jim Morrison was another. (The Paris police had already opened a dossier on his drug-dealing activities.) Jean told Pamela that now they all had to get out of Paris as soon as possible. He and Marianne would leave for Morocco that night. Jean told Pamela that if she could get to Morocco, where his family had great influence, he would be able to protect her if any legal questions arose. Jim had no track marks on his body. Autopsies were only performed in France on suspicion of murder. Jean told Pamela that police would soon be in the house and to flush any drugs she had. She could tell the medical examiner that Jim had heart disease. Pamela asked Jean what to do next.

"Call your other friends," the count said. "Get them to help you. I will see you again before I leave. I'm sorry, darling. I love you. Good-bye."

Jean de Breteuil left 17, rue Beautrellis around seven-thirty on Saturday morning. Pamela padded back into the bathroom to talk things over with Jim Morrison, who had died, miserably and alone, about ninety minutes earlier at the age of twenty-seven.

THE SHORT AFTERLIFE OF DOUGLAS MORRISON

NO ONE KNOWS for sure where Count Jean de Breteuil went after he left Pamela alone with Jim Morrison's body soaking in the bathtub. After being gone for several hours, he arrived back at l'Hôtel, Marianne later said, stoned on heroin but in a very agitated state. He woke her, and she asked what had happened. Jean then dragged her out of bed and beat her up. When he had finished, Marianne lit a cigarette.

"Get packed," he growled. "We're going to Morocco. I want you to meet my mother."

"But we just got here."

"Shut up, damn it."

Marianne was getting the picture. They were blowing town, fast. "What happened over there?" she asked.

"I said, *'Shut up!'*"

Marianne now got it. "Oh, *shit,*" she whispered.

"Yeah," Jean said. "It's fucked."

Marianne: "He was scared for his life. Jim Morrison had OD'd, and he had provided the smack. Jean saw himself as dealer to the stars. Now he was just a small time heroin dealer in big trouble. He was very young. Had he lived, he might have turned into a human being."

There is one clue as to the count's movements after he left Pamela. At an all-night disco called La Bulle, on the rue de la Montaigne-Sainte-Geneviève, there was a weird announcement made over the sound system that morning by the American deejay, Cameron Watson. Sometime around eight o'clock, after a word with a couple of dope dealers who had stopped by his booth, and with only a handful of customers left in the club, Watson stopped the music and said: "Jim Morrison died this morning." Then he repeated the news in French.

He was, mysteriously, the first person to announce Jim Morrison's death.

A GNÈS VARDA'S PHONE RANG at about seven-thirty on Saturday morning. Alain Ronay awoke and answered it, but the line was dead. It rang again a few moments later. Monique Godard, the yoga healer, was calling to say that she was leaving Paris that day, but during the night she had the feeling that Ronay's American friend had to see a doctor immediately. She said, "If your friend wants my help, he must see a doctor first. Does he take drugs? Does he have circulatory problems?"

Ronay said he had contacted her to help Pamela, not Jim.

"Her? I would never take her on. *Never!* Listen—your friend must see a doctor immediately. I feel these things. It could even be too late."

Ronay asked Godard if she had called a few minutes earlier; but she said no, again told Ronay to take care of his friend, and hung up.

The phone immediately rang again. It was Pamela Courson, speaking very softly. Ronay told her to speak up, and then heard the fear in her voice. "Jim is unconscious, Alain . . . he's bleeding. . . . Can you call an ambulance for me? . . . You know I can't speak French. . . . Oh, please hurry . . . I think he may be dying." Pamela couldn't say anything else, because she was sobbing. She hung up.

Ronay dressed and crossed Varda's courtyard to wake her. She immediately called the Paris fire department's emergency line. Their rescue squad was the best chance anyone in a medical crisis in Paris had of staying alive. She ordered Ronay to write down Jim's address for her, and told him to write a note to Bertolucci and the maid that they were leaving in an emergency. She told Ronay to bring his American passport, because he would need it when the police arrived.

Varda drove them in her old VW Beetle. They were delayed by a political demonstration on the Île de la Cité. The students were leafleting the drivers, explaining their grievances. Ronay was almost pissing himself in fear. Weaving through traffic, Varda finally got them to rue Beautrellis at about nine-thirty. Fire trucks, an ambulance, and a small crowd held back by a police officer were in front of No. 17. When they got upstairs, Pamela was in the apartment's foyer, still dressed in her wet djellaba, surrounded by firemen.

"My Jim is dead, Alain," she said. Then: "I want to be alone now. *Please*—leave me alone."

Ronay was stunned. He glanced over at Jim's empty boots in the hallway, one in front of the other, as if he'd just stepped out of them.

When the fire-rescue squad had arrived a few minutes earlier, they had lifted Jim out of the bath and laid him out on the floor. They tried cardiac massage briefly, but the body was already cold. They had carried Jim to his bedroom and placed him on the bed. Pamela covered Jim with a blanket.

Agnès Varda asked the fire chief if he was sure Jim was dead. With tender courtesy, the chief replied that the resident had been dead for at least an hour before they had arrived. Varda went into the bedroom to be with Pamela. A police inspector arrived. When Varda came into the hallway, Ronay whispered to her not to let them know who Jim was, or who she was either. "Don't exaggerate," Varda replied. "Believe me, they have no idea my films even exist."

The inspector began to grill Ronay. "How did you know Mr. Douglas Morrison?" After establishing that Ronay was an American citizen, he asked about Jim's age, nationality, and occupation. What about the girl-friend? Did they use drugs? He turned and asked the paramedics to write a full statement. Ronay then told him: "My friend's name was Douglas Morrison. Douglas James Morrison. An American. He was a poet. He was an alcoholic, but no, he didn't use drugs."

The inspector was skeptical. Looking around the flat, he remarked that poets don't usually live in such bourgeois surroundings. "If he was really a poet, as you say, how could he afford some place like this?" Ronay replied that Mr. Morrison lived on a private income, then pleaded that he was traumatized and couldn't answer questions. The inspector backed off a bit, and said that if the medical examiner's report was satisfactory, the police would certify a death certificate and a burial permit. Otherwise, there would be an inquiry. Then he left.

The bedroom door was closed. A hotel sign, brought back from Morocco, hung from the doorknob. It read DO NOT DISTURB in French and Arabic. Suddenly the door opened and all the firemen filed out and left the apartment. They were alone now. Ronay couldn't bring himself to go in. All he saw were Jim's bare feet, hanging off the end of the bed.

Pamela came into the hall, still in her djellaba. Ronay told her he had reversed Jim's name for the police, and she said she had done the same thing. Agnès Varda came out and took them into the salon.

"Tell us what happened," Ronay urged Pamela. "We won't be alone much longer."

Pamela began to pick at the embroidered silk threads of the sleeves of the djellaba. They went to the movies, she said. They ate and came home. They sniffed heroin. Varda asked, "Who had it—you?"

"Of course," Pam answered, almost proudly. "I'm the one who holds it." She turned to Ronay and said, "Alain, why haven't you seen him yet? My Jim, man, he's so beautiful. You should check this out. Go, see. . . ."

Ronay ignored her. What happened next? Pamela told them about the films, the records, the coughing and breathing problems, and the crisis that led Jim to the bathtub. (She left out the mad scene in the hallway, the bathroom door locked from the inside, and the involvement of Jean de Breteuil.) Both women began to weep. Agnès, overcome, took Pamela's hand. The telephone rang. Varda said something about the phone possibly being tapped. The caller was Jean de Breteuil.

Ronay went out to buy cigarettes. The ambulance was still in front of the building. A few people were still gathered, gossiping about the young foreigner they had often seen walking through the quarter for the past several months, who had died in the night. There was still no idea of who he really was. But two long-haired young dudes in silk scarves and leather jackets were loitering as well, and they followed Alain up the steps. They introduced themselves as Jean and Jean-Louis, and asked to see Pam. When Ronay protested, Jean said, "Look, she called me. And I know everything."

Varda appeared, ready to brook no nonsense. "I lived with Pam for six months," the count blurted. "She wants to see me." Varda told him to get out. But Pamela emerged from the bedroom. She called the count into the other bedroom, where Ronay had slept.

They sat on the bed and talked for a while. Ronay interrupted them. There would be a scandal if the count was there when the medical examiner and the cops arrived. They had to get Jim buried before questions could be asked. As he was leaving, de Breteuil told Ronay that both his London digs and his Moroccan homes were at Pamela's disposal. On his way out, the count tripped over something that was under the carpet in the foyer. It was a hash pipe. Jean put it into his pocket and left with his friend. That evening, he and Marianne Faithfull took the night flight to Casablanca.

THE ROAD TO PÈRE-LACHAISE

BACK AT THE FLAT, PAMELA ASSURED Ronay that all the dope had been flushed. She went into the bedroom, carrying a pile of papers and copies of *An American Prayer,* and locked them in Jim's desk. Agnès said she wanted to leave before the medical examiner arrived, and told Pamela that she could stay at her house.

When Varda left, Pamela started to burn papers in the fireplace. Anything with Jim's name on it went up in smoke. She also burned some of her own letters, a journal, and files relating to Jim's various arrests in Los Angeles. Ronay said he thought the cops would smell the fire, on what was turning out to be the hottest day of the summer, and ask questions. Pamela didn't care. Some of her letters, she explained, were like diary entries about Jim and drugs. She then produced an application for a marriage license from Denver in 1967. She asked, "Will they accept this? Do they know English?" Ronay assured her that it wouldn't work.

Next Pamela broke into Zozo's padlocked bedroom with the fireplace hatchet and emerged wearing a full-length mink coat. "It's *mine* now," she told Ronay. "I'm taking it with me. She'll never give me back all the money we paid her in advance." Ronay said later that he convinced Pamela that she was in enough trouble already, and she hung the fur coat back in the closet.

The doorbell rang. It was the doctor, a short, stocky, middle-aged man carrying a black bag. "Where's the corpse?" he asked. Ronay pointed to the bedroom. Following legal procedure, the doctor demanded that Ronay accompany him to lay out the body. Ronay begged off because he didn't want to see Jim. But then Pamela appeared, apparently in a trance. Speaking in an artificial voice, she took the doctor's arm. "This is my very beautiful man, sir," she said, as she took him into the bedroom.

The exam was completed in less than five minutes. The doctor came out and asked Ronay to translate Pamela's answers to his questions. He asked Jim's age, and was shocked when he was told twenty-seven. "I was going to write *fifty-seven*," the doctor told Ronay. He asked if Jim ever used drugs and was told no, never. Ronay tried to tell him about the coughing spasms, but the doctor waved him off. "All right. I understand," he said. He filled out a form and handed it to Ronay with an envelope. "Take this to the civil registry of the Fourth Arrondissement," he said, "and show it to the clerk. They will give you the death certificate." Then he offered his condolences to Pamela and left abruptly. It was now around noon. Ronay said that they went out for something to eat.

Then they went to get the death certificate. The office was closed, so they went back later. The lone woman on duty on a sleepy Saturday afternoon scanned the papers and told them that their request for a death certificate due to natural causes would be denied. She made a phone call and handed the receiver to Alain. The prefect of police angrily told Ronay to get back to No. 17 within ten minutes.

The police arrived half an hour later. They found Pamela sitting demurely in the bedroom, next to Jim's body. She was holding hands with

Jim, talking to him quietly. The inspector, Captain Berry, was brisk and unsympathetic. Jim had been cleaned up, with no traces of blood or any needle marks. The police quickly inspected the apartment and found nothing. The fresh ashes in the fire grate went unnoticed. But Captain Berry was bothered by the scene. He obviously smelled something very wrong, and twenty years later told an interviewer that he thought Mr. Morrison had overdosed on drugs. He arranged for the senior medical examiner to arrive later to look at the corpse. Finally he told Pamela that if the new doctor found nothing amiss, they would receive the death certificate and burial permit.

Ronay asked when they could remove Jim's body. Captain Berry replied that they couldn't. It might have to be sent to the police morgue for analysis. "The corpse will remain here until further instruction," he told Ronay. "The only problem will be the heat of the next few days." Ronay protested that this would inflict great cruelty on Pamela, but the officer was unmoved. He said certain normal arrangements for this would be made, and that they now had to come with him to the quartier de l'Arsenal police headquarters to make a statement.

Pamela and Alain Ronay sat in the back of the police sedan. Ronay whispered to Pamela to cry a lot, and make it look good. In an office upstairs, a triplicate official form was rolled into the typewriter, and Pamela began telling her story in English, which the inspector now told them he knew perfectly well. Pamela perked up a bit, and spoke with some animation. She said that the movie they had seen was called *Death Valley*. She left out the heroin, Jim's outburst, and the count, and so blundered into several inconsistencies and mistakes. As police sirens sounded outside, Ronay was afraid she was telling too much and could get herself in trouble now.

"So," the inspector asked, disgusted: "You *abandoned* Douglas three times to empty the basin? *Three times?* And where did you empty and wash the basin?"

Pamela said the sink, which Ronay thought was the wrong answer. The inspector looked at her sharply. When she described her violent efforts to arouse Jim by hitting his face, Berry shook his head in obvious contempt. Turning to Ronay, he fired off questions in French. "Let's get this finished. What was this girl to Douglas Morrison?" Ronay answered that she was practically his wife. The cop wrote "concubine," the official word for unmarried spouse. "Did they have sexual relations the night Douglas died?" Pamela answered no. Finished typing, Captain Berry told them to go back to the apartment to receive the new medical examiner.

Once inside the flat, Pamela had a fit. She shouted at Ronay that she couldn't understand what was going on, that he had to make her understand what was being said. Ronay was scared for himself as well. It crossed his mind that if Jim had been murdered, he could be implicated in covering up the crime. (He didn't yet know that Pamela was Jim's sole heir. It's possible also that Pamela didn't know either.) Ronay, trying to control his emotions, told Pamela that she just had to trust him.

DR. MAX VASSILLE ARRIVED AROUND SIX O'CLOCK, carrying a black leather bag. Jim had been dead for twelve hours now. Vassille was an older gentleman, relaxed, and he smiled at them. He walked briskly into Jim's room, and walked out again within a minute. He had a quick look at the bathtub. In the dining room he told Pamela and Ronay that he thought it strange that so young a man, who seemed to be in good condition, should just die in the bathtub like that. Ronay told Dr. Vassille about the heavy drinking and the violent coughing spells he had witnessed.

Vassille stood up. He told them that if their statements were accurate, and could not be immediately proven otherwise, he was inclined to say that Mr. Douglas Morrison had died of a heart attack caused by blood clots in the cardiac artery. He was now going to the Arsenal station to file his report. He advised them to rest for an hour—"You both look very tense"—and then join him at the station. Vassille took Pamela's hand and offered his condolences. He took her wrist to feel her pulse, and nodded that she seemed all right. After he left, and it looked for the first time that day that they might be in the clear with the authorities, Pamela fell apart and began to cry. Then, when her tears were dry, she had a tantrum. "Valium," she screamed at Ronay. "I want *Valium.* Give some to me *now.*" Ronay said he'd flushed his pills down the toilet. Pamela started crashing around the apartment until she found a few that she had stashed herself.

After she calmed down, Pamela said she wanted Jim cremated and his ashes scattered someplace he liked. Ronay said cremation was very rare in France, and that an autopsy was always required first. Ronay told Pamela about Père Lachaise, and suggested they try to bury Jim there, near Chopin, Sarah Bernhardt, Molière, or Claude Debussy. This seemed reasonable to her. Pamela began going through the pockets of Jim's clothes, collecting about two hundred dollars in francs in a glass jar. She would need cash for the funeral. She would have to call one of the people she hated—Bill the manager, Bob the accountant, Max the lawyer—and get some money out of them. And they all hated her too. Ronay pointed out that the American banks were shut until Tuesday because of the Fourth of July holiday. She decided to ask Bill Siddons to bring the money personally.

Ronay suggested calling the Morrisons in Washington. "We don't have to worry about that," Pamela said coldly.

While Pamela leafed through some old photos of Jim, Ronay then called Agnès Varda. When they went to the police station, they would have to reveal the true order of Jim's name. Someone might notice, and the story could leak out and cause an uproar. Varda had a press baron friend, whose wife Ronay had once escorted to a Doors concert in Los Angeles. Ronay says that Varda's connection worked for four straight days to keep Jim's death off the prefecture of police's death roll, and any mention of a major rock star dying suddenly in Paris out of the papers.

Captain Berry received them coolly at the Arsenal station. At seven-thirty he handed them the death certificate (backdated to two-thirty that afternoon) and the burial permit. He asked for Jim's passport, which had to be turned over to the American embassy. To avoid giving Jim's real name, Ronay lied that they had left it in the flat. Besides, the embassy would be closed until Tuesday because of American Independence Day. The inspector said they could return it themselves, and that they were free to go.

"What about the body?" Ronay asked.

"Leave him where he is for now," Berry said, and picked up the phone.

LAST RITES IN PARIS

THE DOORBELL RANG at eight o'clock, only a few moments after Pamela Courson and Alain Ronay returned to the flat where Jim Morrison lay dead. Ronay was making tea, so Pamela answered the door. After a commotion she shouted to Alain, asking if he had ordered some ice cream. When he went to investigate, he found a small mortician in a dark suit, carrying a plastic bag and twenty-five pounds of dry ice. The police inspector had sent him. Shown into Jim's room, he wrapped the corpse in the bag with the ice. On the way out, he gave his card to Ronay, told him he would visit regularly until the funeral. "Believe me," he said, "I'll do my best. But this heat is against us."

Ronay told him that Pam wanted to sleep next to the body. The mortician look pained, and said that he strongly advised against it. Ronay left also to get some badly needed rest.

ON THAT SUNDAY, JULY 4, 1971, no one yet knew that Jim Morrison was dead. Pamela seemed better when Ronay returned late that morning. The iceman had already been and gone. Pamela was exhausted, but told Ronay that having Jim in the house made her feel secure. She said that if she could do it, they would live like this forever.

The iceman came again, late in the day. He repacked Jim and explained to Ronay that, with the continuing heat wave Paris was enduring, the current situation would become impossible to sustain by Tuesday. That evening, Alain Ronay spoke with a well-connected Paris lawyer who had been contacted by Agnès Varda, in case there were problems with the police.

The phone rang for the first time that night. Ronay thought it was someone from Elektra's London office. Pamela said Jim wasn't home, and hung up. Word was getting out. A Radio Luxembourg disk jockey named Jean-Bernard Hébey had heard the announcement at La Bulle and mentioned it on his show, later on Sunday. A Paris party girl told her journalist friend that she had heard the disc jockey at La Bulle announce Jim's death, and she knew that Jim was in Paris. The journalist checked the wire services and found nothing. His editor told him to call the record company for a statement. In London, Elektra executive Clive Selwyn was soon asked if Jim Morrison had died in Paris. Selwyn replied he'd had no idea that Jim was even in Paris. He called Elektra executives in Los Angeles. Someone got him Jim's phone number. There was no answer. Then a woman finally picked up and said that Jim wasn't home. So he called Bill Siddons.

On Monday, after a second night spent lying next to her decomposing boyfriend, Pamela consented to a burial as soon as possible. Ronay walked across the river and found the house of Bigot, the undertaker, in the shadows of the twin spires of Notre Dame Cathedral, where the old monastic cloister had once stood. Mr. Guirard, the director, explained that *everyone* wanted to rest in Père Lachaise, and there were very few spaces left. Ronay pleaded that Douglas Morrison had been a famous young American writer. Guirard brightened. "A writer? I know a space— in Division Eighty-nine, very close to another famous writer—Mr. Oscar Wilde."

Ronay was shocked. "No, I beg you, *not next to Oscar Wilde!* Please— can you find another space?" A small double plot was found, near a memorial to victims of Nazi oppression in Paris, in a less desirable location on the other side of the hill. The funeral was arranged for Wednesday morning, July 7. On Monday afternoon, the undertakers came to the flat, dressed Jim in a too-large dark suit, and stuffed him into a too-small wood-veneer coffin, the cheapest one Bigot offered. Pamela gathered all the pictures of herself that she had, and placed them in the coffin. The coffin was then sealed tightly with screws to retard further decay in the hot, dark apartment.

Pamela later said she had never seen Jim in a suit before. She said she thought he looked kind of cute.

THE PHONE RANG in Bill Siddons's Los Angeles house at four-thirty on Monday morning. Before he picked it up, Cheri Siddons said, "Something's happened to Jim." It was Clive Selwyn calling from London with the worst possible news. Siddons called Jim's Paris number, but no one answered. He tried again at eight in the morning. This time Pamela picked up. She sounded very nervous. Bill told her there were rumors that Jim had died. No, she said, that isn't true. Siddons asked to speak to Jim, and Pamela began to sob. He told her he wanted to help her, and booked a seat on the next plane to Paris.

Then he called Ray Manzarek. Ray said they'd heard these rumors before. Siddons said it seemed different this time. Ray said he couldn't believe it without some proof. Among the other Doors, no one was surprised, and there were not a lot of tears shed for Jim.

THAT MONDAY NIGHT IN MARRAKECH, Jean de Breteuil and Marianne Faithfull were having dinner with his mother and some young American friends of hers, who were living in the city's medina. Roger Steffens and Cynthia Cottle had met in Vietnam, where he was serving in the American army and she was a war correspondent. After dinner, the young people said good-night to the countess and repaired to the tower room. The desert heat had abated, and the windows were open to the cool of the evening. They smoked some kif Roger had brought, and Jean put on his test pressing of *Sticky Fingers*. Marianne was stoned, totally out of it. During "Sister Morphine," Jean suddenly began to blurt out what had happened in Paris on Friday night. He was in a state of confusion and anguish, and spoke in a rush of words. He left nothing out, except that the heroin had come from him.

Roger and Cynthia didn't quite believe him. They listened to the BBC news on the radio every night, and there had been no mention that Jim Morrison died. Jimi Hendrix's death had been headline news only a few months earlier. If anything, they knew, Jim Morrison had sold more records, and was far more controversial. The count explained that he thought they were trying to keep the story quiet until they got Pamela out of the country. Jean de Breteuil also made it clear that he thought Pamela Courson was somehow responsible for Jim Morrison's death. "The whole thing," he sighed. "It's *fucked*."

Later that year, Comte Jean de Breteuil would die in Tangier after a massive overdose of heroin that was considered either a suicide or an unsolved murder by the police magistrate who signed off on the case.

BILL SIDDONS ARRIVED AT 17, rue Beautrellis at nine o'clock on Tuesday morning. He found Pamela with Jim's secretary, Robin

Wertle. They explained that Jim was in his coffin, which had been sealed for health reasons. Pamela was distraught, and preoccupied with getting their things packed so she could go home. Alain Ronay arrived and explained the situation, and they all agreed to keep the death and the funeral secret as long as they could. Robin took Pamela to the American embassy to file a death report and return Jim's passport later in the day. Pamela was listed in the report as James Morrison's girlfriend. No one mentioned anything about "Jim Morrison," and they left quickly and hoped no one noticed. Sometime that day, Siddons opened a small, ornate Chinese box he found on a bureau in the apartment. He tasted the white powder it contained, and later said he thought it was heroin.

Pamela was listed as Jim's cousin on the burial certificate, notarized on Wednesday morning. At eleven o'clock a small procession wound its way up the cobblestones from the main gate of Père Lachaise. Jim was carried up the hill on a noisy, motorized cart, followed by several pallbearers, the undertaker, and his friends: Pamela, Alain Ronay, Agnès Varda, Robin Wertle, and Bill Siddons. They stopped at Grave No. 5, Second Row, Sixth Division. The pallbearers laid the coffin by the grave. There was no priest, no religious observance. Pamela cleared her throat and said in a soft voice that Jim wanted a few lines recited when he died. From memory, she whispered the last lines of "Celebration of the Lizard":

> *Now Night arrives with her purple legion*
> *Retire now to your tents and to your dreams*
> *Tomorrow we enter the town of my birth*
> *I want to be ready.*

The funeral lasted about eight minutes. Then everyone left. No one lingered at the grave to witness the interment. A couple of elderly French widows, tending their late husbands' graves in the same division, witnessed Jim Morrison's funeral. They said they thought the mourners had been in an unseemly hurry. They thought it was a shame to have had a funeral without a priest. They walked over to the abandoned grave when the workmen had finished filling it in. They saw only a small square of freshly turned earth. There was no headstone (and there would be none for many years). One of the women brought over a faded plastic rose from a nearby grave, and laid it on Jim Morrison's. Then there was nothing but the quiet, pretty summer day under the shady trees of the old cemetery.

T HEY ALL HELPED PAMELA to pack her things—except Agnès Varda, who'd had quite enough. (It seems possible that the events of Jim's death percolated into the bleak ending of *Last Tango in Paris,* which was filmed shortly afterward.) It took twenty-five shipping boxes to get Pamela ready to travel, including a metal case containing Jim's manuscripts and notebooks. Even so, she would leave a lot behind.

Bill Siddons was on the last plane to L.A. on Thursday night. When he arrived the next day, he drove to the Doors' workshop and said, "Well, we buried Jim yesterday." Late that night, he called the band's publicists, Gary Stromberg and Bob Gibson. Their answering service found them getting drunk at Dan Tana's. They had to break into their own offices because neither had a key. They asked Robert Hilburn, the pop writer for the *Los Angeles Times,* to come over at three in the morning, and then began working on a press release and a statement from the Doors about the death of Jim Morrison.

Pamela Courson also flew home with Siddons that night, having left her old man in the soil of Paris, along with a lot of unanswered questions. She was the sole heir to Jim Morrison's fortune, but first there would be hell to pay in California.

T HE REPORTER FROM the *Washington Post* reached Admiral Steve Morrison at home in Arlington, Virginia. The reporter asked him for a comment on his son's death in Paris. There was a silence. The admiral said he hadn't heard anything about it. The reporter said he had just confirmed the story with the Doors' manager, Bill Siddons. Admiral Morrison said that if Siddons said it happened, it probably was true. He then asked the reporter to call back with any further information. Admiral Morrison later called the naval attaché at the American embassy in Paris to confirm the story. The Morrison family was said to be very broken up about Jim's death. About a month later, Jim's passport was returned to Steve and Clara Morrison.

*　*　*

ZOZO AND PHILIP DALECKY were enjoying life in Saint-Tropez when they heard on the radio that the American rock star Jim Morrison had died. They flew back to Paris that weekend, arriving on Saturday, July 10. The new graffiti had already started to appear on the walls near the Rock and Roll Circus: *"Jim was a junky."* At 17, rue Beautrellis, they found the front door of the flat ajar.

Philip Dalecky recalled: "I can't really describe the atmosphere, except to say that it was a scene of *intense* anguish. Man! It looked like vandals had wrecked the apartment. It looked like a *civil war* had been fought. It took us forever to clean up. We looked at the bathtub with total disbelief. What had *happened* here? What kind of *nightmare?* A heavy spirit of oppression and anxiety filled the rooms. We tried to burn some incense and air out the flat, clean the house of bad energy, but it never felt the same again."

Over time, Zozo found notebooks, photographs, drugs, and a bloody switchblade that had been left behind in the apartment. She found threatening letters from an American woman who claimed to be Jim Morrison's wife. Over time, most of these papers were lost, or ended up in private collections.

NICO WAS VERY SAD when she heard that Jim had died. She bought all the Paris and London papers and wept as she read the stories. She couldn't believe it. She had just seen him, her former poet/lover, a few days earlier. When the crying stopped, Nico went into the bathroom and began rinsing the red dye out of her hair. It took her several days to wash her long hair back to its natural blond color. Then she dyed it black.

THE COOL REMNANT OF A DREAM

Jim Morrison—it's a strange story—that he drowned in a bathtub in Paris. It seems a Goddamned odd thing to happen. I never believed it for a minute.

—WILLIAM S. BURROUGHS

JIM MORRISON'S death in Paris in July 1971 was the coup de grâce for the American sixties. "Let's change the mood from glad to sadness" had accurately predicted the fading of communitarian sixties ideals—protest, reform, emotional intensity, the transience of nature, the expansion of consciousness—into the harsher realities of the seventies. The main political beneficiary of the wild California sixties would be Ronald Reagan, who rode a conservative backlash to the governorship of the state, and eventually into the White House and into history.

Jim's death was the last of the sequence of rock star extinctions that had begun with Brian Jones and continued with Jimi Hendrix and Janis Joplin. After Jim died, their places were taken by younger musicians who were just coming into their own: Bruce Springsteen, Aerosmith, Bob Marley. In England, David Bowie and T-Rex emerged from the underground "glam" movement; for a while in the early seventies, feminized men ruled the world of pop. By 1975, the rock movement that Jim Morrison helped invent had grown into a mammoth, multibillion-dollar recording, touring, and merchandizing industry that was dominated by Led Zeppelin until the end of the decade.

The Vietnam War that Jim Morrison so despised dragged on until 1975, when it ended in a communist victory. Almost fifty-five thousand Americans and three million Vietnamese had been killed. Immediately a new generation of rockers tried to blot out any memory of the sixties, just as Jim had prophesied, with their new weapon of mass-cult destruction—punk rock.

The specter of Jim Morrison loomed over all of this like a dark shadow from the recent past—or rather from another world age.

Pamela Courson returned to Los Angeles a few days after Jim died, and proceeded to play out a three-year, Ophelia-like mad scene. Reliable information about Pamela in this period is scarce and often unsupported, since she lived as a demimondaine in a shadowy milieu of addiction, grief, and occasional mania.

After recovering from her Parisian ordeal, she tried to resume her life in L.A. as "Pamela Morrison." She talked to her dog as if she were talking to Jim. She always spoke of Jim in the present, as if he were alive. The accountant informed her that Jim's estate, to which she was indeed the sole heir, could not continue to support her boutique until the will was adjudicated, which could go on for years. Themis would have to close. Pamela became so enraged that that she drove a car into the front window of the store. In November 1971, she filed papers formally claiming Jim Morrison's estate, which was reported to include holdings in oil wells and California ranchland. The other Doors immediately sued Jim's estate for what they claimed were large outstanding cash advances that had been paid to Jim. The ensuing litigation left Pamela almost penniless.

Pamela relocated to the Bay Area in 1972. She stayed in Bolinas with Ellen Sander for a while. Then she lived with some friends in Sausalito. Wracked by crippling spasms of guilt, she would sit for hours by the telephone, waiting for "my old man" to call. Ray Manzarek ran into her in Sausalito, and wanted to ask her what had happened in Paris. But when she saw him, she swooned in a paroxysm of grief and could only weep in his arms.

A bit later, she contacted Michael McClure about Jim's remaining poetry. She loaned him the leather portmanteau, which he described as "a doctor's bag," that contained Jim's poems and notes, each filed in a binder and carefully arranged. McClure later returned the bag, expressing surprise at what he later called "a miracle of order," and told Pamela that he felt the works could be published.

Eventually, Pamela returned to Los Angeles. She had affairs with a younger rock star and an older French diplomat. She continued to have serious cash flow problems and a taste for heroin. To survive, she sold her jewelry, Jim's books, and anything that wasn't nailed down. (She managed to keep her small collection of Luger pistols.) She was evicted from her house in the Hollywood Hills for nonpayment of rent and moved into a garden apartment in West Hollywood. Paul Rothchild said that she used to turn up at his house at all hours, well supplied with barbiturates and heroin. She spent much of her time with Rothchild crying. She kept saying, over and over, "I just couldn't control him."

Pamela had a lot of enemies. Some believed she had killed Jim Morrison for his money. There were people who were content to see her in extreme distress. They put out rumors that she was prostituting herself, but tracking these rumors always leads back to people who hated her. (She may have been "kept" for a time by the rich Frenchman.) Others swore to God or wrote in thinly sourced books that Pamela had confessed to killing Jim accidentally, that he had snorted massive lines of what she had told him was cocaine, but which was actually China White. No one put it past her—or stood up to say it couldn't have happened.

The Doors litigated Pamela for years. She had no money at all, and had to be supported by family and friends. Lawsuits flew like bats at sunset until early 1974, when it looked like there would finally be a settlement. Then the Doors sued the estate again, prolonging the agony. In April, the court recognized Pamela as James Douglas Morrison's lawful heir, and a full settlement was reached with the Doors. Pamela's initial cash disbursement, hurried through to relieve obvious financial distress, was twenty thousand dollars.

Friends say Pamela seemed a little better after things were settled. Others say she was more despondent than ever. She bought a cheery chrome-yellow Volkswagen beetle. She went to Saks Fifth Avenue and bought a monogrammed ranch mink stole. She phoned her connection and reportedly ordered an ounce of China White.

The people she lived with found her dead on the living room couch on the afternoon of April 25, 1974. At first they thought she was just taking a nap and let her sleep for hours until it began to get weird. Then they noticed she wasn't breathing. The cops arrived. A man living in the house, who said he used to drive for Jim and Pamela, was questioned about Pamela's use of heroin. He volunteered that her "husband" had died of a heroin overdose in Paris three years earlier, and that Pamela had recently spoken about looking forward to seeing him again soon. When they took her away, her long red hair cascaded over the side of the gurney as she was being lifted into the ambulance. The coroner could have called Pamela's death a suicide, but called it a massive pulmonary edema instead. The autopsy noted she had a severe bladder infection.

Ray Manzarek was asked to play at a memorial service for both Pamela and Jim, organized by the Coursons, at Forest Lawn Cemetery on Monday, April 29. Ray played "When the Music's Over," "Love Street," and "Crystal Ship." (Pamela's apartment was burglarized during the ceremony, and an unknown amount of Jim Morrison's effects were reportedly stolen.) It is not known whether there was talk of burying Pamela's ashes with Jim in Paris, but they were later interred in a memory wall (under the name "Pamela Morrison") in an Orange County cemetery.

A week later, a probate judge officially awarded Pamela a half-million dollars and a quarter of the Doors' future royalty income, making the dead girl a virtual millionaire. It later emerged that her family suspected that Pamela might have been murdered, with suspicion reportedly falling on a former in-law member of the Morrison family. An investigation produced no actionable results. Since Pamela had died without leaving a will, Jim Morrison's entire estate, including the executorship of his literary and artistic remains, passed to Pamela's parents, Corky and Marie Courson. Sometime after Admiral Morrison retired from the navy in 1975, the Morrisons sued for a share of their son's legacy. Several years later, a settlement awarded the Morrisons half of the financial worth of the estate, but left Jim's artistic legacy in the control of the Coursons.

THE DOORS DIDN'T SURVIVE long after Jim died either. Ray Manzarek was angry that Bill Siddons hadn't insisted on seeing Jim's body, and for years Ray seemed not to believe that Jim was actually dead. Jim Morrison resurrections were reported to the band almost immediately. Jim was "seen" in Paris, in Tangier, in New Orleans, and in San Francisco within a year of his death. But when Jim didn't show up for the Doors sessions in the autumn of 1971, they figured he really was out of the band. They recorded two more albums as a trio, and disbanded after a final show in September 1972.

Robby Krieger summed up the fate of the Doors after Jim passed on: "For a long time, it was the three of us against Jim. When we didn't have Jim, we fought among ourselves."

In 1977, Elektra engineer John Haeny rediscovered Jim Morrison's poetry tapes. Using readings mostly from 1969 (and incorporating vocals from other sources), Elektra released *An American Prayer* as a Jim Morrison/Doors album, late in 1978. It was actually a posthumous Jim Morrison solo album, with new music that sounded like the Doors circa *L.A. Woman*. An enclosed album booklet reproduced Jim's notebook entries and doodled scrawls. *An American Prayer* was really just a shallow pastiche; both the mellow power of Jim's vocal delivery and his surreal imagery were diluted by music aptly described by critics as cocktail jazz. Paul Rothchild, who didn't work on the album, called *An American Prayer* "the rape of Jim Morrison."

The end of the seventies and the tenth anniversary of Jim's death saw an uptick in the Morrison legend. Francis Ford Coppola used his former classmate's epic "The End" to bracket his Vietnam War masterpiece, *Apocalypse Now*, reminding people of the Doors' crucial role as an echo of the era's turmoil and violence. (Soundtrack producer David Rubinson discovered Jim's staccato *fuck-fuck-fuck* sequence buried in the master tapes, and remixed the song to spotlight its violence and fervor.) To coincide with *Apocalypse Now*'s 1980 release, Elektra put out a fourth Doors compilation album, *The Doors: Greatest Hits,* that shocked the label by quickly selling two million units to a generation too young to have seen the band.

These high school kids also put the first biography of Jim Morrison on the bestseller lists for months that year. The manuscript of *No One Here Gets Out Alive*, which had been researched by Jerry Hopkins, had been rejected by every major publisher. The text was then reworked by Danny Sugarman (and reportedly Ray Manzarek) to include material that only Doors insiders knew about. Published in 1980, the biography—the first of a major sixties rock star—was an instant success. It cemented in the public mind the image of Jim Morrison as a poetic wild man, a rebel, an asshole, and a tragic American legend. The book ended, stupidly, with the suggestion that Jim Morrison might have faked his death, and might be still alive and in hiding.

Jim Morrison's real friends knew that this was an impossibility. There was, they insisted, *no possible way* that Jim would ever have allowed Pamela Courson to suffer as she did, if he had any means to prevent it. (Some of Jim's close friends still refer to this problematic book as "Nothing Here but Lots of Lies.")

Tom Baker fatally overdosed on drugs in 1984. In 1985, Bono was doing Jim Morrison impressions during performances with his band, U2. In that year the Doors released a video compilation, *Dance on Fire,* that recycled some of Jim's more shamanic moves from *Feast of Friends.* For the first time, younger fans could see the roiling tumult and mania that had characterized Jim's performances with the Doors.

In 1986, at Père-Lachaise Cemetery, where no tombstone protected his uncovered, seemingly abandoned dirt grave, two people were caught trying to dig Jim up. The estate then finally placed a large granite cube over the soil, with Jim's name and dates inscribed on the stone. Then a Yugoslav sculptor took it upon himself to install a hideous granite bust of Jim on the gravestone. This lasted for about a year, defaced with paint and lipstick, until it was stolen. For fifteen years, Jim's grave had been an important stop on the international hippie trail, as young backpackers and nomads included Père Lachaise in their European itineraries. Scabrous, desecrating graffiti throughout the cemetery pointed the way to the obscure grave, where kids gathered to strum guitars, smoke dope, light candles, read Jim's poems aloud, drink wine, and leave offerings of flowers, joints, pills; snapshots, demo tapes, letters; cheap plastic lighters by the thousands.

I N 1988, NICO DIED after falling off her bicycle near her home on the Mediterranean island of Ibiza. In that year, Frank Lisciandro began to edit the notebooks and journals that the Coursons had retrieved from Pamela's jumbled effects. (Her father and uncle had reportedly driven up and down California after she died, trying to retrieve the many cars she had abandoned.) Because *The Lords and The New Creatures* continued to sell several thousand copies every year (very respectable numbers for a contemporary American poet), Jim's estate was able to publish a second volume, *Wilderness: The Lost Writings of Jim Morrison,* in 1989. This volume collected diverse material from notebooks, recordings, and privately published poems such as "Dry Water," "Far Arden," and "Ode to L.A. While Thinking of Brian Jones, Deceased."

Soon after publication, some of Pamela's Bay Area friends attempted to sell a cache of Jim's poems that she had (supposedly) left behind when she returned to Los Angeles. They were contained in a metal box marked "Fascination 127," and were thought to be the remnants of the poems filed and ordered in Paris. Jim's estate sued to stop the sale, and the material was returned to the Coursons. Parts of it, including the despairing "Paris Journal," were published in a second posthumous volume, *The American Night*, in 1990.

By that time, Jim Morrison was becoming recognized as a poet by academia. Wallace Fowlie, the distinguished biographer of Rimbaud, began teaching Jim's poetry at Duke University. Similar courses were offered at Yale, Stanford, and other schools. Fowlie later published a critical study, *Rimbaud and Jim Morrison: The Rebel As Poet*, which sought to legitimize Jim's insistent claim that he wasn't just some chump rock star. He had been a poet, too, one who had immolated himself in pursuit of some greater design that remained unknown to all others.

T HE DEFINING EVENT IN THE DEVELOPMENT of the Jim Morrison legend was Hollywood's treatment of it. Oliver Stone's film *The Doors* was released in early 1991 to great and deserved acclaim. Stone had worked hard to re-create the hazy, druggy atmosphere of Jim Morrison's sojourn through southern California in the sixties, and he adroitly captured some of the magic and chaos of Jim's performances. Val Kilmer played Jim as a too-tall Dionysius. Meg Ryan portrayed Pamela as a bitchy hippie princess. (Stone later said that the Coursons had only allowed him to use Jim's music and lyrics on the condition that there be no suggestion in the movie that Pamela had anything to do with Jim's death.) Cynics said *The Doors* was the first Hollywood biopic in which the movie stars were not as beautiful as the people they portrayed, but the film was a commercial success, and even had a certain vibrational integrity as well. It excited enormous renewed interest in the Doors, especially Jim Morrison, and resulted in a shelf of new books about the band, its singer, and their era.

Typically, *The Doors* was later denounced by Ray Manzarek, who had cooperated with the film. "That was a white-powder movie about a psychedelic band," Ray complained ten years later. "They were two worlds that never met. A white-powder guy has no idea of cosmic consciousness. . . . He made Jim into a humorless drunk. No one laughed in that movie. Hey—we were *potheads*! Jim was funny! We laughed a lot."

There was a major riot in Paris on July 3, 1991, the twentieth anniversary of Jim Morrison's death. The Soviet Union had collapsed two years earlier, and the Iron Curtain that had separated Eastern Europe from the West had come down. That summer, several thousand former inmates of European communism headed to Paris to visit Jim's grave on his death day. They'd been listening to him for almost twenty-five years, with no way to make contact. By noon on July 3, a thousand Poles, Hungarians, Czechs, Slovaks, Latvians, and Russians were mobbing the gravesite. They were drinking vodka, smoking dope, eating, fighting, fornicating on the surrounding tombstones, and just grooving. Jim would have loved it. By three in the afternoon, two thousand more Moldovans, Georgians, Ukrainians, and Romanians had arrived and chased away the guards. The authorities grew alarmed and herded everyone out by closing time at five o'clock. The huge crowds waiting outside couldn't get in to pay homage to their rock god.

The party continued outside the gates when three thousand people sat down in the street. As night fell, the crowd lit bonfires. Everyone got loaded. Jim's songs were chanted in strange accents. At midnight, the crowd set fire to a parked car and tried to ram it through the gates of Père Lachaise so they could hang out with Jim. Suddenly the CRS, the dreaded French riot police, were on top of them. There was mass panic, clouds of tear gas, blood in the streets, many wrecked cars, and a hundred injuries after the riot cops in the black leather raincoats had sorted out Jim Morrison's unruly fans from the former Warsaw Pact.

By then, many places where the Doors had once played no longer existed. The clubs had closed, the psychedelic ballrooms had vanished, and most of the arenas had been torn down or redeveloped. Rock itself died out in the early nineties, and was replaced by alternative music and the heroin-fueled grunge movement that had begun in Seattle. Hundreds of radio stations in America changed their formats to the newer bands (Nirvana, Pearl Jam, Stone Temple Pilots). The old rock bands survived on "classic rock" radio stations that soon grew into regional powerhouses on purely demographic lines. The Doors became staples of the classic rock format, with such late-period masterpieces as "L.A. Woman," "Riders on the Storm," and "Peace Frog" continuing to dominate station request lines—to this day.

"Jim always wanted to be huge," Robby Krieger said recently. "He wanted it to be like the Beatles, with girls falling out of the sky. But it never was like that in those days. But if Jim was here today, he would *love* it. Because right now, it's like—Beatles, Stones, and Doors, you know?"

By the end of the twentieth century, the Doors had sold more than fifty million records.

In 1994, the Doors were inducted into the Rock and Roll Hall of Fame. At the annual induction ceremony, held at the Waldorf-Astoria Hotel in New York, the surviving Doors were joined by Jim's sister, Anne Morrison, who accepted her brother's honor on behalf of the Morrison family. Eddie Vedder, the charismatic lead singer of Pearl Jam, joined the Doors later to sing Jim's parts on "Roadhouse Blues," "Break On Through," and "Light My Fire."

The Doors drifted further apart. John Densmore's 1990 memoir, *Riders on the Storm,* recounted the Doors' career through the eyes of the band's horrified drummer. Ray Manzarek's 1998 memoir, *Light My Fire,* lashed back at Densmore and confirmed Manzarek as a rigid sixties ideologue with little sense of humor, an absurd myth to evangelize, and many axes to grind.

Densmore responded in 2002 with an article in the radical American weekly *The Nation,* in which the Doors' drummer defended his continued, stubborn refusal to sanction the band's classic songs for (extremely lucrative) commercial exploitation. John Densmore declared himself the rightful legatee of Jim Morrison's anarchic stance as an American artist of conscience, and someone who had never sold out.

THROUGH ALL OF THIS, well into the nineties, Jim Morrison rested quietly in his grave. His fans, however, continued to run amok in Père Lachaise, holding daily pot parties and jam sessions over his tomb, until the cemetery was forced to clamp down after Oliver Stone's movie moved the situation into crisis mode. The cemetery's director complained in the Paris press that the situation was getting out of hand. There were reports that Jim would be dug up and evicted when the thirty-year gravesite lease expired, unless his estate paid for erasing all the graffiti on the surrounding tombs, and provided security for his grave.

Sometime in 1995, the estate cleaned up Père Lachaise, and established a fund for a permanent security detail. A large bronze plaque was attached to Jim's gravestone. It bore the Greek inscription "KATA TON ΔAIMONA EAYTOY," which can be translated as "True to His Own Spirit."

In 2003, Ray Manzarek and Robby Krieger regrouped—without John Densmore, who refused to participate. They recruited the former Police drummer Stewart Copeland and British rock singer Ian Astbury (from the postmetal band the Cult) to fill out the new Doors. They played sold-out shows in Los Angeles and a Hell's Angels party in Las Vegas, before lawsuits brought by Densmore and Jim's estate forced them to stop calling themselves the Doors. ("John [Densmore] will destroy the Doors, ultimately," Ray told the press.) Then Copeland broke an arm in a bicycle accident, and (successfully) sued the Doors for loss of income when they replaced him with another drummer so they could tour.

Ray and Robby pressed on with Ian Astbury, a bass player, and a less-than-magic drummer, playing concerts under the street-legal name "the Doors of the Twenty-first Century." They toured America, often playing for packed houses of old Doors fans and young classic rockers. Ian Astbury's brilliant impersonation of Jim Morrison enabled the band to play the *L.A. Woman* songs for the first time in concert. The shows often began with "Roadhouse Blues" and "When the Music's Over," casting an almost trancelike spell over their audiences. Astbury looked like a cleaned-up Jim Morrison might have looked at the age of forty-five, and sang respectful, precise interpretations of Jim's classic songs. A time-tripping, psychedelic light show played on a big screen behind the band, providing visual references to the Doors' old jams. The general effect was astonishing for twenty minutes until Ray began rapping to the audiences to hustle upcoming projects, ruining what had been a near-divine illusion and a more-than-willing suspension of collective disbelief.

"The Doors of the Twenty-first Century" played sold-out shows in Paris in December 2003. On December 8, which would have been Jim's sixtieth birthday, they visited him at Père Lachaise. They lit candles alongside dozens of fans and tourists crowding around the grave. The little ceremony was monitored by a pair of security cameras, and two uniformed guards who discouraged the hundreds of rock pilgrims paying daily homage to Jim from playing music, drinking wine, smoking dope, or sitting on the nearby tombs.

The security precautions remained necessary because, at the end of that year, the French tourism authorities announced that Jim Morrison's grave was, more than thirty years after his death, still one of the most heavily visited tourist sites in Paris.

> *This living hand, now warm and capable*
> *Of earnest grasping, would, if it were cold*
> *And in the icy silence of the tomb,*
> *So haunt thy days and chill thy dreaming nights*
> *That thou would wish thine own heart dry of blood*
> *So in my veins red life might stream again,*
> *And thou be conscious-calmed—see here it is—*
> *I hold it toward you—*
>
> —JOHN KEATS

AUTHOR'S NOTES

IN AUGUST 2001, a month before America was blasted into a new reality, I was reading a copy of *Rolling Stone* by an azure swimming pool in the south of France when I came across "The Unforgettable Fire," Mikal Gilmore's tribute to Jim Morrison on the thirtieth anniversary of his death in Paris. Instead of rounding up the usual suspects—all the clichés about the Doors—Gilmore concentrated on Jim as a fiercely loving and compassionate man who had redeemed his mad, suicidal behavior through the dark and intensely beautiful work he left behind. When I finished the article, I fell into a dream, and remembered seeing Jim Morrison for the first time as he took the stage in a now-demolished theater in Boston, with the peyote-vision sonic aura of the Doors throbbing behind him. The performance was so incendiary, and Jim's approach to putting on a rock concert was so cool, that my life changed that night. *This* was the energy I wanted to be part of, every day, for the rest of my life.

I didn't know at the time that, for Jim Morrison at least, it would prove to be a martyrdom operation.

Back in France, I read Mikal's piece again and decided to look into the Morrison story. So many questions about his life and death remained unanswered, those who knew him then were older and wiser now, and new sources were becoming available in both Los Angeles and Paris. Over the next two years, I interviewed people who knew Jim and was given kind access to various archives and private collections. Jim regarded the interview as an art form, and some of his articulate responses to interviewers' questions proved more revealing over the passage of time. I was able to review nearly all of Jim's recorded work, including unreleased material, unauthorized live recordings, and the wonderful solo recordings of his poems. Collectors, mostly in France, provided copies of Jim's televised appearances, as well as copies of his experimental films. Most crucially, I was able to examine several of Jim's personal journals, now in private hands. When this text ascribes a thought or a feeling to Jim, it is because he said it on tape, or wrote it in a journal or notebook entry.

There have been many books published about Jim Morrison and the Doors, some of whose varying degrees of reliability are noted in the text. Having now made a few leaps of faith of my own, my sympathy for their authors has increased. The books I got the most out of were *The Doors on the Road* by Greg Shaw with David Dalton; *A Feast of Friends* by Frank Lisciandro; and Patricia Butler's biography of Pamela Courson, *Angels Dance and Angels Die*. I must also acknowledge Jerry Hopkins, whose pioneering rock journalism in *Rolling Stone* is responsible for much of what is reliably known about Jim Morrison.

Jim Morrison made friends with a small circle of people during his final months in Paris. Today their memories provide a living link to one of the great mysteries of our era. This book couldn't have been written without Gilles Yéprémian, Hervé Muller, and Philip Dalecky. Jim left a plastic bag full of his stuff with Philip a few days before he died. Decades later, Philip found the forgotten bag in a drawer. In it were Jim's last notebooks, reels of audiotape, and Jim's private photo file, all of which were generously made available to my investigation. Gilles Yéprémian's legendary collection of Doors materials has been equally invaluable. Hervé's photos of Jim in Paris speak volumes by themselves.

I'd also like to thank JHA and the girls, Hana and Howard, Chris Davis, American Airlines (esp. John Spano), Bill Glasser and the good dogs of Topanga Canyon, Helene Lee, Mike Zwerin, Patrick Zerbib, Pamela des Barres, Victor Bockris, David Dalton, Albert Goldman, Paul Rothchild, Gary Stromberg, Bob Gibson, John Gaby, Sugar Katz, Guy Webster, Therese Muller-Stival, Roy Pace, Lev Braunstein, Carol Stocker, Anne-Celeste Dalecky, W.M.H Magicel, Peter Simon, Carly Simon, Joe Perry, John Bionelli, *Rolling Stone,* James Isaacs, David Winner, Maria Evangelinellis, the Michael Ochs Archives (esp. Helen Ashford and Paul Chesne), the Archive of Rock, Vin des Pyrénées, Gli Angeli, Michaelangelo Antonioni, and David Vigliano, the Big Buddha of Broadway.

Special thanks to my intrepid publisher Bill Shinker, my learned editor Brendan Cahill, and the whole star-quality crew at Gotham Books: Patrick Mulligan, Karen Mayer, Lisa Johnson, Melanie Koch, Aline Akelis, Hector de Jean, Ray Lundgren, Susan Schwartz, Bob Wojciechowski, Joseph Mills, Sabrina Bowers, Rachelle Nashner, and Craig Schneider— copy editor extraordinaire.

SELECTED SOURCES

Artaud, Antonin. *The Theater and Its Double.* New York: Grove Press, 1958.

Ashcroft, Linda. *Wild Child: Life with Jim Morrison.* London: Hodder & Stoughton, 1997.

Ashcroft, Linda. *Wild Child: Life with Jim Morrison.* New York: Thunder's Mouth Press, 1997.

Babitz, Eve. "Jim Morrison Is Dead and Living in Hollywood." *Esquire,* March 1991.

Blackburn, Richard. "Jim Morrison's School Days." *Crawdaddy.* May 1976.

Bockris, Victor. Unpublished audiotape transcription of a 1993 conversation with Albert Goldman regarding Jim Morrison.

Boettcher, Thomas D. *Vietnam: The Valor and the Sorrow.* Boston: Little, Brown, 1985.

Butler, Patricia. *Angels Dance and Angels Die.* New York: Schirmer, 1998.

Carpenter, John. "Jim Morrison." *L. A. Free Press.* July 19, 1968.

Celine, Louis-Ferdinand. *Journey to the End of the Night.* Boston: Little, Brown, 1934.

Charlesworth, Chris (ed.) *The Doors* (booklet notes for box set). Elektra Entertainment Group, 1997.

Chorush, Bob. "The Lizard King Reforms." *L. A. Free Press.* January 15, 1971.

Coover, Robert. "A Hell of a Way to Peddle Poems." *An Hour for Magic,* edited by Frank Lisciandro. New York: Delilah, 1982.

Cruz, Merced Valdez. *The Doors: Los Dias Extranos.* Mexico City: Lopez, 1999.

Cuscuna, Michael. "Behind the Doors." Downbeat, May 28, 1970.

Dalton, David. *Mr. Mojo Risin'/Jim Morrison/The Last Holy Fool.* New York: St. Martin's Press, 1991.

Dalton, David. "The Marble Index." *Gadfly,* June 2002.

Densmore, John. *Riders on the Storm: My Life with Jim Morrison and the Doors.* New York: Delacorte Press, 1990.

Densmore, John. "Riders on the Storm." *The Nation,* July 8, 2002.

Des Barres, Pamela. *I'm with the Band.* New York: Beech Tree Books, 1987.

Des Barres, Pamela. *Rock Bottom.* New York: St. Martin's Press, 1996.

Didion, Joan. "Waiting for Morrison." *The Saturday Evening Post,* March 9, 1968.

Diehl, Digby. "Jim Morrison: Love and the Demonic Psyche." *Eye.* April 1968.

Dixon, Willie, with Don Snowden. *I Am the Blues.* New York: Da Capo, 1990.

The Doors. *Dance on Fire: Classic Performances and Greatest Hits* (1985). Universal City (Cal.): Universal Video, 1997.

The Doors. *The Doors Are Open: The Roundhouse, London, Sept. 1968.* Burbank (Cal.): Warner Reprise Video.

The Doors. *Feast of Friends* (1969). Paris (France): Bootleg DVD.

The Doors. *Live in Europe 1968.* Los Angeles: Eagle Rock Video, 1999.

The Doors. *Live at the Hollywood Bowl* (1968). Universal City (Cal.): Universal Video, 1997.

The Doors. *No One Here Gets Out Alive: The Doors' Tribute to Jim Morrison.* Los Angeles: Eagle Vision (DVD).

The Doors. *The Soft Parade—A Retrospective* (1969). Universal City (Cal.): Universal Video, 1997.

Farina, Richard. *Been Down So Long It Looks Like Up to Me.* New York: Dell, 1966.

Fong-Torres, Ben. "Jim Morrison's Got the Blues." *Rolling Stone.* March 4, 1971.

Fowlie, Wallace. *Rimbaud and Jim Morrison.* Durham: Duke University Press, 1993.

Gershman, Mike. "Apathy For The Devil." *Rock,* November 1970.

Gilmore, Mikal. "The Unforgettable Fire." *Rolling Stone,* August 30, 2001.

Ginsberg, Allen. *Collected Poems 1947–1980.* New York: Harper & Row, 1984.

Goldman, Albert. *Freakshow: Misadventures in the Counterculture, 1959–1971.* New York: Cooper Square, 2001.

Goldstein, Richard. "Pop Eye." *Village Voice,* March 23, 1967.

Goldstein, Richard. "Pop Eye," *Village Voice,* June 22, 1967.

Grace, Francine. "Vibrant Jazz Rock Group at Gazzarri's." *Los Angeles Times,* February 28, 1967.

Graham, Bill, and Robert Greenfield. *Bill Graham Presents.* New York: Doubleday, 1992.

Halbert, James. "This Is the End." *Classic Rock.* July 2003.

Holzman, Jac, and Gavan Daws. *Follow the Music.* Santa Monica: First Media Books, 1998.

Hopkins, Jerry. *The Lizard King.* New York: Charles Scribner's Sons, 1992.

Hopkins, Jerry. "The *Rolling Stone* Interview: Jim Morrison." *Rolling Stone,* July 26, 1969.

Hopkins, Jerry, and Danny Sugarman. *No One Here Gets Out Alive.* New York: Warner Books, 1980.

Huxley, Aldous. *The Doors of Perception / Heaven & Hell.* New York: Harper Colophon, 1963.

Jahn, Mike. *Jim Morrison and the Doors.* New York: Grosset & Dunlap, 1969.

Jones, Dylan. *Jim Morrison, Dark Star.* New York: Viking Press, 1990.

Kamp, David. "Live at the Whisky." *Vanity Fair.* November 2000.

Kaufman, Phil, and Colin White. *Road Mangler Deluxe.* Glendale (Cal.): White/Boucke, 1993.

Kerouac, Jack. *On the Road.* New York: Viking Press, 1957.

Kinnealy, Patricia. *Strange Days.* New York: Plume, 1993.

Leary, Tim. *Psychedelic Prayers.* Kerhonkson N.Y.: Poets Press, 1966.

Lesprit, Bruno. "The Doors of the 21st Century: Quand le Rock S'addonne a la Necrophilie." *Le Monde,* Dec. 11, 2003.

Lipton, Lawrence. *The Holy Barbarians.* New York: Grove Press, 1959.

Lisciandro, Frank. *Jim Morrison: An Hour for Magic.* New York: Delilah, 1982.

Lisciandro, Frank. *A Feast of Friends.* New York: Warner Books, 1991.

Mailer, Norman. *An American Dream.* New York: The Dial Press, 1965.

Mailer, Norman. *Why Are We in Vietnam?* New York: G.P. Putnam, 1967.

Manzarek, Ray. *Light My Fire: My Life with the Doors.* New York: Putnam, 1998.

Marsh, Dave. *Before I Get Old—The Story of The Who.* New York: St. Martin's Press, 1983.

McClure, Michael. *The Adept.* New York: Delacorte, 1971.

McClure, Michael. *The Beard.* New York: Grove Press, 1967.

McClure, Michael. *Lightning The Corners.* Albuquerque: University of New Mexico Press, 1993.

Milne, A.A. *When We Were Very Young.* New York: E.P. Dutton, 1924.

Moddemann, Rainer. *Doors.* Koningswinter (Germany): Heel Verlag, 1990.

Moddemann, Rainer, with Gilles Yepremian. *The Doors on Stage.* Geneva: Moving Sound Books, 1996.

Morrison, Jim. *The American Night.* New York: Vintage, 1991.

Morrison, Jim. *Arden Lointain.* Paris: Christian Bourgois, 1988.

Morrison, Jim. *HWY* (1969). Paris: Bootleg DVD.

Morrison, Jim. *The Lords and the New Creatures.* New York: Simon and Schuster, 1970.

Morrison, Jim. *Une Priere Americaine et Autres Ecrits.* Paris: Christian Bourgois, 1985.

Morrison, Jim. *Seigneurs et Nouvelles Creatures.* Paris: Christian Bourgois, 1976.
Morrison, Jim. *Wilderness: The Lost Writings of Jim Morrison.* New York: Vintage, 1989.
Muller, Hervé. "Lord Jim." *Rock & Folk* (France), February 1979.
Muller, Hervé. "Jim Morrison." *Globe* (France), October 15, 1990.
Ortiz, Ricardo. "L.A. Women: Jim Morrison with John Rechy." *The Queer Sixties* (Patricia Smith, ed.). London: Routledge, 1999.
Paglia, Camille. "Cults and Cosmic Consciousness: Religious Vision in the American Sixties." *Arion,* Winter 2003.
Perr, Harvey. "Stage Doors." *L. A. Free Press.* August 8, 1969.
Pinter, Harold. *The Caretaker & The Dumbwaiter.* New York: Grove Press, 1961.
Powledge, Fred. "Wicked Go the Doors." *Life,* April 12, 1968.
Prochnicky, Jerry, and Joe Russo. *Jim Morrison: My Eyes Have Seen You.* San Marcos (Cal.); AM Graphics, 1996.
Reuzeau, Jean-Yves. *Jim Morrison et les Doors.* Paris: Librio Musique, 2001.
Rimbaud, Arthur. *Illuminations.* New York: New Directions, 1966.
Riordan, James, and Jerry Prochnicky. *Break On Through.* New York: Morrow, 1991.
Rocco, John. (ed.). *The Doors Companion.* New York: Schirmer, 1997.
Ronay, Alain. "Jim and I / Friends Until Death." *King* (Italy). July, 1991.
Rush, Robert. "The Doors in Philadelphia." *The Psychedelic News.* July 2000.
Sander, Ellen. *Trips: Rock Life in the Sixties.* New York: Scribners, 1973.
Shaw, Greg. *The Doors on the Road.* London: Omnibus, 1997.
Sparrow, Poe. "The Doors: Re-visited." *The Unabridged Poe Sparrow.* Internet Website. Undated.
Slick, Grace, with Andrea Cagan. *Somebody to Love.* New York: Warner Books, 1998.
Stevenson, Salli. "An Interview with Jim Morrison." *Circus.* January 1971.
Sugarman, Danny, with Benjamin Edmonds. *The Doors: The Illustrated History.* New York: William Morrow, 1983.
Sugarman, Danny. *Wonderland Avenue.* New York: Morrow, 1989.
Sugarman, Danny (ed.). *The Doors / Complete Lyrics.* New York: Hyperion, 1991.
Tobler, John, and Andrew Doe. *The Doors.* London: Proteus, 1984.
Wager, Gregg. "Murray Lerner's Film *Message to Love.*" *The Doors Collector's Magazine.* 2002.
Wallis, Dave. *Only Lovers Left Alive.* New York: E.P. Dutton, 1964.
Warhol, Andy, and Pat Hackett. *POPism: The Warhol '60s.* New York: Harcourt Brace Jovanovich, 1980.
"Warhollywood! Andy in L.A." *LA Weekly,* May 24–30, 2002.
Whitcomb, Ian. *Rock Odyssey: A Musician's Chronicle of the Sixties.* Garden City: Doubleday/Dolphin, 1983.
Zwerin, Michael. "Jazz Journal." *The Village Voice.* March 7, 1968.